William Henry Heymann
Mt. Pleasant Park
Clinton Iowa
Peace Cottage 1928

Wilhelm

J. M. Peebles

THE

SPIRITUAL PILGRIM:

A Biography of

JAMES M. PEEBLES.

By J. O. BARRETT.

"My name is 'Pilgrim;' my religion is Love; my home is the Universe; my soul-effort is to educate and elevate Humanity."

THIRD EDITION.

BOSTON:
WILLIAM WHITE AND COMPANY,
BANNER OF LIGHT OFFICE,
158 Washington Street.
NEW YORK AGENTS:—THE AMERICAN NEWS COMPANY,
119 Nassau Street.
1872.

Printed by William White & Co.

Sacred to the Angel:

MADAME ELIZABETH PHILIPINE MARIE HELLENE,

OF FRANCE.

A FRIENDLY EPISTLE.

Dear Reader, — My object in writing this book is to encourage the world's reformers.

In the fall of 1868, busily engaged in literary work at my residence, Mr. Peebles related some of his experiences by way of pleasantry; when, deeply interested, I playfully said, "Why, James, such incidents have a beautiful moral! you should publish them for others' benefit." Urging the claim with cogent reasons, I succeeded in parrying off his jokes about it, but put myself in a dilemma unexpectedly, for I must be the biographer! Embosomed in the faith of this brother's love, it did seem a natural choice.

Meeting him again the next summer, on the shore of Elkhart Lake, Wis., in that "Wigwam Bower of Prayer," I took the horsocope of his life, — the shadows of fact cast in the light of the spirit. Corresponding with some of his friends — whose kindnesses are gratefully acknowledged — to procure old and new letters, and seizing upon his voluminous writings, I at length had a little mountain of documents; and what a chaos! So checkered did I find his life, my greatest difficulty was to reduce this sketch to consistent bounds. Much remains untold.

A biography, you know, is the hardest portraiture to delineate. It is a slight task to measure by rule, and quite a different art to impress the soul till sentences think with words that burn. The writer must have sympathetically the experience of his hero, — fight his battles, weep with his tears, rejoice with his joy, feel the pulses of his heart.

Oh, for *Nature's* art! The poet's success is what he feels; inspired feeling through a practical mind is divinely eloquent. The painter needs more than an anatomy: he must catch the soul of his subject, and stamp it upon canvas, or his effort is a failure. Sweden's song-birds, Jenny Lind and Christine Nilsson — poor peasant girls once — enchant the nations; for theirs is the *soul of music.*

I never would have undertaken the honored task of writing the actual biography of a man whose life-line threads over all the world, and heaven too, interlacing with the "New Gospel" in its most delicate and refined activities, had I not been guided by a genius higher than my own, by an angel familiar with all the experiences of the "Spiritual Pilgrim." Have I caught it, — the *soul?*

> "Thy song, the joy and sorrow of all races,
> Life's contradictions, harmonized anew"?

J. O. B.

Glen Beulah, Wis.

PREFACE.

BY EMMA HARDINGE.

TIME is the great and original touchstone of truth. When this impartial judge has pronounced his verdict upon movements whose source dates back to periods antecedent to our own, the records that are left us gain force and interest in our minds in exact proportion to our information concerning the personages who were instrumental in creating the events recorded. It is for this reason that biography is esteemed as the most acceptable and analytical form that history can assume. All human transactions originate in the influences of the human spirit, whether in the visible or invisible world; hence we can only approach the problem of causation, when we begin to understand the nature of the spiritual forces that have been brought to bear upon the events we trace. When the great spiritual outpouring of the nineteenth century shall be submitted to the judgment of posterity, and the criterion of time, unbiassed by passion or prejudice, shall determine its true value to mankind, the more precious the record may become, the more eagerly will humanity search for the footprints of its pioneers, preachers, teachers, media, and martyrs. It is this tendency to identify all human interests with human individualities that has led to the errors of hero-worship, and god-men. Perhaps the best corrective that can be devised for this species of idolatry is the calm and strictly human record which biography presents; and therefore we know of no better service that the writers of the present era can perform to posterity than to prepare for their use truthful records of the various individualities that have been engaged in the wonderful and world-wide movement known as "Modern Spiritualism."

Perhaps none of the phenomenal personages of this movement can furnish a more striking, instructive, and interesting theme for the biographer than J. M. Peebles. His early education and connection with the ministry in phases of religious belief utterly opposed to the great modern revelation; his long, patient, and self-sacrificing labors for the promotion of Spiritualism, when, Saul-like, he became inspired as its apostle; his admirable and scholarly contributions to its literature, and the vast geographical areas over which his experiences have been extended in both hemispheres, — all contribute to render this biography at once one of the most interesting and important that the movement can furnish.

Will the bright angelic visitors, whose presence here is now so clearly demonstrated, continue their missionary labors amongst earth's children? Can they, if they would, do so? or are these bright forerunners of our immortal destiny to perform the work of building the temple of the new Zion, and then to pass away from the longing eyes of mortality?

Will Spiritualism be absorbed by sectarian organizations, and used simply as an agent for the promotion of liberal ideas? or will it remain a concrete movement, itself absorbing all other religious associations in the vortex of its irrepressible powers of demonstration and reason?

Will the spirits continue to experiment until they have perfected their glorious telegraph between heaven and earth? or, weary of our apathy, shortcomings, and indifference, will they permit no glimpses only of the possibilities that lie dormant within the human soul, and then leave the earth to await the uprising of a more faithful and spiritually-minded generation?

These are questions upon which the Spiritualists have formed widely diverse opinions, and upon which no Cassandra's voice will be accepted as authority until the results shall be proven in time; but, however these may ultimate, the immense importance of clear, concise histories of what has been done, said, thought, and suffered in the earlier phases of this movement can never be exaggerated.

The causes which operated to convert so many various grades of character and intellect as Spiritualism includes should all be weighed and duly considered. The world's reception of its spiritual teachers, — the effects of their unparalleled labors, and too frequently of their sufferings, in the performance of their mission, — the records of all this should be preserved as milestones on the road of human progress, without which the pilgrims of the future are liable to fall into precisely the same toils and snares as have beset the paths of the pioneers.

The writer has herself proved the impossibility of condensing the events of the world-wide movement known as Spiritualism into any more comprehensive form than a mere compendium; but, to do justice to the personages who have so faithfully and toilfully created the chain of spiritual history, nothing but individualized biographies will suffice.

As a brother laborer in the cause of Spiritualism, as a writer whose pearls of glowing eloquence and gems of historic research always formed felicitous subjects for quotation, the writer has long known and gratefully esteemed J. M. Peebles.

As a laborer on the older soil of Europe, where the fogs of tradition and the stern spirit of religious bigotry and conservatism weave a pall around the mind as fatal to the new life of Spiritualism as the panoply of the grave, Mr. Peebles has been equally bold, indefatigable, and successful.

Returning to his native country, freighted with the rich treasures of knowledge and experience gathered up in many lands and from contact with many minds, Mr. Peebles is eminently fitted to perform his share of the mighty work of knitting together in the ties of divine fatherhood and human brotherhood all the broken and scattered lines of humanity distributed over life's ocean, from the farthest East to the remotest West.

The man that has stood on the last foothold of Western civilization, on the golden sands of California, and wandered amongst the pioneer men whose ancestors first numbered up the mystery of the solemn stars on the plains of Arabia, — the man who has been enabled to compare the influences of the spiritual outpouring over nearly all the vast breadth of the equatorial belt, and speak Spiritualism in the ears of the wandering Arab, the fateful Mussulman, the degenerate Roman, the fickle Frenchman, the sternly orthodox Briton, and the inquisitive cosmopolitan American, — such a Spiritualist, faithful in his belief and its expression to all persons and in all places alike, is an historical man whom the world ought to know, and of whom the ranks of Spiritualism have just cause to be proud.

That a scholar, a thinker, and a man of large heart, broad principles, and high intellectual attainments has been inspired to the work of collating the materials which form the subject of the following pages is also a source of congratulation, and can not fail to secure for their perusal respectful and candid consideration. The writer can not answer for the methods pursued by authors in general; but, in her own case, she has more than once realized the advantage of writing a preface *after* a perusal of the main body of the work.

Of course, this admission implies a recognition of some disadvantages in the *per contra* of this system; still, the knowledge which we possess of the field of resource to be traveled over, and the able hands in which that field of labor has fallen, justifies us in anticipating a rich treat to the student of the following pages.

That the dear angels who have so faithfully and tenderly guided their missionary through the thorny paths of an unpopular reform will themselves superintend and inspire the transcription which bears witness to their divine achievements, we can not doubt; hence we may confidently usher into the world the biography and spiritual experiences of J. M. Peebles as one of the most important and remarkable contributions to the literature of the age of which the nineteenth century can boast.

CONTENTS.

THE SPIRITUAL PILGRIM.

CHAPTER I.

PLANTS, BIRDS, AND FLOWERS.

> "Flood the new heavens and earth, and with thee bring
> All the old virtues."
>
> WHITTIER.

THE rough diamond polished in adversity, the child brained in philosophy, the orator tongued in love, the pilgrim grayed in wintry storms, the seer translated in a chariot of God, the ministering angel now, — such is life, O exiles!

> "Let all harmonies
> Of sound, form, color, motion, wait upon
> The princely guest."

Julius Cæsar forced obedience in Britain, — centuries of discipline. Then a colony of industrious citizens — paternally Roman, maternally Scottish — settled a high elevation on the northern bank of the Tweed, inland from the sea, south from beautiful Edinburgh, Scotland. It was democratically named Peebles, from the Latin *populi*, many people. It was the resort of the Scottish kings and queens during the summer months. Alexander III. sought its hunting-grounds, when tired of war. After the battle of Nevill-Cross, in which David II. was taken prisoner, the town of Peebles contributed so largely for his ransom it was created a royal burgh; when titles were conferred upon the families of Peebles, making them eligible to seats in parliament. This continued till the passage of "The Reform Act." Walter Scott frequently mentions Peebles in his works, and describes "the rashness and impetuosity of John Peebles, an Earl."

Alexander Smith thus improvises a song, entitled "The Tweed at Peebles:" —

"I lay in my bedroom at Peebles,
With the window-curtains drawn,
While there stole over hills of pasture and pine
The unresplendent dawn.

"And in the deep silence I listened,
With a pleased, half-waking heed,
To the sound that ran through the ancient town, —
The shallow, brawling Tweed.

* * * * * *

"Was it absolute truth, or a dreaming
Which the wakeful day disowns,
That I heard something more in the stream as it ran
Than water breaking on stones?"

* * * * * *

About two hundred years ago, a branch of the Peebles family moved into the north of Ireland, where they took an active part with other Protestants against the wrangling Irish papists, and endured much persecution. In 1718 they formed, with others, an emigrant party of one hundred, crossed the ocean, and settled in Massachusetts, where the bigoted inhabitants gathered by night, and destroyed their meeting-house. After this, under the charge of Rev. Abercrombie, they began a settlement in the town of Pelham. Bringing from Londonderry "the necessary material for the manufacture of linen," they were, as the historian avers, "industrious, frugal, and peaceful."

One of these adventurous Peebles's penetrated into Vermont, and "drove down his stakes" in Whitingham, Windham County, near the Green Mountains. Those days the girls were buxom lasses, — muscular, daring, hearts sound as ringing bells. Miss Nancy Brown, daughter of "Deacon Brown," was a towering lady, refined, hazel-eyed, intellectual, — "the school-mistress," dreamy as the morning clouds hugging the shaggy necks of the mountains. James Peebles was sanguine, enthusiastic, intelligent, epicurean, benevolent, popular with the yeomanry, being captain of the militia. What of that romantic courtship, on a granite rock, under the shadow of an ancient elm? There the vows were plighted.

In Whitingham is an old homestead on a hill-side. Babbling near it is a little stream from springs, away to the south, in a nook so cunning. Great-grandparents, so ancient and nervous, graced the wide fireside, — drooping wintry willows, silvered with snow. The mother, young and independent, was socially antipodal to their old notions. So the honey-bees in that domestic hive buzzed with an angular industry. It was magnetic peril to "the welcome child." Did not those maternal tears, redolent with high ambition, psychologically mold the unskilled heart of her pledge of love? The thread of life undulates into solitudes. Is it not inwoven with trying hours, like a telegraph to its battery? But the trial tempered that birdling to daring ere it fluttered on the mother's bosom. Poor, but laborious; distressed, but resolute; pensive, but heroic, she rose superior to her surroundings, and gave the world an indefatigable reformer. Sunbeams and stars, flowers and gurgling waters, cast the germ-child in the dies of beauty. She was nature's guest, — Hagar in the wilderness, lonely, religious. First the blossoming summer, then the quickening autumn, then the winter, white and pure, — these were the "sacred months," under the life-veil of destiny. Prayer, music, and meditation, the ancient clock, keeping vigils, were the "sisters of fate," that wove "a coat of many colors" for the future prophet. Thus she bound her prisoner to a checkered pilgrimage.

James was born the 23d of March, 1822, Jupiter being the reigning star. The angels say they impressed that mother to call her son so, mainly because of the love the apostle John had for his brother James. He was the oldest of five sons and two daughters, all diverse in characteristics. That mother's prayer now, how like Emily Judson's over hers, "the fairest bird of Ind,"—

> "Doubts, hopes, in eager tumult rise.
> Hear, my God! one earnest prayer:
> Room for my bird in Paradise,
> And give him angel plumage there!"

The gospel of childhood, a *blessed* rough and tumble: it whets the edge of character. Checkered as the landscape were those early years, each trivial event limning soul on the canvas of life. One of these may suffice to reveal the chemistry of the colors blending into form.

"Jimmie" had a special liking for troughs, — one such was his cradle when a baby, and about his only plaything when a boy. Growing bigger, seeing the other boys had sleds, he at length looked upon his old trough with a haughty disdain, and importuned his father to make him a sled. That ugly *No!* A sled educates to speed of thought, and a kite to lofty purpose. Both refused.

One winter's afternoon, the snow-crust hard and glary, the lad stole the bread-trough, and took a slide. On it sped with a dash and whirl, and struck against a stone, splitting it in twain. What was to be done? A moment of sad gazing, weighing consequences; and in he rushed, eyes full of tears and heart aching, to make a confession. A sharp crack on the ears, and the boy felt true justice was done. Good orthodoxy that! An ample supply of playthings for children, and *persuasive* discipline, are economies in household furniture.

This restless fellow did not take to muscular industry. He hated grindstones, axes, churns, and hoes, when imposed as *tasks*. Awkward in the use of tools, he could not even construct a top. "We can never make any thing of James," was said more than once with a feeling of despair. The truth was, they did not know the boy, nor touch the pulse of his genius. But he was famous for looking after young lambs. With cold bare feet at daylight in springtime, while the snow mantled the shaded rocks and hollows, he was off into the old pasture, to see if any young lamb had been chilled by the night wind.

His ambition ran in the channel of the brooks, full of babbles and frolics. That wild country enchanted him. The flowers and birds were his companions, maple-poles his ponies, red-sticks his whips to drive them with, chips and leaves his sailing vessels in the eddying pools. He gamboled with the minnows, and owned all the butterflies and robins' eggs. Unwearied were the swift hours as he sat on his native hills, watching every thing, the stilly world at his feet.

What was that undefinable feeling, that mystic consciousness, that genius attending him in all his rambles, which seemed to be a face-image in the water-brooks and flames of fire, — a face bending benignantly over him when locked in slumber on his rickety bed in the attic, close under the roof?

"While yet a boy I sought for ghosts, and sped
Through many a listening chamber, cave, and ruin,
And star-lit wood, with fearful steps pursuing,
High hopes of talk with the departed dead."

CHAPTER II.

SCHOOL DAYS.

"I consider a human soul without education like marble in the quarry; which shows none of its inherent beauties until the skill of the polisher fetches out the colors, makes the surface shine, and discovers every ornamental cloud, spot, and vein that runs through the body of it." — ADDISON.

THAT red schoolhouse, just a mile off, "round by the pond," shingled all over, — what a tale it tells of "lads and lasses O!"— of snow-balls, poutings, whippings, and "turning somersets!" How changed now! The saplings around it are tall trees; the incisions in the bark where the scholars carved their names have grown over, but the marks are there. How like human life! The wounds we make only partially heal. Even the brook where the boys and girls drank and fished, and built dams and saw-mills, once quite a river in their eyes, has become beautifully less. In the soul's picture-gallery is the portrait of all the boys and girls we knew; of all the hills, streams, fields, beasts, birds; of dewy eves and morns; of the stars we chose to rule our destiny; of first dreams, and first lessons of friendship.

A child never loves duties. When the genius of children is better understood, and we employ the love-art of the mother-bird, that, by example, woos her fledgling up into the sky, whippings will be at an end. "Jimmie's tricks," so innocent, so tormenting, were full of morality. They made the school healthy. When five or six years old, his uncle, Dr. Peebles, taught with ferule in hand, a birch-stick on the desk! Almost every day he got a flogging for his pranks: every mishap charged against him. He bore it like a Christian martyr, however, never exposing a secret, unconquerable in his submission. The fighting boys appealed to him for umpire. He was the defender of the weaker party always.

"I help the under dog in the fight."

Being an inveterate stutterer, he could not, or would not, read loud. His temper was kept sharp by the grinding taunts of the "big boys," ever laughing at his awkward articulation. In righteous indignation, he wished a hundred times there were never a school in the world. Justly did he hate the hard-backed bench, so high that his feet hung dangling for hours without rest. Glad we do not have to live but once those flogging, aching, rambling days of *auld lang syne.*

The next summer, Elizabeth Godfrey taught. One day, she sent him with a little tin pail after some water. The path led by Azuba Martin's garden (mother of Dr. O. Martin, a prominent physician of Worcester, Mass.). As he peeped through the fence, his palate could not resist the delicious currants, then red ripe. That little hand again and again plucked the "forbidden fruit"—the first Adamic sin! In vain did he try to wash off the stains that betrayed him. Oh, the agony! Entering the schoolhouse, he demurely went to his seat; when the teacher, noticing his embarrassment, called him up.

"What is the matter with your hand, Jimmie?"

"Nothing, ma'am; not sore!"

"What! currant juice! Been stealing? Now, you go right straight to 'Aunt Zuba,' and confess you stole her currants!"

Exposed before the whole school as a "little thief," what a trying moment! Snail-like, he dragged his heavy feet back to Mrs. Martin's, just the most humble and self-blaming lad, part mad, much ashamed, half-crying. Aunt Zuba caught sight of him, as he entered the gate, and, greeting him with a smile, seeing his sadness, said very patronly, —

"What, my little man, come after more water a-ready?"

"S-s-sch-school-ma'am t-t-old me t-to come, and-and tell you I-I-I-st-stole your currants; and I-I-am sor-s-sor-*sorry!*"

"Why! come here, my darling. Were you hungry? We have of currants plenty to eat. You should not steal, dear boy; but, when you want any more, come and ask me, and you shall have all you wish."

Then she patted him tenderly on the cheek, and laid her hand upon his fevered brow so soothingly! The good aunt understood a boy's heart. A faithful teacher's promptness in correcting the first mistake, and a loving motherly sympathy from Aunt Zuba, impressed at the right moment, gave a moral direction to his restless and persistent spirit,— not to stain the hands with stolen juices, and always confess a fault where it is due. Both these good women, in the higher school of angels now, delight to recall the incident that channeled the little rill of love, swelling since to a river of integrity.

Reason tests the strength of thought. "Jimmie's" mental powers were one day taxed to their utmost tension at a new idea, that made him reticent for many weeks. His father's sister, Aunt Sally Corkings, getting old, suddenly passed away. It was winter time; snow deep. They put the coffin on a stone-boat, and dragged it with oxen to the grave; the white mantle of nature and the black drapery of the mourners forming a strange contrast, weirdly impressive to the lad.

"What did they put her in the ground for?" he silently asked. After the dismal funeral, he soberly went to his mother — always his oracle — with the inquiry, —

"Will Aunt Sally sprout again, like corn and beans?"

"Her body, my son, will come to life again at the resurrection, in the end of time."

"Well, what makes 'em put her in a coffin? She can't get out!"

"The coffin will rot away, my son."

"And not the body rot, mother? Won't something then eat Aunt Sally up, and she won't live again?"

The mother did not anticipate such an argument, and could only answer in the usual orthodox way, —

"Oh, well, my son, these are God's mysteries! we must not ask too many questions."

The next spring, there was a "revival of religion" in Whitingham, and "Aunt Betsey" was converted. Whilst witnessing her baptism, James clung to his mother, and, in a trembling voice, asked, —

"What are they doing with Aunt Betsey, drowning her?"

"She is to be saved, my son."

"Saved? — what is that, mother?"

She then told him about a dismal hell below, and a beautiful heaven above.

"What did God make a hell for, mother?"

Finding his mother evaded this question, he inquired again,—

"Have *you* been baptized?"

It was his turn to be silent, when she answered in the negative. Thinking she should attend to this duty as soon as possible, he wondered what the difference could be between being baptized and "going in swimming."

A few days after, seeing he was thoughtful, and believing he might be under "conviction," she pursued her advantage, and told him about a "recording book kept by a sober angel." This hightened his ideal fancy. "How much," he said to himself, "he will have to write about *me!*" He thought the book had gold covers, and was big as a window. He very orthodoxically conceived God to be a great man, with a long beard, just like the picture of a prophet he saw in the old family Bible. When told about the "all-seeing eye," he imagined it was in the center of God's forehead, looking straight at him. When he pouted, or played the truant (very innocently), that night he dreamed God said to the angel of records, "Put all that down against the boy!" These instilled ideas, bodied forth in corresponding fancy, tinged his first years with a shade of melancholy. "Theological mysteries" produce spiritual fevers.

How dreamily prophetic were the successive sabbaths, when this youth walked beside his mother to church, holding her by the hand, inquiring what it all meant. B. F. Taylor paints the picture of those "meeting-times,"—

"For a sprig of green carroway carries me there,
To the old village church and the old village choir;
When, clear of the floor, my feet slowly swung,
And timed the sweet praise of the song as they sung,
Till the glory aslant from the afternoon sun
Seemed the rafters of gold in God's temple begun.
You may smile at the nasals of old Deacon Brown,
Who followed by scent till he ran the tune down;
And the dear Sister Green, with more goodness than grace,
Rose and fell on the tunes as she stood in her place;
And, where old 'Coronation' exultingly flows,
Tried to reach the high notes on the tips of her toes.
To the land of the leal they went with their song,
Where the choir and the chorus together belong.
Oh, be lifted, ye gates! let me hear them again!
Blessed song! blessed sabbath! for-ever, *amen!*"

Narrow valleys contract the mind. Room, room, is what we need. Seized with a "Western fever," the Peebles Family moved to Smithville, N.Y., then "the West." Here new hardships presented themselves. Under the tuition of Prof. Hurlburt, he was cured of stammering. What a joy! He used to put a pebble under the point of his tongue to keep it down, and not flopping up against the roof of the mouth.

Exuberant over his stammering victory, — scarcely knowing, like a minnow just finned out, what to do with himself, — he thought he would fall in love with a pretty damsel; at the age of thirteen, writing love-sick poetry! After sending the palpitating verses to the bashful girl, who, it seems, was "going to sea," the psychological effusion suddenly vanished. The animus of the poetry indicates at this age the musical genius of the man: so we snatch it from oblivion. The first poetry and first little shoe should always be preserved.

"When the storm-god wildly rages,
And the foaming billows roar;
When thou art far away, my lady,
I'll think of *thee* the more.

Often friends in life deceive us,
Till we know not whom to trust;
But the links of love that bind *us*,
Oh! may they never, *never* rust!

Though oceans may between us roll,
Still will fancy love to trace,
In thy true, devoted soul,
Ever thy remembered face.

I'll think of thee when evening's ray
Is gleaming o'er the sea;
When gentle twilight's shadows play
On mountain, vale, and tree."

At Smithville, James attended a select school, taught by Amos H. Bedient, making rapid progress in geography, elocution, and roguery. Proud of his proficiency, he resolved to return to Vermont in the spring, to make money by teaching elocution! Suddenly appearing in Whitingham, it did cause a wonderful expansion of self-reliance — such as he needed — to hear familiar friends congratulate him on his "lingual improvement." But his "elocutionary fortune," — that was verily "a will-o'-the-wisp." Above all expenses, he earned just fifteen dollars. The disposal of these hard earnings is the sure index of his sweet sympathies, running then quite at random, as do mountain streams, to bless the jagged fern. Meeting a poor, unfortunate traveler one day, lame and sorrowful, his heart was touched; and he impulsively emptied the whole fifteen into the beggar's grateful hand, saying, "I am even now better off than he, the poor lame man!" Here is the key-note to his nature, — sympathetic; sometimes imprudent in giving. No money, no home, hungry and weary, he sat by the roadside, and ate a raw turnip for a supper, the tears flowing freely. Poverty stared him in the face, and haunted him a full year. His clothes were threadbare, his health below par. Poor fellow! he wished himself dead.

CHAPTER III.

GETTING RELIGION — THE MINISTRY.

To the Monkeys:
"Tell me, accursed whelps, what are ye stirring up with the porridge?"
Monkeys:
"We are cooking coarse beggars' broth." — GOETHE'S FAUST.

"Eyes are found in light; ears in auricular air; feet on land; fins in water; wings in air; and each creature where it is wont to be, with a mutual fitness." — EMERSON.

MISFORTUNES in Vermont taught James to go ahead, not backwards. Wiser for the sorrows, he returned to New York a little tamed. Placing himself again under the tuition of Prof. Bedient, he soon won a high recommendation. He was now seventeen; and with bright hopes did he enter upon the experiment of teaching a district school in Pitcher, Chenango Co., N.Y., and was successful. He boarded at the home of a Baptist deacon, who had some very bad children. One morning, whilst the old man was praying with his usual fervor, a boy of his made confusion with his feet, chuckling at the same time. The deacon paused, and, getting roiled at the repeated noise, sprung up from his knees with a flushed face, and shook the "young sauce-box," accompanied with a desperate threat; then knelt down again, and commencing at the "Jews," where he left off, finished the prayer, his son groaning "Amen!" This strange exhibition at a "family altar" repelled the young teacher from religious ceremonials.

About this time, a "revival" breaking out near Mr. Cole's, in Smithville, Jerry Brown, a particular friend, got religion. Others "got it bad." Being the only person who could specially affect "the teacher," Mr. Brown talked with him most pleadingly, warning him to "flee from the wrath to come." At length, he consented to go to meeting. The young converts gathered round him with serious looks and affectionate interrogations, such as, "*Will* you, James, will you not go to heaven with us? Oh, come and kneel at the anxious seats! Oh, seek the overtures of mercy!" The meek-eyed girls besieged him, put their arms around his neck, pleading with him so eloquently to get religion! How could he resist such persuasion? Consenting to make the trial-effort, he took a seat at the front, right under the droppings of the sanctuary. The prayer was furiously impassioned. The magnetic fire began to burn: "And the smoke of their torment ascendeth up for ever and ever!" The pictures drawn from this text were frightful: hell was opened, the devil let loose, the judgment set, the Almighty frowned, the dread sentence thundered forth, "Depart, ye cursed, into everlasting fire!" The scene that followed was terrible: eyes stuck out, hair stood on end, women half-swooned, and men groaned. This part of the job finished, Elder Bush descended from the pulpit with a consequential air, and laid his fat hand upon James's shoulder, saying with a solemn intonation, as if from the vault of despair, "*Young man!* YOUNG MAN! are you prepared for DEATH?" The new converts pressed closer, girls holding his hand, weeping. The magnetic sympathy was contagious. The young man wept too. When the "feeling felt bad," the minister sepulchrally exhorted, —

"Oh, say you believe in Jesus; just say it. Oh, say it, *say* it!"

"Why, yes," replied James, "I believe in Jesus!"

"Yes, *yes!*" shouted the Elder. "Glory, glory! let us shout glory! for another soul is saved! glory, hallelujah!"

The rest laughed for joy; and there was a general hugging-time.

Snuffing the freer air out of doors, the "holy feeling" began to subside, and speedily died out; for the Elder suddenly left his own wife and children, and ran away with his hired girl, when religion there went down to a low ebb. James reflected. It was a lesson. He doubted the sincerity of the clergy, became skeptical, entered deeper and deeper into mental darkness, — a confirmed infidel, regarding all religion as priestly imposture. To indicate his utter disgust against the popular church and "its mock worship," as he called it, he one evening secretly put cayenne-pepper on the hot stove, and smoked the people out, when they assembled for another revival. The choking fumes ventilated, he took his seat with the rest, so self-complacent, when the minister poured forth vengeance upon the head of the perpetrator, and made hell so hellish the house became a general pandemonium.

Re-action from "revivals of religion" is always to skepticism, scorn, defiance. Said the wise Hindoo, "Keep thy soul in moderation; teach thy spirit to be attentive to its good: so shall these, its ministers, be always to thee conveyances of truth."

One winter, where young Peebles was teaching school, notice was given that Rev. N. Doolittle (Universalist) would preach in that locality the next Sunday. If interest be wanting, curiosity may bring us. Always defending the persecuted party, he resolved to attend. When Mr. Doolittle rose to speak, our "infidel" noticed a beautiful sincerity in his countenance, which charmed him to strict attention. The text was, "The Lord is good unto all, and his tender mercies are over all his works." The delivery was easy, the style poetic, the inspiration fervent. The purpose was to show the harmony of the God of nature with the God of the Bible, when interpreted in the light of reason. It made a happy impression: a ray penetrated the inner darkness; a more charitable spirit sprung up in his heart. He read the Bible with candor; read "Ballou on the Atonement," and other Universalist works, and, within a year, became a convert to the "new faith." Attending conventions, then so inspirational, he thought what delight *he* would take in demolishing old dogmas of error. On one occasion, the good Mr. Doolittle, as if moved by an angel, left the desk, came direct to this youth in his seat, and, taking him by the hand, looking deep into his soul, said, "You have a fine forehead: you should make your mark in the world." What did it mean? Was it an angelic appointment?

"Each one hears what he carries in his heart."

Trace back the life-thread that mother wove from angels to her heart, from her heart outward, veiling a soul for mediumship between heaven and earth. Is not effect always true to its cause?

"Let us build altars to the Beautiful Necessity."

Ambition, once so fluctuating and disappointing, now burned with steady fire. Scholarship was James's first aim. Teaching a high school at Upper Lisle, N.Y., he was flushed with brighter hope.

The cloud of skepticism shivered into "silver linings." For several successive spring, summer, and fall terms, he was a close student at Oxford Academy, New York. By close application to books, while yet teaching, he kept along with his classmates who were not compelled to provide for their own physical needs. Here he studied the higher English branches, Latin and Greek. Charmed with the classics, the poetic prophecy whispered in his ear, "Thou shalt visit those lands of heroism and art."

> "The foresight that awaits
> Is the same genius that creates."

He was a constant attendant upon the ministrations of Rev. J. T. Goodrich, pastor of the Oxford Universalist Church. When his parents also found the rising star of Universalism, enthusiasm lent him wings. A walk of ten or fifteen miles to a conference or convention was a delight. Fast young men derided him; for he would not drink, smoke, nor spend his time idly. Where now are those "Young Americas?" Dissipation impoverished them; the few left linger in obscurity; whilst the "student James," frailer in constitution, is still on the rising scale. Our inspired Belle Bush foretells the harvest: —

> "Sow ye on earth the blessed seeds,
> That, springing up and whitening in the field,
> A hundred-fold shall yield
> Of fruits for human needs;
> And men will bless you for those golden seeds,
> And angels call you poet of good deeds."

About this time, he had occasion to act the lawyer. During a revival at Morrill's Creek, under the manipulation of Rev. Mr. Jamieson, two lads were arrested for disturbing the meeting. Disgusted with such proselyting, sympathizing with the boys, he voluntarily plead their cause in court. "They are orphans," earnestly said the fervid defender, "deprived of parental counsel; thoughtless, rather than malicious; their first offense. Justice may condemn, but mercy and forgiveness are more beautiful; for we are commanded to 'forgive even seventy times seven' to save a brother."

It was splendidly done. After reprimanding, the Justice dismissed the boys, whose gratitude to the young attorney knew no bounds.

In the summer of 1842, J. H. Harter, modest and verdant, came to the Academy. Poorly dressed, and Germanic in accent, certain students made fun of him; but he excited James's sympathy, which he showed in acts of encouragement. He persuaded this devoted student to attend a Universalist meeting, Bible in hand, to guard against temptation, and afterwards managed to provoke him into a debate defensive of Universalism, on the question of endless misery. By his side sat his schoolmate, whispering now and then in his ear what Drs. Clarke, Gill, and other doctors of divinity said upon this and that hell-fire passage.

As might be expected, it was a commitment to Universalism. James, now entitled to the appellation of *Mister*, was instrumental in converting him. Their friendship was deep. As he says, "they roomed together, studied together, slept together, prayed together, wept together, worked together in reforms." Revs. J. B. Gilman and J. J. Austin were associate students at Oxford during these terms of studious romance. Young Harter afterwards attended the Clinton Liberal Institute, and finally entered the Universalist ministry, serving with marked ability. Never the breath of slander touched his garments. His ready wit made him a prince in the social circle. After several years of successful labors in the ministry, he was called to take charge of the business department of the "Christian Ambassador," as general agent. Since 1850, having manfully investigated the Spiritual Philosophy, his sermons have been well-spiced with the gospel of angel ministry, for which he has been questioned by his sect, and, as he avers, and others know, "persecuted nigh unto death for his readiness in exposing ecclesiastic corruption." He is now free, having resigned his letter of fellowship, and steps forth a well-skilled officer in the army of Spiritual Reformers.

Writing Mr. Harter concerning those school-days, we received the following affectional testimonial of early and lasting friendship: —

"AUBURN, N.Y., April 8, 1870.

"J. O. BARRETT. *Dear Brother*, — I first made the acquaintance of Mr. Peebles in the summer of 1842, when we were both students in the Oxford Academy at Oxford, Chenango Co., N.Y.

"We soon became warm friends, and have been so from that time to the present, and, without doubt, will so remain throughout the endless ages of eternity. During an intimate acquaintance of nearly thirty years, has never any thing arisen to darken or stain the bright chain of friendship that has bound us together. We have both passed through bitter and severe trials, but have been mutual aids to each other. He is one of the most genial, companionable men I ever knew; strictly honest and upright; and, to be fully appreciated, he is to be fully known.

"He was popular as a man and a minister, when among the Universalists, as our papers and periodicals abundantly show. I hope he may long remain on earth to benefit and bless mankind. Yours truly,

J. H. Harter."

Christmas eve — laden with its happy memories, all faces smiling, all hearts speaking "merry Christmas" — was the auspicious hour of Mr. Peebles's secret thought that had haunted him in dreams and reveries. The church in Oxford was beautifully adorned with evergreens and burning tapers, the congregation large and intelligent. Pale from a momentary agitation, Mr. Goodrich read with a subdued voice the inspirational testimony of the prophet, so appropriate, — "Who hath believed our report?" It was not the minister, nor the prophet, nor the occasion, that so peculiarly stirred him, but the rising thought, finding echo in all these, of a commission to proclaim the gospel. "Who hath believed *our* report?" sounded in his ears as an appeal from Heaven. Responsive to the question, a lady in the gallery, playing upon the organ, sung with inspiring acclaim, —

"There was joy in heaven!
There was joy in heaven!"

It thrilled him through and through. The whole house seemed a Bethlehem of ministering angels. He saw a more golden light than others present. Then and there he resolved to consecrate himself to the Universalist ministry. His purpose fixed, he began his theological studies with Rev. A. G. Clark of McLean, N.Y., and subsequently read with Rev. A. O. Warren, now of Montrose, Pa.

Our anointed candidate was a perfect eye-sore to "revivalists." He attended their worship, speaking, praying; always obeying, "Sit down, sir," when too unorthodox. One day, on the Chenango River, he visited E. H. Tillotson, an old acquaintance, a convert now from Universalism to Spiritualism; and, of course, they must that night attend the Baptist revival. Long cloaks were the fashion those days. A dismal prayer, a nasal melody, singing —

"A charge to keep I have,"

and the spell of revivalism crept on, forcing tears, surging, sighing.

The minister became hoarse, and invited any exhorter or clergyman to come forward and assist.

"That means me," said Peebles in a whisper to Tillotson; and up he rose with such a dignity, marched straight to the desk, and fell upon his knees and prayed. He walked the aisles, put his hands on the heads of the young converts, exhorting and encouraging them to persevere. There was a general weeping. He sat down amid "hallelujahs," the minister thanking him for his "effective work." What a commotion, most blasting to the "revival," when it was afterwards reported that "the young preacher is a Universalist student at Oxford!"

The ministry, oh, the ministry! Were you ever in its ark of safety, locked in, chained, sentineled, pampered, starved, loved, slandered, flattered, rebuked, tempted, betrayed, prayed in and prayed out, proud of the "Rev.," ashamed of it, dying and living, blessed in blessing? The ministry! how grandly perspective — how *real* — how deep a prison — how great a freedom when the spell is broken! "Not as I will, but as thou wilt," — that's the order.

Rev. James Martin Peebles — euphonious! Only twenty years old, tall, slim, light hair, red cheeks, pretty in the eyes of the young maidens, white cravat, and black kid gloves! Thus equipped and qualified, he walked seven miles to a meeting in Gridley Hollow, and on the way got his boots muddy. It was so mortifying to his clerical dignity! He preached his first sermon in McLean, N.Y., in the presence of his theological tutor. That was a trying moment; but, having his manuscript before him, he "did not lose his place." It was a success, as the sequel proved, for he was afterwards pastor of McLean Church five successive years. His first permanent settlement was at Kellogsville, N.Y., for three years. He then had charge also of two other societies at Genoa and Mottville, engaging Rev. Harter and others to supply desks.

Whatever Mr. Peebles undertakes, it is always with enthusiastic zeal. His was an "earnest ministry." A stray leaf from his diary, like the hazel in the hands of the "water-witch," shows where and how deep the fountain is. He sought to improve every possible advantage, to be first in his profession, without jealousy for others. Note the little jets of earnestness: —

"TUESDAY, May 25, 1849.

"Started about eight o'clock for Scipio. Had a pleasant ride; reached there about eleven o'clock. Put up with Bro. Hudson, a noble, good soul.

"Had a fine session of the sabbath school this afternoon. Bro. O. A. Skinner and J. M. Austin's remarks were excellent. Bro. Sawyer preached this evening, and a glorious sermon it was, — *plain, logical*, yet eloquent. His delivery is calm — *sang-froid* — yet impressive. Staid with Malachi Fish, one of God's best specimens of humanity.

"WEDNESDAY, May 26, 1849.

"A fine morning, with Malachi Fish. Bro. O. A. Skinner preached this morning an excellent discourse. I admire his fervidness. It seems to come from the heart. Bro. L. S. Everett preached this afternoon; a good sermon. Oh, how many warm hands I have grasped this day! *Confident I am* that few love their friends as I love mine. Bro. Skinner preached this evening. He is a splendid speaker and a *good man*. There is rich music in his voice. Went home with Selah Cornell. He is a glorious soul."

Being a man of fashion then, — biblical, creedal, "constitutional," — he must, of course, be ordained in the best style. Put on the "yoke of bondage!" Must we not ask the pope or bishop? Ordination in ecclesiastic circles! Alas for the "salt that has lost its savor!" Mr. Peebles received his "Letter of Fellowship" at a session of the Cayuga Association of Universalists, held at McLean, on the 25th and 26th of September, 1844. For several years thereafter, he was standing Clerk of the Association. On the 24th of September, 1846, in Kellogsville, he was ordained to the "work of an Evangelist." The following was the order of services: —

"I. Prayer by Rev. J. H. Harter.
II. Sermon by Rev. J. M. Austin.
III. Ordaining Prayer by Rev. C. S. Brown.
IV. Charge and Delivery of Scriptures by Rev. D. H. Strickland.
V. Address to the Church by Rev. J. M. Peebles.
VI. Benediction by the Candidate."

CHAPTER IV.

THE SPIRITS — RADICAL PREACHING.

"The spirit world is not closed; thy sense is shut; thy heart is dead. Up, acolyte! bathe untired thy earthly breast in the morning red!" — SAGE.

"Hark! for a voice of gentle tone
The answer to our cry hath given,
Soft as Æolian harpstrings blown,
Responsive to the breath of even:
'I have not sought a distant shore;
Lo! I am with you: weep no more!'" — LIZZIE DOTEN.

THE "rappings"! come without our bidding; come to stay. A divine revelation, it is founded in natural law; and those who fight it, fight all tangible knowledge of immortality, fight all natural answers to prayer, fight their loved in heaven, fight spirits, angels, and the Almighty himself! It is a fearful battle. Priests had better at once ground their weapons of rebellion. The church was heart-sick, eaten with a dry rot. Skepticism was sitting in the seat of judgment, ecclesiastical religion begging at her high court. Creeds, sermons, eucharists, baptisms, no longer furnished food for the thinkers. The light on the church altars had gone out. A dark silence brooded there. It was midnight. But a tide was setting in from the other side. The seers saw it coming. At length it touched our shore — electric! "What was *that?*" asked the thinkers. The MYSTIC RAP! It echoed over the land, and "there was joy in heaven." Two decades ago, it startled the world from its long slumber. What of the ministers? They *laughed* at it. What of the philosophers? They *affirmed*, Man is immortal. The rap shivered and burst into sunlight of day, and millions were entranced. Then the church was sober, gathered up its phylacteries, walked on silver slippers to worship God, crying out, "It is the devil!" Shot from a transfiguring cloud, Truth rent the vail of the church from top to bottom. Lo! a shower fell; a river full, "clear as crystal." A refreshed world! "Ho! every one that thirsteth, come ye to the waters!"

Continued imbibation at the denominational tap inebriates the soul. Was this Mr. Peebles's condition? Like many "Liberal Christians" to-day, he was very emphatic about his independence; said so often, "I am open to conviction," but failed somehow in finding the way. The fact is, he did not investigate, "for fear of the Jews." So "*free*" in the pulpit, so *prudent* in word and action, ministers are generally the last to be converted. "Publicans and harlots shall enter the kingdom of heaven before you."

During the last year of his pastorate in Kellogsville, Mr. Peebles was invited by Hon. Vincent Kenyon, a Universalist of Quaker descent, spiritually inclined, to ride with him to Auburn, and hear the spirit rappings. He consented, with the reserve, "that the appointment be fixed for some evening." Nicodemus! The medium was Mrs. Tamlin. The raps heard, he whispered to his friend, "A splendid trick!" "Suppose you expose it," responded Mr. Kenyon. "Please rap on the wall," said Mr. Peebles. To his astonishment, the wall seemed to speak. On his coat collar, on his boots, on his heart-strings! "What?" he asked. That *what* meant a great question. When his spirit-cousin gave thus an intelligible communication, he attributed it to thought-reading. Well, thought-reading is

"The end of a golden string;
Only wind it into a ball,
It will lead you in at heaven's gate,
That invitingly opes for all."

After this, Rhoda Fuller, honest and intelligent, became clairvoyant, giving remarkable tests of spirit-presence. In due time he heard an uneducated boy deliver a masterly lecture, entranced, upon a subject of his own selection, — "The Philosophical Influence of the Nations of Antiquity upon the Civilization and Science of Modern Europe and America." Reporting it, he said, —

"The boy at once stepped forward and commenced, and for one hour and three-quarters one continual stream of history and philosophy fell from his lips. The beauty of the language was astonishing, and the names of well-known and little-known sages of antiquity fell glibly from his lips. He began by speaking of the old Aryan race, and spoke as if he had the whole history of India, Egypt, Greece, and Rome at his fingers' ends. I knew the work necessary to get up sermons before they are preached, and was perfectly astonished at the address given by the boy. I went home thinking that there must be some power at the root of Spiritualism."

Stirred by these discoveries, he ventured to preach a sermon in his church from the text, "Go on unto perfection;" in which he alluded to angels, and the spiritual gifts, as perpetual in inspiration. Mr. Kenyon, hearing it, said to him afterwards, "Our denomination will not stand such sentiment: you will have to leave it. You can fight but poorly in Saul's armor; better cast it off." This advice was startling to our young minister.

> "The crust o' the letter cracks; new life takes wing;
> A strong ground-swell will heave, a wave will break;
> The Eternal grows more visibly awake!"

The eastern star before the morning, the Baptist before Jesus, superstition before science; so radical thinking before spiritual development. Too much light all at once will dazzle us to blindness. Liberty may be driven to death. The greatest virtue is to be qualified for practical use. Be not in haste for angelhood. Excess is equal to the vice of defect. Break not the shell ere the bird is hatched.

> "Those who greedily pursue
> Things wonderful instead of true,
> That in their speculation choose
> To make discoveries strange news,
> And natural history a gazette
> Of tales stupendous and far-fetched,
> Hold no truth worthy to be known,
> That is not huge and overgrown,
> In vain stern nature to suborn,
> And for their pains are paid with scorn."

Those "spiritual exhibitions" unconsciously gave Mr. Peebles a radical tendency of sentiment. "Despise not small beginnings." Mr. Peebles read Volney, Hume, Voltaire, Paine — how audacious! — and Swedenborg, Emerson, Parker, and the like; and was spoiled for the sectarian Church. What was the cause of the new habit, — the argument first, and then the text? Bravo! When a minister puts the text on a sermon after it is written, "look out for breakers."

During the years 1853–55, Mr. Peebles was pastor of the Universalist Church at Elmira, N.Y., where he found a boon companion in Rev. Thos. K. Beecher, half-brother of Henry Ward Beecher. Here were a Universalist and a Congregationalist yoked together, bathing together, lecturing together on temperance, and even together marrying folks; Peebles marrying one of the couple according to Universalism, and Mr. Beecher according to Congregationalism. A clipping from an exchange says, —

"Rev. Thomas K. Beecher, one of the Beechers, who is pastor of a Congregational Church at Elmira, N.Y., has been disfellowshiped by the Ministerial Union of that place."

Mr. Peebles, in chronicling this disfellowshiped brother, thus reviews those novitiated days of the ministry: —

"Being warm personal friends, both of us were considered by the denominations to which we respectively belonged a little 'shaky,' theologically. Brave enough to read different periodicals and reviews, we frequently talked of the progress of 'free thought,' and the disturbing element of Spiritualism. Friend Beecher always said there was '*a fish at the other end of this line;*' but of its real character — saint or demon — he was not so certain.

"Pleasant and sunny the memories of those times. Together we rolled balls in ninepin alleys, practiced gymnastics, took baths in Dr. Gleason's water-cure, hurled stones into the valley at our feet, told mirthful stories of eccentric Christians, lectured on temperance, attended social gatherings for conversation and culture, and mutually, laughingly, accused each other of being the rankest heretic. A dozen years or more buried in the abyssmal past, and lo! we are both outside the 'camp of the Philistines,' and the reach, too, of all such theologians as feed on the crusts and crumbs of a cold, formal, creedal Christianity. Over this chasm of time, we extend the warm right hand, and welcome our old friend Thomas K. into the good and growing fraternity of the '*great unchurched.*' May his shadow lengthen, and his heresy *strengthen!* Amen.

"'Humanity sweeps onward! where to-day the martyr stands,
On the morrow crouches Judas, with the silver in his hands:
Far in front the cross stands ready, and the crackling fragments burn,
While the hooting mob of yesterday in silent awe return,
To glean up the scattered ashes into History's golden urn.

. . . .

Truth for ever on the scaffold, wrong for ever on the throne;
Yet that scaffold sways the future, and behind the dim unknown
Standeth God in the darkness keeping watch above his own."

"Illustrative of Mr. Beecher's style, when a fellow-boarder with us at the Elmira Water-Cure Institution, the following may serve as a sample: Sitting in the parlor one evening, some thirty present, listening to music, Beecher suddenly whirled around, and, putting his eagle eye upon us, said in his own felicitous way, 'I've got an idea — *must* fire it off.'

"'Well, if liable to rust from keeping, let us have it.'

"You, a heretic, speaking after the manner of the fathers, have traveled all over the hills and through the valleys of Chemung County, preaching there's no hell — no hell — no endless hell torments! And I've been around after you, preaching hell and damnation — hell and damnation! Now, we've both gone to extremes. You preach hell — or at least a little more hell — to those Universalists — they need it; and I'll not preach quite so much to my church, and I think we'll both hit nearer the truth.'

"'Wouldn't you call that policy?'

"'Certainly not; but wisdom, — that wisdom which appreciates both justice and love in the divine administration.'"

The brief epistle we here transcribe reveals the expanding force of "our minister's" soul, from loving one to loving all. "Thus in our first years," says Emerson, "are we put in training for a love which knows neither sex, person, nor partiality; but which seeks virtue and wisdom everywhere, to the end of increasing virtue and wisdom."

"ELMIRA, N.Y., Jan. 7, 1853.

"REV. D. S. B——. *Dear Brother*, — . . . Will you now lay aside your commentaries and clerical duties for a few moments, and listen to me? I have been writing upon a sermon from this text, "Verily, I say unto you, there is no man that hath left house, or brethren, or sisters, or father, or mother, or wife, or children, or lands, for my sake and the gospel's, but shall receive a hundred-fold now in this time, and in the world to come eternal life" (Mark x). What was Jesus' real meaning in this passage? It quite puzzles me. Like the young man who had 'kept the law,' I am 'sad at the saying:' for I love my brothers and sisters: there are six of them, — Emery and Elmer (twins), Leonard and Lorenzo, Lovira and Luana, — all good, though in different ways and degrees; and in my very heart I love them with a true fraternal love. Must I, as Jesus commands, leave them? Memories of them are blissful. Are all fleshly ties of kindred temporal and fading? Is spiritual love alone immortal and eternal? Love is the very life of my soul. . . .

J. M. PEEBLES."

During all his public career, Mr. Peebles has been an earnest and unflinching friend and apostle of temperance. He was one of the select committee that drafted the degrees of the Good Templars, and was the National R. W. Grand Chaplain of this order. At an early period he also espoused the anti-slavery reform, Odd Fellowship, the dress-reform, and woman's rights. He has a way, peculiar to himself, of enforcing unfashionable truth in the pulpit, without offending to any great extent. Of all men he is the greatest adept in the art of cutting your head off without hurting, and then growing it on again in better shape.

In May, 1855, resigning his pastoral relations in Elmira, Mr. Peebles felt a rising force to question his *ism*. There is a vein of spirit-life underlying these brief words, addressed to his Bro. Harter, to whom he confided many heart secrets. Were the spirits burning up his theological rubbish? "Don't glory, my brother, in my independence. I want a long talk with you about Universalism, as an *ism*, particularly as taught by the old school."

Mr. Peebles takes to dignity as the pine to the mountain. His pride is in the way. While he was preaching in Oswego, N.Y., vigorous efforts were made to obtain a capacious Orthodox church, for the celebrated Mrs. Bloomer, wherein to lecture upon "dress-reform." The officials refusing it, of course, Mr. Peebles secured the Universalist house of worship. To give it more respectability, he was voted into the courtesy of meeting her at the cars. When on a mission of duty, Mr. Peebles is thoughtless of reputation. This is a marked trait in his make-up. He is of the Fremont stamp, not Lincoln. In his zeal, he sometimes blunders into a pit, but is out ere he touches bottom. He met the lady: she was attired in "*bloomer*." Why had he not thought of her costume before consenting to escort her into the city? But there was no backing out; against the grain. Arm in arm they walked through the principal street, followed by an accumulating crowd of rowdies who encored them with shoutings, whistlings, and jeerings, to the hotel. He, however, bore this "great cross" quite manfully, and had the compensating satisfaction of seeing an enthusiastic congregation gathered in his church, swayed by a woman's eloquent appeal for emancipation from the thralldom of fashion. The victory over rowdyism and Orthodox conservatism was splendid, popularizing his moral independence.

He pressed in his "Literary Herbarium" this floating thistle-flower: —

> "Learn for the sake of your mind's repose,
>   That wealth's a bauble that comes and goes,
> And that proud flesh, wherever it grows,
>   Is subject to irritation."

Mr. Peebles's radicalism cost him much, trying his moral steel in a thousand ways. Under the pressure of Orthodox prejudice and a world of care, he would often fall into despondency, producing physical exhaustion. Needing "school-day companionship," he sent for Bro. Harter, and offered to pay his expenses if he would come and cure him of the "blues." Coming, he commenced his ready wit, — the antidote for such sins, — when the depressed minister, the first time for several weeks, began to laugh; the thermometer of joke rising to so great a heat, Mr. Peebles offered him double pay, "considering lame sides," if he would go home!

"Seek and ye shall find," was his text about this time. So utopian, he needed a balance-wheel, a centripetal force. Thus he reasoned; and so others recommended. In Mary M. Conkey, a teacher of Clinton Liberal Institute, he found a very refined and artistic companion. As a painter, she excelled; and in after years became a spirit artist, whose productions are very beautiful. In a "Pen Sketch of Reformers," published in Moses Hull's "Spiritual Rostrum," Mrs. H. F. M. Brown writes, —

> "Mary Conkey, the wife of our brother, has kept pace with him in all his progressive ideas. However dark and rough the outer world has sometimes seemed, there has always been light, peace, and a loving welcome in a home that Mary has beautified by her own artistic hand. Clouds have overshadowed the home, but they were the shadows of angel wings."

Sir Walter Scott says, — untruthfully? — "From my experience, not one in twenty marries the first love: we build statues of snow, and weep to see them melt." Oliver Goldsmith, adverting to his experience, says, "I chose my wife, as she did her wedding-gown, for qualities that would wear well." Our volatile young preacher had often wept over "the melting snow," but sought "qualities that would wear well."

CHAPTER V.

STEPS TO FREEDOM.

"Out of the eater came forth meat, and out of the strong came forth sweetness." — RIDDLE OF SAMSON.

"Sow ye beside all waters,
Where the dew of heaven may fall:
Ye shall reap if ye be not weary;
For the Spirit breathes o'er all.
Sow, though the thorns may wound thee:
One wore the thorns for thee;
And, though the cold winds scorn thee:
Patient and hopeful be.

Sow, though the rock repel thee,
In its cold and sterile pride:
Some cleft there may be riven,
Where the little seed may hide.
Fear not, some will flourish;
And, though the tares abound,
Like the willows by the waters
Will the scattered grain be found." — FRIENDS' REVIEW.

IN January, 1856, Mr. Peebles accepted a call to the pastorate of the Universalist Society of Baltimore, Md. The query rose in the minds of some of his professed friends, whether he would there freely advocate Northern principles. One "jealous-pated fellow" reported he had the "gag on;" another, that he had "lost his Northern heart." Writing a friend about this, he said, —

"I have *not* lost my Northern heart, nor Northern principles. You *know* I can neither love nor apologize for human slavery. What I believe, I must speak out. There are open opponents of slavery here, as in New York. It was the understanding from the first, that I should be a pastor free and independent."

About this time, Mr. Peebles was already a defender of a certain phase of Spiritualism. Wedded to his denomination, he was very prudent in his language, careful to preserve the precious adjective that renders all things respectable, — Christian, — a "*Christian* Spiritualist." Hopeful! If we only get *spiritual* on the brain, growing, it will soon burst the iron frontispiece of our caste. Evidently our brother had been in good company, being guilty of all the heresies of the day. Note a private epistle dated from Baltimore, —

"I hear many complaints that 'The Ambassador' is filled with such trash as 'Tangle-Town Letters!' The last two articles of the editor are down on the Spiritualists. Brother Reynolds ought to know, and Brother Austin *does* know, that hundreds of Universalists, and patrons, too, of 'The Ambassador,' are *Spiritualists*, — not fanatical Spiritualists, nor 'free-love' Spiritualists, but earnest, candid, *Christian Spiritualists;* such as are Rev. T. J. Smith, and Rev. S. Cobb, of 'The Freeman.' I met several intelligent Universalists in Western New York, that have stopped 'The Ambassador,' and commenced taking 'The Spiritual Telegraph.' This grieved me; because I love 'The Ambassador' and *Brother Austin*, and will ever do all in my power for its advancement among *Universalists!* We have some old fogy Universalists among us, who treat Spiritualists just as the Orthodox have treated us! The truth will finally triumph, call it by what name we may."

Successful, he was regarded by other churches as "a most dangerous man." He issued several doctrinal tracts, which were circulated over the country, and received with general favor by liberal minds. The Orthodox had a "committee on Sunday appointments." Mr. Peebles, addressing a polite note to the same, solicited the favor of having his vacant pulpit supplied, one sabbath, by a Methodist minister. It was refused! He then wrote Bishops Waugh, Scott, and Rev. L. F. Morgan, a pungent, kind epistle, comparing them with the rabbi of the Jewish synagogue, —

"Would to God that the narrow, proscriptive, sectarian spirit, so pointedly condemned in the Pharisees by Christ, had perished with them, instead of living, as it evidently does, the blight and curse of Christendom. Why not exchange pulpit services with Universalists and Unitarians? Can you not preach as much truth to their congregations as they can error to yours? Or are you so popish as to doubt the propriety of 'private judgment,' forbidding your people hearing all denominations, that they may form a correct judgment upon the doctrines of Christianity? If you have the light, why not let it 'shine' from Universalist pulpits? This reminds me of the following circumstance: —

"'John Adams, upon being requested to give for the support of foreign missions, made the following pointed reply: "I have nothing to give for that cause; but there are here in this immediate vicinity sixty ministers, not one of whom will preach in the other's pulpit. Now, I will give as much, and more than any other man, to civilize these clergymen."

"The venerable Adams, with a severity that I would not employ, thought the civilizing of those Massachusetts clergy a pre-requisite to Christianizing them.

"But to the original inquiry, Why refuse a preacher for our pulpit? The apostle says that 'Faith cometh by hearing, and hearing by the word of God.' 'And how shall they hear without a preacher?' And yet you declined sending us one, when you certainly must have had nearly three hundred in the city unemployed, idling away their time. Had the master visibly stepped into his vineyard on Sunday, would he not have repeated his language of old, 'Why stand ye here all the day idle?' And then how can you give an account of your stewardship at the day of 'final adjudication?' May not these neglected Universalists (who are to be damned, admitting your theology true) confront you with the telling words: 'No man hath cared for my soul;' 'Our blood be upon your garments;' 'The harvest is ended, and we are not saved.'

"I believe in God, in Jesus Christ, in the Holy Spirit, in the inspiration of the Scriptures, the necessity of faith, repentance, the new birth, 'experimental religion,' personal piety, and that, 'without holiness, no man shall see the Lord.' I believe in moral freedom, in man's accountability, in a just punishment for sin, the atonement by Christ, the resurrection of the dead, and the restoration of all men, during the mediatorial reign of the Son of God. And, in all my ministrations, I press the importance of obedience to God, a compliance with the conditions of salvation, and a more thorough consecration of all the powers to the love and service of the Father.

"And yet I am not recognized as a Christian, nor permitted to receive the civilities and courtesies of civic life from the Methodist clergymen of Baltimore. 'Father, forgive them.' God looks not at denominational names, but the heart. I cherish no malice toward you. The spirit of my faith, with the Master's lessons, induce me to return love for hatred, good for evil, blessing for cursing, and to 'pray for those who despitefully use me.' I close by renewing the former request to the Conference, to supply my pulpit next Sunday morning and evening.

"Yours, in the gospel of Christ, J. M. PEEBLES."

One orthodox minister, ashamed of his Baltimore brethren, — Rev. H. C. Atwater, of Providence, member of the Methodist Conference, — voluntarily supplied Mr. Peebles's pulpit "with power and eloquence, and, I trust, with the approbation of God."

The mistletoe loves the old oak. If pride of position hold us in a fashionable dead-lock, if pampered priests cajole us into tame submission, then the gods will institute trials, and *compel* our freedom. Mr. Peebles was yet young, volatile, sanguine, companionable, playful as a dancing lamb on the sunny hillside. "He is a mischief," said the staid old women; "very unministerial," said the denominational "iron clads;" "too radical," said the political conservatives. But everybody sought his genial soul. "Envy loves a shining mark." The lecherous like to victimize the poetic. The most suspicious of others' virtue are almost uniformly themselves the most *un*virtuous. The depravity we see in our neighbors is ourselves reflected. Betrayal works when charity is asleep.

"The deepest ice that ever froze
Can only o'er the surface close:
The living stream lies deep below,
And flows, and can not cease to flow."

Free, jovial, heretical, affiliating with Spiritualists, of course, unwarranted suspicions sprung up. "Stories," like snow-balls rolling down hill, gain in volume and momentum. The poor man was unprepared for this first trial: disheartened, he sank into an alarming sickness. Under the circumstances, he resigned his pastoral charge. "The Boston Trumpet" thought "all was not right." "The Ambassador" paid the following just compliment: —

"We learn that Brother J. M. Peebles has tendered his resignation to the society in Baltimore. He does not consider his health sufficiently good to enable him to perform the very great amount of labor required in Baltimore. For several sabbaths past, he has held but one service in consequence. Brother Peebles is an excellent pastor, and therefore will not long be without a society suited to his strength."

"The Baltimore Sun" noticed the resignation thus magnanimously, —

"We understand that the Rev. J. M. Peebles, pastor of the Universalist Church in this city, has handed his resignation to that society. Mr. Peebles has been forced to this step by declining health; and we are sure his society will regret the cause of this determination. During Mr. Peebles's short stay in this city, he has won for himself many warm friends; and the large and increasing attendance in his ministerial labors are sure evidences that his society fully appreciate his talents. He will rest from his labors for at least a year, hoping thereby to re-establish his health and usefulness."

Several leading clergymen, disliking the unwarranted suspicions breathed by "The Trumpet," addressed the following letter to the editor: —

"BROTHER WHITTEMORE,— Having made inquiry concerning the report referred to in your paper of last week concerning Rev. J. M. Peebles, we beg leave to say, that we consider said report not warranted by the circumstances, and founded upon unauthorized and exaggerated statements.

"E. H. CHAPIN.
G. T. FLANDERS.
A. ST. JOHN CHAMBRE.
PORTER THOMAS.
B. PETERS.
HENRY LYON.
EBEN FRANCIS.
And others.

"New York, Oct. 30, 1856."

Finding the report was founded upon "unauthorized and exaggerated statements," the ministerial busy-bodies began to fear they had gone too far for the good of the denomination. There is a point of traffic with unrighteous wares when "forbearance ceases to be a virtue." Not a few of our Universalist ministers can testify to this from personal experience, proving that our hunted brother was not alone in his pilgrimage from bondage to freedom.*

After occupying his pulpit two or three months succeeding his resignation, Mr. Peebles and wife left for Canton, N.Y., the "old homestead," where he soon received letters soliciting him to return and build up a new society in Baltimore. Others urged him to accept his previous charge, as letters from J. L. Camp, Geo. T. White, E. L. Ironmonger, Marston, Marden, &c., at our disposal, testify; but he declined every proffer of the kind, when his old society passed unanimously the following resolutions: —

"BALTIMORE, Oct. 6, 1856.

"REV. J. M. PEEBLES. *Dear Brother,* — At a meeting of the Universalist Society of the city of Baltimore, convened in the church, on Sunday afternoon, Oct. 5, 1856, your resignation was received, and the following action had thereon: —

"*Whereas,* It has become necessary for our pastor, on account of his declining health, to offer his resignatioh to the society over which he has held pastoral relations during the past nine months, therefore, be it

"*Resolved,* That the resignation of Brother J. M. Peebles, as pastor of the second Universalist Society of Baltimore, be received and accepted.

"*Resolved,* That we sincerely deplore the occasion which has led Brother Peebles

---

* Of Universalist ministers persecuted, or ex-communicated, for the heresy of Spiritualism, may be mentioned, Revs. T. L. Harris, E. B. Averill, J. M. Spear, J. P. Averill, S. B. Brittan, T. J. Smith, L. P. Rand, J. B. Dods, Wm. Fishbough, Adin Ballou, Geo. Severance, B. S. Hobbs, J. H. Harter, Rev. Mr. Cravens, A. C. Edmunds, A. J. Fishback, Joseph Baker, J. C. Crawford, R. Connor, &c. Mr. Connor was "cast out of the synagogue" for disbelief in the plenary inspiration of the Bible, the resurrection of the physical body of Christ, and other minor opinions. In February, 1869, by the State Committee of the Illinois Convention of Universalists, the author of this biography, after twelve years ministerial labor with that denomination, was excommunicated from fellowship solely for teaching the gospel of angel ministry! The following was the "bull" passed against us: —

"And be it also known, that said committee, having cited the Rev. J. O. Barrett to appear before them, and show cause, if any he had, why his letter of fellowship should not be withdrawn, he having ceased to use it for the purposes for which it was given, and he not appearing, his case is judged by default; and the committee do hereby decide and declare his letter withdrawn. Be it known, that the above decision is not based upon moral causes.

W. S. RALPH,
T. J. CARNEY,
B. N. WILES,
G. W. HIGGINS,
Committee of Fellowship, Ordination, and Discipline."

Patience, brethren! God is majority! Let us trust while we *act* the poet's idea, —

"Stand back, ye Philistines;
Practice what ye preach to me:
I heed ye not; for I know ye all.
Your creeds are living, burning lies,
In the sight of God's pure truths!"

thus early to dissolve the connection which has so happily existed between us as pastor and people.

"*Resolved*, That, wherever his lot may be cast, when other friends are around him, and when other scenes meet his eyes, our prayers will ascend 'to the Giver of all good gifts' to restore him to health and usefulness, and to lengthen his days on the earth.

"*Resolved*, That in all his relations toward this society, as pastor, friend, and guardian of the sabbath school, he has ever evinced a devotedness and untiring zeal, which have conduced to rivet the bonds of affection between us and him more close and firm; and we will not omit to say, that the cause of Christ has prospered in his hands.

"*Resolved*, That a copy of this preamble and resolutions be signed by the officers, and transmitted to Bro. J. M. Peebles.

"JAS. L. CAMP, *Secretary*.

"RICHARD MARLEY,
President Board of Trustees."

Mr. Peebles never held a pastoral relation with any society or church that did not, at the dissolution, pass resolutions in his favor with unanimous indorsement.

The wounded bird, hit in her own nest, returns not thither. Then a hiding-place is sought, —

"Some boundless contiguity of shade."

Just there the angel finds the pilgrim. Strange, that in misfortune we think to run away from the attendant spirit!

After remaining in Canton a few months, the hours of convalescence, dragging their iron fetters, Mr. Peebles one day resolved to quit the ministry for ever. Was that the first time? How many an apostle has thought it, said it! In a few weeks, he was on the wing, *en route* for the West, to enter into business with his cousin, Col. F. E. Peebles, banker and real-estate dealer, of Winona, Minn. We may go the length of our "cable toe." Any farther? What did this man know about business? A pretty shift for a prophet! Elisha whimpered under the juniper-tree. Oh, if he had only got behind a counter, and dealt in "stocks and stones"! If Jesus had only thrown away his "knot of strong cords," and invested capital in the "money-changers' business!" O Reformers! O poor, persecuted, wandering mediums!

"Happier to chase a flying goal,
Than to sit counting laureled gains;
To *guess* the soul within the soul,
Than to be lord of what remains."

On the way West, thinking to rest a while in Cleveland, Mr. Peebles found there a welcome home at Mr. Odell's, one of his Kellogsville friends. Conversation immediately turned upon Spiritualism, —" that unmanageable element of church discord." In the main, it appeared to him " as glittering, drifting sand, with now and then a particle of gold, roiling the pure gospel."

The Davenport boys were then performing in the city; and, fortunately, a *séance* was appointed in a hall that afternoon. Among the prominent lawyers, physicians, ministers, and other quizzing thinkers, sat Mr. Peebles, eying the machinery with silent suspicion. The ropes were securely tied upon the brothers, flour put into their hands, chalk-marks around their feet, and the room darkened; when instantly the musical instruments moved swiftly round the room, played on by invisible hands. Dreamy suspicion changed to earnest curiosity. He was quite a philosopher now, thinking by what occult agency — odylic, magnetic, earthly, or spiritual — that strange phenomenon was produced. A few, more churchal, trembled, fearful that the devil was playing his tricks upon them; but James felt safe on his shaky plank of bibliolatry. When the circle was in good order, by request of the mediums, the light, subdued and mellow, shone just enough to reveal those instruments passing and repassing over their heads, playing a tune; and there sat the Davenports, snugly tied in their chairs. King, the hero-spirit, then spoke audibly through a trumpet, startling them with the assurance that he would reveal himself to them in bodily shape.

The aural emanations of the circle were favorable to spirit materialization. Does not the germ of the rose, rooted in the warm bosom of " mother nature," sun-fused to its almost pulsing heart, materialize itself, incorporate vital elements around it, forming first the stalk, then the lunged leaves, then the bud, bursting, some summer morning, into the many-tinted flower? What is nature but the material embodiment of spirit? What is spirit doing here but constructing a mirror for the angels to look through? Thus we identify ourselves. Why can not spirits do the same by using like forces, governed by like laws?

An orderly circle, with inquiring affections, evolves a sphere rightly conditioned for the visible picturing of a spirit, — to produce a light within a light, like Manoah's angel in the flame of the altar. A spirit is not obliged to work up gross substance into finer form, as we do;

but, acting through our mediumship, it grasps elements already refined, and invests itself with the spheral aura of physical and spiritual organisms, — organ for organ, function for function, — a *very* spirit manifestation.

Emma Hardinge, in her great work entitled "HISTORY OF MODERN AMERICAN SPIRITUALISM," thus presents the analytical testimony of the spirits upon this subject: —

> "In some long but interesting communications, written in the spirit-room, without human agency, it is said that spirits, in their communion with earth, manifest through two primitive elements; namely, first, an electro-magnetic element, of which the spiritual body is composed; next, a physical aura, which emanates from the medium, or can be collected from material substances, analogous, it is supposed, to the element of 'vitality' described in the preceding chapter. From the combination of these two, — namely, the emanations of the spirit and the medium, — a third, or composite, is formed, which is affected by the atmosphere and human emanations. From the preponderance of the electro-magnetic or spiritual element, the laws of cohesion and gravitation can be overcome; and, through this, spirits are enabled to dissolve and re-compose substances with great rapidity, heave up and carry material bodies through the air, and cause them to float or sink, in proportion to the strength of the battery formed. It is this element which enables some spirits, highly charged with it, to come into contact with matter, and thus to use pencils, pens, etc., in writing, drawing, and playing on musical instruments. By aid of the physical or human aura, — animal magnetism, — they cause concussions, raps, shaking of furniture, and heavy ponderable bodies ; by this, also, they produce spirit-light, gathering it up so as to form an envelope of matter around their own hands, condense sound so as to be heard, singing and speaking, and strike upon the heavier instruments. 'The composite element is used more or less in all modes.'"

Mr. Peebles was not *then* able to understand this "spiritual alchemy," — could not even comprehend the simple fact, that his philosophy of miracles could measure even the materialization of a spirit. He had taught that a miracle, strictly speaking, is the action of a natural but unknown law. Here he actually probed the vein of spirit phenomena. What Universalists and Unitarians had discovered, — that the laws of nature harmonize, and are one and identical with the revealed laws of God, — is, in fact, the magic wand that opens to view all the mysteries in heaven and earth, when, behold! we look therein in the calm light of philosophy.

Mr. Peebles was "struck with conviction," but still trying to "climb up the old way." Scales were before his vision, and spirits were "a wonder in a wonder-making world." He had at first doubted whether those instruments would fly around their heads without hands touching them: then the spirits permitted him to see them moving, as if themselves things of life; yet more wonderful came the promise, that the spirit himself would be seen! He doubted.

The boys again were tied: all was dark, silent, gloomy; when, lo! a flickering glimmer shot out, as a star at midnight, swelling larger into nebulous mist, rolling up fleecy white, growing more and more distinct, till, opening as "a door in heaven," there appeared the spirit form of a strange man in large proportions. The spirits had done even more than they promised. Was he now convinced? Our confounded, confounding brother cast himself again into the "slough of doubt," to cogitate upon "occipital motion," "od force," "unconscious psychology," and the like, — the bed of spikes wilful skeptics delight to dream on.

Mr. Peebles said, "We read that an angel rolled away a stone from Christ's sepulchre, and another angel unlocked Peter's prison-door: if you be spirits, I defy you to do the same, or any thing like it."

At Mr. Odell's, that evening, the room brilliantly lighted with gas, the boys tied, he and all the company saw peacocks' plumes floating over their heads, and books with sheets of paper moving without visible hands. Sensing his mental re-action, the spirits approached him, and suddenly jerked him out of the circle, throwing him upon the floor. This trespass upon his clerical dignity enlivened the circle to a general merriment; which the spirits enjoyed by a more lively play, with the instruments whizzing musically around their ears. Did he now believe? He was sure of this much, that it was "no mesmeric hallucination;" for his side was actually lame.

The Davenport brothers, J. K. Brown of Buffalo, and Mr. Peebles, occupied the same room that auspicious night. Retiring, full of frolic, he playfully, yet seriously, challenged the spirits to make him a visit. When all was still, the blinds of the house open, the moon shining brightly, and balmy sleep began to fold over the eyelids, suddenly they were all roused at the sound of three raps upon the door. "Come in!" said our "chosen apostle," — "Come in!" very respectful in tone of voice. But no one responded. "Come in!" loudly called our brother. Then the door gently opened, and swung back to the wall. He looked up, gazed, scrutinizing through the wide aperture; but nobody appeared. Rap, rap, rap! on the floor, then on the walls. The boys exclaimed, "The spirits are here!" Just then Mr. Peebles remembered his challenge; when a heavy hand struck him on his stomach, and a smart crack on his head. "Oh, that hurts — hurts!" said our hero, in trepidation. The boys laughed, and encouraged an "evening entertainment." The moonlight itself seemed a saucy witness of Mr. Peebles's discomfiture.

The clothes sprung off the bed, the bed itself rocked; and confusion generally ensued. "For Heaven's sake, Peebles," said Brown, "strike a light." Mustering courage, he sprung out; and, as he walked across the room, that same hand hit him solid on the back. The blow was overpowering; and, in alarm and pain, he shouted, "That hurts! Oh! Oh! I know you are spirits! I give it up! I will believe; but don't *hurt* me so!" Frightened, he scrambled into bed, pulling the sheet over his face, like a child at sight of a ghost. One of the boys entranced, a voice from the air said, "You dared us. Get your light: we'll do you no harm. Mrs. Odell, listening joyfully in the hall below, exclaimed, "Good, Brother Peebles, good! they will convert you before morning!" Mr. Peebles inquired, "Why do you handle me thus roughly, if you be good spirits?" The intelligence replied, "To give you evidence of our power, and complete demonstration of conscious immortality, that you may walk no longer by faith, but by sight. You are appointed for a great work: gird up your loins, buckle on your sandals, grasp the sword of truth. Go forth!"

It was to him a genuine knock-down argument. The impression made by that *séance* was deep and lasting, awakening in after years a heart-gratitude to the spirits controlling the Davenport circle, for the solid proof of their presence when he was in most need of angelic light.

Away from Eastern associations, dreamily sauntering along the frozen shore of the "Father of Waters," skimming now and then a pebble over the ice, like a mere child; then at night, after an undefined and undefinable business-attempt that was as awkward as his chopping enterprises in old Vermont, tossing and twisting upon his bed, asleep with one eye on bank-bills and the other on God! — such were our hero's experiences in Minnesota. He was nowhere, yet everywhere; thinking nothing, yet thinking every thing. "James M. Peebles, Banker and Real-Estate Dealer!" was his oft soliloquy; "Ha! ha! ha! — real-estate, litigation, speculation, — money to 'swim in.' All my early ambition leaked out: well, well!" Poor fellow! he dreaded the sign-board strangely. At length, a calm came on, the calm that follows a swift shower, — the time for an angel to unroll the panorama of his life. There it was, all in picture, — boyhood, school-days, romances, mistakes, prayers, deeds, ministries, friends so many, enemies too, the work scarcely begun ere it is blasted; oh, what lights and shades in that review! Then sinking into a half-revery, he questioned himself, — questioned his ability, questioned his fidelity, questioned God, Christ, Bible, every thing, — questioned where he had been accustoned to pray with seeming faith; and, listen! the question was laden with a new, startling answer, that folded down upon him like a sun ray, —

"Go and preach your highest convictions of truth and duty!" — "*Highest* convictions," he repeated, — "highest *convictions!*" There was a meaning here, never before so solemn and impressive. "Have I stifled the truth?" he asked: "have I compromised truth, or shunned duty?" — "Go and preach your highest convictions!" was the response.

Instantly his resolution was fixed. He would be henceforth independent, act the Parker, an agitator! 'Tis easier said than done. It is a great ways out of Egypt. A sect holding us by education, friendship, support, is as bewildering as a wilderness. Its darkness is *visible*, when the soul pants for liberty. What are those cables over the fitful waterfalls? Gossamer threads! What the apprenticeship? Battle, agony, heart-ache! To sever ministerial ties; to turn oneself out of home; to be *un*salaried; to be a lonely Elijah on the Sacred Mount; to be a Jesus tempted, betrayed, crucified; to face a frowning church, full of howling and scorn, — *that* is something to a minister once pampered and flattered. But he must pay this cost! He must traverse the gulf between liberal preaching and liberal practice, losing from his shoulders the respectable burden styled *Christian*. Toleration in the pulpit is debasingly intolerant out of the pulpit. He must be the exception among ministers to equipoise these antagonisms. By a delicate art, the spirits write upon the arms of some of their media electric letters of fire, speaking words of immortal love. Such must now be engraved upon his *soul* by an angel's pen.

"The waters compassed me about, even to the soul: the depth closed me round about; the weeds were wrapped about my head. I went down to the bottoms of the mountains: the earth with her bars was about me for ever; yet hast thou brought up my life from corruption, O Lord! my God. . . . And the Lord spake unto the fish; and it vomited Jonah up on dry land."

Scarcely knowing what to do with himself, he half-concluded to return to Canton. "What for?" he pondered. There is a time in life when the heart hugs its holy purpose with a fear and trembling; when a vail shuts over our vision, and we only *feel* destiny. Is there not an angel of the "Over Soul," who hides future prospects from us, lest our hopes may be too high, making us selfish; and hides adversity, lest we may, in our unschooled faith, refuse to advance?

> "Oh, blindness to the future kindly given,
> That each may fill his station marked by heaven!"

Liberty hangs by a delicate pivot: the slightest touch will tip it. The spirits know this, and watch our vacillation with intense anxiety. Unconscious to ourselves, we may be on the very point of turning; and then come two counter-forces, to try our mettle. "Thoughts, like sun-fires, penetrate the world." Spirits of our plane, feeling the disturbance in our bosoms, foreseeing consequences, drifting to us on the wave-crests of this mental sphere, alarmed at any break in a link of fellowship, rush with impetuous zeal to help their earthly companions keep their brightest stars in their own galaxy. Spirits of higher life, hearing our prayer for deliverance, also gather near, to lift us up to their society. To the candidate, it is a fearful moment, — the neutral ground of battle between the old and the new.

This was our brother's experience now. By a blind instinct, he had arrived at Chicago, where he received letters from influential ministers and other friends, urging him to return to the "Universalist ministry, where he belonged." Why this pleading at this hour? Yes, why? Ask those "powers and principalities of the air." What was the voice from Elmira, Jamestown, N.Y., Baltimore, McLean, Auburn? "Return to your first love! Be less radical: preach good old Universalism!" Ah, James! had you known Delilah then as well as you do now, would you even *thought* of having your locks shaven, that the Philistines might conquer you?

This was Saturday evening. That night, sleepless, worrying, full of pleadings, will never be forgotten. The better angels recorded it; and it will be read, by and by, to note how close came a heavenly heart in an angel's hand to his troubled bosom, but could not enter, for the casket was not yet cleared of impediment.

A stranger in a city on Sunday morning is at liberty to go where his *instincts* lead.

Taking a humble seat in a *Spiritualist* meeting, he looked over the happy audience, noticing prominent citizens, whom he afterwards learned to be such men as Seth Paine, H. M. Higgins, Mr. Green, &c. "Not all fools, I trow," he thought. Soon a gentleman was entranced, and came direct to him. What did it mean? All eyes were riveted on him. No escape! Then the spirit calmly said, with a kind voice of recognition,—

> "I see your devious and winding pathway of life, — thorns and craggy steeps. Recently, you have been on a rough and tempestuous sea: your craft was rickety and unsafe. You leaped from it into the deep! Ah, ha! you are in a better vessel: you are alone in it, — nobody to guide you over all this vast waste. But look above: there it is, a strong hand that controls all! Nothing but a hand I see; and it guides you so safe! You touch the shore; and now your path winds up, up, over rocks! There are precipices and perils; but the hand guides, and you are safe! You are commissioned from ON HIGH! Go, teach the ministry of angels!"

> "Methinks the air
> Throbs with the tolling of harmonious bells,
> Rung by the hands of spirits everywhere:
> We feel the presence of a soft despair,
> And thrill to the voices of divine farewells." — DICKENS.

The prophecy of that medium in Chicago haunted Mr. Peebles night and day. It made him reflective. His purpose seemed uncertain. For what was he waiting? daylight to dawn? Starting for the East, through those busy streets, everybody's step poised to resolution but his own: so it seemed. He soliloquized: "What my fate? Rocks, precipices, perils! Alone I'll climb." — "*Alone?*" asked a voice. Then he thought of his ministerial companions, and recalled a report that Rev. J. P. Averill, of Battle Creek, Mich., a prominent Universalist, in full fellowship, had espoused Spiritualism. The angels know whom to trust, — where the oases are! Experiences not yet arrived at are *spiritually* as real as memories of the past. We step forward where the soul sees. The spider casts its vital thread ahead, to *feel* after a basis of support: so do we; but do not unseen friends watch the forward end, and fasten it on the high cliffs of heaven?

At Battle Creek, he called upon Mr. Averill, and found in him a sympathizing friend, who was also passing through the fire. Notice, without his knowledge, was immediately given that "Rev. J. M.

Peebles would address the Liberalists of Battle Creek, next Sunday morning and evening."

"Why," said Peebles, "I do not want to preach!"

"Talk then," replied Mr. A., — "talk! that's the best kind of preach."

A goodly number gathered in the hall, — Spiritualists, Universalists, Quakers, Free Thinkers, &c., "all of one accord in one place." The congregation intelligent, their greetings so cordial, he was inspired with the electric touch of soul to soul. His text was appropriate: "If the truth shall make you free, ye shall be free indeed." It was handled in a masterly manner, and found a happy response. Closing that ever memorable meeting, the congregation gathering around him, Joseph Merritt and Eli Lapham, both Quaker ministers, and others, gave him their hands, saying, "We want to engage thee. Thee need not call it preaching. Thee shall be free." Then and there he engaged for a year; and he remained six years pastor of "the *First Free Church* of Battle Creek." His now happy wife had a home again. Here they lived many years, dearly affiliated with that faithful people who loved him better than themselves. He shared in their deprivations, and sorrows, — always a harmonizer; and in all their troubles, sicknesses, and bereavements, was the ministering angel.

As the wave on the still lake widens out, so did our brother's work, so arduous, augment upon his hands from year to year; first a town, then a county, then a State. He was a seed-sower; and the gardens he made are in blossom yet.

Those days, as now, many Spiritualists whom he visited in these outgoings did not always remember the just claims of the faithful teacher. Often did he travel miles on foot to his appointments, receiving not a "thank you." As often did he bear his own expense of team. Poor gratitude that! In one of his "foot-appointments," he traveled fourteen miles, after speaking, in a dismal night, and fell into a ditch. "My God!" he exclaimed, "has it come to this? Horses owned by friends in ——, and I in this dilemma?" There is a species of bipeds, in their worm-state, that assume a liberal name to avoid taxation in illiberal relations. When just reward is demanded, they appeal to the example of Jesus and his apostles, who "preached the gospel without money and without price." Was ever insult greater? Do they forget that the Nazarene said, "The laborer is worthy of his hire." If they are *so* apostolic, let *them* "give all their goods to feed the poor," and "take no thought for the morrow." Will *they* deny self? The patience of Mr. Peebles with such "leeches" was sometimes too great to be a virtue. Be not too gentle with rotten teeth. Through all these tribulations, he faltered not. He verily went to the "by-ways and hedges." Where he sowed seed in the cold, the summer bloomed. His was the reward: "He that goeth forth, and weepeth, bearing precious seed, shall doubtless come again with rejoicing, bringing his sheaves with him."

O heart-aching church! feeding on the husks of fashion, what is this power that snatches us from your "close communions," from fine salaries, and drives us forth into thorny paths, to preach "the gospel to every creature," — in barns, halls, groves, and streets? "He that hath an ear, let him hear what the Spirit saith unto the churches." . . . "I counsel thee to buy of me gold, tried in the fire, that thou mayest be rich; and white raiment, that thou mayest be clothed, and that the shame of thy nakedness do not appear."

How can the river be locked in ice, when the summer sun touches it with so many hearts of love? Located among a people who appreciated his radical sentiments, favored with spiritual associations, frequently witnessing new and convincing developments of spirit presence, our brother grew young again, — full of frolic and merriment, as in his school-days at Oxford. How quick clouds vanish when a sensitive soul finds its social home! How grandly the sinking ship of life rises high on the waves, when an angel hovers over it! O blessed heaven! but for those who know and love us, what were our changing world? The cross buds when love is bleeding on it.

"The very flowers that bend and meet,
In sweetening others grow more sweet."

Mr. Peebles continued his well-begun work, winning friends everywhere to the standard of spiritual liberty. One, two, three years rolled on, each laden with seed-time and harvest. Then dawned the hour of reconciliation. Several Universalist ministers, instrumental in circulating "bad currency," having grown more liberal, made the *amende honorable* in private letters to him, asking his forgiveness. Says Lamerais, —

"Love makes all things possible."

The flower blesses the foot that crushes it. What a joy was his, to give back a hand warm with generous feeling! Arm in arm again, joking over the past, they proposed that he return to his denominational motherhood! Aha? His Brother Harter proffered a hand and heart. Other clergymen wrote in similar style.

"CHRISTIAN AMBASSADOR OFFICE,
AUBURN, N.Y., March 19, 1859.

"BRO. JAMES, —Why not come right back into the old Cayuga Association, and get a *letter of fellowship*? I will warrant one for you. I want the *true companion* of my boyhood to be a *Universalist minister*. Let me hear from you.

"J. H. HARTER."

His brother, J. L. Camp, of Baltimore, suggested the same step. We extract from his letter, —

"O Brother Peebles! you did a wrong thing to leave B., where your usefulness was just about being developed; and let me assure you (though I do not want to pamper your vanity, but tell you the solemn truth), that, were our desk vacant to-day, and you could be had again, you could get the unanimous vote of the society (save probably *one*); and, if you do go back into the Universalist ministry, which I pray God you may, do not make any permanent arrangement with any society until we have a chance."

What was Mr. Peebles's reply to these cordial invitations? "Come over and help *us*!" When asked if he thought of returning to the Universalist ministry, he asked, "Do planets go back?"

"Can ye drive young spring from the blossomed earth?"

During all his public labors, Mr. Peebles has never said any thing against, but always for, progressive, liberal Universalism; among whose defenders, he reckons some of his truest friends. No formal denominational charge was ever brought against him: no ecclesiastical tribunal ever arraigned him. He resigned his letter of fellowship in 1856.

Several years after, Mr. Peebles was invited to Baltimore by the Spiritualists: then he went. There he met old friends, — Danskin, Camp, White, and others. How changed! After speaking encouraging words of the spiritual cause, under the ministrations of Mrs. F. O. Hyzer, he wrote, —

"We bid Universalism, as interpreted by its better and broader-souled exponents, Godspeed; but this little picayunish, sectarian Universalism, that says, 'Thus far and no farther,' is only comparable to Martha's representation of Lazarus's body, four days dead. We believe in Universalism still, as a *faith;* and, in becoming a Spiritualist, have only obeyed the apostolic injunction, 'Add to your faith . . . *knowledge.*' Whereas we formerly walked by faith, seeing through a 'glass darkly,' now we walk by sight, *knowing*, that, when this earthly house is dissolved, 'we have a building of God, a house not made with hands, eternal in the heavens.'"

CHAPTER VI.

THE PROPHET MAN.

"All are architects of fate,
  Working in these walls of time;
Some with massive deeds and great,
  Some with ornaments of rhyme." — LONGFELLOW.

THE artist angels select their media for temple-service. Fitness to order is the rule of structure. The man before us, entering now upon a higher work, is public property; and everybody has a right here. There is yet to be a system of "Spiritual Phrenology." Engineers, conductors, treasurers, and other candidates for public positions, to whom the safety of human life and property is intrusted, will be selected with reference to mediumistic abilities.

Mrs. H. F. M. Brown gives the following psychometrical reading: —

"Mr. Peebles's leading characteristic is, perhaps, *individuality*. He is independent in thought and speech; condemns cowardice and jealousies without stint: he commends where he can, never looking to see which way the tide is setting, or waits public approval. But he is quite willing that others should live their lives, if principles are not compromised. He is orderly, generous, social, mirthful, and a great lover of the beautiful. In personal appearance, he is tall, straight, of slender form, brown hair, blue eyes: his face is of Roman mold: his teeth faultless. He dresses with great care, avoiding alike the dandy and the sloven. . . . He is tall and slim as a May-pole; as fair and frail as a delicate woman. Consumption looks him in the face occasionally; but, by sailing the world half round, he has eluded the unwelcome phantom. But, after all, the mistake might have been in putting the right soul into the wrong body. Spiritwise, Mr. Peebles is a mountaineer. He is calm in a storm, laughs at the lightning, and listens to the thunder as friend to friend. His thoughts, like mountain-streams, gush forth with freshness, music, and originality. If he is a thought-borrower, his benefactions are the ferns, the dewy mosses, the wild flowers, the cloud-crowned hills, and green valleys of his native State. I said to my soul, while listening to him, Emerson had this very man in his mind, when he said, —

'In your heart are birds and sunshine: in your thoughts the brooklets flow.'"

In 1858, J. M. Spear, entranced, gave Mr. Peebles the appropriate title of the "Elucidator;" because his "mission is to catch and elucidate thoughts, ideas, and principles." In 1867, at Blue Anchor, N.J., Mr. Spear gave him another reading, discovering material changes in his spiritual organism during the interim of about ten years: —

"The element of reconciliation is just coming into the bud state. It will so open that you will be able to reconcile apparent opposites, and to show the relation which disapprovals must and do bear to approvals, and how a course of the opposites helps open up into the divine and highest action."

In the trance condition, Mr. Spear also advised him to labor in the sphere for which he was then best fitted, — "the ministry of reconciliation," — to harmonize the belligerent forces of Spiritualism, and in social and political life. Travel he must in the Old World, to study institutions, and trace the civilizing relations of nations, — to be no longer a nationalist, but a cosmopolitan. And here stands a prophecy: —

"At a later period, you will have your chair in a contemplated college, where, by your elucidative and reconciliative power, you will become a teacher especially adapted to young women from eighteen to twenty-five years of age. There will be your forte. You are therefore in process of culture for this closing labor of your life."

In 1869, Mrs. S. A. Waterman of Boston, dating from the magnetism of the superscription on his letter, under spirit influence, gave Mr. Peebles a very lucid delineation, indicative of rare mediumistic powers and appreciation of a true life.

Being in Providence, R.I., in 1860, lecturing on Spiritualism, he one evening attended a popular course of lectures on Phrenology, by O. S. Fowler, who, at the close, permitted the audience to select individuals for examination: when Mr. Peebles, then a stranger to the professor, was loudly called to the platform, with results afterwards written as follows: —

"You, sir, have an organization of mark, and can hardly fail to be a man of mark.

"Your largest single organ is firmness; are well nigh obstinate; would be quite so, but that large *caution* enables and disposes you to judge wisely before you decide, but, once decided, are like the laws of the 'Medes and Persians.' So be sure that 'you are right before you go ahead;' for you can turn your attention to almost any thing but bargain-driving. . . . Are a practical skeptic; doubt every thing until it is proved, and worship the Deity in nature, but not at all in *creeds* and *ceremonies*. Are eminently, even *pre-eminently*, *reformatory*, even radical. Have unbounded *benevolence*, and the greatest desire to do *good*, and make those around you *happy*. But, sir, your prayers are short. Are a first best judge of *human nature;* read a *man* right through; take your snap judgment of every thing, of men included; do best on the spur of the moment; so 'take no thought what you shall say; for it shall be given unto *you*, in the hour thereof.' Are *logical, clear-headed*, good in *explaining*, *expounding;* especially good in arguing, by *ridicule*, and '*showing up*.' Are terribly sarcastic, and will be one of the best *abused* and *praised* of men; for your enemies will hate you badly, and friends love you proportionately, even tremendously. Never stop; and, the greater the *obstacles*, the more determined you pursue your course: *obstacles only embolden you.*

"Have all the elements for becoming a soldier, and ought to be a commanding officer. I speak now of bravery, ambition, and endurance; would flinch at neither moral nor physical danger, but face them boldly: yet *moral courage* predominates. Are a most potential advocate of the *truth;* with you, *right* and *truth* are paramount. Are one of the *few* who dare to do their duty, and defy the *consequences*,— dare to speak right out.... Are not naturally mercenary; have no regard for dollars and cents; should learn their value, and cultivate smallness. Ought to have a salary, so that you can graduate your expenses accordingly. Will be cheated every time you try to drive *bargains*. Ought to have an economical wife, and put the purse into her hands; for you are not fit to carry it. Can never 'Jew up or down;' have no commercial talents; could succeed in business only by intellect. Are infinitely better adapted to *intellectual life;* should be a professional man; ought to be a *speaker*. Have really superior *talents* for acquiring knowledge, and imparting it. Have fine descriptive powers; are a little too apt to overdraw your pictures,—I mean, are given to hyperbole; use very strong *expressions;* are versatile in talents" . . . . . .

James Burns of London, England, in a philosophical dissertation upon climatic conditions as molding mind, writes in his excellent monthly, entitled "Human Nature," of July 1, 1870,—

"In America, we find a marked blending of the religious views of the native Indian with the best parts of Aryan philosophy. The keen, natural intuitions of the red man, his monotheistic creed, and consciousness of the 'Great Spirit,' are ingrafted upon the white man's culture and rationalistic tendencies; and, as a result, we have an improved combination of the primary and recent, the natural and attained, the intuitive and rationalistic, the spiritual and intellectual. And where did these influences come from? They have been derived from two sources: First, from the psychological influences impressed on the soil, atmosphere, and objects of the country by its former inhabitants, and unconsciously perceived and absorbed by the present population. Second, from the spirit-world, through the action of the spirits of the departed race upon those who this day occupy their places. We repeat, these considerations must become leading features in the investigations of ethnologists before the secrets of the wonderful transformations which are going on, and have taken place, amongst mankind can be accounted for. While anthropologists are mere physicists,—materialists,—they can only deceive themselves, and mislead the world. Their anatomical facts and incidental narratives are all good, so far as they go; but they are only children's stories and old women's fables, when compared with that form of knowledge which exposes the hidden causes from which objective phenomena proceed.

"We preface these remarks to a delineation of J. M. Peebles, as he is a well-marked example of the law we are endeavoring to point out. He is almost immediately descended from Scotch and English ancestors; yet, while he retains in the deeper strata of his character some of the features of both, but more particularly the Scotch, he very prominently exhibits peculiarities that belong to neither. The more we see of American mediums and Spiritualists, and the deeper we dive into their psychological experiences, the more are we impressed by the fact, that the unsectarian, natural, free influence of Indian spirits has much to do with the broad liberality and untrammeled love of spiritual truth which characterizes advanced Americans; and the work is yet going on, intensifying from year to year. And, as new means of communication open up between the various countries of the earth, we shall behold a wider extension of this great principle of psychological action, which we believe is the great modifier of humanity.

"Your brain [speaking of Mr. Peebles] is exceedingly active. The organs are sharply developed, and few of them are in a dormant state. Your body is eminently fitted for action. It is the servant of the brain in every particular; and your bodily organs and passions are entirely under the control of the mind, and subservient to its highest behests. You are lacking in vitality: you do not love life sufficiently for its own sake. Physical wants and animal necessities are disregarded by you; and you are entirely removed from the sphere of sensuous pleasure and animal indulgence. You have scarcely sufficient lung power, or arterial blood; but your peculiar temperament enables you to derive more from spiritual than physical sources. You do not feel the want of these deficiencies of the vital apparatus in the same degree as others would, of a grosser temperament. Your nervous system is excellently harmonized and balanced by your locomotive apparatus, which is long in development, and exercises much power of equilibrium over your exceedingly excitable nervous system; hence you can expend all your nerve-power in useful acts, and are inclined to be busy, continually carrying your thoughts into action, and doing a great deal of work with a very little wear and tear.

. . . .

"The social organs are very fully marked. This region of the brain is indicative of the feminine type. You have all the feelings of a mother, and, as it were, take a maternal interest in those with whom you come in contact. Your affections are more of the domestic than social type; hence you take everybody with whom you sympathize into the close relationship of brotherhood, and take a real interest in all with whom you become acquainted. . . . .

"You are very considerate towards woman. You harmonize with her spirit very truly, and can influence the female mind quite favorably, if it is on the same plane as your own. You are capable of making many female friends.

"Industry and promptness are striking characteristics. You are always busy, and can not waste time, or take sufficient rest. You would be better with more hardness and aggressiveness of character, to resist encroachments and protect self. Were it not for the fact that you have very little fear and restraining power generally, you would not have sufficient resolution to accomplish the work of your life; but your mind is free from apprehension or fear: hence you can advance with very little friction.

"You are exceedingly deficient in that which leads to policy, equivocation, and suspicion. You are too open and unguarded. You have moral forethought, which keeps you straight with your conscience. You likewise manifest that quality of reserve and depth of mind which keeps you from opening up your character at once to the greater number of those you meet with; hence, though familiar with many, they may not know you thoroughly, because of a certain delicacy which restrains you from manifesting yourself beyond the limits of strict propriety.

. . . .

"You are naturally proud and elevated, and conduct yourself with dignity and manliness; but you are somewhat deficient in self-reliance, and like to have a positive companion with whom you can associate and take counsel.

"The summit of your character culminates in your great integrity and stability of moral principle, perseverance, and sense of duty; though you may, for a moment, feel absorbed in individuals, and apparently succumb to their opinions, yet you maintain a fixed inflexibility of purpose.

"You are not one of those circumspect people, who make every day of their life accord with the others; but you are ready to renounce every thing you profess, if your discoveries of truth indicate such a course.

. . . .

"You feel as if too much of the success of the world's struggles depended upon yourself and upon your works. Thus you do not enjoy so much spiritual beatitude and divine fellowship as you find pleasure in doing the work and promoting the interests of humanity. Your benevolence is exceedingly large and active: your sympathies are susceptible, almost to an abnormal extent. You can not come within the sphere of necessity without feeling it as your own. Yours is the spirit of the true philanthropist.

"You have a prophetic and intuitive perception of the course of things, which leads you on when your want of faith and hope would cause you to flag, and give up the contest. Your mind is looking forward and backward at the same time. You see very clearly the relations between the past and the future; and the present is to you a sphere of progressive activity. . . . .

"Ingenious and versatile, you can readily turn your attention to a great variety of subjects. You have much taste and literary ability; and, as the inspirational faculty is very active, you readily find material to cover the necessities of your case. You gather knowledge accurately and to the purpose; and, having great power of recollection, you have an inexhaustible fund of literary matter to fall back upon. You readily distinguish special features of thought, and can make your selections according to your requirements.

. . . .

"Your love of music and desire for harmony is intense.

"You are a great chronologist. Your sense of time, and your ability to determine the relative dates of events, is good. Thus you are historical, and can mark epochs and the lapse of eras almost intuitively. You are also a traveler: you love to peregrinate, and visit the various parts of the world to collect their mental products. You do not notice so much the phenomena of nature as you do those of mind. Your mechanical skill takes a mental form; and you readily sketch out a subject as a builder would a house, and see all the adjustments of your work. Your sense of perspective, order, and arrangement are very good; and there is an exquisiteness and artistic beauty about your speeches and literary works.

"Your command of language is moderately good; but there is a greater fund of matter than there is a specialty of words in which to clothe it.

"Feminine and eminently spiritual in temperament, you are, from brain development, constituted to view spiritual and religious subjects from the secular or humanitarian side. Thus, while your inspirations are intensely religious and spiritual, your method is for truth against priestly devices, and favorable to the unity of all human interests."

Buffon says, "Style is the man himself." In a man's writings do we discover his fiber and ring of genius. In 1859, Mr. Peebles wrote a popular pamphlet, entitled, "Signs of the Times," in which he defends Parker and Beecher, contrasts the "old with the new," with a scalpel opens the sore of Orthodoxy, to "cleanse the body politic." These extracts show the pith of his thought:—

"As well hush the winds of heaven as bid the currents of free thought cease circulating 'mong the inquiring masses that walk 'neath the noonday sun of the nineteenth century. 'Light, more light!' is humanity's motto. And yet every newly-conceived truth, whether scientific, philosophic, or spiritual, must not merely be cradled in a manger, but baptized in tears, and crucified between the two thieves, authority and popularity, ere it can become an acknowledged power in the world. An ancient conservatism gave Socrates hemlock, and crowned Jesus with thorns. And the same spirit of intolerance that burned Huss, Servetus, and Latimer, in the name of Christianity, persecuted and hung the Quakers, accused and mobbed the Wesleys, stoned Murray, and dragged Garrison through the streets, still lives, — lives to vilify and slander Spiritualists, Reformers, and all those liberal-minded Christians who are laboring for the redemption of humanity. . . . .

"There is nothing more evident than the immutability of God's laws; and, if it were ever possible or ever permitted spiritual beings to communicate, the same law permits them now. This principle is admitted by the inspired preacher: Eccl. iii. 15. — 'That which hath been is now; and that which is to be hath already been: and God requires that which is past.' Not only is it possible, but probable; for the spirit, relieved of its gross earth garments, retains all its faculties, forces, mental characteristics, and moral qualities. It is a substantial, organized, individualized, and conscious entity, living, thinking, reasoning, and loving the same as before the transition. Pure love is imperishable, and can not cease; immortal, and can not die: and would not the mother, freighted with those warm, gushing emotions peculiar to her affectionate nature, delight, though in spirit-spheres, to watch over her children? Would she be herself, or would heaven be such to her in reality, if she could not? Would not the good father rejoice in being a counselor to his sons in earth-land? and, free to roam the universe, would not the wisely-ordained law of parental attraction oft call him into their presence? The spirit-world is not located afar, in some infinitely remote region. It is all around us, as is the atmosphere we breathe; and intercourse between spirits in the body and out of it is just as probable and natural also, as the oceanic commerce between America and the isles of the Pacific."

CHAPTER VII.

"THY SINS ARE FORGIVEN THEE!"

"Go ye into all the world, and preach the gospel to every creature.... And these signs shall follow them that believe: In my name shall they cast out devils; they shall speak with new tongues; they shall take up serpents; and, if they eat any deadly thing, it shall not hurt them: they shall lay hands on the sick, and they shall recover."—JESUS.

"I have heard of a mystic organ, which God's own hand has sealed:
Not a single note from its silent keys through the dim years has pealed.
The hands of angels are searching to waken the strains sublime
That shall make glad tidings re-echo through the corridors of time."

NIGHT reveals the stars. Mud is the mother-bosom of the lily. The slime of a damp, over-trodden path in the outskirts of a neighboring town, composed of clay, sand, and soot, by the process of individualization and co-operation, when left free to follow its own instinct, becomes in time a sapphire, an opal, and a diamond, "set in the midst of a star of snow."

About twenty-five years ago, a horde of bandits stole a bright-eyed lad of obscure birth, and carried him to their retreat in "Black Swamp," Ohio, to serve as their spy and chore-boy. Their business was to steal horses, forge money, and pillage the country generally. Active and clownish, intelligent and shrewd, he soon learned and excelled all their tricks. Twining vines around the daggers of the robbers, he was the youthful Bacchus, whose waving spear cowed all the game of the woods into silence. Satyrs, nymphs, and demons were his guards, holding nightly orgies in the bandits' den. He was frequently shot at by citizens, whose marks are indelible. He was schooled in the arts of profanity, gambling, and forgery. Poor boy! he was not responsible for his early associations. When these fierce men scattered, he connected himself a while with a band of traveling minstrels, and was a perfect adept in exciting the crowd, and procuring money. For two summers after, he was a circus-boy and ventriloquist. Educated at these popular colleges of vice, he became a "wild, gay, rollicking, good-hearted, demoniac, affectionate, fast young man." Having served such an apprenticeship, satiated with wandering, he settled down in Battle Creek, a companion of the dissipating classes, of which he was an acknowledged leader.

No man attracted his attention like Mr. Peebles, nor was so often the subject of satire. Seeing him on horseback, riding to his appointments, noticing his towering, gaunt form, he would dance a jig at the door of the saloon, and, with a low chuckle to the "boys," shout, "See old grandsir long legs!" The English language was never before so tortured into ludicrous blackguardism as against this "long-haired Spiritualist," and in so harmless, mimicking way too.

Some time in the winter of 1858, Prof. I. Stearns visited Battle Creek, and commenced a series of popular lectures on Psychology. The interest increasing, this quizzing youngster, taking the world to be "a grand humbug," proposed to his coadjutors, that, the pending evening, he would "explode the whole thing;" and the programme was mapped out accordingly. He was to go on to the stand, the boys backing him, and feign magnetic sleep for a while, and then betray the professor.

When all was ready, he stepped to the platform with an air of resolution, and, facing the vast crowd, gave the boys the wink. The professor scanned him a moment, and ordered him off, stating that he wanted to experiment with his old subjects, whom he required to be immediately seated. Young Dunn gave the wink, so well understood, and took a seat with the rest. The professor ignored him entirely.

"Why not me, sir?"

"Because I have enough without you: leave the stand."

"Just as I expected: you *dare* not try me; you are a humbug,—a *humbug!*" chimed in the youngster, glancing significantly towards his chuckling companions in the secret.

"Perhaps not, sir; perhaps not! I'll try you: sit down here, *sir!*"

That was what the young man wanted, negatively yielding. The operator made a few passes, and ordered him to close his eyes, exclaiming, "You can't open them!" The subject thought he would just slyly peep out of one, and, making the effort, behold, they were sealed! He was then caused to hunt, fish, dance, &c. Soon he began to lose consciousness, indicating psychological phases entirely outside the programme. Using all his will-force, Mr. Stearns shouted, "All right!" No response. Another influence held the boy! What did it mean? "All right!" came the command again, but no obedience. In a moment, he was in a fit, — a species of trance peculiar to disorderly mediumship. The people were excited. Soon his hand moved, as if writing, when Mrs. A. A. Whitney, comprehending the secret, came to the stand, and said, "The spirit wants to write." Making a few passes, to induce a more harmonious action, she gave him paper on which he wrote, bottom-side up, a dashing sentence. Several hinted, "That is all gibberish!" Others, "An unknown tongue!" Reversing the paper, Mr. Peebles deciphered this, —

"I was killed on the Great Western Railroad, near Hamilton, C.W., two hours ago. I have a wife and two children in Buffalo.

"JOHN MORGAN."

On the following morning, the papers brought the news of the accident: two days later came confirming intelligence; and among the names of persons killed was that of the very man who, the evening before, made himself known as a spirit.

Ere the influence left the medium, a spirit beckoned Mr. Peebles to come forward again; for there was something important to communicate. Obeying the summons, the invisible intelligence with much earnestness said through the lips of the medium, —

"We want you to invite this young man into your study to-morrow, when we will entrance him; and the object shall be made known to you."

When returned to external consciousness, Mr. Peebles took him cordially by the hand, and spoke kindly; run his fingers through his short hair, cut in pugilistic style, and, with soothing words, such as a kind friend only can utter, added, "You have a good head; you can make a man of yourself," and pressed his hand again with the warmth of a brother's sympathy. Such tenderness was new to his ear; and strange was the quivering in his soul. Mr. Peebles publicly asked him to call at his house the next day. That was a sleepless night to this initiated medium: a spirit was trying to touch the tremulous chords of his heart, heretofore so cold and dead.

On the morrow, finding he did not appear at the appointed hour,

Mr. Peebles, impressed by a spirit-intelligence, sought him in the shop where he was working, and, not upbraiding him, asked why he did not come, his eyes at the same time filling with tears. The young man was embarrassed, and stammered out a half-conscious excuse about work. Taking a walk with him, Mr. Peebles, asking no questions about his antecedents, portrayed the beauty and joy of an educated and upright life, with the persuasion of that confidence which an angel feels in a mortal's latent goodness.

A few days after this, the young man, attiring himself as best he could with his thin, coarse garments, knocked at the door of the man he almost dreaded to see. Mr. Peebles was cordial, giving the bewildered medium a little self-reliance. As he passed the pictures and library in his "study," his emotions were so odd, for it was indeed a new world to him. When sufficiently composed, he entered the trance-state with perfect facility, under Mr. Peebles's magnetism.

> "So gaze met gaze,
> And heart saw heart, translucent through the rays, —
> One same harmonious, universal law,
> Atom to atom, star to star, can draw:
> And mind to mind swift darts, as from the sun,
> The strong attraction and the charm is done."

A spirit then addressed Mr. Peebles as follows: —

"I am a stranger to you, but not you to me. My name is Aaron Nite. My birthplace is Yorkshire, England. I departed this life when nineteen, and have been in the spirit-world about one hundred and seventy years. No fame attached itself to my career; but my ancestors were in high repute. My brother, Rev. James Knight, was a distinguished clergyman of the English Church. Some time hereafter, I will tell you of my beautiful surroundings, — of the River Ouse, St. Mary's Abbey, York Minster, the old rocks, lawns, and hunting-grounds.

"We have at last brought about this meeting of yourself and medium. Organically, he is mediumistic. His tricks and athletic exercises were aided by spirits on his plane. Through the psychological power of Prof. Stearns, he was thrown into our sphere; and we have now a partial control. He is susceptible of great improvement. We place him in your care. Be a father and elder brother to him on the earthly side; educate him; lift him up: he will stand by you in old age; and many blessings will return to you."

After this, a beloved sister of the medium, who departed when he was an infant, took possession of him, manifesting the tenderest joy, and with whispered words, set to poetry, so soft and melting, pleaded with Mr. Peebles to be a faithful guardian to her "dear brother." Such persuasion! such tearful pity! such solicitude and faith! coming from heaven as the summer sun to wintry hopes! Then and there, in the presence of those ministering spirits, Mr. Peebles solemnly pledged himself to be to the young man a friend, a brother, a father, under all circumstances, confident, as they averred, that he had the ingermed elements of a superior mediumship and manhood.

Soon after this happy interview, Mr. Peebles's moral fortitude was put to a test. Obsessing influences, generated by evil habits, absorbed the medium's very life-blood. He was reckless. Many a time did this "spiritual father" sigh and weep over those unfulfilled promises; till, at length, he entered serious complaints against the spirits having the medium in charge, declaring, that, "were I a spirit, I would *compel* this young man to desist from such practices!" Then, in one of those deep trances, Mr. Peebles would get a lecture that always made him ashamed of his own littleness and want of charity and of faith in God. Those wise, calm angels would say to him, —

> "Remember, Friend Peebles, how much better have been your associations in life than those of this young man. Had your lot been cast in the same channel as his, over which you could have had no control, consider what might now be your character. He has his failings in one direction, and you yours in another direction. Who shall judge between you, as to moral worth? Measure his early advantages: measure yours. Are *your* garments all clean and white? Were your eyes open, you would discover as great distinction between an angel's robe and yours, as between yours and the medium's. Though *you* should sink into pollution, we will never forsake you. If you would have an angel lead you, be an angel to this young man."

Such lectures, so beautifully variegated, melted the proud man to a meditative silence, awakening the holier emotions of the soul; when he would rise from such communion a wiser and better man.

When conscious of being in the wrong, that his complaints were self-righteous, that he had caused distress by hasty remarks, his sorrow was deep; and no peace could he find, till his arms were around the neck of his boy, in mutual, tearful forgiveness.

One night, being at Hastings, Mich., in the beautiful home of Dr. Russell, the medium became clairvoyant. Far in the distance, he saw a star of intense brilliancy, magnifying and approaching him. When nearer, it widened out in the form of a cross with golden and silvery colors, held in the hands of an Italian spirit, who gave his name as *Perasee Lendanta*, and threw a magnetic, flowering wreath around their necks, saying, —

"In this, we emblemize the soul-sympathy uniting spiritual father and son in a life-long fellowship. Walk hand in hand, thus encircled, and nothing shall separate you."

When a mortal, or immortal, is quickened for a higher life, the consciousness of defect is most painful. The holiest angels have a soul-agony inexpressible, when they discover in their affections the least stain; and rest not till it is bleached out by reform. Light only reveals darkness. So with our "chosen vessel." Heavenly inspirations burned down into his soul, awakening a moral torture, followed by weeping.

"O Mr. Peebles!" he would say, "I am a poor, miserable devil, not fit to be associated with you: your loftiness of character shames me." Then a warm hand grasped his, and another rested in benediction upon his head, with words so like the man, "No, my Charlie, not a devil: you are my brother. Your tears are tests of virtue and capacity."

"There are poems unwritten, and songs unsung,
  Sweeter than any that ever were heard,—
Poems that wait for an angel tongue,
  Songs that but long for a paradise bird.

Poems that ripple through lowliest lives,
  Poems unnoted, and hidden away
Down in souls, where the beautiful thrives
  Sweetly as flowers in the airs of May.

Poems that only the angels above us,
  Looking down deep in our hearts may behold;
Felt, though unseen, by the beings who love us,
  Written on lives all in letters of gold."

The following private letter to young Dunn, written about this period of his spiritual growth, is an index of paternal care and affection, breathing sentiments most encouraging to us all: —

"*My dear Brother*, — For some reason, unknown to myself, I feel inspired to write you this morning. Nothing else can I think of. This thought comes to my mind: the certainty of success if coupled with effort, and directed by *wisdom*. You or I may choose any honorable calling in life, and we are certain of success, though that success may be reached only through poverty and thorny paths. Rogers, Cranmer, Ridley, Latimer, reached their success through a martyr's fire; Jesus, through the *tears* of Gethsemane to the crown of thorns; Howard, and Payne, the author of the song, 'Home, sweet Home,' through persecution and poverty. Often what we, in our childishness, call success, is *defeat*. Ease, wealth, luxury, praise, flattery, are all guide-boards on the road of defeat, and sometimes disgrace added thereto. Were there no ocean-storms, there would be no skillful sailors. One of the grandest truths Jesus uttered to his discouraged disciples is this: 'He that would *lose* his life shall *save* it.' You may have often asked yourself: 'Shall I succeed?' If you do not, with your exalted spirit-circle, the fault will be entirely your own. No power in the universe can put me down but myself. Enemies can never defeat us. They often benefit us, by holding up our faults to public gaze: thus seeing them, they disgust us; and we forsake the wrong. The worst real enemies we have are within our own non-unfolded natures. Hence, he that conquers himself is greater in the eyes of angels than he who conquers cities, or wears kingly crowns. Accordingly, what are frequently termed defeats are eternal victories, and are so registered in heaven. Saplings would like to be oaks, without the pressure of wintry winds or snows. I have wished to stand on John's plane, without treading the rugged road of study, effort, and self-sacrifice that have made him an angel; but how childish the wish! Your dear angel-guide, you know: in me, too, you will ever find a brother's hand, a brother's heart, and a brother's love, joying in your joys, and weeping in your tears. Added to these, my soul's desire is, that you may ever have the approbation of your own conscience in every thought, plan, deed, act.

"Yes, Charlie, you will certainly succeed in every worthy undertaking of life. Every good deed done, every virtuous and beautiful seed sown, will surely germinate and ripen. I shall succeed, even though I walk through peril, poverty, and persecution. Then let us take heart, and be happy. 'We walk the wilderness to-day; the promised land to-morrow.' "Good-morning, brother,

"J. M. PEEBLES."

When it was generally known that Mr. Peebles had chosen young Dunn for his traveling companion in the ministry, there was a great cry against him in fashionable circles: "Your master eateth with publicans and sinners!" The Orthodox spoke of it very eloquently, trying to weep big tears, but failed, saying, —

"What a shame! — Well, he's a Spiritualist! the legitimate fruits of his teachings, — scapegoats and harlots for company!"

Even some of his own friends, catching the contagion, apprehensive that Spiritualism might re-act into disgrace, warned and entreated him, "not to make so much of that medium." His prompt reply was, —

"I am pledged to stand by him till death; and all the powers in earth and hell can not sever this sympathy."

How beautiful is justice! This pupil began a new life. His angel-guides, so prudent, warned him, mortified him, baffled him in his impolitic schemes, strengthened him by adversities, through a bitter experience led him higher. Under the fostering care of his "elder brother," with spirit-light burning in his heart, he girded himself, redeeming and redeemed from dissipation, to be a swift herald of the angels' gospel; then apprehension became admiration; and Mr. Peebles at last was honored for his long-suffering charity, which "thinketh no evil," and "endureth all things." Those faith-ful spirits say so feelingly to Mr. Peebles, "The crowning act of your life is the redemption of this young man."

> "The shaken tree grows faster at the root;
> And love grows firmer for some blasts of doubt."

For many weary years, Mr. Peebles had been sickly, and was pronounced by the physicians as of short life. One of his lungs nearly wasted away, leaving a large cavity in his chest to this day. He spat blood quite profusely at times. Consumption set her red signet upon him. But, when those healing spirits reached him, they turned his dial back more than ten degrees, and promised him "a long and trying pilgrimage."

A few years prior to this event, the spirit of the veritable Powhattan, of the early history of Virginia, visited Mr. Peebles, through the mediumship of a lady in Albion, Mich., and thereby kept him posted in the Indian wars, four or five weeks ere the news appeared in the journals. In due time, he promised to find another medium. One evening, he suddenly rang the war-whoop through young Dunn, identifying his name and history, saying, —

"Me promise you medie: me come now!"

Powhattan is always full of life, wit, and frolic; delights to picture the spirit hunting-grounds; warms into fervid eloquence, when speaking of the Indian's forgiveness for the wrongs of the whites. Such fun, "big talk," and "shaking up" magnetically, were verily a balm of Gilead to Mr. Peebles. Dr. Willis, formerly an eminent physician of Brooklyn, N.Y., and Dr. Schwailbach of Germany, celebrated in his time, are also in this healing circle; and, through their art, his lungs were comparatively restored, and his whole system renovated into electric action.

The medium had been accustomed to fits even before Prof. Stearns psychologized him: these Powhattan effectually cured. Whenever either of them was sick or exhausted, this Indian, duly commissioned in the spirit-world for this purpose, was always ready to direct and find the right remedies. By association with these medical spirits, the medium was developed to be a successful healer; when they honored him with the title of "Dr. E. C. Dunn," duly diplomatized in the medical schools of the spirit-world. Powhattan had control of the medicine-bags, and used the doctor's right hand (in a trance-state) to select the right kind of medicine, giving Mr. Peebles directions in preparing it for the patient. The woods, fields, and gardens were their laboratories.

> "The silent ministers of healing crowd
> About the broken heart and spirit bowed,
> To stay the bleeding with immortal balm,
> And still the cries with wings of blessed calm;
> Out of the old death make the new life spring,
> Our earthly, buried hopes take homeward wing;
> And, to each blinding tear that dimmed our sight,
> They give a starrier self, — a spirit of light."

Powhattan named Mr. Peebles "*Preach.*" One night he was quite ill; when this Indian, always on the alert, ordered medicine.

"Take times (three fingers), once great dark" (midnight).

Mr. Peebles objected, stating he could not wake at that hour.

"Me risk," was the reply: "me wake you," ordering him to put his watch on the table.

Just at midnight broke forth a voice, "*Preach! Preach!!* up get: time by the tick thing."

Rousing, he at first thought he had been dreaming; when it spoke again in his wakeful consciousness, —

"Up get, Preach! tick thing, time up. *Preach!*"

Taking the medicine in hand, he drank a toast to the faithful spirit, and in a moment was locked in

> "Nature's sweet restorer, balmy sleep."

During the healing and lecturing peregrinations, the uniform custom was, after retiring, to entrance the medium. "Be not disturbed," said the spirits: "we know our own business." Perfectly entranced, an invisible silver chord flickering over the silent body, Mr. Peebles holding the pulseless hand, deeply anxious lest death might rob its tenant, the spirits, taking the medium to lower planes, would teach him lessons of warning, and thence higher, into medical temples, instruct him in the laws of spiritual science and better modes of healing.

The true spiritual teacher is a physician of souls. The leaf is nourished by the root; so is the spirit-world by our healthful conditions. The body is the crystal of spirit. Heal at the life-springs. Bring the balm of an angel's love. This healing band, in cases of obsession, scattered the dark influences, regenerated the self-abandoned, brought wandering spirits into light. Being at Port Huron, Mich., Mr. Peebles was introduced to Dr. Hawkins, healing spirit for Dr. S. D. Pace, a successful physician, who purposely permitted several suicides to control him, that Mr. Peebles might address them from the earthly side to which they gravitated. With words of hope, tenderly he alluded to their early days under the paternal roof, to the moral uses of temptation resisted, closing with these words, "If you would be angels, you must seek to make others angels." They listened; and how hallowed was their joy!

The curative agencies for obsession are thus happily delineated by Mr. Peebles in one of his late pen-productions, —

> "Kindness and firmness, aspiration and self-reliance, pleasant physical, social, and mental surroundings, with gentle harmonizing magnetic influences from circles of exalted spirits, through noble, pure-minded media, — these are the remedies. Speak to the obsessing intelligences as men, brothers, sisters, friends; reason with them as members of a common Father's family; and at the same time, demagnetizing the subject, bring a healthier, purer magnetism, and calmer, higher, and more elevating influences to the patient's relief. This was Jesus' method: it should be ours."

Powhattan, once a fierce warrior, was converted to peace principles in the spirit-world. He was at first very shy of the whites, retaining a strong antipathy for many years. Occasionally, William Penn, with his benignant face, with form so beautiful, crossed his path on those "hunting-grounds;" but his selfish resolution not to speak to him was at length conquered by so much sweetness of sphere. Penn all this while was seeking to reach his heart, "so incased in the vestment of blood." Powhattan listened to his words, felt their love, was softened and converted; since which time, he has ever endeavored to inspire Indians with love of peace among themselves and the whites. Every 4th of July, the day when first he revealed himself to Mr. Peebles, he wished to celebrate the advent of universal peace with him and his medium, and such other spirits and earthly friends as chose to be there. They used to assemble in the woods, engage in solemn worship; Powhattan addressing the "red brethren" in the Indian dialect, and Mr. Peebles the "pale faces" in English. The first celebration of the kind was held near Leonidas, Mich.; where about forty citizens commingled their orisons with those of a host of Indians gathered from the spirit country in peace council. These were memorable anniversaries, ever fraught with subdued inspiration, bringing the sympathizing whites nearer the brotherly heart of the lone Indian.

CHAPTER VIII.

EL DORADO.

"Weary souls
By thee have been led up unto the fountains
Whence the deep tide of living waters flow,
And into that fair light of heavenly truth
Which like a blessed rainbow spans the future,
And bridges all the dark abyss of death." — FANNY GREEN.

NEARLY four years of toil in Battle Creek, each widening in influence, when the spirits advised a change of climate, to recuperate his wasted health. "Whither?" was the question. "California," was the response. That land had long haunted him. "Go I must," was his resolute talk.

Upon the temporary suspension of his pastoral relations with the "Free Church," resolutions were passed, speaking of him as "a true teacher," having "purity of life and honesty of purpose;" and prayers were breathed upon him amid tears that welled up from many hearts.

"The Jeffersonian," a secular paper of Battle Creek, thus noticed his departure: —

"While we part with him, it is our desire to say, that few better persons are found in this mundane sphere than Mr. Peebles and his amiable lady; for we know that this resolution on their part will effect a vacancy in our midst quite hard to be filled."

During his absence, his desk was supplied by such personages as Warren Chase, Benj. Todd, Bell Scougal, F. L. Wadsworth, of whose labors he spoke with grateful credit.

Amid farewells and waving of handkerchiefs, he embarked for California, on New Year's, 1860, in steamer "Ariel."

Ocean and island scenery invigorated him. When sea-sick, the angels visited him. He said in a letter to "Clark's Spiritual Clarion," —

"Whilst suffering from sea-sickness, I felt my spirit-friends continually around me; and how delightful the delicate touches of their fingers upon my forehead; their impressions how calming!

"Crossing the isthmus of Panama, ideally reveling amid those groves of lemons, cocoas, and palms, I coasted the Pacific, recalling the words of Shelley,—

"'My soul is an enchanted boat,
Which, like a sleeping swan, doth float
Upon the silver waves of thy sweet singing;
And thine doth like an *angel* sit
Beside the helm, conducting it.'"

At San Francisco, he made himself known to Rev. A. C. Edmunds, editor of "The Star of the Pacific" (Universalist), who represented him as a "Universalist-Unitarian-Spiritualist," with encomiums as follows:—

"Mr. J. M. Peebles, of Battle Creek, Mich., arrived in San Francisco on the 25th ult. (March, 1861), and is now temporarily tarrying in Sacramento. We bid him welcome to California. He comes among us, not as the bearer of parchments from ecclesiastical associations, but as one divinely commissioned by the Father to speak the truth according to the measure of his understanding, imparted by the Spirit and the inspiration which the Fountain of Good has given to every man. We admire the platform of Brother Peebles, believing that every man should think and act for himself.

"Bound to no party, to no sect confined,
The world our home, our brethren all mankind:
Love truth, do good, be just and fair with all;
Exalt the right, though every ism fall."

Among the friends that greeted him, there were Judge Robinson, Senator E. H. Burton, V. B. Post and family; Fanny Green, the poetess, who addressed him burning words of encouragement in his reforms; and T. Starr King, the patriot and spiritualistic Unitarian, received him with heart warm as the baptism of that tropical clime.

Mr. Peebles wrote several valuable articles for "The Star of the Pacific," in which he gave spiritual interpretation to biblical lore, for the benefit of the Universalist community, with a view of converting some to "a knowledge of the truth;" and was also a correspondent of A. J. Davis's "Herald of Progress," in which he reported his spiritual experiences in California. Seeing the favorable notices in "The Star," the Universalist papers of the Atlantic States reported him "as preaching Universalism in California!" "The Chicago New Covenant" (D. P. Livermore) noticed him thus:—

"Rev. J. M. Peebles, of Battle Creek, Mich., formerly of our communion, and now advocating a phase of Spiritualism that in no way conflicts with Universalism, is to leave for California in November or December. He will probably locate at Sacramento. His first object is health: that restored, he will resume preaching."

"The Universalist Companion," a statistical pamphlet, said, —

"The Rev. J. M. Peebles was preaching Universalist sentiments in San Francisco, by last advices."

This insult, "*by last advices*," Mr. Peebles reviewed in a letter to "The Ambassador."

"Advices and reports are unreliable just in the ratio of individual negligence and depravity. The millennium will be near when advices are correct, and men *report* what they positively *know*. . . . The phrase, 'preaching Universalist sentiments' is correct, allowing the Protestant's privilege of private judgment and free expression. So do Unitarians proclaim 'Universalist sentiments;' so do most of the Swedenborgian clergy; so do lecturers upon the Harmonial Philosophy; so do all spiritualistic mediums, whether normal or abnormal; so does Henry Ward Beecher, when in his highest and happiest pulpit moments: and what of it? Simply this: It demonstrates the moral growth of the race, and a general tendency of the thinking masses to embrace broader theological views, touching the attributes of God, the administration of the divine government, the soul's educational capacity, and the final destination of humanity; and certainly no enlightened Christian gentleman, especially of the liberal school, would forbid the casting out of devils; i.e., the evils and errors of old sectarian theology, though under other names than the one he may have seen fit to adopt."

Seeing favorable notices in Universalist papers, certain Spiritualists alleged he had renounced Spiritualism; and he drew the sword also on such. Writing "The Herald of Progress," he said, —

"Supposing I had, the sun would shine, the stars glisten, the world move, — truth would be truth, and bigots bigoted. No! I have not renounced Spiritualism, Universalism, Unitarianism, Quakerism, or rather the *truths* that underlie them: for each symbolizes a central truth; and all truths manifest the harmonic law of unity. Octave notes do not jar; nor does unripe fruit contradict the mellowed fruitage of autumn. There are a few one-idea, one-sided 'Spiritualists,' who can perceive no truth in the universe, unless christened *Spiritualism;* and they seem to think themselves heaven-appointed watchmen, to gruffly growl around, and guard their imperfectly-conceived notion of that '*ism*.' It becomes a 'hobby;' and they ride the poor thing hoofless. I would as soon accept the teachings of Pius IX., or sectarian churchdom, as *authoritative*, as communications from spirits. . . . Every thinker, given to meditation, will discriminate between *use* and *abuse*. To affirm there have been no abuses, no 'froth nor scum,' under the name of Spiritualism, manifests not only a most deplorable ignorance and imbecility, but the very quintessence of impudence. . . . I am indebted to spirit intercourse for my knowledge — I say *knowledge* — of immortality, the location of the spirit-world, the condition of the immortalized, the occupation of the loved gone before, and their progressing toward the infinite. Those love-messages that have greeted me from the thither side of death's peaceful river, I cherish above all price, and shall till I reach the sunny shore of that 'island home.' Still, I can be the exponent of no *ism*, to the exclusion of other and all great reforms that begin to glow upon the brow of this illustrious age."

Nor was Mr. Peebles exempt from the missiles of slander in California. Envy follows the brave. Those of shaky reputations are anxious to pull others down to their own level. "That red-mouthed Irishman," as Capt. Soule of Sacramento termed him, who peddled the story, was forced to sign a paper, certifying he had libeled Mr. Peebles. Since returning to the States, Mr. Peebles has regretted that he did not compel two or three pseudo-Spiritualists to do the same. Every attempt of this kind to put him down has re-acted upon the guilty parties. Virtue needs never be disturbed. Slander is its own advertisement. Henry Ward Beecher says, "He who stops to kick at a barking cur delays his own progress."

Those times, California was Hades descended. People found themselves there. The "New-England Puritan churchite" donned his "Mokanna veil." That tropical clime quickened the animal instincts, chilled by Northern conventionalities, as burning sands do crocodiles' eggs. But what of our brother there? The same reformer. Commissioned a district deputy of the Good Templars, he stormed the strongholds of Bacchus. The "Dashaways" felt the force of his arrows. He culled truths and beauties from caves, mines, mountains, extinct volcanoes, mammoth trees, waterfalls, thermal springs, &c. Traveling in coaches, steamers, and on mules' backs, among representatives from all human races, he lectured all up and down those mountain fastnesses; and his trumpet voice seems to be re-echoing in San Francisco, Sacramento, Petaluma, Santa Rosa, Sonora, Santa Cruz, San Jose, Stockton, Montezuma, Jacksonville, Columbia, Auburn, Eldorado, Clarksville, Folsom, and other cities, villages, and mining districts. Speaking of his strange experiences there, he writes, —

"I have slept under the nightly sky, and the roofs of almost palatial mansions; have collected specimens for a choice cabinet; have descended into mining-shafts; visited vineyards, one, Col. Haraszthy's, containing five hundred acres, with three hundred and fifty thousand vines; and roamed amid the ruins of old adobe cathedrals, erected by the Spaniards long prior to the gold discoveries. I have met scores of noble souls; in brief, have been blamed and blessed, occasionally 'damned,' and quite often enough deified. Such is pilgrim life. Lights and shadows are indispensable to pictures. Our enemies work by inverse methods, to benefit us. Joseph's brethren, meaning evil, made him a hero. Perfection precludes progression; and yet we ever meet self-voted saints, who, in their 'imputed righteousness' and excessive piety, are apt, as Artemas Ward says, to '*slop over*.' To wit, a Tuolumne County editor, in October last, complimented me thus highly:—

'A long-bearded, cracked-brained fellow, calling himself *Peebles*, has been edifying our citizens upon the new-fangled philosophy, that men sprang from trilobites and tadpoles; that ghosts range the earth, muttering through mediums; and that the salvation of the soul comes by lifting one's self upwards, regardless of the grace of God, the blood of the Lord Jesus, and church ordinances. . . . Such doctrines can only demoralize. Has not Stockton Lunatic Asylum recently lost an inmate?'"

Being invited to lecture near the foot-hills of the Nevadas, — the mining town about ten miles distant, — he adjusted his carpet-sack, nomadic style, and, mounting a mule, off he rode in such dignity! his feet dangling nearly to the ground, his long hair streaming out behind in wizard confusion; and his whole appearance so provokingly ludicrous, the miners shouted after him, "There goes old Pilgrim's Progress! — old Pilgrim's Progress on a donkey!"

A few extracts from private letters to confiding friends are the openings of an El Dorado in his very soul:—

"SACRAMENTO, July 25, 1861.

. . . "On the 4th of July, I delivered an oration in Yolo City, and made the Secessionists quite angry. Yet I do not justify the war. I am opposed to all war. It brutalizes men and nations, and places a low estimate on human life; arouses a degrading martial spirit in our children; inspires our youth to employ fire-arms; creates standing armies; increases taxation; rushes thousands prematurely into the spirit-world, to say nothing of the widows' groans and orphans' tears. . . . All bloody wars are wrong; only dogs and animal men delight in blood, battle, and death. The devil can not cast out devils."

"COLUMBIA, CAL., Nov. 12, 1861.

. . . "My California life is strange. Hundreds of miles among the mountain ranges have I wended my way on a Spanish horse, dispensing words of truth to the mountaineers, sometimes not paid one cent, and then again fairly remunerated. In Sonora, they called me the 'Prince of Fools.' So goes the world with the reformer. . . Only a few weeks since, I talked with a learned Chinaman upon theology and the sacred books of the Chinese. His name is Le Can. He made me ashamed of our boasted American civilization and religion, when we claim, as we have, that it is so superior to the ancients. I feel that I must travel in Oriental lands, to learn the rudiments of Spiritualism."

"CLARKSVILLE, CAL., Dec. 17, 1861.

"*My Brother, A. Smith:* Thy very welcome epistle of September reached me after five weeks. It was thankfully received, and perused with a greedy gusto; for a friendly letter from a friend and brother is ever a wellspring of pleasure to my soul. Nellie's was also excellent, bearing the marks of inspiration, both *celestial and terrestrial.* My good letters I tie up in a package with a ribbon, now soiled with frequent handlings; and, during these long evenings, I untie and re-peruse them, and, for the time, live with *loved ones* far away: and my affectionate nature, tuned sensitively as the wind-lute, alternately weeps or smiles. Human *hearts* are little known. Only the Infinite can sound their deeps of bitterness, count their pain-throbs, plumb their wells of agony. Man is a strange entity. He only partially comprehends himself and his surroundings. Had you looked hither the 9th of December, three o'clock, P.M., you would have seen me in the city of Sacramento, numbering sixteen or eighteen thousand, upon a housetop, with the water rapidly approaching the edges of the shingles. There were twenty-two persons in the upper chamber. The whole city was flooded, the water ranging from four to twelve feet deep, caused by a three-days' rain and the bursting away of mill-dams, embankments, levees, &c. A million and a half of property and some lives were lost. My trunk, with contents, was submerged two days. I lost all my books and nearly all of my manuscripts, lectures, &c., with a part of my clothes. But I have my *head* left me, and good *health;* so it will all end well. It made me a little sad for a few days. Oh, the charms of home and loved friends! A ranger in foreign lands appreciates such. Well said the poet, —

'Take the bright shell from its home on the lea,
And, wherever it goes, it will sing of the sea:
So take the fond heart from its home and its hearth,
'Twill sing of the loved to the ends of the earth.'

"I feel that my mission to this country has not been in vain.

"I know that I have made some souls glad. . . . Poor Mrs. Munson (the trance-speaker here), how much she suffered from slanderous tongues! She has since married Dr. Webber, and retired. Sorrowingly the poet sings, —

'Many a friendship has been broken,
Many a family's peace o'erthrown,
Many a bitter word been spoken,
By the slander-loving tongue.'"

Already the angels had taken to their heavenly nurseries the three undeveloped buds of our pilgrim, too frail to blossom on earthly soil. In that home at Battle Creek was weeping over broken links, as if tears might possibly weld them; but when the angels, returning, told the disappointed parents about the matronly spirits nursing and educating their children, — that from the sacred moment of incarnation, when generative principles blend, a child is immortal, — a sweeter sunlight dusted all the soul's dark drapery with living gold. But what is home without an earthly angel in it? They thought an adopted child might live. "Louie," as he was tenderly called, was the precious gift of Rev. J. R. Sage, a dearly-beloved Universalist minister. Whilst recuperating in California, news came that this boy had suddenly passed to the spirit-world. It struck a tremor through his whole being, giving it a silent polarity heavenward. For the moment, he complained.

"Oh, I loved Louie!" said he.

"So did we," was the reply of the angel.

"But he was necessary to my happiness."

"So he was to others."

"I had superior claims."

"You think so, brother? Where is your philosophy in the superiority of the spiritual over the material?"

"I could have made him spiritual here."

"Suppose it be proved that Louie's departure is a mutual and eternal blessing?"

"But I loved him from my soul's depths."

"No doubt you did: the angels, however, loving him better, transplanted him into their heavenly gardens.

'The angels have need of these youthful buds
In their gardens so fair:
They graft them on immortal stems,
To bloom for ever there.'"

"Well, I go mourning over the world, now that Louie is gone."

"Go mourning, O philosopher! to render him and you more unhappy? So many beautiful buds, flowering out on the immortal shore to prepare a paradise for you? So unhappy over it, child?"

This spiritual interview calmed him to a star-like silence, sweet as the night-rest. Hear what he says in letters to friends, and note how the angel rules the human at the saddest of losses: —

"SACRAMENTO, CAL., March, 1861.

"*Dear Mrs. Brown*, . . . I am sad, oh, so sad and tearful, to-night, Frances! None, however, see my tears. There may be something of pride in this; but I long ago resolved that no shadow upon my face should ever filch the sunshine from others. Why sad, do you ask? Aye, last week's mail brought the tidings of the severe sickness and departure to the better land of our darling Louis, — a precious bud, transplanted to bloom in the garden of God. Oh, how I pity my poor wife! Lonely must she be without the echoes of his dancing feet, and the lyric cadence of his voice. He was a promising, a beautiful child of hardly ten summers, and the very idol of our hearts.

"This deep affliction will weigh heavily upon my wife. I shall hasten home on her account. Home! how many sweet associations cluster around the endearing word! Put me in my library-room, and I'm happy; and yet, dearly as I love books, family, home, and home-comforts, a divine voice is ever saying to me, 'Go forth, — go among all nations; preaching the ministry of spirits, and the principles of the Spiritual Philosophy.' . . .

"Though gifted in intellect, Frances, you are equally sympathetic, and will readily understand the sorrow that will come over me like a cloud upon crossing my threshold in Battle Creek, — my wife glad to welcome me, gratified with my improved health, but mourning for Louis. It is all *well*. He has gone to join and become a companion of our own *three* dear little ones, who left the mortal ere earth's ills had tinged the gossamer of their spirit-garments with a single stain. Angels are their teachers; progress their eternal destiny. Oh, how blessed is Spiritualism in all the trying scenes of life! Would I had a thousand tongues to tell its glories and sing its praises! To its promulgation under the inspiration of a circling band of spirits, I have consecrated my powers, dedicated my life. So have you, and many, many, other noble souls.

"Deeply do I sympathize with reform-workers, lecturers, and *media*, negative and sensitized from the heavens. Oft-times their sorrows are many, their joys few. Beautiful are the crowns that await them in the glorious hereafter.

"Were it not for the feeble health of my wife, and sudden departure of Louis, I should remain here at least a year, and do earnest missionary work in behalf of Spiritualism. I am stopping in an excellent family, Victor B. Post's; the spirits have named them 'Peace and Harmony.' These, with many other dear friends, entreat me to remain another year; but duty calls me home.

"I must tell you, by the way, that I have formed the acquaintance of Mrs. Eliza W. Farnham; met her in the lunatic asylum, Stockton, California. She is the matron; and her brilliant, solid intellect, boundless benevolence, and deep comprehension of principles, charmed me. During several evenings, she read from unpublished volumes she is preparing, — read me select passages from Walt Whitman's 'Leaves of Grass,' and several European poets. She told me she delivered the first lecture upon Spiritualism ever given in California. She spoke highly of you, Mary F. Davis, and others of her sex laboring for woman and the great interests of reform. And, only think, — little, anxious, jealous souls, hardly worthy to unloose her shoe-latches, have tried to traduce this great, noble woman. Blessings upon her! I'm proud I ever clasped her hand, a prelude to abiding friendship."

"PETOLUMA, CAL., Jan. 15, '62.

"*Dear Charlie,* — Accept my thanks for the *love-message* sent me from 'Louie' through you. Oh, the dear pet child, how I want to clasp him to my bosom upon my return home! You know, Charlie, that I am enthusiastic in my love nature; loving not only children, but music, flowers, and friends, almost to distraction.

"The news of Louie's leaving the earth-life almost overcame me at first. I was not prepared for it; for I had just been to a mountain-village, by stage, to preach a funeral sermon, and had gatherings in my ears, making me nearly sick: but I was sustained by two spirits, and made to feel that it was not only right, but '*all for the best,*' as my dear brother Nite says. I have heard from him through J. V. Mansfield of Boston. Accept my thanks for the promise that I shall hear from Louie often through you. It will cheer me in my lonely pilgrimage along the Pacific coast."

CHAPTER IX.

THE CHAIN OF PEARLS AND SPIRIT BANDS.

"Have ye heard, have ye heard, of the angel of love,
Who, with glory of princess and grace of a dove,
Leaves her seraph abode in the sunsets of even,
Gathering pearls on earth for crowns in heaven, —
Have ye heard of this angel of love?" — SPIRITUAL PILGRIM.

"The mortal world may be divided, but the nobility of intellect of the spirit-world is one." — HUDSON TUTTLE.

MANY a spirit outside of Mr. Peebles's band had promised him great things, — decking his pathway with prophetic flowers. The intention may be as pure as a little child's, that brings us the roses without the thorns; but it indicates that such ministration is unschooled in the moralizing rudiments of adversity, and unreliable. A flattering spirit, so far from being a guide, should be guided.

About a year and six months in California, and Mr. Peebles returned to Battle Creek, greatly recuperated, and was received with hearty welcome. Absence only strengthened the bonds of fellowship.

When he stepped upon the stand to renew his ministerial labors, amid so many smiling faces, the choir sung two original songs, composed by Mrs. D. M. Brown, reviewing the departure and return: —

"We would welcome thee, our brother, —
Welcome thee from o'er the sea;
From the perils and the trials
That we know attended thee.
And we come, we come, to greet thee,
Safe returned from distant lands;
Feeling thy inspiring presence
Binds us close in friendship's bands.
And we love, we love, to welcome,
Welcome thee from distant lands."

It was a thrilling moment. The words and the music of "welcome" and "response" changed thought to heart; and heart was in the hand of greeting to their dear pastor.

When once more put in direct communication with the spirits, through his long-tried medium, he felt confident that the way would open more propitiously. Thus far, he had battled for a certain attainment of spirituality, so often required by his heavenly guards. Now that his health had improved, he sanguinely asked them if the life-line would not be straighter, drawing him nearer a sunny experience.

"I have been to California," he added, "under your approval; have done my work there; have a more practical appreciation of human needs; have returned, as you see, quite vigorous and full of faith, — what say you now? are not matters more promising?"

Perasee had mentally forecast the trial-scenes rising in view, and showed them to his brother Nite, then speaker for the silent band: —

"No, friend Peebles," said Mr. Nite, "your pathway is begirt with thorns, and jagged rocks will pierce your feet: your horoscope just before us is rough and stormy. We throw around your neck a chain of pearls, — pearls which reflect your life, your plans, thoughts, purposes, deeds. All things are dual. These spiritually reflect your outer life, as your spiritual sensorium reflects your inner life. Symbolically, you are chained by these beautiful pearls.

"A lady friend of yours, clad in robes of purity, known among us as, 'Queen of Morn,' and in your world as 'Madame Elizabeth,' sister of Louis XVI. of France, from this chain, which I put around your neck, has suspended a cross, indicative of trials and crucifixions in your pilgrimage. But be of good cheer, you shall overcome, and every sorrow will give fragrance to the bud that blossoms over your heart."

Not many months after, Madame d'Obeney, a celebrated traveler and Spiritualist, met Mr. Peebles in the East, and surprised him with a gift, significant of the pearls mentioned by the spirits, consisting of a string of beads, carved from the wood of an olive-tree that grew on Mt. Olivet, in the very garden of Gethsemane, where Jesus had his "strong crying and tears." He then had a cross made, after the pattern shown by the spirits, — the front of it of beautiful pearl, the back of pure gold, on which were engraved the names of spirits in his band: —

Lorenzo Peebles.	Hosea Ballou.
Cana.	Mozart.
James Leonard.	Perasee Lendanta.
Madame Elizabeth.	Aaron Nite.

John W. Leonard.

This circle of sympathizing spirits are not authority to him whom they inspire. Constitutionally skeptical, he can accept *no* authority but the God of truth and wisdom, love and purity, manifest in himself. "Judge ye of yourselves," said Jesus, "what is right."

Mr. Peebles wears the string of olive beads around his neck, screened from the public eye, but the cross is exposed. Many an iconoclast has jeered at his cross, taunting him with the sobriquet of "Catholic," "Episcopal priest," "Your Christian Highness," and the like; and in one instance a jealous aspirant proposed to send him a string of Catholic beads. From all such Mr. Peebles kept his own secret, conscious it is imprudent to "cast your pearls before swine." Those olive beads continually remind him of the spiritual chain of pearls which the spirits put around his neck, admonishing him as to his "life, thoughts, purposes, and deeds," — how to keep these unstained. Oh, the cross! the pearl of wisdom, the gold of love! every name thereon engraved is associated with trying and hallowed associations. It has ever been to him his *Urim* and *Thummim*, — life light and shade. These he will wear to the end of this rudimental pilgrimage, when, tendered to another worthy of the trust, he will behold its counterpart, — the living pearls, the "treasures laid up in heaven," — what spiritual beauties he has unfolded amid earth's tears and self-denials.

Let the profane jeer at these symbols; the good and true will revere this sibylline oracle which only the pure in heart can interpret. But whose the hand that wove the chain and twined it 'round his neck? whose the voice that bade him be "hopeful, trustful, faithful?" whose the heart throbbing in those pearls?

When in New York, soon after this interview with spirits, Mr. Peebles called on W. P. Anderson, spirit-artist, who drew a likeness of Madame Elizabeth. To his surprise, a chain, similar to the one she had pictured to his mental vision, was around her neck. The artist paints her in one of her aspirational moods, wearing upon her beautiful brow a gemmed crown.

Soon after procuring the much-prized likeness, Mr. Peebles was one day indifferently walking the streets of Boston, when, of a sudden, he wheeled into an antiquarian library, having no thought of being spiritually influenced, and was impressed to search for the Bhagavat Geeta. Failing to find it, he turned to go out, and, in passing, was drawn instinctively to the "French Department." There he was whirled round with a shock, and caused to stoop down and put his hand on a history of Louis XVI., in which was a likeness of himself and his sister Elizabeth, resembling that of her in the spirit-painting, — hair the same, chain of pearls around her neck, with a cross attached. Dr. G. Haskell and others, being present, saw in a moment the correspondence between the two pictures. This strengthened Mr. Peebles's faith in his guides, and made him buoyant in spirit. The question recurs, Whose the hand that led him to that history? The same that twined the cross with the string of pearls?

"Love reflects the things beloved."

Spiritually, our fathers and mothers, — Who are they? who our educators? "Wiser than we know," by birthright we are represented in the high councils of immortals. Many-fold as nature is, sphered in spheres derived from all planes of life, past and present, we are constitutionally banded with spirits of other races and ages, just as the webs of our being run.

"Our echoes roll from soul to soul,
And grow for ever and for ever."

After Mr. Peebles became more conscious of angel-presence, he began to inquire into the history and identity of spirit-bands and their special work.

Through the trance-mediumship of Dr. A. P. Pierce of Boston, by whom ancient spirits are writing histories and philosophies unknown in the libraries, he conversed with erudite spirits of millennian ages, and with Jehovah, the Lord of the Hebrews, identified as an Egyptian priest, who instructed him in the ministries of angels at that remote period. At other times he talked with Brahman seers, Egyptian hierophants, Chinese moralists, Persian fire-worshipers, Druidic priests, Platonic philosophers. Associated with these ancients, under their inspiration, he has for years been on a pilgrimage to caves, ruins, geological relics, moss-grown records on monuments and obelisks, and antiquarian libraries. From instinct he is thus a student of Nature, ruins, and arts. Force of circumstances also molds his love to flow in such channels. Organically spiritual, battling with adversities, so often assailed, so disappointed in a thousand expectations, he courts solitude, and finds in pensive meditations a soul-joy. In that beautiful story of "Paul and Virginia," over which we all used to weep when boys and girls, the historian says, "All suffering creatures, from a sort of common instinct, fly for refuge amidst their pains to haunts the most wild and desolate; as if rocks could form a rampart against social misfortune; as if the calm of Nature could hush the tumult of the soul." Is there not also a "Virginia" for our Pilgrim? Surely some angel leads him, a wanderer over the earth, a child-learner, dusted with the undimmed truth-light that sparkles even under the *débris* of extinct civilization. Dreamily he there studies, gathering up the precious lore, bringing it forth into the living present, till it breathes again, and thinks and loves. Thus his reading, up into the spirit-world, casts him into the cycles of the golden past, when lo, he says, "Immortality blossoms all around, and Eternity is *Now!*"

There are two intertwining bands associated with our Pilgrim's sphere of life acting mainly through the mediumship of Dr. Dunn, — one more physical, the other spiritual, corresponding with the body and spirit. The first is hygienic, practical, perceptive; the other interior, souled in love, "God with us." Conspicuous in this physico-spirit-band are, Aaron Nite the Speaker, Powhattan the Magnetic Cleanser, Pawnee Chief the Assistant, and Drs. Schwailbach and Willis the Analyzers; all of whom guard his forces of body and brain with the strictest vigilance, infusing the very beds and rooms he sleeps in, and the food he eats, with the aura of spirit-presence.

We must not forget to mention Michael O'Brien, — a quaint, witty Irishman, — who, years ago, disturbed Mr. Peebles by his slang words and obtrusive designs, sometimes driven off when too boisterous, but afterwards tamed down by the voice of our brother's love to educate himself. Such gratitude as he shows towards his earthly benefactor! His rollicking wit is most refreshing. He obeys Aaron Nite with the trust of a child. Orderly, principled in integrity, the discipline of this band is most excellent, ranging up, as flowers from the root, into administrative affiliation with the more *interior* band.

These spirits have been identified repeatedly by different media. Betsey Howard, whose funeral discourse Mr. Peebles preached in California, once controlled J. V. Mansfield, in 1863, and clearly manifested herself with gratitude for his favors. There appeared in this band — having their names written in dazzling, electric light on their foreheads — Henry Ware, Jun., Ephraim Peabody, W. E. Channing, and Eliza W. Farnham, who addressed him in vigorous words, with this closing admonition, "Oh, my brother, be true to the light within you! Say the same to Bros. Davis, Mansfield, Harter, and others; that they have for their purpose truth!"

The spirits whose names are engraved upon Mr. Peebles's cross of gold and pearl are more intimately his "guardian angels." Lorenzo Peebles is a loving brother; Hosea Ballou is the sermonizer; Canà, the positivist; Aaron Nite, the elucidator; Madame Elizabeth, the love-angel; Mozart, the musical harmonizer; Perasee Lendanta, the scientist; John, the beloved, around whom the whole band revolves as planets around their central sun. This spirit, controlling John W. Leonard, a clergyman, of Edinburgh, Scotland, whose identity has been traced in history, so signed himself for years, lest the real, when given, might engender a pampering pride in Mr. Peebles's mind. He prefers to be impersonal. We have no permission thus to announce his name; but from a sense of justice we take the responsibility, the better to unveil the wonderful discipline of spirits. "John" was first discovered through the mediumship of Mrs. W. P. Anderson. Scores of other mediums said the same; but Mr. Peebles doubted, until, by accumulating evidences from myriad sources, the statement was confirmed, that this is none other than John, the beloved disciple, who leaned on the bosom of Jesus.

The characteristics of the leading spirits in this dual band are plainly indicated by their sentiments, tinged more or less by the mediumistic channel. These were communicated in Rockford, Ill.

We take each communication from the world of spirits for what it is worth to us. Reason is the voice of God in our soul, and no truth is truth to us till born into our self-consciousness as such.

It will be seen from the following, that each spirit retains, to a certain extent, the peculiarities of the earth-life. The Indian is the Indian still. The poet is the poet still. The philosopher delights to pursue his philosophic investigations; the astronomer, to measure those stellar worlds which dot infinity, and sift their silvery beams through unfathomless space. So the artful, scheming, sordid, and malignant of earth are such upon the other shore, till, through remorse, repentance, restitution, and varied experiences, they progress to higher and holier conditions.

"Let love be the diadem upon thy brow,—a comfort and an inspiration to thy spirit in earth-life, and a beacon-light to guide thee in the pearly paths of wisdom along the infinite future." — JOHN.

"Prepare yourself to live, and in the noble work of preparation you become prepared to die." — AARON NITE.

"Earth's poetry is Heaven's prose: strive, therefore, to perfect thyself in earth's poetry." — QUEEN OF MORN.

"Have confidence in the Father; for in thus doing you have confidence in humanity, as they are but parts of the universal whole." — HOSEA BALLOU.

"Endeavor, brother, to chase the wolf of discord from thine own soul, as the musician would chase it to the remotest portion of the instrument." — MOZART.

"This life is but the horoscope of the future: try then and make the present as glad and golden as the future you would like to see." — MORNING STAR.

"Let thy brain be a pool of knowledge, and desire the angel of wisdom to often trouble it." — JAMES.

"Let the council-fires of peace burn brightly in thy breast; for the tomahawk is ever buried with the warrior." — POWHATTAN.

"Master mind, and you've mastered the universe." — PERASÉE LENDANTA.

"Let the chase for the wild deer be done, and the chase for wild thoughts and Nature's higher truths be begun." — PAWNEE CHIEF.

"Strive to make thyself a master-builder; and, ever baring thy breast to the sharp point of truth, let each stone be a word of kindness, and the key-stone to the arch, wisdom." — DR. WILLIS, the mason.

"Man is a species of flower that buds in earth, to bloom on spirit-shores; and as the flower-bud is nurtured, so will the blossom testify." — MADAME THERESA.

"Wouldst thou study geology, physiology, astronomy, and the deeply hidden sciences of matter and mind, study the wonderful combinations of man."

SCHWAILBACH.

"Remember that the heaven of man is the harmony of his own soul: then prepare thy heaven now, that thou mayest enjoy it the more in the grand hereafter."

THY BROTHER.

"As there is coin in the golden bar yet to be coined, so thou, living in the world, are yet *to be born*; then prepare thyself for the higher birth and the mint immortal."

CANA.

Mr. Peebles is quite a critic with the spirits of his band, but yields to them as a child for instruction. He is not infected with the "aching palm" to *control* the spirits, — as our Halleck sarcastically says, to —

"Check and chide
The ærial angels, as they float about us
With robes of a so-called wisdom, till they grow
The same tame slaves to custom and the world."

CHAPTER X.

"GONE TO THE WARS."

" War is the concentration of all crimes." — CHANNING.

" War is a denial of human brotherhood, and justice is in no respect promoted by it."
SENATOR SUMNER.

WHEN in California, popular with the soldiers, a regiment of that State voted him their chaplain. On visiting them at their "Camp Donney," noticing the machinery of battle, he courteously declined, convicted in his own conscience that a commission of this kind would make him an accomplice of bloodshed. Returning home, he found the very air charged with war. Every thing centered here, to crush the rebellion. Though a lover of his country, patriotic, the idea of shedding a brother's blood shocked his love of peace. Long he pondered upon his duty, and came to the sober conclusion that he must go, — a clerk under Capt. D. Y. Kilgore. He wished to see life in all its phases, and administer comfort to the sick, wounded, and dying soldiers. The following extracts from his letters tell the story of his experiences and moral impressions of war: —

"BRIDGEPORT, ALA., Dec. 7, 1863.

"I can only write to-night from the text, 'And in hell he lifted up his eyes, being in torment!' . . . There are over twenty thousand soldiers encamped here now, all in cloth tents. I am now writing in a tent, with the top of a valise for a writing-desk. The soldiers are on half-rations. It is almost impossible to get food for so many. Destruction lines the wagon-roads. The weather is warm and beautiful. Blue-birds sing in the morning. How homesick I have been! . . . I went to work the next day after my arrival, copying papers, drawing orders, issuing forage, &c., &c. It is perfectly earthly and worldly. I look into no book; see no 'Banner of Light,' nor 'Herald,' nor Northern paper of any description. . . . Soldiers and officers gamble and drink horridly. . . . I saw four thousand of the rebels that Gen. Grant took in one squad, and talked with a number of them. They looked dirty, ragged, and homesick. Poor brothers! How strange my life-experiences! Poor prodigal I, from John's and Aaron's house, spiritually speaking. Say nothing to my wife about the hardships and exposures before me."

"NASHVILLE, TENN., Jan. 14, 1864.

. . . "Oh, 'tis sweet to be alone! Never did I so long for solitude. The eternal bustle of business, of jarrings, antagonisms, swearing, cheating, that so prevail, make me sick in soul. My body is wearing away under the pressure. I feel it, *know* it. Either I must leave, or my bones will whiten under an Alabama sun. . . . Tell Powhattan to help his 'Preach.' . . . Oh, the deceit and hypocrisy of certain spirits who promise officers great positions! They purport to be Washington, Jackson, Clay, controlling a young medium here. How intensely I love and appreciate Bro. Nite for his honesty! He came to me, not a god, or a Franklin, or a Washington; but simply Aaron Nite,—once a poor coach-driver in England. Now he is an angel, and I would gladly sit at his feet for instruction. . . . Rebel soldiers, erring yet sincere, lie frozen to death on our hands. A poor woman was frozen,—is dead. The dead carcasses of mules are lying over the graves of our soldiers. Only those that have seen have any idea of this war."

"BRIDGEPORT, ALA., Jan. 21, 1864.

. . . "Last evening, about 9 o'clock, I returned from Chattanooga in a private car, with Bishop Simpson, Gen. Howard, Gen. Cook, Col. Donaldson, and several chaplains. . . . I went up the Tennessee River, in charge of some commissary stores, by order of Capt. Kilgore. Capt. Jett, a Mississippian professor, went with me on to 'Lookout Mountain,' over the late battle-field. Picked up bullets, pieces of shell, and other trophies. He and several soldiers engaged in the battle told me all about it. I went several times to Gen. Howard's head-quarters. Generals were as thick as were the frogs in Egypt.' I have no respect for gaudy trappings. . . . Heaven help our poor soldiers! Their sufferings are terrible. Oh, the effects of army life upon two-thirds that go thither! . . . The weather is pleasant now. The birds sing. The ground is covered with dead mules and horses. Reckless soldiers travel this way and that, day and night. . . . I can not write. The office is full of folks; some for gain, some for clothes, some to have unruly soldiers arrested. It is 'Babel!' the last place on earth for a refined organization. My only happy moments are when I walk away from every human being. I am alone, all alone, although in the midst of an army of men!"

In response to a letter of inquiry, we received this cordial testimonial from his army friend and brother, who is one of our sterling Spiritualists,—a reform lawyer, defending justice and truth:—

"605 WALNUT ST., PHILADELPHIA, Jan. 1, 1871.

"J. O. BARRETT: *Dear Sir*,—In answer to your note of inquiry respecting the army life of James M. Peebles, it affords me pleasure to say it was unexceptionable and thoroughly consistent with his peace principles.

"In the winter of 1863–4, he was employed by me as a clerk in the quarter-master's department at Bridgeport, Ala. During the time he continued in the service of the Government, we occupied the same tent, and most of the time the same couch.

"Such was my confidence in him, that he was intrusted with the most responsible duties; and although property amounting to tens of thousands of dollars passed through his hands daily, no mistakes were found in his accounts, and not a penny stuck. Though often placed in the most trying circumstances, he never lost his equanimity, nor evidenced a disposition of retaliation toward those who had wronged him; but, on the contrary, he everywhere manifested, by word and deed, a gentle, forgiving, and loving spirit, coupled with that sterling integrity which never sanctions wrong.

"The example of such a man is always good; but in the rough experiences of army life it is invaluable.

"At the end of about three months' service, his health declining, he was obliged to return home, much to the disappointment of all who knew him. I am glad to hear you are preparing his biography; for the life of such a man will be of service to humanity. He is one of the saviors of the nineteenth century.

"Faithfully yours, DAMON Y. KILGORE."

CHAPTER XI.

MEDIUMSHIP.

"Each ounce of dross costs its ounce of gold." — LOWELL.

"And he set the rods which he had peeled before the flocks in the gutters; . . . and the flocks conceived before the rods, and brought forth cattle, ring-streaked, speckled, and spotted." — BIBLE.

"It seems that every creed or tribe of earth
Conceives a God, and gives him form and birth
Possessing all the traits of every tribe:
Thus, while portraying God, themselves describe;
And as they each advance in reason's light,
And have more just conceptions of the right,
A God of like improvement then appears." — BARLOW'S "VOICES."

SPLICE the hemlock, oak, and pine, can we make a new tree? Wait till each, fulfilling its mission, crumbles into dust: now there is a union of the elements; out of the improved soil rises another species of tree, — matter progressed, — which no art can construct.

At a Universalist Convention held in Janesville, Wis., in the summer of 1864, were three radical ministers, Revs. R. S. Sanborn, A. J. Fishback, and J. O. Barrett. Having spiced and peppered the "bread of life" quite successfully, we sinned "the sin of heresy." Secreting ourselves, we attempted to draw up a platform for a new religious movement; but the spirits dashed the creed-making business to the ground. Thinking we had not got the right patterns, we concluded to "wait on the Lord" by calling a convention of "Liberal Christians" in Beaver Dam, Wis., Rev. H. A. Reid (Unitarian) being afterward enlisted as a co-operator. But who would bring in the Spiritualists? Note how the spirits came to our rescue. We went to Palmyra to preach a chowdered theology. By invitation of Dr. Ridell, an old schoolmate, Mr. Peebles was announced to speak there the next Tuesday evening. "Mr. Peebles," we asked, "of Battle Creek, the writer of Spiritualism in Universalist papers?

That's the man we must see." He had just closed a month's labor in Milwaukie. We clasped hands for the first time at the residence of Rev. C. F. Dodge of Palmyra, Wis. Being then a "respectable Universalist minister," we looked him over very carefully, endeavoring to call him out, particularly upon the subject of "free love;" for we staidly asked, if "Spiritualists generally are free lovers!" Agreeably surprised at his positive remarks, advocating a moral life far above our actuality, we were taken back again by a most awkward Indian jump he made, with a war-whoop yell, when we spoke kindly of the Indians; but the next moment all this "ministerial impropriety" (in our estimation) vanished, when he discoursed so feelingly about the rights of the Indians, and of the down-trodden of all races. When we had inspected each other, — he with a sort of careless sociability, we with a coy and *very* churchal questioning, — he said, when alone, to test the heart-blending, "Bro. Barrett, I see your inner life and struggles, the drift of your love, and impending fate as a Universalist minister. My sympathy goes out to you: we are brothers in oneness of spirit." The manner of this remark, tinged in every cadence with a sweet confidence, shot through us a sunbeam. Then and there we laid before him our darling project, soliciting co-operation. He responded with a hearty readiness, consenting to represent the Spiritualists, and enlist all possible influence from that source. This happy interview was introductory to a most enlivening correspondence with him, which became the principal agency in emancipating us from a sectarian prison. In the mean while, the prime actors, noticing the great meeting in the churchal and spiritual presses, received responsive letters from eminent divines of the Unitarian sect, — such as David Wasson, Drs. Ellis, Livermore, Clarke, Bellows, E. C. Towne; and from J. S. Loveland, Moses Hull, Adin Ballou, and others of the Spiritual ranks; but none of marked note from the Universalists — except Revs. J. H. Harter and George Severance — who gave any encouragement to the undertaking.

Soon after, attending a convention of Spiritualists at St. Charles, Ill., we publicly stated the object, advocated union, and invited Spiritualists present to attend our meeting at Beaver Dam, when E. V. Wilson sprung to his feet, and lashed the proposition with a commendable fury, shouting the prophecy home, that brought a laugh from the electrified audience and a blush to our cheek, pointing at us with a rebuking sarcasm, "And you, sir, kicked out of the Universalist sect, where you deserve to be!"

The auspicious hour arriving, these "heretics" (Peebles and Fishback absent on other engagements) met at Beaver Dam, — five Unitarian clergymen, two Universalists, one lone Spiritualist representative (Dr. J. E. Morrison of Illinois). The convention was meager, — a mongrel. The batteries opened; all was brotherly, when, of a sudden, a growl was heard. The true symbol of the meeting was a spotted hyena. Mr. Morrison was covertly ignored. Spiritualism must be cast out of the kingdom, "the dirty thing!" Rev. ——— of Janesville had "conscientious dislikes against Spiritualists: they are loose, seditious. Mr. Peebles and other restless clergymen are a fair specimen, having been for years under the ban of their denomination." No proof was adduced to substantiate this statement. It was cowardly, FALSE. Indignant, we poured in grapeshot. A battle ensued. The fire was hot. Injustice had been done, and the rebuking angels scattered us. Blasted in this our most sanguine effort, but hoping for union in another State, we fled to Battle Creek, where Mr. Peebles had been trying his art of cementing liberal elements in conventional fellowship. Pursuant to due notice, the people assembled. Any Universalist ministers? any Unitarian? Not one, except our heretical self. The meeting was mainly Spiritualistic in representation. Moses Hull, William Baldwin, and others, gave a ready hand of support. It was inspiring, embosomed this time in the loves of the angels. The folly of amalgamating incongruous elements was apparent. The lesson which the spirits taught us was severe, but beautiful. "No alliance with the dead!" "What fellowship hath Christ with Belial?" is written on ruins. Exhume no damaged titles! "Let the dead bury their dead!" So we both said, "and so endeth the second lesson."

The morality of mediumship depends upon the plane to which we key it. If sensuous in motive, developed by "filthy communications," its mold of character is of the same low degree, — "carnal and devilish." No stream can rise higher than its source. Descending from the spiritual, cultured in the moral, restraining in the passional: then we have what holy angels expect, — reform and progress. Said the pure-minded Nazarene, looking to the mediumistic discipline of his apostles, "In this rejoice not, that the spirits are subject unto you; but rather rejoice because your names are written in heaven." On the arches of the spiritual temple faithful mediums have such names engraved: PURITY, CHASTITY, FIDELITY, CHARITY, PATIENCE, — just as our leading virtues are.

Stormy, blasting — shivered by lightnings: March winds from melting winter! So Mr. Peebles's mediumistic experiences during 1857–63. What of his horoscope? Clouded with doubts, red with battles, purpled with victories!

Such is the way for all of us. Jesus had his seasons of temptation, destruction, "strong crying and tears," martyrdom; the after calm of "Father, into thy hands I commend my spirit." What of Pythagoras, Socrates, Plotinus, Apollonius of Tyana, Hildebrand, Friar Bacon, Joan d' Arc, George Fox the Quaker, Swedenborg the Mystic, Murray the Preacher? — lights in the zodiac of solar truth, mingling their glory with the new-made planets of our age, they shine at last over the chaos of their pilgrimage. Thither the journey lies; through the hells of self, up the heights; veterans of moral heroism! "Thou art the anointed cherub that covereth; I have set thee so: thou wast upon the holy mountain of God; thou hast walked up and down in the midst of stones of fire."

"E'en his vices leaned to virtue's side."

Unsuspecting as a child, confiding as a woman, believing humanity is divine, Mr. Peebles awoke from soul-slumber in objective life to plunge into the magnetic whirlpools, tempest-tost, and riven as a lost mariner at sea. "He is mine," said a voice; "nay, mine," said a loving angel. Oh, the "conflict of ages"! Here our brother fought against spirits, against mortals, — himself the chief enemy to himself. The following letter to a friend betrays the secret of every spiritual soul, — the balancing pivot, — Mohammed's hair-bridge stretched over the abyss on which Allah's children must walk to heaven: —

"DEC. 28, 1861.

. . . "It may be that my conscience is becoming exceedingly sensitive; for at times I feel impelled to rush along the track of my whole past earth-life, unsaying and undoing every thing said and done amiss. Forgiveness is out of the question. Restoration and reconciliation, crowned with wisdom, are the only *saviors*. The very things, that, in the depths of my soul, I *hate*, I am tempted to do; thus being a puzzle to myself. It is quite clear that we must die to the earthly before we can live to the spiritual. My aspirations, Heaven knows, are high enough; but they are never realized: and yet I complain of no one but myself; nor would I make others miserable on my account. The world shall only see my smiles.

"'I am weary, I am weary,
I am longing for my home,
Looking through life's wildering mazes
For the rest which ne'er doth come;

But sometimes there cometh visions,
Faint, yet beautiful to me,
Of the home for which I'm longing,
In "the land beyond the sea."'

"True, there are some flowers blooming along my pilgrim pathway; but they grow fresh in Nature's garden, and jut out from the mountain sides, rather than from the masses of souls I meet.

"'Grief is deepest laid
On hearts that deepest feel and deepest love.
"Perfect thro' suffering," mounting thus above
The sense of wrong, the soul is steadfast made.'"

Must we have experience on the plane where we stoop, ere we can sympathize with the fallen? Must we explore every hell, ere we can open a full, free heaven to the unfortunate? Does the human heart select a life of shame, or is it forced by circumstances? Ask the gamblers. Ask our erring sisters. Ask the blasted hopes, the aching consciences, the bitterness of hearts. Cherish it, — the sweet truth, — that human nature is pure by birthright as the budding rose; or will you reckon that its beauty is to blame for the blighting frost or heat?

Mediumship! what a power this, that touches all the souls in the world; that feels all that mortals and angels feel, drawing the pilgrim up to higher love: but oh, the perils, the *perils!* Can the medium, confiding as a child, descend into the hells of self and not be contaminated, or tempted to err? Such may sin, and not be sinful; may be snared, to learn wisdom! O beautiful charity! drop a tear on every heart-stain, and out of the roots of woe will spring the truest love. Afterward the descent can be made by an angel of light, the mental darkness furnishing fuel for a greater moral splendor.

Muscular contortions, painful trance, the Dervish dance, are not criterions of evil influences, but simply the processes of removing obstructions. The mediumistic phases vary according to organization. Frenzy of body may prevent injury to the inner life. Too much illumination of the spiritual senses might induce phantasy. The opening of the spiritual forces, until we are wholly balanced, subtracts from the material. There is a magnetism in a smile, a frown, a gesture, a kiss, a heart-throb. Psychological action of the nerve-organs mediumizes for the supremacy of the spirit.

About this time, Mr. Peebles was easily controlled. In psychological, half-dreaming consciousness, he often traveled miles, and found himself in strange localities, whither he had no intention of going. Thus led to libraries, he took down books, and turned to passages utterly foreign to any plan of his own, the purpose of which he afterward discovered. Unconscious of the fact at first, he was known to give excellent spirit-tests, as in the instance of a funeral discourse. Whilst picturing the glories of the future life, over the lifeless remains of Dr. A. S. Hayward's wife's mother, in Boston, he seemed to hear the spirit-voices; for he repeated, word for word, the dying testimony of the departed.

This mediumistic sensitiveness, quickening every latent force of character, giving preponderance to his organic spirituality, awoke an over-anxiety to gain a moral victory in angel-life, incidentally inducing a wish, thousands of times expressed, to die, and ascend to the celestial heavens; as if a closer contact with spirits, the very causes of his battles to develop him, would be a safer retreat! The road to wisdom is the knowledge of our weaknesses.

When in Oswego, engaged to lecture, guest of J. L. Pool, a lady friend, simply relating the current news, said to him, —

"Well, Brother Peebles, we used to think you were a good man when pastor of our Universalist society here; but we hear terrible stories about you in the West."

"What's up now?" asked Mr. Peebles.

"They say you have got to be a drunkard, a beastly drunkard, wallowing in the streets of Battle Creek."

Astonished and morally indignant, Mr. Peebles exclaimed, "It is a lie, a malicious, vindictive lie! I belong to the Good Templars of Battle Creek, and am Chaplain of the Lodge. This is a lying, wicked, slanderous world. I am sick of it. I wish I were in the spirit-world, away from all this social corruption!"

When these two brothers were alone, Aaron Nite approached, deeply entranced Dr. Dunn, and said, —

"Well, Friend Peebles, we have been listening to your description of the slandering, wicked, backbiting world in which you live; and, while hearing, we thought of our own, so beautiful, orderly, loving, and happy."

"I know that," answered our Pilgrim; "I understand all that: hence my desire to die and be with you in your spirit-home."

"Ah, Friend Peebles!" replied the spirit, smiling through the medium's face, "we don't like to pluck green fruit in our country. You never saw an apple want to fall from the bough in July, when it is sour, green, bitter, unfit for use; but, seemingly wiser than you, wants to hang on till long in October or November, — till it gets ripe, full, luscious, matured, when there comes an opportune breeze, and it drops off, born into individuality, a natural and beautiful separation. So we want you to hang to the bough of life on earth till your work is done, and you are fully ripe for the spirit-world; then we shall call for you, and meet you at the entering in."

After this lesson, so aptly given, the "Spiritual Pilgrim" was not in such a hurry to die; but to live as long as he could, battle bravely, face all slanders and falsehood with heroic fortitude, and remember "green fruit."

In these earlier stages of Mr. Peebles's mediumship, we discover the same mistakes we all have made. Fear of mischief from a spirit engenders a spheral antagonism; a weakness this, which entangles worse than the snarl of such relationship. When we are spiritually self-poised, whether in this or the next world, we can neither be insulted nor imperiled nor injured. The balanced mind is invulnerable. If we fear no evil, think no evil, harbor no evil, nothing but the good will seek us for protection. If we are balanced up, every force of life coronated in the flower of spirituality, our sphere is so sweet and sunny, so like the lily with a golden heart full of fragrance, whatever touches us then is transformed into divine likenesses.

Lecturing in Portland, his eyes inflamed from over-reading, and otherwise ill, he was led blind-folded to the hall every Sunday. Taking advantage of this condition, a cunning spirit, not of his band, introduced himself through a friendly medium, proposing certain plausible schemes. Mr. Peebles writes to Dr. Dunn, —

"Though K. brought his medium one hundred and sixty miles on purpose to see me, I did not stay with him a night, — refused to sit in a circle with him, refused to be magnetized by him, refused to ask him into the desk with me; in fact, dreaded his magnetic influence. This figure comes to me: though the spirit did not enter my premises, or my house, he stood aloof and threw mud on it. The medium is naturally a good man, and interested me deeply in his travels in spirit-life.

"You ask, 'What will K. do next?' Perhaps injure me! You say, 'Had we not better yield before it goes farther?' Why did you write that? Do you know me? Have you not had enough exhibitions of my firmness? I am never conquered, *never defeated;* and, if subdued, love only can do it. I know not that I ever attempted to reach a moral stand-point in my life and failed. Oh that word 'yield!' — no, *never!* My fraternal love for you is deeper than the ocean, divine as God. Millions of K.'s can not change it. Why do you indulge him in those talks? He thinks he is holier and wiser than John. I have no fears of his breaking our friendship; for the angels encircled us in a wreath of immortal love."

Note the following incidents, as reported in his private letters, indicative of the special care of angels over their brother at this period of his mediumship: —

"MILWAUKIE, WIS., April, 1865.

"Last night the hall was densely packed; and when pronouncing the benediction, I felt a hand upon my shoulder, and supposed it to be Mr. B.'s, the sexton who lights the gas. For a moment it annoyed me; and yet I felt inspired to pronounce a much longer benediction than usual. When through, I turned round to speak to him; and lo! nobody was there, nor had there been anybody on the platform. It was a spirit-hand, probably Perasee's, as I had been speaking of his putting your hand into a blaze of fire without injury. . . . I am a strange creature, — perhaps, a medium. The other day, my window being raised, a dollar-bill dropped down before me. In Chicago, a man (almost an entire stranger) handed me twenty dollars. I refused it. He said, 'You are a medium, working for humanity: take it!' and I did. Two men in New York did the same thing, and one lady. Why is it? Is it their spirit-friends, or mine?"

The experience of our brother is not uncommon. Many a medium, when distressed for means, has been likewise favored in ways unmistakably proving a spiritual agency. In our saddest hours — if we lose not our faith to draw them — angels interpose in our behalf. Thousands can testify to this. Was Elijah fed by the ravens under spirit direction? Was the widow's cruse of oil replenished through the mediumship of that prophet? About a century since, lived a Catholic medium in Paris, the 'Curé of Ars,' by whom the spirits supplied bread to starving children. Money was also tendered, if we may credit the historian: —

"He recommended his dear little ones to the compassionate heart of the holy mother of God, who is also the mother of the poor. His prayer was speedily answered; for suddenly a female form appeared to him, and said, 'Are you the Curé of Ars?' — 'Yes my good lady.' — 'Here is some money which I am desired to give to you.' — Are they for masses?' said the curé. 'No: it is sent in answer to your prayers.' Having emptied her purse into his hands, she left him without saying where she came from, or whither she was going. In this way, says M. Monnin, did money come providentially, in some secret way, at the very time when it was most urgently needed."

Lecturing in Indiana, among philosophical minds, the question incidentally suggested itself, whether Christ did really walk upon the water. The spirits declaring it probable, Mr. Peebles demanded a test. Assenting, they added, "Certain conditions are first essential: the medium must fast several days, and avoid hard labor. This will clear the brain, and fit the whole system for proper control." Appreciating the necessity of the mind's being free from worldly cares, Mr. Peebles would slyly put a dollar or more, every night, into the medium's pocket. Fitness to use is when the mediums are justly protected. Having faithfully complied with the required conditions, one evening, the light burning, Mr. Peebles and others had the satisfaction of seeing the medium carried up by spirits, perfectly afloat between the bed and ceiling. The test called to mind the words of the Nazarene: "All power is given me in heaven and earth."

> "Powers there are
> That touch each other to the quick, in modes
> Which the gross world no sense hath to perceive,
> No soul to dream of."

On another occasion, Mr. Peebles inquired of the spirits if the three Hebrew children (Daniel iii.) did actually pass through the fire unharmed, as is stated in the Bible. Perasee assured him the event was a probability, being in consonance with spirit-law. Mr. Peebles demanded a test; and the Italian chemist again demanded in turn a faithful compliance with the conditions of fasting. This obeyed, one afternoon the medium was deeply entranced in Mr. Peebles's library room, and his hand held in the burning flame of a kerosene lamp for five minutes. The smoke was on the hand; which, being removed, lo, not a particle of the skin was burned or blistered! The test satisfactory, Mr. Peebles asked for the philosophy. Perasee, informing him of the barrenness of our language to elucidate the truth, gave an analysis of the chemical ingredients, stating that "light, heat, electricity, are modifications of a fluid held in common, individualized as separate existences. We gathered from the atmosphere an antidotal element that neutralized the effects of the fire. Coating the hand with this, we protected it safely. This is the subtile substance, embodying itself in vision to Nebuchadnezzar, as the 'fourth like the son of man.'"

One June evening, in Rockford, Ill., Mr. Peebles and his medium were sitting side by side, holding each by the hand, enjoying the fresh breeze laden with fragrance. Instantly what seemed a summer bug flew in, circling round and round from wall to ceiling, with a musical buzz, and at length lit on the vest of the doctor. Noticing it carefully, Mr. Peebles exclaimed, "Don't brush it away! why, it's not a bug!" Two beautiful fresh buds fell to the floor, both on one stem, plucked by the spirits from an adjoining garden. How gratefully were they cherished, pressed between the leaves of the Bible!

Lock the "sweet Pleiades" in silver chains; bind all waters and gases, the odors of leaf and flower, the gushes of music, and the arts of beauty! This is the business of mother Nature to educe birth, change, and progress. No escape from the law that holds us? None. The divine government is inexorable in justice. License is abhorred by wise spirits. Eternal vigilance to order is the path to "the perfect law of liberty." There are "spirits in prison," "locked in chains of darkness," kept under strict guard for the protection of the innocent and their own redemption.

> "And I will give unto thee the keys of the kingdom of heaven; and whatsoever thou shalt bind on earth shall be bound in heaven; and whatsoever thou shalt loose on earth shall be loosed in heaven."

This truth was happily illustrated in frequent instances where certain departed clergymen, not yet outgrown their Church dogmas, would enter Mr. Peebles's congregations with designs to enforce their sentiments inspirationally through his mediumship. Whenever such could succeed in forming a battery, the effort of Mr. Peebles was labored. The presence of such spirits, — whom, of course, we should invite, when sufficiently positive to control ourselves, — accounts for failures with some of our more negative speakers in mixed audiences. Spiritualists are largely responsible here, in neglecting to form counter-acting batteries. The churches have their confederates in the first spheres of the spirit-world, who, unseen save by our media, seek the control of our inspirational forces; and do sometimes drag, now and then, an unguarded negative victim into their fold, when they are inevitably lost, their identity swallowed up.

One Sunday, lecturing in Sturgis, Mr. Peebles stormed the old citadel of the "Christian Atonement," Aaron Nite being the presiding genius of the spirit audience. The medium, clairvoyant, saw at the right, in the distance, a spirit dressed in black, with a white cravat, — a very dignified clergyman, who was gesticulating, and gathering around him a few friends, and influencing others in the audience, pointing with serious scorn at Mr. Peebles, and quoting Scripture with eloquent gravity, saying, "That man is preaching damnable heresies. Hear what saith the word: 'But there were false prophets also among the people, even as there shall be false teachers among you, who privily shall bring in damnable heresies, even denying the Lord that bought them, and bring upon themselves swift destruction.'" This spirit then preached to his auditors about the resurrection of the body, the second coming of Christ, and the atoning blood. "As proof," said he, "that I am of God, see those long-bearded Grecians listening approvingly to the ribaldry of that speaker. No heathen philosopher hath part with Christ." The effect of this harangue was a division of sentiment in the meeting, and a general feeling of social jar.

When about to commence a lecture in Oswego, noticing his medium (seated with him in the desk as usual) was clairvoyant, and gazing round the room as if spying every nook and corner, Mr. Peebles asked him what he saw.

"An old, positive man," was the reply, "ugly and fierce, approaching the desk." The spirit took a seat in the third chair, when the doctor conversed with him, unknown to the gathering audience.

"Who is there, Charlie?" inquired Mr. Peebles.

"I know him," answered the spirit: "I used to discuss with him in the streets of this city, when he preached here as a Universalist."

The medium described him accurately, "Positive, dogmatic, still a member of the same church, one-eyed" —

"Yes, I know him well," broke in Mr. Peebles; "he annoyed me much: what is he here for?"

A commotion among the spirits: that man's friends pressed nearer, and insisted that Mr. Peebles should be controlled by him (this very one-eyed minister), and be "*compelled* to tell the truth this time!" Mr. Peebles's spirit-friends were disturbed, for the wrong man was in the circle. Instantly one of his faithful guides telegraphed to Perasee Lendanta, who was then busily engaged in a distant portion of the sidereal heavens. The telegram was charged with a feeling of imperative urgency, — the very *soul* of thought which spirits easily sense, — and he hastened to obey the summons, bringing with him a band of ancient spirits, supposed to be mainly Persians, for they wore the Persian spirit-costume, long robes, shining girdles, and white, snowy pyramidal hats, or plumes. A large company of Indian spirits also assembled, amused and wondering, ready to obey orders. In a moment the nucleus of a battery was formed; and the magnetism of the atmosphere changed to a positive condition, involving belligerent forces. Trembling from exhaustion, the medium turned to Mr. Peebles with the startling statement, "You will doubtless break down!"

This remark made Mr. Peebles nervous and apprehensive, producing a more negative state, when the "one-eyed" spirit, seeing his advantage, rose and pressed his hand toward Mr. Peebles's shoulder, unable to touch him, yet succeeding in imparting a mental force that caused confusion of ideas, dragging him, as with chains, — a captive! He shuddered and shook, and prayed for deliverance.

Watching the sequel, the medium saw the appearance of a wall, rising slowly in vivid compactness, as if alive, forming at length a high cone-like rampart. Aaron Nite stepped inside, taking both Peebles and his medium with him, safely inclosed from all intrusion. The moment the top of this cone folded up, as if a netted sheet, Perasee drew his hand down quick, and cut off that old fellow's magnetism, pushed him one side, made another cone around him, then moved him in his prison off to one corner, where he chafed like a caged tiger, under the eye of Indian sentinels. Mr. Peebles, now free again, opened grandly with his discourse under the loving inspiration of John, Perasee presiding, and governing the batteries of mind. The lecture closed, those spirits let their prisoner out, when Perasee gave him some good advice, "Never to undertake again what he had no capacity for or association with." The ashamed minister, receiving a blessing to be for ever remembered, and quailing under a just criticism, went off shivering in every nerve to find his own place.

This is not the only instance where it was morally necessary to imprison, or control, interfering spirits. Deceiving spirits, seeking to decoy, were struck dumb and blind for the time being, as Paul did Elymas the sorcerer, till "there fell on him a mist and a darkness." How beautiful and startling are the uses of the psychological laws! They are the constitutions, the codes, the enforcements, of the republics of spirits. We no longer wonder at John's vision, when he "saw an angel come down from heaven, having the key of the bottomless pit and a *great chain* in his hand," with which he bound a deceiving spirit in power, — "bound him a thousand years."

> "All my soul
> Was thrilled and filled with music, and I prayed
> To be let loose, that I might cast myself
> Upon the mighty tides, and give my life
> To the supernal raptures."

Fly with electric life the fiery steeds, the red blood in the human body, to vitalize every part. Carrying the spheres of angels, impelled to action, the spiritual heralds have circled through all the country, shocking the bigoted, fighting effete theology, sowing precious seed watered with tears. A large moral experience and a large charity: true ratio this. To minister to mortals on their diverse planes of suffering, we must "be touched with the feeling of their infirmity." To understand the spirit-world and its claims in wholeness, representatives of every plane of life need be introduced to us; and thence we gravitate where we belong, serving as we are served. This was our Pilgrim's discipline now. Let the sequel show how well he conned the lessons. By the mediumship of Dr. Dunn, the spirits taught him every possible art of spiritual health and culture; by Nellie J. T. Brigham, Sarah M. Thompson, Mrs. S. A. Horton, Mrs. Reid Knowles, Emma Martin, Jennie S. Rudd, they breathed into his soul the music-words of immortality; by the Andersons and Mumlers they revealed the artistic galleries of the better world; by Maggie Patterson they portrayed perils to escape and successes to gain; by L. G. Smedley, H. Slade, and A. P. Pierce they instructed him in the laws of spiritual healing; by A. B. Whiting they showed him glimpses of the superior wisdom of ancient seers; by S. B. Brittan they proved how a sunny heart sweetens the home till the angels nestle there; by Mrs. Victor Post they impressed in stillness of thought the peace-words of a happy life; by Nettie M. Pease they visioned him in the flash of heaven that veils the face in the beauty of hope; by E. V. Wilson they were repeatedly identified, saying "Doubt not;" by Mrs. J. H. Conant they inspired him with the heroism of the Parkers and Pierponts; by Sarah A. Byrnes and Mrs. J. G. Wait they rimmed the solitudes of his life with the rainbows of trust; by Fannie B. Felton they sent into his bosom the merry heart-beats of healthful spirit ministrants; by Mrs. F. O. Hyzer they demonstrated that perseverance conquers, and

> "Love is the transmuter of all outer things;"

by the Davenports, Annie Lord Chamberlin, and Maud Lord they materialized themselves comprehensible to every sense; by L. C. Howe they opened to view the divine of Nature and the harmonies of worlds; by Abraham James they apprenticed him in the more practical of the spiritual gospel; by Mrs. M. S. Townsend Hoadley they revealed the beauty and grace of freedom; by Elvira Wheelock Ruggles they disciplined him in the gospel of woman's fidelity and independence; by Thomas Gales Forster they demonstrated to him the correlation of matter and spirit; by Hudson Tuttle they read to him the philosophical solution of historic problems of religions; by Mrs. Cora L. V. Tappan, they unveiled the mysteries of mind and the glories of the upper kingdoms of God; by Olive — too modest to be known — they promised an "Eden of rest for the weary Pilgrim;" by Nellie Smith they sung the melodies of the fair enchantress who is preparing a home "up there;" by Emma Tuttle they exemplified how fidelity wins, how the ideal must be "my Jesus," in the *real* man of sunny soul, to whom she sings, —

"Ye won it by no false pretense;
Ye did not daze by gems and gold,
Nor buy by flatteries sweetly told;
But by the soul's magnificence
And kinship to thy God maintained,
Our spirits unto thine are chained."

Remembering these lessons, he often quotes his friend Preuss, —

"With weak and mole-ish vision.
We work our way below;
But sure our souls are building
Much wiser than we know."

One day, at Albion, Mich., Mr. Peebles fell into a most frightful dilemma, whilst magnetizing Dr. H. Slade, the celebrated test medium and healer. Asking Wassoo, the Indian spirit controlling the doctor, about the method, he was permitted to make a trial of his skill, the spirits retiring to a distance. Mr. Peebles commenced operations, and threw his subject into a perfect trance; when, to his astonishment, the medium imitated his every motion, repeated his words, articulated his ideas, till he seemed to be a part of himself, — verily, himself repeated. Getting somewhat alarmed, he made reverse vertical passes, but to no purpose! In his bewilderment, he invoked the aid of Perasee, who, coming to the rescue, taking possession of the medium, instructed him to make passes horizontal as well as vertical; "for," said the Italian, "in the perfect trance, like this, the psychological rays center from all directions; hence the counter-currents must be made in reverse lines to scatter the entrancing sphere." The success of the ever-to-be remembered lesson was beautiful.

Up to 1864, Mr. Peebles, like the rest of us, maintained that the age in which *we* live casts all other ages into the shadow of its knowledge. Everywhere he was grandiloquent about "the greatness of the nineteenth century." At a lecture in Princeton, Ill., on the subject of Progress, he wound up his electric lecture with a splendid peroration upon the inferiority of the past and the superiority of the present; and went to his boarding-place elated with the proud consciousness that he had done something really worthy of the flattery he received. When alone in his room, his medium, suddenly entranced, made a strange bow, after the Asiatic style, and, after a series of earnest devotions, stood up before Mr. Peebles with closed eyes, and inspecting him from head to foot, with a pungent sarcasm, said, —

"Well, you are about the homeliest man I ever saw. What's your name?"

"Name?" replied Mr. P., with a wit in his cadence; "my name is *Pee*-bles."

"What does *Pee*-bles mean?" said the spirit with gravity.

"Don't know."

"Don't know your own name? you a teacher, and don't know the meaning of your *own name?* Well!"

"Is that any thing strange? You seem to be thunder-struck at a mere name. All people have names. In China the people are called *Chinese*."

"What does *Chinese* mean?"

"I don't know."

"Why use words you do not know the meaning of?"

"What may I call *your* name?" asked Mr. Peebles.

"No matter as to that: you seem to have but little knowledge of names; but you may call me *Aphelion*, if you like. Do you know the meaning of that word?"

"I think it is an astronomical word, signifying the greatest or least distance from the sun; I forget which."

The spirit betrayed not an emotion, but looked him over again very gravely, and said, —

"I lived on your earth, in an Asian province, about sixteen thousand years ago. We wrote in what corresponds with the Egyptian hieroglyphs: every dot, point, symbol, and curve meaning something, conveying some distinct idea. Sixteen thousand years ago was the dark age of which you spoke so eloquently to-night."

When the spirit said "sixteen thousand years ago," Mr. Peebles laughed outright.

"What do you laugh for? Philosophers seldom laugh. Imbeciles giggle much. You disgust me with your *ha, ha, ha!* — mouth wide open."

"Have not you, as a spirit, a brain," asked Mr. Peebles, "and an organ of mirthfulness?"

"Yes," said *Aphelion* with dignity.

"How do you exercise it?"

"In a calm, pleasurable sensation, that permeates our whole being. . . . I momentarily listened to your temperance lecture, the other evening. The people cheered you by shouting, and stamping, and clapping hands; and you were proud. Such appreciation disgusted me. When on your earth, I was a medium, teacher, and lecturer; and, when uttering a great truth, the people rose and stood silent, gazing with an inspired, enraptured look that seemed to penetrate the very heavens. They would shade their eyes under the palms of their hands, as if the better to see and examine the truth. . . . On the 4th of July, that sultry day, I heard you speak on Independence, during which you said defiantly, 'I care not what the people say: I will be myself, —*free*.' There you stood with thick boots on, and black coat, sweltering in the sun. You should have been barefooted, or, at least, sandaled, wearing a white, trailing robe. But you do not care what the people say! In glancing over your country, I have not seen a true man or woman. None live up to their highest ideal. You are a nation of cowards. . . . You are aware that the ancients had a cement of which the moderns know nothing; that they could transfuse color through glass, which you moderns can not; that there are many lost arts and sciences; that the sculpture of three and four thousand years since is copied by modern artists. Sixteen thousand years ago, our navigators propelled vessels by electricity. . . . Plato's account of the sinking of the New Atlantis Isle is nearly correct. I was acquainted with several inhabitants of that island, then so famous for its fine arts and high degree of civilization. Records establishing the facts may yet be found in the hieroglyphs of ancient Egypt, or in the beds of the ocean. Cities buried by sand or volcanoes will yet be exhumed and re-inhabited. History is ever repeating itself, and progress is in cycles."

Taken down to a more modest mein, Mr. Peebles, after this, was less boastful and boisterous about modern civilizations. He then began the study of ancient spiritual literature and science with a keener relish than ever. His exclamation was: —

"Let no one presume originality. Let us pierce the inflated balloons of Bros. Davis, Brittan, Denton, Tuttle, Owen, Howitt, and *Peebles especially;* sit at the feet of the Neo-Platonists, Hindoo Gymnosophists, Egyptian Hierophants, Persian Magi, Chinese Philosophers, and learn wisdom; for 'of such is the kingdom of heaven.'"

CHAPTER XII.

THE GOLD THAT WEARS.

"And the preaching of this preacher
  Stirs the pulses of the world.
Tyranny has curbed its pride;
Errors that were deified,
  Into darkness have been hurled;
Slavery and Liberty,
  And the Wrong and Right, have met
To decide their ancient quarrel.
  Onward, preacher; onward yet!
There are pens to tell your progress,
  There are eyes that pine to read,
There are hearts that burn to aid you,
  There are arms in hour of need.
Onward, preacher! Onward, nations!
  Will must ripen into deed." — NEWRY EXAMINER (IRELAND).

When Mr. Peebles had labored six years in Battle Creek, the spirits impressed Warren Chase to say, "You are prepared for greater work. Go East, West, North, South, and teach this gospel to all the people." It was reiterated through other media. Earnestly did he obey. Humanity needs magnetizers,* as the earth needs comets.

* Talking with Mr. Peebles one day, about our speakers and "magnetizers," he said, —

"Proud of them, sir, *proud* of them, they have vim; have I not worked with them? When the 'Angel of Accounts' demands the jewels, I shall hand in such a list of names! and among them will be Joel Tiffany, S. J. Finney, Warren Chase, Dean Clark, E. S. Wheeler, Frank H. N. White, C. B. Lynn, A. C. Robinson, Lydia Ann Pearsall, A. J. Kutz, Mrs. F. A. Logan, Wm. H. Johnson, Mary J. Wilcoxson, W. F. Jamieson, J. T. Rouse, A. C. and E. C. Woodruff, Laura Cuppy Smith (whom I helped into spirit-light), E. V. Wilson, Addie L. Ballou, E. Winchester Stevens, Joseph Baker, Thomas Gales Forster, A. A. Wheelock, Lizzie Doten, Hudson Tuttle, L. C. Howe, Abraham James, E Whipple, A. B. French, A. J. Davis and his Mary, Wm. Denton, Adin Ballou, J. O. Barrett, H. P. Fairfield, A. T. Foss, J. G. Fish, F. O. Hyzer, I. P. Greenleaf, S. B. Brittan, M. H. Houghton, E. C. Dunn, Moses Hull, A. B. Whiting, John Mayhew, J. H. Powell, H. B. Storer, A. E. Carpenter, Cora L. V. Tappan, H. F. M. Brown, Emma Hardinge, M. S. Townsend Hoadly, Elvira Wheelock Ruggles, Susie M. Johnson, Laura de Force Gordon, Nettie M. Pease, C. M. Stowe, Lois Waisbroker, S. A. Horton; and ascended saints, such as Henry C. Wright, J. B. Ferguson, Alcinda Wilhelm Slade, John Pierpont, Achsa C. Sprague, L. Judd Pardee; and I shall hand in some of our poetical jewels too, — E. S. Ledsham, L. B. Brown, T. L. Harris, Mrs. C. A. Fenn, Mrs. C. J. Osborn (who sung to me the song of the 'Spiritual Harp') Mrs. H. N. Green, Mrs. M. A. Archer, Mrs. J. S.

All over the country his trumpet voice has rung, — an Ezekiel prophesying in "the valley of dry bones," breathing the breath of the Spirit that brought forth life from the dead. Everywhere a resurrectionist, he has made verdure spring from the desert and water from the rock. Having, these later years of his spiritual mission, become a constructionist, he studiously avoids the "revival system," falsely ycleped "spiritual lectures," believing it engenders an unstable and intemperate social character. His is the calm argument now of loving wisdom; and it strikes deep in the soul like the silent sunlight that warms all hearts to life and beauty. He maintains that a speaker should never swallow up his listeners in a whirlpool of psychological sensation, but use this law with prudence, appeal to the rational judgment with a serious reverence for truth, and, by the sweet persuasion of reason and love, draw the people to a higher altitude of character. An audience should be induced to discriminate. A speaker who drives an unbeliever farther away from Spiritualism fails, — *signally* fails, — however great the sensation he creates. Whilst we are aggressive against error, is it not a nobler accomplishment to attract into higher light, to set souls aglow with loftier aspiration, and lead the truth-seeking with a loving hand into the temple of heavenly wisdom?

Wherever he has spoken, he has been cordially invited to come again. He has lectured in all States of the American Union but three, — New York, Brooklyn, Philadelphia, Washington, Baltimore, Boston, Charlestown, Lowell, Portland, Worcester, Troy, Rochester, Buffalo, Cleveland, Detroit, Chicago, Rockford, Milwaukie, Springfield, St. Louis, Topeka, Lawrence, Omaha, Cincinnati, Indianapolis, Louisville, Nashville, San Francisco, Sacramento, New Orleans, Mobile, — the principal cities, and in innumerable villages and country districts in every compass of the land, — also in Canada West. He has attended nearly all the National conventions, multitudes of State conventions, associations, and mass meetings. He is scarcely ever enabled to supply

Adams, Frances D. Gage, H. Clay Preuss, Mrs. J. H. Conant, Emma Tuttle, S. C. Coffinberry, Amanda T. Jones, Belle Bush, and Lita Barney Sayles who charges me, —

"'Guard well thy head; nor trust thy life's refrain
To Reason cold.
Consult the heart; their verdict then shall keep
Thee young when old."

All these, I know, have a friendly word for the 'Pilgrim,' their wandering brother.

the demand upon his services. In some places he has spoken the third, fourth, fifth, and even sixth time at monthly engagements, and in no city is he so popular as in Battle Creek. He has exchanged pulpits with a Congregationalist, with Rev. Mumford and other Unitarians, and with Universalists; but in other instances the latter refused their pulpits in Milford, Mass., Neenah, Wis., and Auburn, N.Y., &c. During an able speech delivered in the latter city, in the opera-house, reported by "The Daily News," he aptly said, "Ordained by a former pastor of that congregation in this city, and cherishing a home-like feeling for the citizens of this section, I am reminded of the Nazarene's words, 'He came to his own, and his own received him not.' If universal salvation shuts out men from the churches here, would it not, narrowed down in its creedal tendencies, shut out men from the great Church triumphant in the heaven of heavens?" Incident to so vast a work, he recoils within himself at times, patient in his impatience, but trustful as Polycarp, who, going to martyrdom, heard a spirit-voice say, "Polycarp, be firm!" In a letter to a friend, he says, —

"I will drink the cup that destiny holds to my lips, and labor on manfully and bravely, till the earth-life is finished, and those harpstrings from the summer land beyond the river welcome me home."

In the fall of 1867, Mr. and Mrs. Peebles moved from Battle Creek to Hammonton, New Jersey, hoping for a more lucrative locality for a living. The parting hour will never be forgotten: the "good-byes" were genuine, such as angels never say but ever feel. A slip from "The Banner of Light" expresses the deep love the friends there always cherish for them both: —

"BATTLE CREEK, MICH., Nov. 4, 1867.

"MESSRS. EDITORS, — The name of J. M. Peebles has long been inscribed on the folds of "The Banner of Light;" and I now ask you to let that of his excellent wife occupy a small space for a brief season, as it has long held a high place in the hearts of her friends here, where they have so long made their home. Mrs. Peebles is an efficient co-worker in the cause of truth with her most able and widely-known husband, though in a more contracted sphere; and we feel that our society is losing one of its brightest ornaments in her departure for her new home in the East.

"A few evenings since a 'surprise' was given her by a few of her friends, and a small 'token' of regard was presented on the occasion, when the following address was read, and very neatly and appropriately replied to by Mrs. Peebles: —

"MRS. PEEBLES, — We, your friends of the society with which you have so long been identified, have met here this evening to express our sorrow that you are no more to be with us in our meetings or social gatherings. During the years you have been with us, we have ever felt that your noble and true life shed a holy influence on all with whom you were brought in contact; and, that in you we had a faithful adviser, a genial companion, and a true friend. You have ever been earnest to aid us in every good work, and we know we shall not soon cease to regret your absence from our midst, or find your place adequately filled in our association. We beg you to accept this slight token of our affectionate regard. May you, in your new home, find contentment and happiness amid other friends who will appreciate your true worth.

" 'It seems appropriate that one so much beloved should receive this notice.

D. M. B."

"November has come, and with it dreary autumn days, — days of gloom and sorrow to some, brought around by every departing summer. But a deeper, darker cloud has come over us, — the departure of Brother Peebles and his dear wife for a new home in New Jersey. Brother Peebles has been with us most of the time nearly eleven years, and during all those years has been steadily gaining influence and friends among all classes of citizens, and, I will say, all who ever 'progressed upwards.' J. B."

From the many testimonies of love, we clip this little gem written by Hudson Tuttle, then editor-in-chief of "The American Spiritualist:" —

"J. M. Peebles. — This well known author, student, and speaker is the St. John of the New Dispensation. If we desired a portrait of that loved disciple of Jesus, Brother Peebles should sit for it. We hope the beloved of Old equaled that of the New in all-embracing charity, unselfishness of character, and a love which extends from the highest to the lowest." . . .

George A. Bacon, of the editorial corps in same paper, says of our "Pilgrim:" —

"We now recall no other writer in all our ranks who has given so many smoothly-flowing, richly-colored and beauty-laden expressions. They thickly adorn his every page, as the glittering stars gem the heavens. His sentences are replete with musical cadences, and seem to flow as naturally as birds warble. They are not only rhetorically felicitous, but what is additionally better, they bear the seed-grains of deep thought and profound truth. . . .

"Infinitely superior to all the dazzling sheen of verbal euphony, is the simplest utterance of an eternal, immortal truth. Our brother does not forget this cardinal point. Notwithstanding his tendency to pictorial speech, he believes with St. Jerome, that 'truth told inelegantly is better than eloquent falsehood.'"

Corresponding with friends to glean facts for this work, we received the following: —

"Battle Creek, Mich.

"Brother Barrett, — . . . When Mr. Peebles took charge of our society in 1857, we *were* proud, — proud of our leader and members. He has always been an honor to Spiritualism. I do not know of an exception where any one that ever knew him, however low or inferior, so called, but felt he was a friend. . . . I would to God the world had more such men! May his star never grow dim! . . .

"Your Sister, Rhoda A. Loomis."

"DEAR BROTHER BARRETT, — . . . Indentified from its early day with the cause of modern Spiritualism, with unparalleled fidelity, Mr. Peebles has adhered to and announced the convictions of his soul, manfully braving the battles of opposition through which this new and blessed religion, by the help of the angels, has been developed into a moral and spiritual power now infiltrating spiritual life, strength, and vitality into all organized religious bodies of whatever name, character, or profession, — and that, too, though they despised, denied, and rejected these glorious truths.

"Endowed with fine natural qualifications as a poet, moralist, reformer, and teacher, he has also added the rare graces of scholarship and culture; and, better still, has beautifully developed those inward graces of the spirit which exalt and refine life, and make expression, thought, and act, lofty, loving, and true.

"With admirable zeal, all these rich endowments and choice attainments are consecrated to the good of humanity and the cause of truth and right everywhere. What better consecration than this? What brighter fulfillment of the soul's highest promise? A life of aspiration, love, prayer, purity, and earnest practical work will always lead to the heavenly paradise prepared for the sainted upon earth.

"Your friend with esteem,

"ELVIRA WHEELOCK RUGGLES."

"J. O. BARRETT: My Dear Friend, — . . . J. M. Peebles has been instrumental in leading me, as he has a host of others, into spiritual freedom. He is a full-orbed man, versatile. His secret forte as a speaker and writer, and his success in building up spiritual societies and banding our people together in great brotherhoods and sisterhoods of peace and harmony, lie in the fact that he blends the excellence of intellect and culture with the sublimities of the ideal and spiritual. His many disinterested kindnesses and tender charities have blessed hundreds; his broad, fraternal sympathies have given him a wonderful universality, endearing him to thousands. He ever succors the weak, strengthens the weary, encourages the down-trodden, resurrects into newness of life the morally dead. He is an advocate of temperance, woman's equality with man, freedom, — social, political, and religious; and, soaring aloft into the pure ether of love, he takes strong ground against war. Yours, very fraternally,

"CEPHAS B. LYNN."

"DEAR BRO. BARRETT. . . . Pre-eminent among Bro. Peebles's public services are his great and indefatigable labors in the cause of Spiritualism. With voice and pen he has been one of its foremost as well as ablest advocates and defenders. Brave and fearless, where many have been proved cowards; faithful among the faithless, let the fair-browed angel of memory plant a rose-wreath of sweet recollections, gathered from the holy inspirations of love, truth, and beauty, which, for all time, the bright examples of a noble, pure life must ever inspire. Sincerely yours,

"ADDISON A. WHEELOCK."

Recounting the agencies at work in the Great West, Emma Hardinge says, in her estimable work, "The History of Modern Spiritualism in America," —

"Another of the 'Western Institutions,' and one which has wrought an incalculable amount of good and use in the community, is Mr. J. M. Peebles. By his scholarly writings, and indefatigable labors as a lecturer, Mr. Peebles has been a gigantic lever in moving public opinion in favor of spiritual belief, and the repudiation of the effete superstition of old orthodoxy. Being a graceful and accomplished orator, Mr. Peebles's services are in eager demand throughout the whole community; but, as the scene of his earliest and most widely-diffused efforts, the West undoubtedly claims him for her own, and as such he is numbered amongst her jewels, and forms a distinguished part of her spiritual wealth."

If Mr. Peebles is injured, he lays it to heart, grieves over it, feels resistance and the "late remorse of love," defends the right, confesses the wrong; but is sure to forgive and ask forgiveness, when the good angel attends in the way of reconciliation. His is the spirit of the venerable Victor Hugo, in his address to the German people, when they were sending an army to bombard Paris: —

"If you assault Paris, we shall defend it to the last extremity; we shall fight with all our strength against you; but we declare we shall continue to be your brothers. And your wounded, do you know where we shall place them? in the palace of the Nation. We shall assign the Tuilleries in advance as a hospital for wounded Prussians. There will be the field-hospital of your brave, imprisoned soldiers, and it is there our women shall go to care for and succor them. Your wounded shall be our guests; we will treat them loyally, and Paris will receive them into her Louvre."

Writing Dr. Dunn, who had lost valuable property by fire, Mr. Peebles, sealing his promise with a generous donation of life-long duration, says, —

"As flax never begins to be useful till pulled and laid out to die and rot, so I intend to be of more service to you when my old body is rotting than I possibly can be now. . . . You lost not a truth, not a useful fact, nor scientific formula. Your furniture is gone, but not your reputation. This latter is much harder to gain than the former. Your books may have been burned; but so much of their contents as by faithful application you had stored away in your brain remains unharmed. All the disappointments and losses of life teach us the importance of laying up treasures in the intellect and soul. Such are beyond the destroying hand of earthly elements. Such only can serve us when the death-angel knocks, bidding us lay down the pilgrim-staff, and plunge beneath the waves of the rolling Jordan."

Again he says, in another letter, intended only for the eye of the recipient: —

"I wept when reading your letter. It took me back to Battle Creek, where first I met you and showered upon you my very soul-tenderness. Even the occasional thorns of those times have faded from remembrance, and only the flowers freshen into sweet remembered realities."

A healing physician, of great success, tried to tempt him by proffer of money to travel with him in Europe. The man was gaining at the rate of sixty dollars per day. Mr. Peebles declined. His reasons were given to a bosom friend in a private note: —

"He certainly performs most wonderful cures; but his sphere is morally repellent. He smokes, drinks, &c. I will sooner go without money than form the alliance. In a few years, I shall be where money is of no account. Purity and goodness are the coin of heaven."

These jets of loving sarcasm, falling like quickening shivers of lightning from the cloud, engraving the image of soul upon paper, were called out by our trials in the Universalist ministry, when, like a little boy, we sought a hand that had been sinewed by similar storms and labors. What buoyancy in the words which Mr. Peebles showered upon us! We recall them into form for the benefit of others who may be likewise sentenced to crucifixion: —

"PROVIDENCE, R.I., Oct. 26, 1865.

"MY SON JOSEPH, — You *ought* to be persecuted, — accused of being a 'wine-bibber and a seducer;' ought to be compelled to wander about in 'sheepskins and goatskins,' to be 'cast into prison,' and then let out to eat 'grass' like your brother Nebuchadnezzar. Then you would begin to be worth something for the use of God and his angels. . . .

"All *higher births* are through sorrow and suffering. Such is the divine order. Hence my prayer is, '*Mortals*, pierce him; *angels*, give him thorns to tread upon: for feet that bleed are on the way to see the head crowned! Great Father in heaven, hold him tenderly, lovingly, in thy hands; for he is a dear child of thine and brother of mine, just pluming his wings for a flight into the realms of the gods! Amen.'"

Again he writes, in a letter from Cincinnati, dated Dec. 5, 1866: —

. . . "Your trials, my dear brother, have truly commenced. You will find God's grace sufficient, and his angels ever, *ever* present. They never forsake the true soul. You say you have 'already been sold, betrayed.' Jesus was betrayed before you. Yes, persecution must come; and I feel just now like preaching a sermon to you from this text in Rev. i. 9: 'I, John, who also am your brother in tribulation, and in the kingdom and patience of Jesus Christ.'

"And did not Jesus say to the disciples, 'In the world ye shall have tribulation; but be of good cheer, I have overcome the world'? 'Which of the prophets have not your fathers persecuted?' asks one of the anciently-inspired men. My brother, you must *expect* all these things. It is God's method. Martyrs' feet have always bled; but oh, the brilliancy of their crowns in heaven!

"This life, at best, is but the shadow of that more substantial life to come. Let us live for the future by being *patient*, *true*, *brave*, and *independent* in the present."

Trials make heroes. Tempted, yet sinless, is true progress. Sublime is Mr. Peebles's moral indignation. He spares not a shred of enmity to right. During his lecturing in Detroit, — vast congregations, working in beautiful order, — the new constitution of the Spiritual Society was sent to the Detroit "Tribune" for publication, when the editor appended some belittling criticisms to please the Church, no doubt. Taking these comments into the desk, Mr. Peebles lashed that editor with a whip of scorpions. When wrought up, his sarcasm and invective are scathing as lightning! Earnest in his righteous wrath, he threw the paper upon the floor, stamped upon it, and shouted home the charge: "*Republicans*, take the 'Post'! *Democrats*, take the 'Times'!" Then the crowd, electrified, hurrahed with a vim.

Glancing into a letter addressed by Mr. Peebles to Mr. Wilson, of Harmonia, 1859, we clipped out the following: —

... "By the way, one of the last slanders on the docket is this: I was seen to get off from the cars in Detroit with a woman, and go with her on board the steamer for the Canada side. Horrid! This occurred last summer: it leaked out a while since, and turned out to be my wife on her way to St. Lawrence County. The Presbyterian 'babbler,' when *faced* about it, confessed that he did not know Mrs. Peebles, but thought it was some strange woman. Surely, if the best fruit is the most clubbed, I am ripe, mellow, fallen, and ready to be eaten. No matter, let us comfort ourselves with the words, 'Blessed are ye when men shall revile,' &c. How beautiful God's law that sends slanderer and slandered, the wrong-doer and the wronged, each to his appropriate place. The heavens and the hells await each and all." ...

Hearing of wicked conduct practiced in certain circles, Mr. Peebles severely rebuked the parties. One of these, envious and "filthy still," trying to screen himself, reported Mr. Peebles as a patron of such circles! His indignation knew no bounds. When the leerish fellow also declared that Mr. Peebles had forsaken his wife, making it common talk, he reviewed the man and his villainy before his audience, and gave him such a "dressing-down," and all connected with him, that the congregation surged like the stormy sea. That was the last of the story. The culprit wished a millstone were around his neck to carry him down to oblivion.

"Outlooking eyes that seek and scan,
Ready to love what they behold;
Quick reverence for his brother man;
Quick sense where gilding is not gold."

On another occasion, whilst in an Eastern city, a Unitarian minister, professionally liberal and radical, careful not to spot his garments by touching against a Spiritualist, reported him as infidel to his domestic responsibilities, and a "brazen free-lover, who did not live with his wife!" Coming from such a source, it had its influence, of course, to forestall his success. Hearing of the lie, and believing that mincing minister morally needed a lesson to study (having before learned of his cunning to entrap Spiritualists, in Janesville, Wis., by promising a free house to *them*, as well as others, if they would help build it, and afterward shut the door in their faces, and virtually drove them out), he went direct to a distinguished lawyer, who addressed the "divine" a letter. The sequel is described by a pure and noble woman, — Mother Whittier, of Fox Lake, Wis., — in a communication to "The Spiritualist:" —

"All honor to that wise man, J. M. Peebles! While in an Eastern town, about to lecture, one of the present Sanhedrim, — just as potent as the old Jewish — said to individuals, 'Don't go to hear that man; he is licentious, lives with another man's wife,' &c. Brother Peebles just stepped into a lawyer's office and commenced an action. The result: a humble acknowledgment, which condemned the man as a liar and slanderer."

Mr. Peebles was invited to lecture in Earl's Grove, Ill., just after a revival of religion. Instigated by the manipulations of the Church, the boys hurled stones at the schoolhouse, and, peeping in at the windows, yelled, "Put him out, — put out the old blasphemer!" Mr. Peebles then poured grape-shot upon the falses of the Church-system in so heroic a manner persecution changed to admiration.

Whilst lecturing in Princeton, Ill., on the "atonement," — arguing that Jesus was begotten like other men, in harmony with the relational laws of life, and that he would be ashamed to slide into heaven on the merits of another, — a churchman, scenting heresy, bounded to his feet, brandishing a green umbrella, and exclaimed, —

"You are a bold blasphemer, an infidel: you will have to answer for this in the day of judgment. I wonder the Almighty does not strike you speechless!"

"I hope the brother," calmly remarked Mr. Peebles, "feels better after being relieved of so much pious nausea."

This exasperated him; and he rushed out, stamping his feet, slamming the door after him as he departed. The confusion having subsided, Mr. Peebles playfully said, —

"The chaff always flies before the gospel fan!"

Notwithstanding a rare refinement of character, and a deep sense of politeness, Mr. Peebles is awkwardly forgetful and habitually absent-minded, being absorbed in the ideal kingdom which sucks him up like a sponge.

He had an appointment in Indiana, — was then at Chicago; the train would start at ten o'clock precisely. Having an hour at his command, he seated himself in the sitting-room of the Union depot, reading a book of ancient religion, and forgot appointment and cars; oblivious to the confusion around him, till one hour beyond the time.

"Pretty business this!" he exclaimed; "this living in two worlds, fitted for neither." When he has "just peeped out of the *shell*," as he calls the dying process, and happens to find an ancient history "lying round loose," it is conjectural whether he will not miss the train for heaven. We suggested such a fate to him; and his answer was, —

"Well, the other place, then! to build an under-ground railroad up to the New Jerusalem!"

"Maybe they'll make you superintendent of that department," we added, — "an appointment you are well qualified to fill." Looking at us from head to foot, he rapturously replied, —

"And I will appoint you prime-conductor of the train loaded with spirits from hell bound for eternal glory! Did not Jesus preach to spirits in prison? Then let us bear a hand in their redemption."

Being at our residence one summer, the weather wet and chilly, the wind blowing in upon him through a broken glass, he took a sheet of paper, whistling and thinking, and beating time with his foot, and nicely pinned it to the sash.

"There, Olive," he said at last, "see how well I have fixed the window for you!"

Olive, glancing at it, laughed outright.

"What are you laughing at, girl?"

"Why, you have fixed the wrong pane: that one is whole!"

"So I have," he replied, jumping up, Indian style; so I have, — just like me! Don't tell Joseph."

During a lecturing June month, in Rockford, Ill., he and Dr. Dunn boarded at T. M. Clark's, an earnest Spiritualist. Greens were a great rarity then. Succeeding in getting barely enough for dinner, Mrs. Clark nicely prepared them, that each might have a share from the big pie-plate on which they were richly piled. Mr. Peebles was earnestly descanting upon Mohammed's flight to heaven. Passing the plate to him, Mr. Clark asked, —

"Have some greens, Mr. Peebles?"

"Oh, yes! I'm very fond of greens, — thank you;" and politely took the plate, set it beside his own, put on pepper and vinegar, and deliberately devoured the whole contents. The doctor looked; Mrs. Clark blushed; Mr. Clark thought, "How queer he is!" Nothing was said, of course, about the impoliteness; but when these two pilgrims were in their room, the doctor asked, "Peebles, how's greens?"

"How's greens! what do you mean?"

"Why, you ate up all the greens: I wanted some, and so did the rest."

"Did I do that? I did, Charlie, — what shall I do? Eat all the greens, — all, — all?"

The joke was too good to be suppressed; and Mr. Peebles made an apology so handsome, that it became a by-word to say, "Peebles, how's greens?"

One winter's evening at Galva, Ill., Mr. Peebles and his medium were sitting together in their room, awaiting the lecture-service. About an hour before the time, a spirit said, —

"You should center your mind on your subject: we inspire only the *active* brain."

"What subject?" thought Mr. Peebles.

"The relations of the finite with the infinite."

He paced the floor, catching the light, for a few moments; and put on his overcoat, gloves, and furs, head drooping in meditation. Starting at a brisk pace, they passed three or four blocks, when the doctor chanced to look up.

"Ha, ha, ha, J. M.! where's your hat?"

"Sure enough, no hat on!" and back he ran through the busy street, like a frightened boy.

Returning, he laughingly said, "The foxes have holes, and the birds of the air have nests, but the son of man hath no hat for his head! What's a hat? You are all after hats and gewgaws. 'The head is not for the hat, but the hat is for the head,' says Henry C. Wright; and have we not a right to take it off, or put it on, as we do theology? In the 'day of judgment' it will not be asked, 'How's your hat?' remember that, my boy!"

Lecturing in Sturgis, Mr. Peebles discoursed upon "hell." In the heat of his eloquence, he exclaimed, "Were I a saint in heaven, and friends, humanity, not there, I would look down the battlements into hell, lay aside my golden robe, cast my crown at the feet of the Almighty, shock the heirs of glory, rush into the fires of damnation, and seize my doomed brother!" —

Grasping the doctor by the hair of his head, he lifted him with one hand from the sofa. The congregation in a titter, Mr. Peebles seemed to rush the angels in, transporting hell to heaven!

"Macaulay remarks that absent-mindedness is the mark of either a genius or a fool. A man's mind may be so intensely occupied with lofty intuitions and inspirations, that his senses, seemingly, are scarcely awake to the realities of this tangible world."

Sir Isaac Newton, it is said, being intent on some great subject, requested that the fire be moved. "It would be easier for you to move," said his servant. "Oh, I did not think of that!" replied the philosopher. One day, Père Gratry, director of the academy in Paris, when going to the Sorbonne, where he lectured on theology, imagined he had forgotten his watch, and took it out of his pocket to see if he had time to go and fetch it. But this hardly beats Mr. Peebles. In Philadelphia, he purchased a new work, entitled, "The Bible in India," by Louis Jacolliot, a French judge. Waiting for the cars in the depot, he became completely absorbed in it, when, hearing the bustle, he rushed up to the ticket-master, and, looking him staringly in the eye, exclaimed, —

"The Bible in India!"

"What?" said the ticket-master.

"Price of the Bible in India!"

Just then another gentleman asked for a ticket, and he came to himself, so chagrined; and blushingly and meekly he said, —

"Ticket, good sir, for Chicago."

Mr. Peebles besieges heaven and earth for truth. He moves the Spirit, that the Spirit may move him. His devotions rise into fire-flashing billows that bear him aloft. He pens what he gleans, and voices them in speech and papers and books. He is a spiritual economist, making all his wares think. He speaks by inspiration; but the nimble pen is sure to indite what saith the Spirit. By such discipline he is able to stir the people, and engrave his identity upon the age. In the effort to hide himself, he finds himself. This modest verse of Emma S. Ledsham's pleases his ideal of impersonality: —

"Names and titles are but snowflakes
 Melting on Time's storm-swept shore:
When we cross the silent river,
 They are known no more."

What Mr. Peebles reads must be practical, — have a moral significance for the age. Time is too precious to peruse defunct theology. He admires the good sense of Ernestine L. Rose. Professor Bush once made her a present of Swedenborg's treatise on "Heaven and Hell." "Thank you, Professor," said she, putting the book under the cushion of the sofa, "my daily duties are enough for me: I shall attend to heaven or hell when I find myself in either."

In style, it is said, Mr. Peebles's writings resemble the floridness and diction of S. B. Brittan's. He almost lives on books. He has by far the best library containing the philosophies of the "Mystics" and Neo-Platonists, in America. Ensconced in his library, with his angel, he is just the happiest man, — like a child in a garden of flowers. Never shall we forget his joy, which he actually indicated in kisses upon the books, when he received from England, at a great expense, the "Anacalypsis," "Bhagavat Geeta," "Rig Veda Sanhita," "Asiatic Researches," "Divine Pymander," "Proclus," "Plotinus," and several volumes of the Mystics.

CHAPTER XIII.

CORRESPONDENCE WITH SPIRITS.

"There's a land far away 'mid the stars, we are told,
Where they know not the sorrows of time;
Where the pure waters wander through valleys of gold,
And life is a treasure sublime.
'Tis the land of our God, 'tis the home of the soul,
Where ages of splendor eternally roll,
Where the way-weary traveler reaches his goal,
On the evergreen mountains of life." — JAMES G. CLARK.

MORE childlike in habits, the law of mental telegraphing practically understood, and correspondence with spirits will be as common and reliable as is our every-day life. It is something worth the struggle and the cost of social purification, to establish spirit-batteries in different parts of our globe, as news-depots from the heavenly countries, concerning the new institutions, expeditions, conventions, world-congresses, arts, sciences, children's convocations, discoveries, and general improvements peculiar to spirit-life. Such intelligence, constantly opening upon us, will quicken the inhabitants of earth to loftier, diviner ambition. It is coming! let us be patient in well-doing.

The few letters subjoined are both real and beautiful, throbbing with living thought most fascinating to the reader who loves to feel the very souls of the angels breathing around us. Mr. Peebles frequently held correspondence with spirits through J. V. Mansfield, but these we give were through the mediumship of Dr. Dunn: —

"EARTH-LIFE, PAINESVILLE, OHIO, July 9, 1864.

"BROTHER OF THE BETTER LAND, — . . . The name of your spirit home, 'Pear-Grove Cottage,' charms me; it is musical with thought. Plant me a tree near the borders of the garden, fronting your cottage, that, when I drop the staff and put off the pilgrim sandals, I may sit in your presence, beneath its foliage, listening to your words of wisdom. . . . What of pre-existence? I believe it. What of re-incarnation? It's a question. . . . Am glad you spoke of my impressions. Could I draw the line of demarcation between impressions of spirits and the workings of my own mind, it would be more satisfactory. But I can not, *will* not, palm off my own for those of spirits. It will not be honest. Until I can draw it, I must remain silent. . . . All worldly things are as husks, shells. Earthly fame, popularity, honor, fashion, glory, will fade away as mists. I am sick of fame and flattery; but sigh, oh! how my soul doth sigh for knowledge, truth, all things substantial and eternal! I beg of you, as a circle, pursue that course with me that will result in the greatest good to humanity, and my own spiritual unfoldment; be it thorns, chains, or prisons, it will be for the best, — the cup I drink! . . . Bear my love to John: he is my soul's divine ideal. Wonder if he will permit me to examine his massive library? if Perasee will allow me to accompany him on exploring expeditions to the stars? if you, — Aaron Nite, will assist me to control the medium, and continue the converse with humanity? . . . Having heard your voice so much, I feel well acquainted with you; but of John, I must say with the poet, —

" 'I know thee not, — I never heard thy voice;
Yet could I choose a friend from all mankind,
Thy spirit high should be my spirit's choice,
Thy heart should guide my heart,
Thy mind, my mind.'

"A word to dear Powhattan: Did you not walk with me on that stroll into the woods, the other day, where I plucked the red berries and wild flowers, cut the hemlock bough, and preached to the forest trees? Oh, when shall I clasp your shining hand, look into your calm eyes, handle your spirit-bow, plumed with peace arrows? . . . I have lately received a letter from Father Beeson of Washington, asking me to devote more time to the benefit of the Indians. Yes, I will do all in my power. God bless the Indians! Remember me to the 'Pawnee Chief,' 'Red Jacket,' 'Black Hawk,' and others. Good night, precious brothers! Affectionately,

"J. M. PEEBLES."

Traveling so extensively, and taking on so many diverse influences, Mr. Peebles was perplexed relative to the promised wonders of different media. Pleased with the wisdom of certain spirits, and contrasting it with pretended revelations, he exclaims, —

"Oh, the twaddle and flowery flattery in certain circles! I am strongly inclined to Swedenborg's position. Great men are modest. When they come from the spirit world egotistic and dictatorial, the reflective mind naturally doubts. Now, 'by their fruits ye shall know them.' This the equation: spirits the unknown quantity, media the known quantity, what the result? Are we not justifiable in asking, Do not media, accustomed to control, reflect in their lives the moral status of their spirit-guides?"

These moral queries, suggested to Aaron Nite, drew out the following response: —

"MORNING LAND, PEAR GROVE COTTAGE,
In the year of earth-life 1867, 5th month, and 16th day.

"FRIEND PEEBLES, — . . . You say you are growing skeptical. This is a very essential element in the soul of man. When a man ceases to doubt relative to men and spirits, he must attribute to them more than fallibility. . . . You speak despairingly of the cause you have espoused. Do you remember the prediction I made several years since, respecting the separation of the good from the evil? The difference can only be learned by each one's serving in his true position. . . . *The faith of thousands must yet be shaken*, ere they can awake to the moral necessity of this sifting. You often mentally ask, 'What shall we do?' I answer, *move;* sooner the better. You have 'overdone' in your spiritual organizations; re-action *must* come: remember what I say! You have ignored from your platforms articles right in principle and necessary to union. When a man becomes a guest of your house, are you not morally responsible for his acts? Apply this rule to society. It is not the name, or claim of a man, that gives him caste in society, but a majority of his acts. . . . Spiritualism has suffered more at the hands of its friends than from its opposers. A large proportion of your present manifestations is the voice of spirits from the lower planes. There are flattering spirits from our side as from yours: therefore, 'try the spirits;' exercise your own judgment upon their teachings. Think of these things, my dear friend. Trim your lamp; for the night cometh, and beyond the darkest night is the morning. Thy brother,

"AARON NITE.†"

In silence Mr. Peebles often questioned "John." Without any verbal solicitation, Aaron Nite, acting as spirit-medium, communicated the answers through Dr. Dunn: —

"ROCKFORD, Nov. 8, 1864.

"BROTHER OF EARTH, — Often do I approach thee, listening to thy soul-questions. Even though thou hast not asked, I will answer.

"1. Yes, my brother, I am grateful to the Father for the experiences of a lengthened earth-life. Had I the power to re-live those years, I would strive to have them more in harmony with divine law. But, as eternity rolls on, I more clearly see how the soul-trials which imbittered earth, only served to sweeten the delicious draughts of heaven.

"2. Yes, I was educated in a Jewish school, my governor being an eminent sage, within whose bosom were locked the mysteries and symbols of the past.

"3. Certainly, I have been thy real spirit-guide from thy birth, though not so direct during thy early years of diverse disciplines; for then thou wert passing through the initiative steps preparatory to the higher principles of wisdom. Thy many disappointments, developing a sterner manhood, will achieve for thee the crown of life.

"4. In regard to the Gospels, I will briefly answer: We, the apostles, so called, never wrote the purported histories of Christ. The imperfect records you have are the treasured sayings of the apostles, as kept in the memories of Jewish scribes and sympathizing Galileans.

"5. Thou askest, 'Could not Joshua, now called Jesus, write?' Certainly. But you say, 'Then why did he not, and why did not the apostles?' Because in that period there were scribes appointed to this calling. Thou canst set type; but this business is left entirely to printers.

"6. Thou askest me about the Eleusinian mysteries. Schooled in the Aryan philosophies, I had knowledge of those Egyptian and Grecian rites, and understood many of the ancient dialects.

"Brother, complain not of thy abiding-place, the earth; for it is well that thou shouldst see the cloud bedimmed sun, also hard and diverse experiences, that thy very soul's sinews may be wrought upon, preparing thee for the tasks that await thee in the future. Work well thy mission, then, while on earth, and sweet shall be thy reward in heaven; and bright shall be thy hopes, and light thy burden in days yet thine, which mortality has not numbered; and sweet thy *rest*, leaning upon the bosom of thy brother — when thou art worthy. Thy guide, "JOHN."

Spirit-power is always limited by the organism through which it is manifest, and therefore has the mental measure and idiosyncracies of its media. One evening in September, 1863, Mr. Peebles being at home in his library-room, the medium was entranced, when Hosea Ballou appeared, took down the Bible, turned to the 9th chapter of Daniel, where it speaks of the angel Gabriel who touched the prophet "about the time of the evening oblation," and added, with a sweet dignity in his manner, "So, my brother, shall an angel appear to thee this night." This spirit retiring, another descended to the medium, giving his name "John," at that time unknown to Mr. Peebles, who delivered the following address to Aaron Nite, and Aaron Nite to Powhattan, and Powhattan word for word in labored accents to Dr. Dunn, and he to Mr. Peebles, requiring two hours in its articulation: —

"BROTHER OF EARTH, — I come from the Elysian fields of the blest to greet a brother bound to me closely by the infinite law of attraction, — bound by a golden-textured web, woven from those ethereal substances that float in the ocean realms of space, which can never be decomposed or changed, only to bind more firmly the cords of affection.

"Brother, I delight to descend from the spirit-regions of beatific bliss to aid and instruct you. The cord of affection that unites us is divine. It can never be severed; but the rapidity of your ascension must necessarily be in exact ratio with your aspirations and minglings with me in purity, love, and wisdom.

"Dear brother, let not thy rising spirit sink. In moral, as in mathematical equations, opposites are indispensable. The universe must be balanced; pictures must have shadings; only stormy seas can make skillful mariners, and thou, consciously gifted with soul-power, shouldst master the lesser circumstances, control conditions, and defy moral defects. Sometimes thou thinkest thy pathway strewn with piercing thorns; then again in visions thou perceivest that fragrant blossoms outnumber them, and confess that thou art blessed beyond all blessing. Remember, that sufferings are the chariots that bear balms and beatitudes to the super-sensuous man, dwelling in the courts of the inner temple. The sweetest flowers are mingled with briars; and why shouldst not thou, O child! occasionally suffer the stings that may pierce thy hands, when permitted to look forward to the beautiful roses thou shalt ultimately pluck along the margins of summer-land gardens, — roses moistened by dewdrops from the angel-world, and leaflets fanned by the waving of angelic wings? Oh, that I could portray, or give thee some faint conception of, the surpassing splendor and beauty of the objective scenery that makes so radiant the table-lands of *immortality!* But the winged pen of imagination tires, and mortal language utterly fails to impress upon the physical retina the brilliant and resplendent homes of the 'pure in heart.' Nought but the divinest ideas can interpermeate the ever-increasing loveliness and imagery of our celestial abodes.

"'It doth not yet appear what we shall be.' Angelic beings hardly recognize time or space, — their garments have been washed to crystal whiteness in the baptismal font of self-sacrifice; and, in the quiet of dewy evenings, they delight to sail adown the electric streams that thread the spirit-land, freighted with love's sweetest messages to gladden the inhabitants of earth. Encircling and embowering their harmonial habitations in deathless foliage of ever-varying hue, — flowers that shed perfumes sweeter than those 'vials of odors' seen by an anciently inspired one in heaven; landscapes, begemmed with rubies and carpeted with emerald; and pearly streams ever flowing o'er glittering sands, every gurgle of which is like psalms from seraphic choirs.

"Brother of earth, go on; thy mission is beautiful: bear all thy trials and tribulations with a strong, manly heart; for, as 'twas said in the past, by the 'sweat of thy brow shalt *thou* earn thy bread;' merit the reputation of a moral hero, — a walking epistle of well doing, and that, too, though thou treadest the wine-press alone. When wearying in thy earthly pilgrimage, and tiring of thy uneven journey, reflect upon the New Jerusalem that awaits thee. Let thine eyes be cast toward heaven: let the key-note to thy nature be love; thy guiding star, wisdom. Let thy soul go forth in aspirations of purity, holiness, and truth. Let thy hands be extended toward angels to 'bear thee up;' and though the earth should cease to move, and stars to shine, thy spirit shall ever shine like those brilliant stars of night that receive light and warmth from the many central suns of the great univercœlum; and this central sun illumining thy spirit shall be *inspiration*, poured from the spiritual world, to guide thee to the portals of peace, where, when thine earth-mission shall have been well wrought, thou shalt recline on mounds of velvety moss, thy brow be intwined with myrtle, and decorated with rose-buds, and in the golden future thou shalt partake of the honeydew of eternal life and blessedness.

"Now, my dear brother, go on thy way rejoicing, for, though I depart from thy physical senses, I ever dwell with thee in thy spiritual or inmost sphere; and, in a few short years of ripening experiences at most, thou shalt travel the shining shores of the heavenly existence, hand in hand with *me*, and thine attending spirit-band.

"JOHN ——."

In Portland, 1865, whilst physically sick, Mr. Peebles employed a leisure hour in writing the following reminder of spirit-presence. Weeping and praying as he wrote, there came at last this missive of love, his "Guide John responding:" "Souls, like flocks of white winged doves, descend, that they may ascend, leading others upward and homeward to Paradise."

MY SPIRIT-GUIDE.

"In celestial spheres above me,
There's a spirit bright that loves me,
And, white-robed, he turns earthward in evening-time;
When surrounding souls are cheerful,
Mine all sorrowing and tearful,
He speaks musical as sainted vesper chime:

"'Tell me, brother dear, why weep ye,
Since a *teacher* comes to greet ye
With seraphic words of love from realms afar?'
Then with shining hand upon me,
He pointed starward, above me,
E'en to a golden temple with gates ajar.

"Domes I saw, with arch and portal,
Shimmering o'er a home immortal,
Where bridal harpers breathed music soft for them,
Who, through soul-felt aspirations,
Trials deep and tribulations,
Were found 'worthy' of the New Jerusalem.

"There, 'neath skies serene and golden,
With saints, seers, and sages olden,
Dwells an angel-brother, my immortal guide;
And though his soul circle throneward,
And his upward march is onward,
He comes to cheer in the gray of eventide.

"His calm presence now is near me,
And his magic touch infills me
With a harmony so holy and divine,
That my soul with his seems blending,
While a pleading prayer's ascending:
O thou blest inspirer! seal me ever thine.

"As a brother speaks to brothers:
'Thou art *mine*, and not another's,
And I'll guide thee till life's journeyings are o'er;
When thy mortal's tending earthward,
And thy spirit bounding birthward,
I will meet thee at my open temple door.'

"Then was gone all earthly sadness,
And I sung for very gladness,
When fell the promise, as evangels of yore,
Soft as dews on eastern mountains,
Sweet as flowers by Kedron's fountains,
Still breathing, 'Brother, I guide thee evermore.'"

VISION.

One evening in 1865, weary and nervous, Mr. Peebles sat in his study, sighing for light and rest, when a spirit, flooding the room with a golden atmosphere, pictured before the medium an arch, under which was unrolled a scroll, whereon was inscribed, —

"PILGRIM BROTHER, — Be not discouraged while traveling in the valley of doubt and despair; for though the uncongenial rays of disappointment's sun may shine upon thee in thy wearied journey, and though hard may be thy tempest-tossed barque and storm-exposed couch, still thou dost gather bright pebbles of experience along thy unwelcome journey."

Looking beyond, the medium saw this "Pilgrim" under a shade, fainting in his journey, and over him stood an angel, bathing his forehead with crystal water, and pointing upward to fruit on the over-shadowing tree; and she said, —

"Then, O Pilgrim Brother! having passed the valley of doubt and despair, and having so long gazed upon the evergreens that bedeck the mountain-sides of peace and rest, thou shalt in the bright *hereafter* be sheltered beneath the branches of fadeless foliaged leaves upon those mountain-sides of peace and love, there to partake of the fruits of everlasting life, and drink from the crystal fountains of wisdom and love. These, *all these*, shall be thine, when thy weary earth-pilgrimage shall have been ended, and the explorations of satisfactory *research* shall its unending course begin. E."

CHAPTER XIV.

THE MOSAIC OF WIT.

"True sympathy, a light that grows
And broadens like the Summer morn's;
A hope that trusts before it knows,
Being out of tune with all the scorns.

. . . .

"For such a leader lifts his times
Out of the limits of the night,
And, falling grandly, while he climbs,
Falls with his face towards the hight." — M. B. SMEDLEY.

SINCE becoming a Spiritualist, Mr. Peebles has a wonderful tact at balancing himself, as an eagle poised for battle. If his brain is exhausted and a playmate is handy, instantly he is in a frolic, boisterous as the whirlpool-winds of summer. Then he is refreshed for another mental labor. Often have we sat with him at a table, writing, intent upon some great subject of value to us both, waiting, and thinking to see it in its true light for incorporation into expressive words, when there would come the quaintest joke or the sharpest hit of the ludicrous, that would seem to scatter the ideal into shreds, till it appeared so little! When the uproarious season subsided, then the brain was luminous with new force, and back would rush the exiled thought clothed in golden drapery so enchanting, as if it had just bathed itself in a fresh fountain of immortal beauty.

His correspondence abounds in witticisms. When alluding to trials or disappointments, he often turns all into a focus of sunlight to burn up the darkness, and in this way keeps himself in better balance.

Burns is one of his favorite poets; and he delights to quote his hits against popular theology like this: —

"Auld Orthodoxy lang did grapple,
But now she's got an unco ripple;
Haste, gie her name up i' the chapel,
Nigh unto death.
See how she fetches at the thropple,
And gasps for breath!"

Addressing us a letter reviewing the checkered scenes of life, he says, —

"I am a pilgrim. Have here no continuing city. God is my father; Earth is my mother; Jesus, my elder brother; John, my spirit-guide; and among my very distant cousins is Je-ho-ka, the ancient spirit-guide of Moses."

Finding him more attached to Pagan philosophers than Christian churchmen building up sects, we playfully criticised him in a private letter, which suggested the following: —

"A clerical brother, for whom we cherish a deep heart-fellowship, writing us a while since, commenced his fraternal epistle thus, '*My Dear Heathen Brother.*' The appellation charmed us. If we are to find the legitimate meaning of 'Christian' in the prevailing Christianity of this age, with its wars and pious wickedness, and if Pythagoras and Democritus, Empedocles and Aristides, Confucius and the Neo-Platonists of later times, were types of heathenism, count us ever a '*heathen.*'

"Will not our 'Christian' brother join with us in singing a new doxology? —

"'To *Chrishna, Plato, Jesus,*
With mystics, seers, and sages,
Be honor and glory given
Through everlasting ages.'"

Mr. Peebles is an Aristomenes, sure to escape caverns of his own digging by the leadership of some stray fox. During one of his speeches in Decatur, Mich., he ascended to a pitch of defiant eloquence, and then thundered down upon his hearers after this style: "Let no man who swears come within four feet of me; six feet, who chews tobacco; ten feet, who drinks whisky."

After this explosion, he cooled down a little, and touched the kinder sympathies of his auditors. In the rear of the house, sat a dignified judge, somewhat "over the bay," amusing himself at the orator's somersets. Rising, he deliberately came toward the desk, commented upon "the eloquence of the speaker just seated," and suggested that he be paid for his services, "as no man can travel and work so without money, and I propose to make him a donation." Putting his huge hand into his pocket, he drew out a half-eagle, and stepped back from the desk just four feet, saying, "I sometimes swear." Then stepped back six feet, — "I chew tobacco;" then ten feet, — "I drink whisky;" and at that distance held out his long arm toward Mr. Peebles, looking him complaisantly in the eye, squealing out, "Here is a half-eagle, sir!" and then quietly put it into his pocket, with the air of a Chinese sovereign. There was no chance for a retort; the house was in a perfect uproar, his own laughter loud as the rest; and, when still again, he dignifiedly thanked the judge for his "generous donation, — a gentleman whom he would never forget." And he never did. The severe joke taught him not to defy men by measure of distances; but to take them by the hand, and hold upon their hearts till they twain shall be one spirit.

As is his custom in visiting places where he had previously labored, he called, at Oswego, upon a dear old woman whom everybody styled "grandmother," and, after the usual greeting, she said, —

"Why, Mr. Peebles, I knew you when a little boy! Your folks were Baptists; and *you* were a *blessed* Baptist. After you grew up to a man, you came here a Universalist minister; and now you've come again, this time a Spiritualist. Well, I never! and where will you go next?"

Peebles was too full of a roguish courtesy to disturb her mind, except by an occasional encouraging word: —

"Free your mind, grandmother: it will do you good."

"Why, you will drag us *all* down to hell!"

"No danger of you, grandmother," he coaxingly said, patting her on the shoulder: "don't you believe the Bible? We nowhere read of the damnation or salvation of women."

"Well, now, that's just like you; always turning sacred things into fun; always just as full of your sin as you can be. Dear James, why don't you repent? Why don't you, before it is too late? A Baptist, a Universalist, a SPIRITUALIST! where *will* you go next?"

"Where? ha, ha! if there *is* any thing better, I am going; come on! I am going, going, *going, for ever* going!"

Seated in our wigwam on the shore of Elkhart Lake, one afternoon, he full of frolic, we in serious intent of feeling, for we were talking about the hour of death, when he exclaimed, —

"When I kick out of this old shell, I want my head cut off, and, after being cleaned up, the skull given to Dr. Dunn for use in his lectures, he stating to the audience whose it once was, whilst hitting it a ringing crack to arrest attention. This disposal of my head is understood by my wife and sister, Mrs. C. C. Beach, who consented to my plea, amid tears, at which I laughed. At my funeral, I want a brass band playing a lively air; and for bearers I want an Indian, a Scotchman, a German, a Frenchman, an Englishman, an Italian, an American, and as many other national representatives as can conveniently be selected. Now, remember! Put the body in a white coffin. Be sure and have singing at the grave. Engage two inspirational speakers, one of whom I shall entrance to address the people. You may be there, J. H. Harter, Elder Evans, Dr. Dunn, and Mrs. S. A. Horton; and I shall be there! Will not that be a good time? Then plant upon my grave no marble slab or monument, but simply flowers and a fruit-tree, that even my very dust may be of practical use still in blessing those who stand there and wonder whose the owner."

Writing a poetical article for "The Banner of Light," Mr. Peebles says, —

"WHEN I GO HENCE.

"Life and death are two golden links in the chain of endless being; demonstrating the goodness of the Divine Existence. That was a beautiful superstition, those ever-burning lamps in ancient tombs, imaging immortality, and the upward tendency of all things. Death is but the severing of the physical and the spiritual, — a passing point in the drama of each soul's endless experiences, — a withdrawing of the curtain to show us those we love. It may be likened to a *star*, that, fading from our skies, illumes some summer clime in the sidereal *heavens;* or to a rose twining up the garden wall to bloom the other side; or to a grand triumphal archway, through which millions yearly walk to those sunlit islands of God, where, among the mountains of the beautiful and delicious perfumes, praises ascend with matin and vesper. Musing thus, I sung in better *rhyme* than *rhythm:* —

"When I go, let no wail in the mansion be heard,
No wavelet on soul-sea or heart-chord be stirred;
But may calmness and trust their faith-offerings bring,
To blend with the triumph, 'O death! where's thy sting?"

"Let the hour be morn: while the first breeze is stealing
O'er forest and flower, in sweet voices revealing
The soul's aspirations, like hymns in the air,
That rise with the incense of flowers bent in prayer.

"O'er the tomb let no willow in minor tones moan,
Nor the false phrase, 'died,' be carved on the stone;
For such breathe not the *truths* that gleam through the portals,
That gladden evermore the homes of immortals.

"Oh, these death-scenes are sweet! for the soul then receives
Vast volumes of thought on its unwritten leaves;
While each throe of despair, of sorrow and pain,
Will have burnished the links in Life's mystical chain.

"Let the *harp* of the 'morn-queen' be newly re-strung;
There's mirth to be made, there are songs to be sung;
For a mortal has passed from the care-lands of earth
To the realms of the loved, where music had birth.

"Oh! 'tis joy to stand near this glorified throng,
Whose goodness and love are the themes of each song;
Where the *cross* proved a *crown*, that to angels is given,
With the 'worthy' who glide through the azure of heaven.

"*Rockford, Ill.*, 1864."

CHAPTER XV.

LITERARY LIFE.

"He finds the laurel budding yet,
From Love transfigured and tear-wet:
They are his life drops turned to flowers
That make so sweet this world of ours!"

In June, 1866, Mr. Peebles was unexpectedly invited to the editorship of the Western department of "The Banner of Light." The spirits as the oracles of this stable paper so ordered. Adapted to this work, heartily sympathizing with the reforms of this journal, he entered upon his mission here with enthusiasm, winning laurels by his pen, touched with burning love. "The Banner" became more popular than ever. It was a success. We extract from his editorials some of his thoughts, bubbling with the freshness of insoiration: —

"SALUTATORY.

"Readers, grace be with you from the Infinite, peace from the angel-world, blessings from those beautiful spirits commissioned to minister unto mortals, and a conscious fellowship with the good, the beautiful, and the true, be yours now and evermore! . . .

"Earnest in the advocacy of what I deem *right*, *true*, and *reformatory*, I shall be tolerant to differences of opinion; holding the olive-branch of peace; exercising that charity which thinketh no evil; encouraging all mediatorial persons whose aims are highly purposed; and glorying ever in that freedom of discussion so natural to Western life and enterprise, — yet insisting that it be conducted in the spirit of sincerity, kindness, and brotherly love; considering myself responsible for only such articles as I may furnish." . . .

The "Banner" firm — Wm. White, chairman of circle-room; Luther Colby, editor-in-chief; Isaac B. Rich, treasurer; in connection with the others interested editorially or officially with this leading spiritual journal, and Mr. Peebles "editor of the Western department" — were indeed a "band of brothers," confiding as school-fellows, faithful as teachers, true to the polarity of that institution — the ministry of spirits — to which they ever appealed for advice in matters of importance. The reminiscences of those councils together in the "circle-rooms," whose central figure is Mrs. J. H. Conant, are all beautiful with affections best known and felt in the heaven of heavens.

"MEDIUMSHIP.

"As friction from the contact of flint and steel eliminates the spark, so mind is the result of two conditions of substance, physical and spiritual. Essential spirit, the positive principle, is everywhere dependent upon matter for the production of manifestations, and the molding of forms visible to the sensuous eye. Births from blendings is the universal law.

"Though absolute spirit can not become less than spirit, and though philosophically true that nothing can affect it in its nature and essence, it is equally true that it may be buried, clogged, and its legitimate aims and efforts for a season be thwarted. It is generally conceded by sound thinkers and scientists, that gross thoughts, gaming saloons, alcoholic drinks, and licentious practices, not only destroy the health and harmonies of the body, but ruin the mind; that is, ruin it practically for high, divine uses.

"The organ that manifests mind in the highest degree is the brain, and the nerves are the channels through which it transmits to, and receives impressions from, all parts of the vital domain. Moreover, the delicate tissues, nerves, fluids, and forces of the human mechanism are so connected with the brain, that whatever affects one must necessarily affect the other. Mediumship, as well as physiology and psychology, demonstrate this. Psychologic, impressional, and inspirational mediumship has vastly more to do with the brain than the body; but the brain can not be well balanced, healthy in action, and harmonious in relation, when the body is physically diseased or contaminated with immoral practices. It is very important that mediums understand this. Some have already lost, while others have greatly impaired, their mediumistic gifts, through perverted appetites and passions; while others, from love of gain, for selfish ends, and varied misdirections, have come into sympathetic relations with less unfolded, *evil spirits*, opening the way for obsessions and temporary mental shipwreck. Compensation is certain; as mortals make their beds, whether of thorns or roses, so they must lie.

"The blessed spirits, the very tread of whose white feet make music in the heavens that overshadow us, are anxious, oh! *so* anxious to have their mediums live in strict accordance with the physical, mental, and spiritual laws of their being; for upon favorable conditions and the purity of mediumistic life depends, to a very great extent, the character of the communications, — the body being the sounding-board, and the brain-organs the keys and strings to the instrument.

"Place in the hands of Vieux Temps an elegantly made, rich-toned, four-stringed violin, and give to Ole Bull a broken, rickety, shattered, ill-fashioned fiddle: while one would discourse most delicious music, the other would only grate out wretched discord; and yet both excellent musicians. Well, the body is that exquisite instrument upon which the mind plays; and both body and mind combined as one — wheel within a wheel — constitute a mediumistic instrument for angelic fingers to touch in demonstration of immortality, and sweet communion, too, from the loved dwellers of the heavenly land."

"GO FORTH.

"The apostles did not wait in Jerusalem for 'calls' to go and preach the gospel of the risen Nazarene, but a divine enthusiasm, streaming like golden glory into their souls, forced them to go into all the world, dispensing evangels of truth and love. Did Peter the Hermit, with bared head and sandaled feet, wait for a 'call' to go and rescue that sainted Syrian tomb from the ruthless hand of the Turk? Did those Jesuit fathers in Louis's time, all afire with the missionary spirit, wait for invitations from India and China? This waiting to be invited, waiting to get a call, is hardly in keeping with the glowing inspiration of the new dispensation.

"My brother, start, strike out; take up your carpet-sack and walk! Up and away, making every school-house, hall, and church resound! . . . Cold hearts require re-kindling; the dead, buried in worldliness, need raising; the sleepy, awakening; the shiftless, arousing; the indifferent, a new baptism. The time is auspicious. The world is crying for our liberal, loving gospel, fresh from the spirit-world. It does not want doubt and fear, but demonstrations of immortality, devotion, trust, love. . . . Here's our hand, brother, warm, cordial. List, go forth, work for the truth; live it each day; rise to the height of the occasion; lift and bear others' burdens; make full proof of your ministry, — and friends will flock around you, while, from the arched heavens, angels will shower upon you unfading blooms and immortal blessings."

"YOUNG SPEAKERS.

"We desire to see more encouragement given to our young speakers, those just coming before the public. Many in the field are bearing the marks of age, — will soon pass to the land of the 'Hereafter;' and our young brothers and sisters must be encouraged and supported. Committees should give them warm hands, and cheering words of hope and confidence. Among lecturers and mediums there should be no envy, no jealousy, and no rivalries, save only as to who shall do the most good. We are all workers upon the spiritual temple. Frescoing and tinseling are less important than laying the foundation stones. Each in place, and all for the general good. Such life-consecration should be the divine aim. . . .

"Charles Dickens, writing of Thackeray the humorist, says, 'He had a particular delight in young boys, always wanting to give them sovereigns to aid them in their literary course.' There are young men and women in the range of our acquaintance, gifted, inspired, entranced at times by spirits, waiting for some friendly hand to be extended, helping them to start, helping them to finance and the means of culture, preparatory to achieving distinction in the lecture-field. Will not wealthy Spiritualists help such? A little aid at the proper time, and these young media may become stars in the horizon of thought, lighting, beckoning others up the mountains of the beautiful.

"Our older speakers, — those long in our ranks, — banishing all jealousies and unworthy ambitions, should manifest a deeper interest in young lecturers. Youth is no crime. The more aged are doubtless the better counselors; but all the gathered lore of the ages is not hived in their craniums. Under the entrancing and inspiring power of angels, these youth often completely eclipse their seniors; and this should and *will* gladden the soul of every true disciple of the Spiritual Philosophy."

"ONLY FIRST-CLASS ENGAGEMENTS.

"Not wise and energetic, as most of our sister-lecturers, a brother speaker writes from the East: —

"'Can't you get me a series of *first class* engagements in the West? If so, I should like to undertake the journey as far as the Mississippi. . . . What do they pay per Sunday, and provide entertainment?'

"The phrase 'first-class engagements' seriously puzzles us. Were Jesus' of this character, when, with a Syrian sun-scorched face and sandaled feet, he walked homeless by Galilee's shores doing good? Were Peter the Hermit's, who, thrilled by the inspirations of the hour, traveled, fasted, and preached till fainting by the wayside? Were Wesley's, preaching by roadsides and in the graveyards of England? Were John Murray's, lifting up his voice in mud-hovels, school-houses, and 'stoned' at that? Pray, what your grade of clay? what the superior constituents of your being?

"Brother, get up from your bed of ease: pray the gods to infill you with wisdom, energy, enthusiasm; then, putting your 'pants in your boots,' taking your carpet-sack in your hand, start light-hearted as a bird for the great, glorious West. The angels know their commissioned; the people are sensible and appreciative. The way will open as you journey. The 'pay' is generally good, — considered spiritually, it is absolutely splendid. The entertainment, though diverse, is excellent; social circles are cordial, and Western hearts warm. The moral fields are white, and hundreds of harvesters are needed Any true and faithful man or woman could build up and sustain a congregation in almost any locality. But that sentence, 'first-class engagements,' rings in our ears. Had we been privileged a walk in Judea some twenty centuries since, we should have hinted to Jesus the addition of another beatitude, — *Blessed are the modest, for they shall be promoted.*"

"FOLLOW YOUR STRONGEST ATTRACTIONS.

"Yes, follow them, and go to the 'd——.' 'Do not rivers flow toward the ocean?' Do not steel and magnet follow the law of attraction?' 'Do not birds in spring-time, and four-footed beasts mating, follow the law of attraction?' Certainly.

"If men and women are nothing more than rivers, magnets, needles, and four-footed beasts, *they* will do well also to follow their attractions. Are they no more? To ask, is to answer the inquiry.

"Men and women are moral actors, made in the divine image. They are conscious beings, endowed with reasoning and rational faculties; and, instead of being psychologized, or blindly following their attractions, they should be *guided by reason*, and the spirit's highest, purest promptings. Weighing every motive, exercising the best judgment, and following the Arabula, — the Christ within, — they should be careful to distinguish between the voice of God and the voice of passion.

"Rocks roll down hill because they are rocks. Obedient to gravitation, they follow their 'strongest attractions.' It is well for alkalies and acids, well for minerals, to seek their affinities. Such seeking becomes the mineral plane of existence. Birds, beasts of the forests, and the Adamic propensities, sitting like sirens in the back-brain department of the soul-house, are ever clamorously inclined to follow their attractions. There are diviner counsels. God, Christ, angels, philosophy, and science, considering men and women intellectual, moral, and responsible beings, unite in saying, *Be guided by reason and the soundest practical judgment.*"

"CAPITAL PUNISHMENT.

"Capital punishment, a relic of barbarism, as a governmental policy, is at once mistaken, ruinous, and unwarranted. The history of criminality proves its inefficiency to secure the results desired; and, moreover, every sympathetic prompting of our nature inclines us to intercede in behalf of the unfortunate murderer, that he may live out his natural life. A prison punishment, disciplinary and reformatory, is not only more efficacious for good, but infinitely more in keeping with the gentle spirit of Jesus and the humane tendencies of the age.

"Hanging kills no one. It is simply a retaliatory Mosaic method of punishment, — an unnatural process of severing the co-partnership existing between the earthly organ ism and the real spiritual man. Parties thus thrust into the spirit-world, sometimes *innocently*, and then again all dimmed, stained, and blackened o'er with crime, retain their individualities, and follow, too, their leading bent of mind, till they learn by observation and experience, with the unfolding of the wisdom-principle, that happiness is attained only through obedience and right-doing. And the phrase *learn*, implies effort, process, time.

"Hence, hanging people to get them *out* of the world, is, more literally, getting them into the world by widening their range among men for the exercise of such influences as they may choose to exert. This life determines the commencement of the future. All, 'over there,' gravitate by virtue of fixed spiritual law to their own appropriate planes of action; *act* they *will*, and the effect of such action is felt in both the mortal and immortal realms. . . .

"The highest inspiration of the hour, the genius of the age, and the progressive tendencies of all nations, are against it. This method of punishment is entirely abolished in Tuscany, Portugal, Oldenburg, Bremen, Venezuela, the Danubian Principalities, and in the Swiss Cantons of Freiburg and Nurenburg; in Michigan, Wisconsin, Rhode Island, and, we think, one or two other States. There have been no executions in Portugal for ten years; in Freiburg for thirty-four years; and in Tuscany for thirty-five years. Russia, standing as it were, with one foot upon the frozen ocean of the North, the other well along toward Central Europe, has not only abolished capital punishment, but flogging with the knout. Thus moves the car of Progression, bearing onward the cause of humanity."

"THE ORTHODOX CLERGY.

"Are not evangelical clergymen guilty of serious derelictions of duty for not dwelling more fervently upon the 'terrors of the Lord,' and the torments of sinners doomed to hell? They seldom preach *hell* now as in our forefathers' day. Though taught in their creeds, they pass it over trippingly. Perhaps the mitigation, softening down, and bridging over of hell, form no exception to the general improvements of the age.

"The Orthodox clergy, — 'fat, oily men, with a roguish twinkle in their eyes,' — opening gold-clasped Bibles, and preaching to drowsy people pressing softly-cushioned pews, certainly take the matter very easy. Why, they smile, walking right over this crust of hell; they crack jokes; some of them drive good bargains; others loan money, almost forcing 'infidels' to believe them insincere.

"Poetry, painting, music, art, science, commerce, telegraphic communication, in connection with the phenomena and philosophy of Spiritualism, have all exerted their liberalizing tendencies upon the times. The monstrous dogmas of 'endless hell-torments,' 'personality of the devil,' 'total depravity,' and kindred falsities, are being cast away as rubbish from the minds of the truly enlightened; have become effete, barren, dead. This living age calls for original thoughts, sublime ideas, and broader, grander truths than were ever conceived of by Scribe or Pharisee, Moses or Calvin.

"'Ring out the old, ring in the new,
Ring, happy bells, across the snow:
The age is going, let it go;
Ring out the *false*, ring in the *new*.'"

"SILENT GOSPELS.

"Every individual we meet, every emergency into which we are thrown, leaves its impress, slight or powerful, upon the soul, just as every particle of food we take and every breath we inhale contributes to the support or injury of the physical organism. Of this we may be unconscious, as we are of the play of the lungs, the flow of the blood, and the operation of the forces that digest and assimilate our food. So our moral natures derive the elements of health or injurious growth from each of the occasions of life. We absorb from those with whom we associate. What we see, hear, think of, converse about, aspire to, — all these moral elements are digested and worked into our spiritual natures, the very substance of our being, by forces that play without our knowledge, and quite independent of the control of the human will. . . .

"There is not a pure purpose breathed, nor earnest desire uttered, in the sacred sanctuary of home, but that steals through the walls and infills the atmosphere. Thought impregnates thought, and sphere the spheral surroundings. Words of sympathy and gifts of charity in lonely streets sprinkle genial influences upon the frosty air that beats around the dwellings of the sordid. Nothing is lost. Kind deeds crystallized into character make the presence of those thus doing more sweet and divine."

"SPHERES.

"Each mortal has an aura peculiarly his own; so has each mountain, tree, and flower, and rocky stratum. The atmosphere of some houses is fresh with the elixir of life. It is wholesome to breathe it, for the very breath of the inmates is aglow with the balm of health and harmony.

"Who does not delight to meet good souls? When allowed their intimate fellowship, you feel a personal baptism. You come away better from magnetic association, your heart beats lighter, and your hands seem cleaner from having shaken theirs. Such choice souls are the star-rays and sun-beams that gladden the earth. Send us more, Father! . . .

"Those particles of musk, permeating the walls and floating in the atmosphere of the room, so impinge upon and impregnate adjoining particles, the odor is retained for years. In a method somewhat analogous, mortals magnetize their beds, rooms, dwell ings. Magnetism is refined, etherealized substance. Sensitives sense its grade. It remains in rooms after the occupants have left. This proffers the key to unlock the mysteries of haunted houses."

"THE CHILDREN'S PROGRESSIVE LYCEUM.

"Youth is the golden time, the impressional period. The child's mind, like the daguerreotypist's polished plate, naturally receives impressions from the surrounding objective and subjective worlds; hence the necessity of liberal and exalted teachings to beautify youthful natures, preparatory to the Harmonial Age, of which the Spiritual is but the John the Baptist. Thanks to the angels for the inauguration of these Lyceums, —schools in celestial lands; and thanks to A. J. Davis for being the mediumistic instrument of importation to earth, and translation of these educational principles into form, making them interesting and practical for the growth of the young in their earlier years!

"The aim of the Children's Progressive Lyceum is to cultivate the whole being, physical, mental, and spiritual, in harmony with music, law, science, — with the beautiful principles of nature."

"STRIKE!

"Inconoclasts will be necessary so long as there's rubbish to be removed. Jesus came anciently to abrogate the ceremonial law, and abolish Jewish rites and creeds, leaving not 'one stone of the temple upon another.' Now Christ, the *spirit*, comes again; comes in the 'clouds of heaven;' comes attended by 'ministering angels;' comes in the influx of ideas and principles; comes the grand constructor of the age. The temple is spiritual. These are the progressive steps: investigation, phenomena, knowledge, dissolution, recombination, inspiration, progression, brotherhood, harmony. Out from these sectarian schisms, political partisanships, and social antagonisms, — out from the chrysalis of old forms, trembling, tumbling, are emerging living men and women, armed and winged to do the work demanded, during the closing decades of the Nineteenth Century."

"FLOWERS ON DESKS.

"Blessings upon the fingers that pluck, weave, and decorate the home, the schoolhouse, and the church. Flowers are God's divine bibles; and sweetly do they inspire speakers with loftier thought, uttered with deeper fervency of soul. Jeremiah Brown, a prominent Spiritualist of Battle Creek, his home embowered with shrubbery and roses, appreciates the beautiful as well as the utilitarian. His good lady-companion, famous for refined taste, conscious of our needs, fowarded by express, each Saturday, bouquets and baskets of flowers for the speaker's stand in Library Hall, Chicago. Accompanying one of them were these impromptu lines: —

"'May their beauty weave a spell
'Round thee, in which naught can dwell
But the purest, holiest feelings,
Wrought from truth's divine revealings!'"

"PRAYING.

"'*Pray for me!*' How horribly shiftless that sounds! Would you not like to have us prepare your food, fan you to sleep, dust your pathway, and carry your groceries? To one constitutionally lazy, is it not sweetly bewitching to trust in a vicarious atonement that saves through the 'merits' of Jesus Christ? Is not this one secret of Orthodox success in cooping converts?

"Pray for you! No: pray for yourself; pray with your hands, feet, legs, — Fred Douglass-like; macadamize your own roads; construct your own bridges; plow your own fields; earn the bread you eat; digest your own pabulum; heal your own hurts; get to heaven by your own merits; work out your own salvation, — *be somebody!*"

"SPIRITUALISTS AT FUNERALS.

'When the mortal sleeps the sleep of death, and the soul is marching on to the sunnier homes of the angels, the eyes of the loving left behind are tearful, and their hearts heave and ache. It may be a tender father or mother, sister or brother, that in life professed and prized the blessed principles of Spiritualism. The day of burial comes; and who ministers at the altar of consolation? A Spiritualist teacher? a seer with vision open to the glories that glitter in the temple of the Eternal? Oh, *no!* but a sectarian clergyman is invited, — a man that knows nothing of the nature of death; nothing of the condition of the departed, or of the activities and heavenly beauties that make radiant the spiritual world. Is this showing a proper respect to the ascended soul? is it honoring the truth? is it honoring our principles? and, unless *we* honor them, how can we expect others to?

"From our soul's depths we forbid any sectarist shooting off his sepulchral mouth at or over our corpse, charged with the doubts, dogmas, and superstitions of the past. If Spiritualists desire or claim the respect of a thinking, cultured community, they must first respect themselves, respect their principles, and practice them in letter and spirit. Enthusiasm for an idea, enthusiasm for eternal principles, is grand beyond description. The public speakers employed in voicing the truths of the harmonial philosophy are peculiarly adapted to minister words of comfort at *funerals*, and words of beauty at the marriage altar."

"PRE-EXISTENCE. — ETERNAL EXISTENCE.

"Souls, as mathematics, have their axioms. Circles only are endless. Geometry is of universal application. Every particle of substance follows the line of its strongest attraction. All subjects, modes of motion, proceed in straight lines, unless controlled by intervening forces. That can not be spiritually or philosophically false which is mathematically true. Parallel lines can never meet. Beginnings imply endings. Conditions that form may, by the introduction of foreign conditions, depolarize. Could circumstances constitute or create living, conscious entities, other and mightier circumstances might 'uncreate.' An eternal past existence, then, is the only basic foundation upon which to place the fulcrum to demonstrate a future endless existence. . . .

"What is man? Analytically, he is body, soul, spirit. The least of him is body; the most, spirit, the essential inmost. The best of man, then, is spirit. But what is spirit, human spirit? It is both substance and form, — essential primal substance and essential form, — God the Infinite finited.

"Man, as body and soul merely, is the man of the theologic schools. As such, he is mortal, sinful, dies. But the divine *eternal man* is neither mortal, sinful, nor dies; that is, man in the third, the Deific degree. The scale runs, beginning with the lower, outermost, intermediate, innermost, a trinity in a seven-fold organization. If God is the fountain, man is the drop. If God is the infinite soul, the infinite consciousness of the universe, man is the finite. Man, then, in the best and divinest definition, is the synonym of God, and necessarily as eternal. This is the

'Divinity that stirs within,'

the quenchless fire that burns on the celestial altar, the eternal potency that incarnates itself for mighty destinies. The universe alive with God, and embodying the positive and negative, something as the opposites of a mathematical equation, descension and ascension, must of necessity be the methods of evolution, — the ever-continuous modes of infoldment along the segments and up the spiral circle of endless being. Synthetically, man is *unitary*, and trifold in manifestation.

"Man being, then, what we have defined him, his strict eternity follows as a matter of necessity, and his pre-existence is clearly proven. All conscious mortals, in their inmost spirits, being essentially Deific, they must have existed during the whole past eternity, and will, for the same reason, through the whole future eternity. Analogy, revelation, manifestation, have little to do with future immortality, except to illustrate and make it known to the outer and sensuous. They do not create the *truth*. In fact, pre-existence itself, when logically and fully demonstrated, is not positive proof of immortality, in the sense of endlessness, disconnected from the Deific; for the idea of pre-existence itself goes no further back into principle than the creation of *essential man*, which, once admitted, his dissolution is just as logical, and follows as a matter of course. From nothing, nothing comes. Creation and annihilation are but necessary counterparts of each other. Admit the one, and you embrace the other. Creation is only apparent, not real; annihilation is the same. What is termed creation is merely incarnation, formation, or change of state. It is the clothings that spirit gives itself in its descending cycles of movement.

"That men live on when their mortal bodies are dissolved, Spiritualism abundantly demonstrates. But this fact affords only the feeblest proof of their immortality, in the sense of eternity; for, though they live after physical dissolution as they lived before birth, yet, being created, and having a beginning, they may, yea, *should*, for the same reason, have an end. Absolute endlessness can be affirmed only of circled being. All that begins, ends. The line that has a beginning has its ending. If doubted, extend the line till imagination tires; tread it till you faint, then retrace your steps and you find an end. The sea ebbs and flows. The sun that rises has its setting. All that *is*, is substance, spirit. Matter is phenomenal, and was precipitated from spirit. It ends again in spirit. The darkest worlds opaque started from spirit,—translucent, transparent, making their grand cycle of movement. As worlds, they end; end because they began. It is their nature. It is law; the law of change, precipitation and ascension, outflowing and inflowing, electrical and magnetic,—the latter relating more to the soul, the former to the body constantly, the ponderables gathering from the imponderables, and as constantly the ponderables becoming imponderables again.

"For ever man goes forth. Outgoing, incoming, is the eternal law; descension and ascension following each other in eternal movement, and in orderly succession. Thus ever onward lies the progressive pathway of man, taking on the more etherealized in each grand cycle of his being, yet never exhausting the eternal fountain, for it is infinite.

"Celestial man grows outwardly from himself as *spirit* into six degrees of expression, his seventh degree being himself, most internal, most *Deific* in the special or analytical sense. But man is most Deific, in the unitary sense, when making his upward cycle of movement; for then he excretes his negatives, his superficial and artificial characteristics, and makes himself more consciously immortal in wholeness,—in the seven degrees of his trifold being, conscious of his past consciousness,—a harmonic trinity in unity. How wide the circular sweep! how vast, how mighty, the destiny of humanity!"

While Mr. Peebles was editorially connected with "The Banner of Light," he took strong grounds, as the above article shows, in favor of pre-existence. His positions were pointedly but kindly criticised by W. A. Danskin, Baltimore, Md., a sound thinker and able writer. In reviewing the reviewer, Mr. P. said,—

"Do not connect this position of ours, relating to pre-existence and eternal existence, with transmigration as taught in China, with the metempsychosis of Egypt, and the theories of old Asiatics. It has little or nothing common with those superstitions, from which originated the Christian doctrine of the resurrection of the body. Matter, through processes diverse and inverse, continually ascends to higher degrees of refinement; but souls, divine souls, allied to the *infinite* something, as drops to an ever-flowing fountain, descend." . . .

Quoting Jesus and Plato, the most distinguished philosophers, seers, poets, and authors of antiquity, with several writers of the present favoring the hypothesis, he continued,—

"Against this strong array of positive testimony, from representative minds both in the past and present, all the negations to the contrary ever breathed, or booked, amount to no more than the hum of passing insects. What is it to astronomers, though a thousand blind men testify they never saw dark spots upon the sun's surface? That Homer was sightless was Homer's misfortune.

"*Something* or *nothing* are the only two possible postulates. If something, substance; if substance, eternal; for all substance has in itself the divine energy or quality of endlessness. Therefore, once in existence, always in existence. Forms only change. The converse is equally true: once out of existence, never in existence. '*Ex nihilo nihil fit;*' from nothing, nothing can come. If an individual, then, were absolutely once out of existence, as a conscious individuality, tell us how he 'got' into existence. The telling will solve the startling and heretofore inexplicable phenomenon of something from nothing, — somebody from nobody.

"Again, if a fortuitous concourse of atoms, or pre-arranged conditions, circumstances, or relational incidents, conspired to make this thinking, conscious individuality, MAN, — 'mark well,' *man* (not his physical tenement, not his more etherealized, spiritual body, but *man*, — essential, divine man), — may not future, pre-arranged conditions, or more potent circumstances, conspire to unmake him? May not beginnings have endings? Our position remains then: man a *pre-existent* being; man an *eternal being!*"

"'NEITHER DO I CONDEMN THEE.'

"'Abandoned women,' — that's the phrase in common parlance. Abandoned of whom? Not of God, for owning, loving all, — 'his mercy endureth for ever;' not of Jesus, for from that pure, affectional soul there still comes the gentle words, 'Neither do I condemn thee, go and sin no more;' not of the angels, for there continues to be 'joy in heaven' when, through angelic pleadings and intercedings, an erring one is brought to repentance; not of the spirits of the 'just made perfect,' for they delight to minister to the least and lowest for redemptive purposes; not of philanthropists or reformers, of the good or the true. Abandoned of whom? If by anybody, by those passional men instrumental in their temporary ruin, and such of their sister sex as, from a vivid consciousness of being themselves human, with a taking tendency to the weakness of yielded temptation, put on the extraneous airs of a purity too exalted to touch, or snatch from further degradation, a sister once pure as the crystal snow, and still God's child, bearing the divine image. These pretensions, not Jesusonion, are thoroughly Shakespearian, —'If thou hast no virtue, assume to have it.'

"In the sight of God, angels, heavenly hosts, and constellations of philanthropists on earth quite unknown to fame, there are no abandoned women, no abandoned men; for God, heaven, sympathy, mercy, love, and redemptive efforts are over and around all.

"Under the oily crust of city life, there lies half-concealed a huge, hideous vice, that often those who are too delicate to talk about it are not to delicate to practice. It is frequently termed the 'social cancer.' With venemous roots pushing out and down in every direction, it is the destroyer of inward peace, the enemy of happy households, and fatal to the mental and spiritual growth of the soul. . . .

"With the more positive and guiltier sex, it is generally animal indulgence and violent outbreaks of passion, rooted in ante-natal perversions, often intensified by rich diet, tobacco, liquors, and other stimulants. Relative to the other sex, in a majority of cases, the primal causes are ante-natal tendencies, psychological susceptibilities, and stern life-necessities. Not choice, but poverty, love of costly dress, temptations to indolence, harsh treatment of parents, sensual grossness of husbands, and the wiles and false promises of seducers, — *these* are the more immediate and prominent causes.

"Full one-third of the women wandering in towns and cities, under the gaslight, are driven into the streets, and dens of pollution, from pressure of poverty and extreme want. Think of it! Woman, with the original seal of innocence and sweetness upon her countenance, compelled to choose between starvation and prostitution!

"Society, — another name for gilded sham, — and even women in the higher walks of life, of whom we are heartily ashamed, will, while smiling upon, waltzing and flirting with the libertine, full-fed and gay, turn sneeringly away or mercilessly trample upon the starved victim of his lust. To the fallen sister their language virtually is, 'I am holier than thou!' Heaven save us from a pharisaic self-righteousness! 'None is *good*' (absolutely good) said Jesus, 'but *one;* that is God.' A boasting, satisfied, selfish, do-nothing purity will find itself outside the walls of the city celestial, long after negative, erring women have, through fiery trials and severest discipline, been permitted to pass into those upper kingdoms of God to put on robes of beauty. Sainted sisters, ye who are safe from terrible temptations, because moving in circles above penury, and walking in the sunlight of noble souls, be sparing of the stones you hurl at those who fell, through miserable wages, psychological influences, and a fashionable world's crushing coldness!

"Efforts of Magdalen Societies in this country have done something; but the 'Midnight Meetings' of London have done more for this class in England. A living writer tells us that, —

"'To one of these meetings an afflicted mother sent her own daguerreotype, in hopes that her erring daughter would recognize the face, and be won by its mute pleadings to a better life. The picture was passed around in several meetings, until at last it met the eye for which it was intended, and the guilty girl burst into tears and set off for the home of her childhood.'

"The evil is patent. Where and what the remedy? Centralized into a sentence, it is this, —*The independence of woman!* Make her, or help her to make herself, socially, maritally, politically, and financially independent, and you have laid the ax at the root of this deadly upas-tree. Systematized, the method will bear this general statement: *A full recognition of woman's primal equality with man.* . . .

"The constituents of our social edifice should not be cemented by the force of interest, habit, or circumstance, but by virtue, integrity, purity, justice, sympathy, and love,— the mightiest principles in the universe of God. Society, constituted of individuals, should look after the highest interests of each member, remembering that whatever benefits even the least, benefits a world-wide humanity.

"Theorists must make their reform-theories practical. 'What have you done?' is the question the angels ask. To gossip, tea-party fashion, about these 'unfortunate women upon the town' amounts to nothing. Up, and do something! To talk about their condition deploringly, to pray for them devotedly, to think of them tenderly, to shun them in the streets gracefully, to speak of them sisterly, is *talk*, — cheap talk! nothing more. Away with this silver-tongued hypocrisy! Do something. Redeem them; and the blessings of the angel world shall be yours!"

"MY PEACE.

"This is recorded of Jesus, in the tenth chapter of Matthew, 'Into whatsoever town or city ye shall enter, inquire who in it is worthy, and there abide till ye go thence. . . . And, if the house be worthy, let your peace come upon it; but, if it be not worthy, let your peace return to you.' Whenever the inmates of a house are exacting, selfish, angular, and inharmonious, — when their rooms are badly ventilated, beds unwholesome, apartments tobacco-scented, dishes pork-pickled, and pastry even swimming in swine juice, 'my peace returns to me,' and I can not 'there abide;' for six things, to speak biblically, 'doth my soul hate,' yea, *seven* things are an abomination unto me, viz., tobacco, whisky, pork, feather-beds, coffee, razors, and sectarian theology. And when the fragmentary letters and epistles of the spiritual dispensation are collected and voted canonical by those who in future years shall minister at the altar of freedom, may the above portion of *gospel* according to *Peebles* share no such fate as did many of the 'manuscripts' at the Nicene Council. Amen."

"WHY AWAY FROM THE SPIRITUALISTS' MEETING?

"'Because they act so!' Who are *they?* If you are all right, holding papers of canonization, the greater the necessity of your being an active worker among the 'they,' helping them to become right also. A retired saint is something new under the sun. Would it not be wise to widen the influence of your saintship, thus aiding others to become saintly? Jesus ate with sinners, and God's sun shines into marshes and miry pools. We are not scolding our inconsistent brother; for, by way of contrast, we love him, — love him something as we admire the background to a picture, or the mud from which spring and bloom beautiful lilies.

"'Well, I attend when they have a very fine speaker.' Indeed! what a condescension. The fastidious prince that sought the golden chariot sat on the sod. Quakers frequently consider their 'silent meetings' the most profitable. You, my brother, are not only devoid of principle, but have yet to take your first lessons in the school of moral obligation, and the inspiring effects of right influences and examples."

"CHURCH INFIDELS.

"Christians swallowing all the scriptural camels of the Jewish ages: believing that God made the world in six days; that he walked in the garden in the cool of the day; that he came down to see the city and the tower; that he made woman from one of Adam's ribs; cast down great stones out of heaven; took off the Egyptian's chariot wheels, and sent the she-bears to eat the children; believing that the waters of the Red Sea opened for the passage of the Israelites; that the quails fell around the camp some three feet in a single night; that the walls of Jericho fell at the sounding of a ram's horn; that Samson caught the foxes, and carried the gates of Gaza; that Elisha's ax was made to swim, and the sun and moon to stand still: believing, too, that the *whale* swallowed *Jonah*, and all because booked and labeled *holy!* They believe those ancient occurrences, though purporting to have happened two, three, and four thousand years ago, among those old, selfish, warlike, and murderous Jews, and then traveling down to us through a corrupt Roman Catholic priesthood! And yet, while piously believing the *above*, with other theological monstrosities, they reject the evidences of their senses; reject the *trances*, visions, healings, and spiritual gifts of the present; reject the candid testimony of Thomas Say; reject the testimony of Judge Edmonds, Robert Dale Owen, Senator Wade, yea, hundreds, thousands, and tens of thousands, in our midst whose integrity, eminent social positions, and high moral worth are an honor even to this Nineteenth Century. Great God, have mercy on the souls of these *Church Infidels!* For them, we promise to 'pray without ceasing,' as enjoined by the sainted apostle."

"MARRIAGE.

"'True marriage is the strictest tie of perpetual friendship; and there can be no friendship without confidence, and no confidence without integrity, and no integrity without love. Love *is* marriage, and without it there is *no marriage.*'

"Steel to magnet, bud to sunbeam, require no chemical formula; neither does soul no soul need a Romish ritual or mere formal ceremony; for what God by the fiat of omnipotence has joined together will remain together, and what he has *not*, no priestly mummery or conventional legislation can keep together only in the *external*. The letter killeth, said the apostle. But beautiful, divine, holy, the true monogamic marriage,—man and woman; positive and negative; two halves of a circle! own to own; heart to heart; soul to soul, in a sweet, divine duality, embosomed each in each."

"HUMAN RIGHTS.

"Ignoring such specials as 'woman's rights,' 'man's rights,' 'freedmen's rights,' 'Indians' rights,' 'Chinamen's rights,' 'children's rights,' we prefer that better term, at once broad and comprehensive, HUMAN RIGHTS! As related to woman, they may be classified in this wise:—

"I. The right to vote, hold office, and select that life-vocation best adapted to her glowing genius.

"II. The justice and moral necessity of paying her the same wages paid to men for the same amount of labor accomplished.

"III. The exercise of the same privileges that are granted to men in such civic advances as look to friendship, courtship, love, and the marriage relation.

"IV. The creation of such a high public sentiment as shall gladly guarantee equal rights to all, with no rivalry save that which would strive to build up, beautify, and bless the most souls."

Immediately after returning from the war, Mr. Peebles was called by S. S. Jones, Esq., to a great meeting of Spiritualists in St. Charles, Ill., where he delivered an earnest speech, of which the following is an extract, published in "The Religio-Philosophical Journal:"—

"Wars darken the horizon in every direction. They are the *seeming* necessities of existing conditions. Destruction ever precedes the diviner construction. Wars have their uses on certain planes. Nevertheless, my soul shrinks from war and all inharmonies. The divine within me calls for peace. War can never quench the war-spirit. The North, its armies and navies, has not yet taken the first step toward subduing the South. You may conquer, or even exterminate, the sons of the South; but that is not subduing them.

"Bonaparte conquered, but did not subdue, Europe; Russia conquered Poland; Austria, Hungary; and England, Ireland: but so long as an Irish heart can throb, or a sprig of shamrock remains green, so long will the sons of Erin hate English oppressive rule. Only love and wisdom can subdue. Moral power only is employed by God and angels to uplift humanity. . . . All the races compose one universal brotherhood, and armies with white banners, palms, and olive-branches would tend to make the atmosphere so positive with goodness,—yea, they would so infill the air with the moral magnetism of love, justice, and truth, that the rebels would be struck dumb as by flashes of light from angel hosts. It was this power that felled Saul to the earth, and turned the prodigal to his father's house. It is the Christ within,—the mightiest redemptive power in the universe."

"REFRESHING PREACHING.

"The clergy frequently announce their subjects these days, as a sort of stool-pigeon enticement to draw in the fluttering, floating crowd. A late Washington Sunday Morning 'Chronicle,' — a paper, by the way, that refuses to publish notices of Spiritualist meetings under the head of '*religious meetings*,' — contained the following notice under the head of 'religious intelligence:' —

"Subject of discourse at Dr. Gray's church (E-street Baptist), to-night will be: 'The incidents of the flood; the ark; the builder; description of the ark itself; its stormy passage; the place where it anchored; the first morning of a new day.'

"Important 'religious intelligence,' truly! — incidents of the flood; the ark; the builders of the ark, and its stormy passage! This and similar evangelical intelligence the Washington 'Chronicle' generously publishes.

"With all due deference, we seriously inquire what the people of this country care about Noah's Ark, or other of those old myths and legends that characterized the Jews. Is it not more legitimate to deal and do with American steamers, their passages, the accidents occurring, loss of life, and causes of the same?

"No matter how the Israelites were fed: are the poor of this country — each city, hamlet, neighborhood — all fed? No matter about the number of horns on John's mystic beast, or the mechanism of Paul's tents. We have to do with the living present; the lessons of this day; the necessities of this age. Oh, for living men and women to occupy the pulpits and rostrums of this hour! speaking words that flame with holy fire; words that convince; words that touch the heart's deepest affections, moving the masses up on to that broad humanitarian plane of toleration and justice, sympathy and fraternity."

"THE PRISONER MY BROTHER.

"Loitering, a few days since, with a friend in a rear yard of Auburn State Penitentiary, I saw, jutting through the window-grates of a prisoner's cell, trailing vines, and flowers in full bloom, placed there by pale hands in morning's time, to catch the sunshine; and I said, 'He can not be a bad man!' My sympathies were touched. I wanted to extend to him a warm hand, call him my brother, tell him I loved him, and would fain come unto him. Be sure, in an impulsive moment, he may have committed a crime, and infinitely greater criminals may have pronounced upon him the stern sentence. Did not Jesus say, 'Go and sin no more?' Gladly would I have borne him on loving wings into the realm of better conditions, placing him amid summer surroundings, and, calling angels to guard him, bid him look hopefully toward a smiling and peaceful future."

"GOD, FATHER AND MOTHER.

"Ignoring the fetich gods of Africa, the repenting, jealous God of Judaism, the changing, angry-getting God of Catholicism, the partial, malicious God of Calvinism, the masculine, miracle-working God of Universalism, we find infinitely higher conceptions of Deity in the definitions of Plato, Proclus, Jesus, Parker, and Davis: —

"'Of *good* there is one eternal, definite, and universal cause, — the infinite soul.'

"'God is spirit, and spirit is causation underlying all things.'

"'God is a Spirit, and they that worship him must worship him in spirit and in truth.'

"'To God, our Father, and our mother too, will we ascribe all praise.'

"'The great positive mind of the universe, Father God, and Mother Nature.'

"Spiritualists believe in the Divine Existence, the Infinite *Esse*, embodying and enzoning all principles of mind and properties of matter; all wisdom and love; life and motion: 'God manifest in the flesh,' and every thing else, from sands to solar systems. This is the spontaneous concession of the world's consciousness. Egypt's Osiris, India's Brahma, Judea's Jehovah, the Grecian's Jupiter, the Mussulman's Allah, the Platonist's All-Good, the Theist's Deity, the Christian's Our Father, the Northman's Odin, the

Indian's Great Spirit, express more than glimmerings of universal beliefs in that God whose altars are mountains and oceans, and whose pulpits are fields, earths, orbs, and circling systems, perfect in order, musical in their marches, and flaming with holiest praises.

"Rejecting the human-shaped, prayer-hearing, personal God of evangelical theologians, — because personality logically implies locality, and whatever becomes localized in space is necessarily limited and imperfect, — to *us*, God is the *Infinite Spirit;* soul of all things; the incarnate Life-Principle of the universe, immanent in dewdrops that glitter, and shells that shine; in stars that sail through silver seas, and angels that delight to do the Eternal's will. When we designate God as the Infinite spirit-presence and substance of universal Nature, from whose eternally-flowing life wondrous systems have been evolved, we mean to imply in the affirmation all divine principles, attributes, qualities, and forces, positive and negative, — spirit, and matter as a solidified form of force, the former depending upon the latter for its manifestations. The masculine can not create. There was never a higher formation without the two forces, positive and negative."

"CONCEPTIVE IMMORTALITY.

"All newer and higher formations result from the blending of positives and negatives. So, upon the plane of humanity, when the positive and negative relational forces unite, then and there is the divine incarnation. From that moment, the embryonic child is an immortal being; the divinity has taken on humanity; God is manifest in the flesh. Whoever destroys that germinal man or woman is a criminal in the eyes of all seers on earth and angels in heaven. Nature absolutely never takes a retrogressive step."

"MISCELLANEOUS EXTRACTS.

"Better to be deceived by mortals, now and then, than deprived of the real joy and beauty of calm, deep faith, in our kindred kind. All have their angel side."

"Have you portions of God's green earth you call your own? Do you rent, even? Put out the choicest fruit-trees, decorate them with rare and symmetrical shade-trees, and embower them in trailing vines and roses. Angels delight to visit such beautiful homes."

"The system of evangelical religion, toggled up in the dark ages of popery, is purely a *policy* religion, full of adaptations and worldly expediences, counting on *profits* and *losses* at the *judgment-day*, and is completely mechanical, having *hells* and *devils* for motive powers."

"The highest and holiest are tinged with melancholy. . . . Seers are sadder than others."

"As Spiritualists, we regard dancing, at proper hours and places, a harmless and pleasant amusement, conducive to health and a genial flow of the soul-forces. It imparts an animating influence to the brain, and conduces to a proper balance between the muscular system and mental activity."

"Grand is God's old *rock-book*, — a Bible that never required a 'revision;' a gospel never bound in calf, nor man-labelled 'Holy.' The masses, with open eyes, go blindly through the world, kicking aside the stones that reveal in their formations the history of countless ages past."

"It is terrible, — this chaining by law a living, progressive, spiritual woman to a dead, masculine corpse!"

"DEATH.

"Death, a divine method, is sleep's gentler brother.

"Death, a severing of the physical and spiritual copartnership, is life's holiest prophecy of future progress.

"Death is the rusted key that unlocks the shining portals of immortality.

"Death is the glittering hyphen-link that conjoins the two worlds of conscious existence and holy communion.

"Death is like opening rosebuds, that, in ever-recurring Junes, climb up on garden walls, and, blooming, shed their sweetest fragance upon the other side.

"Just as well ask the blade of wheat to return to the kernel, or the singing bird to its old shell, as a freed, immortalized spirit to the disintegrated physical body at some supposed future resurrection-day.

"Behold Faith, trimming her lamps in the darkness of the grave! Tears are crystallizing into celestial dews.

"All of earth's mortals enter the future state of existence mentally, morally, spiritually, as they left this, retaining their identity. Death imparts no new faculties. It is no saviour; only a transitional agent, introducing pilgrims and students into some higher department of the Father's mansions. Salvation is a process, a divine method of the soul's unfoldment, attained through obedience to the perfect laws of God."

"THE DEPARTURE OF CHILDREN.

"'Did the angels have a funeral, mother, when I left heaven, and came to earth to live?' asked a precocious child. It was a soul question, a cognition of pre-existence. The coming and going of infants, like descending and ascending waves upon a measureless ocean, are parts of the Infinite purpose. Nature would not have all the buds and blossoms of orchards mature in ripened fruitage: so the tree of life lets some of its tenderest buds droop and fall, to bloom in the gardens of the angels. Those airs are more soft and balmy, those climes more sunny. There is no lovelier sight than an infant's form encoffined for the tomb. Spirits, through trance and inspirational media, should speak upon such occasions. The burial should be in morning time. No dark procession, no tolling of bells, no gloomy looks, should mark the quiet passage to the grave; but, dressed in holiday attire, and garlanded with the freshest, brightest flowers of spring, the sleeping body should be borne to rest. Glad songs should be sung; joyous music should ring out upon the air; and pleasantly, as to a festival, the gathered group should go its way, feeling that the child is not dead, but gone before, — gone to the loveland lyceums of heaven.

"Weeping, mourning, and darkened drapery are no signs of intense sorrow; but rather of doubt and atheism. Much of mourning is rooted in selfishness. The more external, the more conspicuous the weeping. Displays at funerals are as common as unchristian; sham and show, going with the superficial to the very threshold of the sepulcher. There are sorrows too deep for tears, as there are prayers too divine for utterance. The fond Mexican mother, relying upon weird, ancestral traditions and the teachings of Nature, 'who has household treasures laid away in the *campo santo*, — God's sacred field, — breathes a sweet faith only heard elsewhere in the poet's utterance,' or the Spiritualist's philosophy of immortality. Ask her how many children bless her house, and she will answer, 'Five; two here and three yonder:' so, notwithstanding death and the grave, it is yet an unbroken household; and the trusting mother ever lives the thought, —

"'We are all here, — father, mother,
Sister, brother, all who hold each other dear.'

"When children are disrobed of the earthly, their spirits are borne to spheres of innocence, and there received by heavenly matrons and good angels to be educated. Oh, how those angelic beings, full of affection, delight to teach infants and little children, such as Jesus took in his arms, saying, 'Of such is the kingdom of heaven'! Variety is a necessity in all worlds. Heaven would not be heaven without children. It would lack the joyousness of childish innocence and educational progress. Our departed children, — aye, ours still, — buds of spirit-beauty; lights in the windows of heaven; the angels of the future!"

"A SONG FOR THE SAD.

"'Our heart is brimming with songs to-night. We would sing them to the sad. Take my hand, weary pilgrim: it is a brother's. Off with all masks; away with reserve. Tell me of life's uneven voyage, — its blighted hopes, piercing thorns, trials, losses, defeats, struggles, and disappointments. There is profit in confessions that bare soul to soul. Neither of us has secrets. All lives are unrolled scrolls, open to spirit inspection. Each is his own recording angel, and memories are immortal. What you are, I am, or have been. What you have felt, I have felt in my dual life-experience along some segmentary portion of the endless circle of being. Go on: I sense, feel, your life-history. It is wild, weird, witching, and big with the blessings of suffering. Now, all told, the good and ill measured, with their necessary compensations, has it not been glorious to live, — to live a thinking, reasoning, conscious, and immortal individuality, with infinite possibilities before you? Could you afford to lose the rusted links even from the chain that connects past and present? Have you not gathered and treasured rich experiences, that will serve, through you, to strengthen others in their weakness and their peril? Have you not seen more flowers than thorns; smiles, than tears; suns, than clouds; and have you not heard more blessings than cursings, and a thousand merry peals of laughter for a single groan?

"Has thy life been stained and blemished? None are perfect; the best have their failings: despair not; the good of earth, and the sainted in the heavens, delight to aid the aspirational. 'Come unto me,' said Jesus. The angels echo the song, come, 'Come up higher.' Look not to the past with painful regrets. In ascending a ladder, the wise never look down to the broken rounds. Every step the prodigal son took in the outward from his father's house was spiritually a step toward it. Husks helped bring him to 'himself.' When himself, he was right, human nature being innately good. This prodigal's bitter experiences of hunger, want, suffering, proved eminently salvatory. The good father loved the repentant son none the less for his wanderings. God, angels, all good men, love the erring. A mother's prayers pierce dungeon bars. The philanthropist hopes for all, loves all, has faith in all.

"No oak, lifting its head, catching and kissing the sunbeams, regrets that it was once an acorn, and fell, — fell into the mud, to be buried, bruised, chilled, and frosted with snows. Progression implies a lower condition to progress from. It was wisdom not to commence conscious life on the physical side perfect. Those fixed stars, that gild measureless distances, shine and sing all the sweeter from having been nebulous fire-mists, floating in oceanic space: so noble-purposed souls, tempted, falling like the child in the effort to walk, yet rising, wiser for the pain, stronger in will-power, treading the winepress of the world's wrath alone to-day, stopping by the wayside to-morrow to help the more unfortunate, will find their path ultimately widening, brightening, and opening at last into the shining portals of immortality, where peals of victory shall blend with the grand oratorios of souls long housed in the heavens: —

"'Men saw the thorns on Jesus' brow,
But angels saw the roses.'

"The Nazarene, though ever attended by ministering angels, shrank from the pain of the thorn-crown. Father, 'Let the cup pass;' thus he prayed: thus ever prays earthly weakness. 'Not my will, but thine, be done,' responded the divinity, the Christ-principle within.

"Carbon shrinks from the fierce chemical fires that transform it to diamonds. Flax-fields tremble at the transitional methods necessary to white linen napkins; and youthful sailors would fain shun the rough oceans requisite to making them skillful mariners. Mortals are but children in the eyes of the angels. Beautiful is the divine plan, with its infinitely-diversified methods of soul-discipline. There was never a birth without agony; a beautiful bloom without an aching, swelling bud; a musical instrument, — lute, lyre, or harp, — without grating, tuning processes; and even 'craftsmen,' and mystics in their upward pilgrimages, meet with 'ruffians,' rough roads, repulses, and fiery ordeals, ere they pass the 'vails,' sit in the council chambers of the worthy, or rest in patriarchal tents. Aspiration and effort are the soul's jewels. Courage, brave ones: the gods help those that help themselves. Oh, it is grand to build the road we travel on; erect the ladders by which we ascend; carve our own mental statues on living, conscious forms; and construct our own homes in the upper kingdoms of beauty and blessedness!

"Come, then, barbed arrows and dark-winged sorrows! Ye are all masked angels, leading souls oft by strange, inverse ways through thorn-encircled doorways into the inner courts of the beatified; the golden temples of the gods, whose every soul-tear will be transformed to a pearl; every groan die away into music; every sigh prove to have been a fore-gleam of a seraphic smile, and the sweetest, divinest ideals of earth, the imperishable reals of eternity! Courage, then, fainting soul! Every winter hath its spring; every ocean, its glittering gems; every frost, its shining crystals; every thunder-storm, its compensating health; every cloud, its silver lining; every ruin, its twining vines; every wave-tossed ark, its dove; every blood-stained cross, its flower-wreathed crown; and for every paradise lost, there are thousands to be gained! Patiently wait, then; wait and labor; wait and trust. Yea, be courageous, brave, hopeful, joyous, happy; for a good God reigns. Eternity with its infinite glories is stretching in mellowed radiance before you; ministering angels are beckoning you onward, upward; and loving archangels, standing upon evergreen mountains, and amid the matchless splendors of summer-land scenes, with wreaths, palms, and glistening robes, are inviting and singing, 'Here's rest for the weary, and crowns for the worthy.' 'All these, and infinitely more than tongue can tell, shall be thine, O children of earth! when ye are worthy,' saith my angel. Good-night, dear pilgrim friends. Sweet dreams to you, and kind angel-watchers. We shall meet again."

CHAPTER XVI.

HEART-ECHOES.

> "It is a little thing to speak a word of common comfort,
> That by daily use hath almost lost its sense;
> Yet, on the ear of him who thought to die unmourned,
> 'Twill fall like choicest music."

LETTERS to our loved ones, not intended for the public eye, like words spoken in the ear with the music of love, always have soul in them. Artless is friendship; and how beautiful are its life-pictures! No one surely has a right to refuse the world the aroma of these flowers, all a-drip with the morning light.

Mr. Peebles's private correspondence has been immense, with people of every profession of life. One of his bosom friends, with whom he has had intimate relation, both in letters and direct co-operation, is Hon. J. G. Wait of Sturgis, Mich., of whom he delights to speak "as a counselor and solid pillar in the spiritual temple." He loves to recall the happy interviews with Revs. Higginson, Towne, Frothingham, Henry Ward Beecher, and with the political honorables who rendered him favors connected with the spiritual gospel, — Sec. Fish, Howard of Michigan, Harris of Louisiana, and Prof. Worthen, state geologist of Illinois.

"COURTLAND, N.Y., Jan. 31, 1863.

"DEAR MR. PEEBLES, — Have you forgotten taking a young man aside in Courtland, several years ago, and telling him the very thoughts of his soul? Oh, those kind, hopeful words! God only knows how much I owe you for the interest you manifested at that trying period of my life. All that I am, or nearly so, I am indebted to you for. . . . Our publishing house is in a flourishing condition.

"Most sincerely, H. S. CLARKE."

"LA CROSSE, WIS., Sept. 3, 1863.

"MY DEAR PEEBLES, — This morning I received a kind letter from you, which took me in the arms of memory like a child back to the olden days of budding anticipations. Am glad to hear from you. My heart sinks down into old scenes, memories, and incidents, as one sinks to rest in a bed of down. The printing-office; the ride to Athens;

the scared woman whose babies and pigs we *did not* run over; the visit to Towanda; the *improvement* to your sermon! Well, well, time has borne those days to the rear, and still the fight goes on.

"I am older than when last we met. My eyes are *wider open.* The world and I have skirmished and battled; but, on the whole, I am ahead. Glad to hear you are coming out this way. The heart is still in the same friendly place for you as of yore. . . .

"I shall publish one or two books before spring; and, as you will read them, you will have an idea of what kind of a man (in theory) the *boy* you used to speak so kindly to in the East makes in the West. Write me. . . .

"With the best, earnest wishes for your health, happiness, and prosperity,

"I am the same, MARK M. POMEROY,

"Otherwise 'Brick' Pomeroy."

A lady friend, M. E. Tillotson, of Binghamton, N.Y., in a letter of Oct. 2, 1864, recalling the dreamy past, sends Mr. Peebles this poetic *billet-doux :* —

"I mind me of a quiet home
By sweet affection warm;
I mind me of a cozy nook
All sheltered from the storm,
Where oft in childhood's hour I sat,
And mused upon the story
Of a Saviour in a manger born,
The cross his crowning glory."

The following note from Bishop Clark (Episcopalian) was addressed our "Peace Brother," L. K. Joslyn, who introduced Mr. Peebles to him as a "Representative Spiritualist:" —

"PROVIDENCE, Dec. 10, 1864.

"DEAR SIR, — I shall be happy to see the Rev. Mr. Peebles at any time that he may find it convenient to call. I expect to be absent from town on Tuesday, and until the latter part of the week. I mention this in order that he may not call while I am away

"Respectfully yours, THOMAS M. CLARK."

Speaking of the conversation with Mr. Clark, about the truth of spirit manifestation, Mr. Peebles reports him as saying, —

"'*You* are just designed to traverse the country, and scatter seed to get the golden fruit: but I,' said the bishop, 'instead of scattering the seed, am content to graft into the old trunk; and, if I put in too many grafts, they will absorb the juices and spoil the whole tree.'"

The author of this is the wife of Rev. C. F. Dodge (Universalist). She accompanied it with an accurate and interesting psychometric delineation of our Pilgrim's attributes of character: —

"PALMYRA, WIS., June 19, 1865.

"DEAR BROTHER AND FRIEND, — . . . I thank you for the interest manifest in our behalf. I hear the words, 'Come up higher;' but the way I know not. I felt strengthened by your presence and teachings, during the brief visit, and felt then as if I would say '*out loud*,' 'I am a Spiritualist.' If I understand my own heart, I have but little sympathy with the creeds now prevailing, — can not feel the interest in denominational matters that I once did. *The scale* seems to me an ascending one. . . . Your visit here was a streak of sunshine to my sister, Mrs. Bunker, as well as to us.

"Truly yours, C. H. DODGE."

Wishing to post himself in the standard ancient works, Mr. Peebles, in the fall of 1865, called on Ralph Waldo Emerson, the New-England Plato, whose life-philosophy is so spiritual. Giving him the desired literary information, these moralizers talked about the "Spiritual movement." Writing of this happy interview, Mr. Peebles reports, —

"This 'Sage of Concord' said, 'The *universe* is to me one grand spirit manifestation; . . . but as to the minor, the specialities so to speak, I shall have to refer you to Mrs. Emerson, who is much interested in these spiritual matters.'"

"CHICAGO, March 10, 1866.

"DEAR BROTHER, — I was just thinking how patient God must have been to wait so long for fullest working out of ultimates from commingling primates. And then I thought the reason why is obvious enough; because He sees a *principle*. Those only lack faith and get out of patience, who have not entered into 'the holy of holies' of ever-unfolding life. To *understand* a *principle* is *eternal life*. No man can have pure 'Platonic love,' unless he has climbed the topmost peak of unfolded *principle*. . . .

"'The truth shall make you free.' The unfolding of principle shall make you free. Nobody can bear and forbear, up to the divine standard of human needs, unless he sees clearly into, and all the way through, the *principle*, or the *nature*, of things. Nobody can comprehend the divine standard which turns the 'other cheek,' except him who has learned beyond the region of approximates. . . . You are the vacuum of appreciation into which my spirit can flow and find a resting-place. SETH PAINE."

"STURGIS, MICH., June 24, 1866.

. . . "MY DEAR BROTHER PEEBLES, — Yes: I think we shall have a good time at the State Convention in Battle Creek. We certainly shall if we are all in the right spirit; if we seek not any personal end, but only the amelioration and elevation of ourselves and our fellow-men. I know *you*, at least, will so seek the precious good of our dear humanity. My country is the world; my kindred, all mankind; and, though we are all imperfect, I feel that most of us who will gather there will come to the great work of the age.

"Cordially, SELDEN J. FINNEY."

"CHICAGO, Sept. 21, 1866.

"ESTEEMED BROTHER J. M. PEEBLES, — . . . How cheering! we have in our midst noble souls, whose tested morality, purified sympathies, and holy affections combine in earnest, practical work, — whose influence casts the shadow of sunshine. . . Were it not for this fact, the bitterness of the dark side of Spiritualism would cause us to retire from public labors, sorrowful at the tardy movements of so-called reformers. But the issues of the hour bid us be faithful at the post of duty, discriminating between the true and the false, within and without. ALCINDA WILHELM."

"PUTNAM, Oct 9, 1866.

"DEAR BROTHER PEEBLES, — God bless you for your kind letter, so much needed. How I love your beautiful teachings! It seems as though you are my elder brother; and I can come to you for counsel. . . . Thine, A. E. CARPENTER." *

"BRIDGEWATER, VT., Oct. 12, 1866.

"BROTHER PEEBLES, — . . . You say you are 'almost a Shaker in theory, perfectly so in practice;' that the idea of freedom of the affections 'has been a bone of contention,'" &c. I believe in freedom of affection; but not indulgence of *lusts* under the name of *Love*. . . . To me, the honest recognition of this philosophy of soul-union is of the utmost importance. When men believe it, they will not degrade their manhood, and *insult* the brute creation with such indulgences as now fill the land with depravity. . . . There *then* will not be as many divorce cases as now. . . . May the dear angels bless you and keep you as pure, true, and good as I know your soul desires to be!

"M. S. TOWNSEND."

The following extract was written just after the stormy convention of Spiritualists in Chicago. The author was formerly one of the editors of "The Spiritual Age." Has not the able brother told us the truth? Has there not been a "daubing with untempered mortar?"

"WASHINGTON, D.C., Oct. 25.

"DEAR BROTHER PEEBLES, — . . . An organization is not to come by throwing together a heterogeneous mass of antagonistic materials, expecting them to fall into order and harmonious combinations. Nature's method, God's method, is different. A little seed, or nucleus of life, is deposited; and this attracts to itself such materials as are fit and proper to constitute the body to be built. So, if there is to be an organization among the crude materials of the Spiritualistic field, it must come of the deposit of a germ of vital truth, first in individual hearts, — or, perhaps, in *an* individual heart, — so vital as to attract around it by slow concretion the individual particles that will form a living and powerful body. I have no faith in the *Convention*-al method. It will eventuate in nothing but the formation of, at best, a lifeless body, an external shell, not pervaded by the living spirit. Let these little *nuclei* begin to be formed, and I shall have some hope. But these must not be mere *financial* organizations, — "to sustain a free platform," — on which a babel of contradictions may be enunciated. There must be a basis or center of vital yet catholic truth, — something *positive*, and not merely *negative*, — something which shall be esteemed of more value than all things else, — something which shall pervade and control the *daily life* of the believer. . . .

"Our meetings are got up too much on the *star* system of theatrical managers. Speakers are employed to *draw*, not to tell practical truths, or to develop a practical form of faith, or lead the way to a divine life. . . . I earnestly recommend you for Washington, and am glad you are engaged. I anticipate much from your coming.

"Yours truly, A. E. NEWTON."

* This brother has been for years the efficient missionary for the Spiritualists of Massachusetts.

These words of our sister, an efficient physician, have a ring of perfect steel, pure and clear in fiber, divinely practical. Millions will thank "Lucinda" for this beautiful letter, thus, to her surprise, made justly public: —

"DETROIT, MICH., Nov. 28, 1866.

"DEAR BROTHER PEEBLES, — Your last two sermons in Detroit gave me inexpressible joy and hope; because of their plainness upon that subject which, it seems to me, lies at the foundation of human progress. I mean the righteous generation of human beings. I want to bless you for your bravery in ascribing the beauty of Christ's character, to some extent at least, to his antenatal conditions.

"But (pardon me) in the evening, when you spoke so forcibly, and I think so truly, of the sin against blasted human buds, did you not stop just where it might be inferred that the guilt rested mainly on the mother?

"I know your heart is right here as everywhere, and doubtless your head too; and I will not say it is your duty to go farther in public: you and your guides know best. But I have felt impelled, for the sake of the thousands of overtaxed, unloved, suffering, must I say *outraged* wives, to beseech you to be faithful to husbands. If not in public, then in private, arrest their attention in some way. Men can control this whole matter if they will; and I have faith enough in human nature to believe 'tis not so much depravity as ignorance that prevents. Then give them light. When women have no unasked children, there will be no more murdered ones. If the soul becomes immortal at conception, 'tis but a step to the truth that there should be no waste of the life-forces. I am glad, thrice glad, that you accept that truth. I almost think, when that is generally accepted in heart and life, the world will be saved.

"Am I presuming in giving you these hints? if so, my love for humanity, my earnest desire to see the race lifted from ignorance and death into light, life, and happiness, must be my apology.

"Now, permit me to say, not to flatter, but to inspire, — few, *very* few are so well prepared to handle this whole subject as yourself. Your psychological power over an audience, your personal purity and delicacy, fit you admirably for the task. I can not but feel that this duty, in a peculiar manner, is resting upon you, and, when well performed, one of the brightest, sweetest buds in the wreath placed by the archangel on the brow of the youth, will have unfolded to shed its beauty and fragrance on a grateful world.

God bless you, in the inner and the outer man, and make you ever more and more useful, is the prayer of Your friend,

"LUCINDA S. WILCOX."

"CROWN POINT, IND., Feb. 15, 1867.

"MY DEAR BROTHER, — . . . As time bears us on through this world, I feel more and more your brotherly spirit. There is one soul linked with another in golden chains, riveted with the saintly hands of angels. All that I am I owe to you.

"LT. H. E. LUTHER."

"MOUNT LEBANON, May 17, 1867.

"J. M. PEEBLES: *My Esteemed Friend*, — I have just read an article in the Western Department of "The Banner of Light," which no man in the outer court of the temple of the Lord on earth but yourself could write.

"You are a blessing to your race, a living spring in the desert of Korah. It is truly comforting to my sin-wearied soul to read such words as the article referred to contains.

"Go on; and be it your mission to teach the holy truth of the existence of a *Resurrection Order*, of which Jesus was but the type to this generation; and many will hear and read, and believe and bless. When they find that on earth they may rise with Christ, or rather Jesus, into an angelic estate to love God with all their hearts, and that they have no need of any lust of the flesh or mind to make them complete in happiness in time as in eternity.

"I send you my love, for your love of purity.

"We have just received a visit from an editor of the Agriculturist Department of "The Tribune," N. C. Meeker, a man like minded with yourself.

"Your friend, F. W. EVANS."

"PENN YAN, N.Y., Nov. 5, 1867.

"MY DEAR BROTHER J. M. PEEBLES, — It is now nearly ten years since you came to me in Battle Creek, and kindly laid your hand upon my shoulder, speaking in my ear the first words of true, manly friendship that I ever heard. I then doubted you. I judged you by my past experiences; but you taught me the world is not all pretension. I oftentimes think that my life was a stupendous vision, or half-wakeful dream, up to the very hour I first met you. Then and there the sunlight of usefulness shone upon me. Then my guiding star wheeled me into a new orbit, while over your luminous path I cast a dark shadow. Faithful to the charge intrusted to your care by the angel 'Morning Star,' you held out firm to the end, until time by its reward proved your labors not in vain. With a heart overflowing with deepest gratitude, I remember all this. . . .

"My audiences are increasing. May the blessings of God's ministering angels rest upon you!

"Thank God and the good angels, the battle is past, the race is won, and the victory is ours! "Your sincere brother, E. C. DUNN."

"BUFFALO, N.Y., Jan. 17, 1868.

"J. M. PEEBLES: *Dear Sir*, — . . . I must tell you how deeply I have been pondering your little sermon, 'An apple is good for nothing, if it falls off before it ripens.' So I mean to hang on; for Heaven knows I am green enough. . . .

"You spoke to me of a volume you expect to issue, 'Spiritualism among the poets.' Pardon me for asking if your attention has been particularly directed to William Blake, artist and poet of Queen Elizabeth's day, I think. He claimed to get both poems and pictures, you recollect, from angels; and gave proof enough in his works, I should judge, of the verity of his claim.

"When I was a little girl, his simple rhymes that prefaced 'Mary had a little lamb,' were sweet to me as wild honey. You recollect, —

'Piping down the valleys wild, —
Piping songs of pleasant glee, —
On a cloud I saw a child,
And he, laughing, said to me,' &c.

Fit beginning for a poem with so heavenly a moral, 'Why, Mary loves the lamb, you know.' "Very respectfully, AMANDA T. JONES."

"NEW YORK, Sept. 11, 1868.

"MY DEAR BROTHER J. M. PEEBLES, — . . . If you can use me in any way, only say so. Time, money, the legal profession, any thing at your command that man can accomplish, I will promise to do for you. . . . With the help of higher power, ere long,

I trust, you may hear of your young disciple, whom you caused first to look into this great and glorious subject of Spiritualism. . . .

"Yours fraternally, GEO. M. DANFORTH."

"NEW YORK, Sept. 26, 1868.

"DEAR FRIEND PEEBLES, — How often I think of you, of your blessed work. You saved me spiritually. . . . Your articles in "The Banner," replete with thoughts ennobling, afford me much happiness. The one concerning 'Demons, obsessions,' &c., I read with great interest. *Bless you*, brother! The angels, I believe, from the *choice* fields of thought and wisdom, cull for you both *blossoms* and the *sweets* to shed upon your life, — so full and abundant does it appear.

"Your very true friend, MILTON RATHBUN."

Rev. Geo. Severance, of Glover, Vt., Universalist, corresponded with Mr. Peebles. In a letter of June 13, 1869, after a kind allusion to Rev. Eli Ballou, editor of "The (Universalist) Repository," as a Spiritualistic brother, whom Mr. Peebles favorably noticed, he said, —

"The value of Spiritualism consists in the fact, we have access to the other world, and can judge of the nature and character of its inhabitants. The revelations of Spiritualism on this point are worth more than all the bibles and treatises that have been written from the old point of view. We can see now how the sacred books of the Oriental nations originated. We can look upon Buddha, Zoroaster, Moses, Mohammed, and all the old worthies, not as impostors, but as men moved and inspired by the spirit-hosts of the departed of their respective nations."

When N. B. Starr had painted "John" for Mr. Peebles, he, the artist, gave him these words: —

"Go forth, my son, in the might and power of truth. Dare and *do* all things for God and humanity; and so am I ever with thee. Amen! JOHN."

"EAGLE HARBOR, N.Y., Sept. 26, 1870.

"MY DEAR BROTHER PEEBLES, — . . . You speak of my being at McLean, the scene of your labors. Yes: I heard of you everywhere; and, in preparing for your saintship, it would be well to settle the still open question, where you preached your first sermon? I was assured, at Kelloggsville, that it was there. At McLean, I was informed by several, that your first public utterance was heard there; and when I got to Mr. Larned's, at Peruville, he assured me that I was in the house and the identical room in which the said first sermon was delivered. Well, wheresoever it was, I was delighted at so much hearty appreciation. . . . "Yours truly, A. C. WOODRUFF."

Emma C. Odiorne and her friend Carrie M. Grimes, "literary, and pure in heart," called Mr. Peebles "Spiritual Father," because of his kind counsel and moral instruction. "Emma," now living in the spirit-world, addressed him beautiful poetry, from which we quote: —

> "Steady, earnest, firm of purpose,
> Thine the power to aid and guide
> Souls, that, wavering, stand beside thee,
> Trembling on Life's rolling tide."

Mediums — dear sufferers in this fighting world, precious links in the living chain let down from angels — everywhere receive Mr. Peebles's deepest sympathy and co-operation. Better than all others, they sun themselves in the spheres of the benevolent.

CHAPTER XVII.

THE WORKER AND HIS WORKS.

"Some souls are descended directly from the line of archangels who have tasted the fruits of the gods, and are alone immortal." — CORA L. V. TAPPAN.

THOUGH taxed with labors in a thousand ways, connected with "The Banner of Light," correspondence, lecturing, and other duties, Mr. Peebles resolved to edit a book on "Spiritualism," whose historic materials he had been gleaning for years. We suggested that another work was then more essential for the spiritual public, — a singing-book. Both of us seemed to be blind to the responsibility. A certain angel was accustomed to play upon a *harp;* so he said "Call it '*The Spiritual Harp.*'" One year of great toil, with the co-operation of Prof. E. H. Bailey, and the brain-wearying task was performed. It appeared in the market Sept. 1, 1868: Wm. White & Co., publishers. "It is a success," said Theodore Tilton, of the New-York "Independent;" and so it has proved.

The "Harp" finished, Mr. Peebles immediately wrote a sparkling pamphlet, entitled, "The Practical of Spiritualism: a Biographical Sketch of Abraham James, and Historic Description of his Oil-Well Discoveries in Pleasantville, Pa., through Spirit Direction." Here was a happy blending of the spiritual with the practical, demonstrating that the spiritual philosophy is destined to open up the hidden wealth of earth in mines, oils, gases, plants, jewels, and be, in the hands of inventors and mechanics, the science and rule of new improvements in human industries.

In September of 1868, full of enthusiasm as ever, Mr. Peebles determined to complete his great work, and came to our "sweet home" in Sycamore, Ill., with his huge piles of manuscripts and monster trunk, whose weight of precious books has caused many a hackman and porter to swear with an unction of blessing right in his face, one fellow suggesting that his punishment be to "carry that trunk on his back all over hell once a year!" Traveling with many books *is* a sin against muscles and economy. "Light luggage as possible with convenience" was the after motto of the "Pilgrim:" "beware how we provoke profanity!" Sundays he lectured in Chicago to increasing audiences; week-days he was at our table, both working, *vis-a-vis*, under a power of inspiration that seemed to open the flood-gates of heaven. In four weeks the manuscripts of the "Seers of the Ages" were in the hands of the printers. *Presto change!* Off again he flew to St. Louis for a masterly effort there, lecturing on the angel gospels. "Seers of the Ages" is read in every part of the enlightened world, and is cherished with gratitude to the author for his "pure and lofty sentiment."

When all these books were in the market, another duty was imposed by the angels. It was a "Thus saith John." We both felt a cloud of tears that burst overhead.

The "Lyceum Guide," whose name "suggested itself," is "the prophetic charge, battle, and victory." With this promise we pressed forward, the angels selecting for us the necessary help to give it diversity. James G. Clark, the American ballad-singer, and Emma Tuttle, the sweet poetess of Berlin Heights, Ohio, were added to the band of authors. With perfect harmony we all wrought, each in an appropriate sphere, for a full year; the patterns being given "on the Mount," with instructions to preserve the Lyceum system, projected from the spirit-world, and impressed upon the sensitive mind of A. J. Davis and others. It has made its debut in the critical market, and is running the race demarked by the heavenly counsellors: Adams & Co. of Boston, with J. Burns of London, imprint, its guardian publishers.

We extract from "The Banner of Light," Mr. Peebles's summing up of labors, simply for one year: —

After alluding to his public writings and private correspondence, and the books just mentioned, he says, —

"Have attended several grove-meetings, three State conventions, and the National convention in Rochester, N.Y. Lecturing each Sunday, save one, have spoken in these different localities: Hammonton, Philadelphia, New York, Brooklyn, Charlestown, Boston, Worcester, Buffalo, Pleasantville, Titusville, Milan, Battle Creek, Omaha, Springfield, Topeka, Chicago, and these last two months in St. Louis. Have attended twenty-nine funerals, and have been present at eight weddings, performing the ceremony.

"Hope to accomplish more during 1869. The field is the world. Spiritualism is the great living movement of the age. Its watchword progress, its triumph is certain. What the recompense for untiring labors in the reform-fields of the times? Let the patriotic and self-sacrificing Garibaldi answer: 'In recompense for the love you may show your country, I offer you hunger, thirst, cold, war, and death; who accepts these terms, let them follow me.'.

"The future is all star-gemmed and rainbow-crowned. Let us on, then, brave soldiers, fighting the good fight of faith, wielding the sword of the Spirit. Under and in sympathy with the bannered hosts of God over us, let us on to victory."

The following, from friendly letters meant only for private eyes, index the business of the man in the sphere he fills; whose example here will certainly evoke ambition to "Go thou, and do likewise:" —

"BATTLE CREEK, Dec. 29, 1858.

. . . "The day is dark and dull, but my spirit is bright and strong to battle for the right, and the upbuilding of the Harmonial Dispensation. Last Sunday, labored in Chicago. Had a good time. Saw Mr. and Mrs. Anderson of Lasalle, Ill., mediums. He is a spirit portrait-painter. Through him, in an hour and about three minutes, I got a picture of Powhattan, my dear Indian friend. He is a noble-looking spirit, though an Indian all over. Tell 'Nellie' to send back my sister's heart. Spiritualists should not steal."

"NORTH COLLINS, PA., July 5, 1864.

"MY DEAR CHARLIE, — . . . My lectures in New York (thanks to John and the circle) were a perfect success. When I was through the second evening, Brother A. J. Davis came on to the rostrum, and said these kind words: 'You dear brother, you have baptized us with the very love-dews of heaven. You have twined yourself around all our hearts, and left your blessing with us for ever.' I had a splendid time at his house. His nature combines the simplicity of a child with the metaphysical acumen of the philosopher. I spent some time with Judge Edmonds and Madame d'Obeney, the greatest woman traveler of the age. Her description of Mt. Vesuvius and the Pyramids was grand. Oh, I almost want to run away, and travel in Asia!"

"PROVIDENCE, Dec. 14, 1864.

. . . "Senator Sprague is a Liberalist; his mother, a very devoted Spiritualist. To-morrow I spend the afternoon at their green-house. In winter a green-house is next door to heaven."

"NEW YORK, Feb. 9, 1865.

"J. M. is himself again. Has passed the 'second watch, and, though roughly handled, trusting in his guide, reached 'Mount Repose.' . . .

"Last Sunday, ten mediums gave me their cards, offering to give me their 'sittings;' but I think some of them, *in their souls*, wanted me to 'puff' them in 'The Banner of Light' more than any thing else. Still, I appreciate their kindness, and should more, if they did not 'daub' on the *flattery* so thick. I am not 'an angel scattering sunshine,' but an angular and inharmonious man, doing what I can, as aided by my circle, for humanity. . . .

"Oh, that I had a body that my soul could use! The truth is, I am too submitting, too much afraid of making people trouble. . . . It was very kind in you, brother, to inquire after my 'purse.' I need somebody to keep it for me, and always did. It costs me nearly all I make to pay traveling expenses.

"Be cautious, my brother, what you say to women and men. Think before you speak."

"MILWAUKIE, April 10, 1865.

. . . "The bells are ringing and cannon thundering in honor of the surrender of Lee's army to Grant. Well, I shall rejoice in peace; for deep in my soul do I love it."

"SHEBOYGAN FALLS, WIS., April 20, 1865.

. . . "My life has been a struggle, a battle. It probably ever will be, though mediums are continually volunteering their services to point out flowers, smiles, and prosperity just ahead. I am coldly unmoved and skeptical to their beautiful pictures. It is Emersonian to accommodate one's self to fate. . . . I would rather talk with Aaron Nite than eat, or drink when thirsty; but I find I can live and enjoy myself without any verbal conversation with him. It is probably at times best, as it inspires me to entertain myself, and further acquaint myself with the knowledge and book-wisdom of this world, knowing there is an eternity for me 'Over the River' to study its mysteries under the teachership of 'John the Beloved.' I suppose the self-poised, well-balanced man is never alone, never inclined to give up or despair; for he feels that law, destiny, fate, are over all, and 'all is for the best.' . . . I laugh at each pang. 'Better that I suffer than cause any one else to suffer;' so says John."

"BATTLE CREEK, June 16, 1865.

. . . "My more ancient spirit-friends have kept me among the rubbish of old historians with reference to the ancient civilizations, say twelve and fifteen thousand years ago. . . .

"I am crowded with business, — so crowded that I know not which way to turn. During last week, I had invitations to attend four grove-meetings (Dewitt, Charlotte, Livonia, and one in Indiana). I refused them *all*, and also a pressing invitation to attend the two-days' anniversary in Sturgis this week, — Saturday and Sunday. Must write, instead of tramp, tramp, so much!

"On the Fourth, I deliver an oration in Laphamville, Mich.; am also urged to give a temperance address in Valparaiso, at a festival. There's no end to these *calls:* I should like to be in the spirit-world, and have about five mediums to control; think I could keep them all busy, after getting the 'hang' of the *machines.*"

. . . "I like some of Dr. C. A. Andros's spirit-controls much. One, an ancient Jew, is keen and sharp as steel, and he fairly got the better of me on one point in an argument."

"BOSTON, MASS., Monday after Convention at Providence, R.I.

. . . "Am weary and worn out, tired of shaking hands, tired of being on committees, tired of talking, and sigh for the quiet of a pleasant old pine forest. The convention was a great success: you ought to have been present. It accomplished much. Report will be in the 'Banner.' . . . The convention was high-toned. Father Pierpont was in his glory. He has since gone to glory! Dear saint, he: I loved, — still love him."

"WORCESTER, Aug. 23, 1865.

. . . "I have visited my dear parents, spending several days, and shall go again. Father is feeble. . . . I am with Dr. O. Martin, where I always enjoy myself gloriously. His garden is full of pears, reminding me constantly of Brother Nite; his house full of books; he has always a seat for me in his carriage. He has removed the obstruction in my ear, just forward of the tympanum, with an instrument and by syringing with warm water, so that I can hear all right. The doctor knows something; but I would give any thing to have Dr. Schwailbach take him 'down the banks' — medically — just once.

"Next Sunday I am to speak in Plymouth, ever memorable as the landing-place of the Pilgrims. It is the Mecca of the Congregationalists."

"BATTLE CREEK, Dec. 20, 1865.

"BROTHER * * * * — Home at last; dearest spot too. . . . Found your letter awaiting me. God bless you, preserve you, and angels hold you in charge! You are my soul-brother. I love you, and can not help it: hence there is no merit, is there? Wish you were here to 'lay hands' on my weak eyes; that would test your apostleship. They are some better, however. You say 'rest, *rest*.' Dear brother, there's no rest this side the grave. Calls and correspondence are continually widening. How true, '*Life is real!*' My unseen angel and inspiring influence tell me, that we have yet a work to do in concert: I believe it."

"BATTLE CREEK, Aug. 3, 1866.

. . . "The State Convention passed off finely. Finney, Whipple, Jameison, Wadsworth, Barrett, Wheelock, Harrison, Andros, were present as speakers; and all spoke well. Being sick, I rode down to every session, and sat in a rocking-chair. I fully appreciate what you say about my body's being frail and tender. More and more I am conscious of it; and I tell you, it is not worth 'fussing' with much longer. Only think, forty-four years I have borne around the *shell*. It's about time I 'kicked' out of it. Only the consideration of work undone reconciles me to patch up the frame and tarry."

"WASHINGTON, D.C., Jan. 18, 1867.

. . . "Last week I went to the President's reception; shook his hand. To-morrow, I go to his residence with Maj. —— a friend at court, to spend a couple of hours in conversation. Senators, and more or less members of the lower house, attend our Sunday meetings regularly. Ross, chief of the Cherokees, called on me night before last. He brought with him 'Bushy Head,' and another Indian chief."

"BATTLE CREEK, April 19, 1867.

. . . "I shall expect to edit a paper for earth, when I cross Jordan, — why not? . . . I went to Chicago the first of this week — sent for in haste — to be a pacificator. They are all in a 'mux' in 'The Spiritual Republic.'"

"DETROIT, Aug. 13, 1867.

. . "Sunday evening, after I was through speaking in Detroit, I was so weak — my lungs sore — I could hardly get home to my room. It annoys me, because I will not be able to do much, or say much, at the Cleveland convention. Already I have received several letters, asking me to frame certain resolutions, and put forward certain matters of importance. These conventions are far below my ideal."

"BATTLE CREEK, Oct. 22, 1867.

. . . "Am engaged 'packing up' for Hammonton, N.J. Out into the world! It chills me. I go West to-morrow; first to Springfield, then to St. Louis. . . . Have had a good time speaking here this month. Sunday evening they could not all get into the hall. Had I been a stranger-speaker here, it would have been natural enough; but living here eleven years, and speaking so much, it seemed good — or queer. The work broadens. Where is the end? . . . Some time in December next, the young men (Unitarians) of Meadville College want me to come and give them a course of lectures on Spiritualism. . . . Say to Brother Nite that he will post himself in regard to Zoroaster. I propose to ask him to let his light shine.

"BUFFALO, Dec. 7, 1867.

. . . "Christmas Eve, I am to marry a couple in Boston; Christmas Day, the spirit-artist, N. B. Starr, comes to meet me. Next day shall be in 'Banner' office, settling up year's account. Friday eve, lecture before a literary society in Ashland. Sunday, speak in Taunton. New Year's, in New York; marry a couple there, — Dr. M. H. Houghton to an interesting lady of Vermont. Then to Hammonton, N. J., to see family; and thence to Washington for a month. So I go through the world, writing on the wing."

"DETROIT, Feb. 6, 1869.

. . . "Am in the midst of a spiritual revival. The Lord is on the 'giving hand. Our choir is magnificent, — congregational singing. Read a service from the 'Harp, morning and evening. It is beautiful."

It is a spiritual law, that whom we defend in adversity we love. There is a place in our Pilgrim's soul for the names of Charles A. Hayden and Herman Snow. Speaking of them in a private note, Mr. Peebles says, —

"Brother Hayden, good and aspiring. It is noble in him, or any young man or lady, to seek the advantages of scholarship. The shield of character is all the tougher for some shafts of scorn. . . . We have bled in the same cause. . . . And there is Brother Herman Snow, — brother of our Lyceum sister, Mrs. J. S. Dodge of Chelsea, Mass., — once a Unitarian clergyman, now a Spiritualist of practical good sense. . . . We have fought in the same army, under official commissions from the angels. Up there, I shall be a witness on the defensive when the celestial court tries him! And this will be my plea: 'Worthy of admission, for he belongs to the divine church of humanity, having prayed in deeds of love. Let him in, Brother Peter!"

"BOSTON, June 4, 1869.

. . . "Why don't you write an editorial in 'The American Spiritualist' defensive of the poor Indians? See Hudson Tuttle's late article. Let us have all sides of the question. The Indians are God's natural children, and my brothers. They are fading away, however, as the red sunsets of autumn." . . .

"LOWELL, MASS., May, 1869.

. . . "Sunday in Lowell, city of spindles! Had a good meeting. Saw your friend, S. W. Foster. . . . I am more and more interested in the Shakers: they are so quiet, unassuming, neat, and pure-minded. . . . I pray God to keep me out of the lower strata of Boston magnetism. Oh, I look beyond for my support! and find repose, as J. H. Powell so gracefully says, in his 'Life Pictures,'—

"'In bowers of God, — where the citron and pearl,
Coral and crystal, diamond and beryl,
Passion-flower, pride of the spirit! and rose,
Gleam in a glory for ever that glows, —
Bright angels are waiting with love in their eyes;
Waiting for thee,
Where cedar and myrtle and lemon arise,
Under deep azure and gold-gleaming skies;
Waiting and singing, gayly and free,
Waiting for thee.'"

"St. Louis, Dec. 16, 1869.

"Friend Joseph, — On thy forehead the angels have written the words, '*True and faithful.*' The world is full of good men, good women. Why did you send me that proof just now? My inspiration is at a low ebb. Each has at times his Gethsemane. Just at present I am under a terrible cross-fire from the East and West, because of my articles defending the Indians. Kansas Spiritualists think my charity for the Indians is in excess of my justice or wisdom. There is seemingly a legion of Indian spirits about me now. They are to me physical life. . . . Have the within 'Memorial' in behalf of the Indians filled as soon as you can, and forward to Washington."

Naturally the query rises, What is the power that enables a frail mortal to accomplish so much? What the love-genius whispering, "Thus only canst thou win the heart of the angel who is thine?"

"'The battle of life,' says our Pilgrim, 'in a majority of cases must necessarily be fought up hill. To win the victory without a struggle would be to win it without honor. While difficulties intimidate the weak, they act only as stimulants to men of energy and resolution. A whining shiftlessness is absolutely despicable! Give us a *stirring* demon in preference to an easy, slow, sluggish, self-righteous saint.

"Upward evolutions are through effort. Every thing that grows — grasses, grains, forests — pushes upward against the law of gravitation. The higher is attained only through struggle. All the diverse experiences of life serve to demonstrate, that the impediments thrown in the way of individual advancement may be overcome by steady good conduct, honest convictions, active perseverance, and a determined resolution to surmount all difficulties, and stand up manfully against all misfortunes.

"Leaning, everlastingly leaning, upon somebody is soft and waxy as putty. Would to heaven we could infuse a moral decoction of spinal stiffening into the American multitude! Bless the man or woman that dares say *no*, and say it squarely! Strike out! Planting your feet upon the platform of eternal principles, fight Life's moral battles earnestly, sincerely, bravely; certain then will be the victory.

"'By the thorn-road, and no other,
Is the mount of triumph won.
Tread it without shrinking, brother:
Jesus trod it; press thou on!'"

Comparatively, Mr. Peebles is poor as to this world's goods. He loves not money, only for its beneficent use. He is a spiritual artist, —

"Building better than he knew,
The conscious stones to beauty grew."

There is a story told of a poor man of unbefriended association, honest and modest, faithful and pure-hearted, who was one day visited by a heavenly guest, a charming angel, clothed in the glories of exalted mind. He could find no language to picture such beauty to delight the world; and yet he felt a rising purpose thus to invite his fellows into the heaven he had entered by enraptured sight. With overwhelming inspiration, he attempted to carve out an image of that angel from the pure marble. He never lost the heavenly expression; for that angel came again and again, in divine posture, for him to copy. Long years he toiled, with diligent hand and delicate touches, and yet it was not finished; for a life-time could not thus delineate such beauty. One morning, his neighbors found the poor man dead beside his statue: his spirit had fled, his body was cold as his marble. Everybody said, "What a fool, to spend so much time so vainly!" But the angel looked into his soul, and lo! the image was there, fully developed; and he took it away to the heavenly temple, where it belonged, — a living form of spiritual beauty. Is not our Pilgrim working on the marble of character? Behold it, by and by!

"Build thee more stately mansions, O my soul!
As the swift seasons roll,
Leave thy low-vaulted Past!
Let each new temple, nobler than the last,
Shut thee from heaven with a dome more vast,
Till thou at length art free,
Leaving thine outworn shell by Life's unresting sea!"

CHAPTER XVIII.

THE OBSESSED WOMAN.

"Pause! her story soon is told:
Once a lamb within the fold;
Stranger voices lured her thence
In her spotless innocence."

Oh, the life-drifts of the human heart! oh, its tempest-tost waves, shivering cold upon the rocks! Whither bound upon this sea? A feeling may be the compass; a look enspheres. The smile that intoxicates makes room for a tear.

"Those tears will run
Soon in long rivers down the lifted face,
And leave the vision clear for stars and sun."

Read the inward law, so fearfully moral: "He that looketh on a woman to lust after her hath committed adultery already with her in his heart." The commerce of spheres, even in thought, is illicit, if the heart is lustful. Beware of the web the wary spirit weaves to steal virtue!

William Howitt, clear-headed and morally religious, after summing up an array of stubborn facts, says, in reference to "infestation:" —

"Nothing has become better known through the physico-spiritual experiences which have been taking place in thousands of spots on almost every quarter of the globe during the last twenty years, than that we can not only 'call spirits from the vasty deep,' but that they can come, when we do call (*and too often when we do not*), if they can but once quaff the vital spirit of the blood through us as mediums. They will come in legions, and in armies, only too glad to renew their connection with the material world. . . . They will come as if delighted to feel their hold once more on material force. . . . They will come with all their old characters, passions, and weaknesses, and revel in lies, in pretenses, in mystifications, and often in lawless fun, or even wicked and diabolical annoyances; showing that the regions lying close on the other side of the invisible boundary betwixt matter and spirit are still the counterpart of the regions on this side.

"Nothing is clearer than that those spirits who are haunting the very edge of this earth are still too much allied to it; are still earthly in mind and desire; are still longing, with a backward glance, 'for the flesh-pots of Egypt.' Like the souls of Gray's 'Elegy,' they have left the warm precincts of the cheerful day, but cast a longing, lingering look behind. As the tree falls, so it lies. As on earth they cultivated only the spirit and tone of the earth; as they gave up to it their whole soul, hope, ambition, and exertion; as they molded and incorporated their tastes, feelings, yearnings, and passions into its nature; as they heaped up its riches as an eternal trophy from which nothing could sever them, — they have stepped into the spirit-regions as aliens, having no possible heritage or enjoyment in them, except in so far as these resemble those from which they have lately been ejected. An intense and agonizing yearning draws them back to the old haunts and conditions of being; and they snatch with frenzied and convulsive fingers at whatever and whoever affords them the mediumistic means of regaining something, more or less, of the taste and consciousness of earth-life. Hence all the phenomena of possession and obsession which history has recorded, and which modern times have shown terrible examples of; hence the wild and frantic demonstrations of Morzine; hence cases of the most awful spiritual persecutions of particularly susceptible persons of to-day. These woful spirits, drenched with the sensuous elements of the life which they led on earth, — selfish as they were then to the very inmost depths of their natures, — rush with a reckless and gluttonness appetite into the tissues of unfortunately open constitutions, and exult in breathing, drinking in, gustating, with a cruel and relentless ardor, the sensations and odors of this mortal life once more. . . . But the vast inspirations from the malevolent and destructive which we have been remarking on result from no cultivation of Spiritualism. They operate unconsciously and independently on the masses, credulous or incredulous, educated or uneducated, refined or vulgar. The calamities of war, of intoxication, and the other self or mutually inflicted crimes and follies of mankind, are too hideous and extraordinary to result from any mere natural cause. They are, as the apostles tell us, set on fire by hell, and by the 'powers and principalities against whom we wrestle, not against mere flesh and blood; by the rulers of the darkness of this world, the spiritual wickedness in high places.' Those human excesses which pollute and desolate the earth from age to age, in spite of religion, and in spite of the highest reach of civilization, are too monstrous and too mad to result from any simple incentives of human infirmity. They proclaim their origin from the accumulated sorceries of the pandemoniums of the past."

Whilst in Boston, in the summer of 1868, editing "The Spiritual Harp," we had frequent opportunities of being with Mr. Peebles in many an interesting experience. One day, he called at the office of "The Banner of Light," asking if we would like to "see a case of perfect obsession." Arm-in-arm, we threaded our way through the crazy crowds, and entered a boarding-house kept by a Spiritualist lady. We knocked at the door of the room occupied by the unfortunate woman. No response. We pressed the door open; and there she lay alone on the hard floor, covered with her shawl (her kind attendant sister being absent for a moment), frothing at the mouth, and muttering strange sounds. "Pity, oh, pity!" was our mutual ejaculation. The landlady could not have her there: "she must leave!" Who would befriend her? We roused her from her stupor; and Mr. Peebles, kindly offering his arm, accompanied her to the United States Hotel, assuring the clerk that the bills should be paid. Procuring a suitable room, we endeavored magnetically to soothe the poor creature, and succeeded to that degree that she calmly told her history with tears of sorrow.

A fascinating girl, she had many suitors, who flattered her with vain ideals of life. One she loved as woman's heart can love.

Parents refused the banns, and by social considerations consummated a marriage with one she instinctively repelled, though he was rich and high-bred. The loss of her own lover, killed on board "The Essex," in the late rebellion, and marriage with her oppressor, who compelled her to murder her babes, ere they breathed the air, to gratify his insatiate lusts, at length fell crushing her soul, maddened to gloom and despair. In her sorrow, she sought the spirits. Ignorant of magnetic subtilties, corrupted by promiscuous circles, cast off a lost woman by the Christian Church, stained by forced lusts till the very fountains of life were the nest of Eden's serpent, she incidently entangled herself in poisoned influences, and finally was completely enveloped in the magnetic coils of demoniac possessions. The manifestations were plainly spiritual, but disorderly.

In a moment of sanity, she caught an impression, doubtless from a spirit, that she and her sister must go to Boston, and, if possible, secure the aid of the spiritual battery of "The Banner of Light." It would not do. The editor of that paper saw the peril of such a sphere, introduced for covert designs. Mr. Colby was guard against that influence, like a faithful sentinel; Mr. White, full of charity, pondered upon his duty; Mr. Crowell was severe, and determined to expel that medium and her band from the city. The general caution, however, linked us all into a mutual responsibility. We engaged a healing physician, Dr. Greenwood of Boston, to expel the obsessing spirits; but the spirits saw the intent, and threw her into spasms to baffle our purpose. The poor girl, as if conscious of one open valve of escape from the serpentine spheres of her obsessors, entwined her arms around Mr. Peebles's neck, and chained him fast, breathing into his face, and winding those fiery cords around him, till at last she imparted to him the burning in her soul; when he tore away, burdened with the dark miasma,—the moral death-sphere of Hades itself. He was the clean cup to drain the poison, eating the body and soul of the poor woman. With a quick step he rushed into the open air, evoked his orderly spirits, went to his room in Charlestown, bathed himself, prayed for divine help, and fell asleep so trustfully; when the angels overshadowed him with folding wings, awaking hopeful dreams till morn, when he rose refreshed and happy. Meeting us the next day with a cordial hand, he said, "Come, Joseph, we must go to another house, that our spiritual strength may not break under this awful pressure." He led us to the residence of Dr. A. P. Pierce, a spirit-healer, by whose mediumship obsessed persons and houses are cleansed, and better influences introduced; and here we rested, as if baptized in dews of the summer land! Thus rejuvenated, Mr. Peebles, a few days after, was urgently sent for to see this poor woman at the United States Hotel. The very hells had broken loose upon her; madness, fury, insanity, were as "legion" in her brain; her husband cursed, her departed lover invoked, her helplessness deplored, her clothes torn and ruined, and the despair of horror stamped upon her face. But the presence of Mr. Peebles partially calmed her; when she gave, at her better moments, beautiful tests, described spirits, presented fine drawings, improvised and sung exquisite poetry under spirit-influence. Mr. Peebles advised them to return home to Connecticut. She and her sister yielded at last. Messrs. White & Co., with Mr. Peebles, paid the bills. Having destroyed her bonnet, she asked for something to protect her head; and Mr. Peebles tied his handkerchief over it, and then, with hair dishevelled and glaring eyes, she took his offered arm for the cars across the street. In the mean while, the police had gathered into the hotel; and all the clerks, maids, and waiters were on the *qui vive* at the confusion of the "insane woman," — the "fruit of Spiritualism!" as the genteel orthodox said of it. As Mr. Peebles and the woman, attended by her weeping sister, passed through the office, the crowd jeering in suppressed jokes, one of the clerks exclaimed, "There goes the old, long-haired Israelite!" No chance for a just rebuke, he silently led her out, provoked at the taunts, but resolute to protect the unfortunate till the cars started. We both resolved, "We will never patronize that hotel again." The next morning, he was astonished to receive a telegram from Warren Chase of New York, asking him, in emphatic words, why he had sent that crazy person to him. Mr. Rich, of "The Banner of Light," promptly exonerated Mr. Peebles from any blame, assuring him that she was expected to have gone home. But the spirits were evidently wiser than the rest. The obsessed was influenced to say, "Send me to S. B. Brittan." This experienced Spiritualist, thoroughly comprehending the case, immediately sought the assistance of Dr. A. S. Haywood, who undertook the task of restoring order. Meanwhile, a prudish lady (?) of New York, whose services were sought as a necessity, declared, "The woman is base; and here is the evidence of it," she added, with a toss of the head, "in this handkerchief: see the name of a man on it, — Peebles!" So she reported Mr. Peebles to her slandering associates "a bad man." Did not that handkerchief tell the story? Could wickedness descend to greater depths? Thus do the vile seek to turn our *good* against us. Dr. Haywood was successful. The obsessing influences left her: she was in her right mind, and soon after wrote a letter of great gratitude to Mr. Peebles for his philanthropic protection during her days of distress. From reliable authority we learn she is now happy. Thus self-sacrifice is always rewarded; and every kind act, like a wandering minstrel, blesses some dependent soul.

Writing on the subject of demons in his "Seers of the Ages," Mr. Peebles says, —

"Like attracts like. Every door must have a hinge to swing upon. No evil spirit can approach us unless — morally weak — we possess a magnet within, attracting corresponding influences. This, so painful to endure, is the lesson of our frailty, teaching the moral necessity of fostering better conditions for more heavenly relations.

"Sensitiveness to psychological influx, susceptibility to mediumistic control, implies higher and lower use and abuse. Will not the tender flower be touched by the frost as well as by the sunbeam? The greater the capacity to rise involves a similar capacity to fall. The charm of a darkened demon is as potent as an angel's, where a point of ingress is possible. Then, according to the apostolic injunction of John, trust not, "believe not every spirit, but *try* the spirits!"

"If spirits uncultured and evil impress, and at times completely obsess, mortals, is not the practice of phenomenal Spiritualism dangerous? Yes, dangerous as the sunshine, that, falling alike on flowers and thorns, the just and the unjust, produces an occasional sun-stroke; dangerous as the spring rain, that, sweeping away old rickety bridges, carries rich alluvial to the valley below; dangerous as steamers, that now and then send bodies down to find graves under green sea-weeds, whilst on their beneficent missions of international commerce; dangerous as mining, railroading, telegraphing, which develop the hidden wealth of a nation. Shall we therefore dispense with them? Shall none pursue geological pursuits because Hugh Miller committed suicide? Briars abound where berries grow. It is one of the offices of guardian angels to protect their mediums from the inharmonious magnetisms of unwise, perverse spirits, and the psychological attractions of depraved mortals."

Respecting the curative agencies of obsession, a Christ-like spirit thus speaks through the mediumship of Emma Hardinge: —

"A good spirit will not attempt to take and hold unwarrantable possession of a mediumistic organization: hence you may rest assured of what class it is from whence the phenomenon of obsession proceeds. Now, if the infesting spirit were not magnetically stronger than his subject, he could not maintain possession, however he might once gain a temporary ascendency. The true processes of cure, therefore, are obvious and dual. First, let all possible means be taken to strengthen the health of the subjects, and render their minds positive to the control of others. Good air, good diet, change of scene, association, and constant employment, pleasant society, and cheerful, active occupations, are the physical means, which steadily resorted to may alone effect a cure. If these fail, use in connection with them the aid of a strong-willed, powerful, and virtuous magnetizer. Let him continue with unflinching constancy to exert his will, and add thereto magnetic passes over his subject, and we will pledge our faith and word that he will speedily dispossess the enemy, though he were the fabled Beelzebub *in propria personæ*."

CHAPTER XIX.

INDIAN SPIRITS AND THEIR BRETHREN WEST.

> "Better trust all, and be deceived,
> And weep that trust and that deceiving,
> Than doubt one heart, that, if believed,
> Had blest one's life with true believing."
>
> FRANCES ANNE KEMBLE.

WHEN alone in Nature's solitudes, Mr. Peebles frequently talks aloud with the spirits. One evening in California, stars as sentinels, he ascended a terrace of the Nevadas, and, standing there rapt in mystery, as an Apollo, addressed a vast concourse of spirits. His voice of persuasion echoed wildly through the rocky caverns and arches, leaping up into heaven, till it verily seemed that the entranced angels heard it, trembling. Several miners, passing the trail beneath, startled at the strange ideas, reported, as Aaron Nite afterwards said, that they "heard a crazy man on a mountain talking with the ghosts."

In July, 1869, Mr. Peebles, Dean Clark, and ourself were the speakers at a mass meeting of three thousand persons held in Plymouth, Wis., — H. S. Benjamin, President, and E. W. McGraw, Secretary. Just as Mr. Peebles composed himself for a rest of brain, he was suddenly called on to speak. For a moment it roused a feeling of murmuring; he was about declining, when a gentle wave of inspiration swept over him. Hidden from the waiting crowd, tears trickled down his cheeks. He was listening to spirit-voices, which said so tenderly in sad music words, —

"James, have we been so long with you, and yet you doubt our presence to aid you? See these hungry souls: rise, and speak;" and he obeyed with a power. "Have we been so long with you?" rang in his ears for hours.

During his visit at our rustic home on the forest shore of Elkhart

Lake, Wis., near Glen Beulah, he made a speech to the Indian spirits who years agone inhabited that picturesque locality. Here we built a wigwam for literary work. He thus describes it: —

"Impressed from the heavenly 'hunting-grounds' of the Indians, Brother Barrett had been moved, ere we reached those regions, to fashion a quiet and beautiful retreat near the margin of these musical waters, by bending and twisting saplings, shrubs, and larger trees into a crowning cone-form, constituting a wigwam bower of prayer, a veritable temple of inspiration."

One starry evening, prior to the mass meeting, the lake waves patting the wood-tangled banks, the leaves overhead keeping up a rustling tenor, several friends assembled in this wigwam; when, after a few moments of silence, he rose, and, facing the lake, gazing off into the peopled space, addressed the Indian spirits, reminded them of their sufferings, of the bloody resolution of the whites to exterminate their brethren in the West, and of his determination to defend their rights by the establishment of industrial systems of peace. How strange it seemed, that speech! and yet responsive to the soul. After the Plymouth meeting, Brother Clark was entranced by an Indian spirit who most cordially thanked the "pale-face" for his "big talk in wigwam." Such gratitude!

Were there responses to these speeches? yea, in the deep silence of impression, too eloquent for human language. But how often did the Indian spirits talk to the "pale-face" through a medium, telling him all his words and deeds of love were known in the "hunting-lands," where they were making a "fine wigwam" for him, where a "pretty squaw was waiting till he come!"

Being at a séance when Mr. Peebles was present, with Dr. Dunn for medium, we asked Powhattan about his earth and spirit life: —

"Me had one squaw," he said; "one pappoose, *Kanawaubish*, 'pretty water:' you call my pappoose *Poc-a-hon-tas!*

"Me Indian; me no speak like white man; me got nice wigwam, nice canoe, and bow and arrow; me hunt; me sleep under sky; me have for me bed the Big Spirit Hunting-Ground; me blanket is the blue heaven; me music is the breath of the Big Spirit, as he blows leaves of trees. In morning time, the Big Spirit look out from his windows [eyes], and the Indian kiss the dew from his forehead."

In the winter of 1868, Mr. Peebles lectured in St. Louis and cities farther west, where his whole soul was stirred to intense action in defense of the Indians, whom the whites in all that region were determined to exterminate. It called down upon him the ire of officials and pseudo-Spiritualists. He had been years before vice-president of the Universal Peace Society, and a most efficient worker. True to his instincts, he went forth on his love-errand. He wrote the following letter to his friend, A. H. Love, president of the society: —

"Passing down the main street of Leavenworth, I saw a recruiting office; and reaching Topeka, on board the train for Lawrence were four cars loaded with cavalry officers. I saw the whitened tents of the soldiery. The army was awaiting orders to march upon the Indians. Oh, how my heart ached and my soul bled! Constituting myself a peace commissioner, I immediately called upon Gov. Crawford and the State marshal, and protested, in kindness yet in *great firmness*, against this proposed movement to be conducted by Gen. Sheridan. I went on still west from Topeka, towards Colorado, conversing with Judge Humphrey, Col. Smith, and other army officers. It seemed as though God's angels aided me in thought and speech. These officers admitted the wisdom and beauty of my humanitarian position; but they were 'Utopian, and *impracticable*,' they said; 'and adapted to times a hundred years hence.' . . .

"Perhaps I am too enthusiastic for the red man, our brother, God's child. Perhaps I am too enthusiastic for peace throughout the world. But my soul's sympathies are stirred; and now, while I pen these lines, my eyes are suffused with tears.

"Can not there be something done to flank this Western war-movement? It must start in the East. The extreme West is red for blood.

"I am sorely tried. The Commissioners, save Col. S. F. Tappan, seem inclined to take retrograde steps. It is impossible to get to the Indians now personally: they suspect every body. If there could be a *delegation* gotten up in some way, in connection with the 'Peace Commissioners,' having the sanction of Government, I think something might be done; but between now and spring, how many will be shot down by a barbarous soldiery! I sometimes feel like flying away from this Christian civilization, so false to justice and benevolence, and going off alone into their country, devoting my life to their good."

About this time, reporting his Western experiences to "The Banner of Light," he tells the story in these stinging words: —

"Stopping at the Planters' Hotel, Leavenworth, Kan., a very intelligent gentleman, just from Denver City, informed us, that, in an adjacent village, the citizens a few weeks previous had 'burned Gen. Sherman in effigy,' because connected with the Indian Peace Commission. He further said, it was the general purpose of the people in that region to kill indiscriminately Indian men, women, and children; for, he added, it takes but a little time for 'pappooses to make warriors.'"

"In several Kansas cities recruiting offices were in full operation. Our train from Leavenworth to Lawrence had four cars filled with cavalry horses, for the coming war of extermination. Just to the north-east of Topeka, in full view, was the tented soldiery of the 19th Kansas, waiting the arrival of other companies for further orders. Inviting a gentleman to accompany us to the Indian country and the Western forts, he refused, because of the nightly depredations of the soldiers tenting near Topeka. 'Why,' said he, 'they are stealing every thing they can lay their hands on!' Strange, thought we, that Government should send out a thieving Christian soldiery to exterminate thieving Indians. It is the old Bible story and practice of the Israelites going into the lands of the Canaanites and Moabites to pillage and destroy. Our Christianity is galvanized Judaism; and our political policy, greedy for power and pelf, winks approval at the most horrid injustice. Whither are we drifting?

"Gov. Crawford of Kansas recently issued a proclamation savoring little of the tender, loving, forgiving spirit of Jesus, — good for evil, love for hate, blessing for cursing. Here follows the closing paragraph: —

"'Longer to forbear with these *bloody fiends* would be a crime against civilization, and against the peace, security, and lives of all the people upon the frontier. The time has come when they must be met by an adequate force, not only to prevent the repetition of these outrages, but to penetrate their haunts, break up their organizations, and either *exterminate* the tribes, or confine them upon reservations set apart for their occupancy. To this end the Major-General commanding this department has called upon the Executive for a regiment of cavalry from this State.

"Mark the phrase, '*bloody fiends*,' and the executive threat of 'extermination,' if they are not forced on to reservations!

"A professed Spiritualist of Lawrence, in a tongue-battle with us touching the solution of the Indian question, exclaimed, '*I would to God that every one of those Indian Peace Commissioners [among which were Gens. Sherman, Harney, Augur, Terry, and others] was obliged to go out on the plains, and be scalped by the red-skins!*' Are such sentiments in accordance with the genius of Spiritualism? Would it not be wisdom in Spiritualist lecturers to devote more time to educating and spiritualizing thousands of nominal Spiritualists, rather than encompassing sea and land to make new converts, who, when converted, often need re-converting every six months by a fresh batch of tests? Quality is often preferable to quantity."

The next winter, Mr. Peebles, lecturing in Washington, D.C., was invited to a position as volunteer in the "Congressional Indian Peace Commission," — consisting of Gens. Harney, Sheridan, Sherman, Sanborn, Taylor, Col. Parker, and Col. S. F. Tappan, — to visit the Indians, then fighting with the whites in the Sioux and Rocky Mountain regions; for the purpose of organizing treaties, stopping the shedding of blood, and befriending them in their natural rights to a living on the American continent. He gathered up the testimony of Senators Doolittle, Foster, Nesbith, Sherman, Gen. Pope, and others, who averred, that, if the facts of the whites' rascality to the Indians "were published to the world, they would disgrace us in the eyes of all civilized nations." He quoted from the speeches of Indian chiefs, asking for justice; talked with W. P. Ross, chief of Cherokees, and other educated Indians, who demonstrate their capacity to be civilized; consulted John Beeson, the Indian's friend; and, with burning words, said, in an editorial of "The Banner of Light," —

"Our Saxon face is mantled with shame, and soul humbled in deepest humiliation, at the individual and associate crimes that blot the escutcheon of this great, wicked

Christian country, called United States of America. Crimes red as blood, vindictive as death, and black as the cinders of Pluto's pit; crimes willful, determined, and continuous too, against the Indian tribes of the West, North-west, and South-west! Is justice, is philanthropy, dead? Is progress a dream? and sympathy a mere historic legend? Our heart aches; our tears flow. God, angels, American citizens of the better thought and life, tell us what we can, what we *ought*, to do to check this nation from further cheating, swindling, sacking, shooting, slaughtering, and murdering, through its officers, superintendents, and agents, the three hundred thousand remaining aborigines of this country? A government is responsible for the agents it employs and pays. In this country the people, with ballot in hand, are the government: accordingly *you*, readers, directly or indirectly, are responsible for the defrauding and murdering of those red men west of the Mississippi.

"This Indian question is all the more grave at present from the consideration that the two waves of population between the Pacific and Atlantic coasts are soon to meet. Way-stations will dot Western mountains. A railroad will span the extremes, and a peaceable transit through these mountainous regions will be indispensable. The only way to secure such will be by the exercise of blended justice and kindness, — kindness and sympathy, not revenge; love, not hate; mercy, not vindictiveness; integrity, sincerity, and peace; deeds of purity and fraternity, rather than murderous acts of extermination.

"William Penn had no difficulty with the Indians. They knew — know — their friends. The English government in Canada has never had an Indian war, nor has a life been lost by an Indian massacre. They live in peaceful relations with their white neighbors. Tribes have centered into Indian villages, around which the grass is green, and orchards bud, bloom, and bear their fruitage.

"Our Government must give those three hundred thousand Indians the protection of law; must give them a civil-rights bill; must treat them as men; must give them individual and permanent right in the soil; must grant them their annuities, and guard them against thieving agents, trafficking vagabonds, and a murderous soldiery: for they are God's children, and our brothers. This course pursued, and a continuous *peace* is secured with our red brothers of the West, — brothers originally noble in nature, firm in their friendships, and keen in their perceptions of the principles of natural justice.

"Though treated as they have been by the whites, those that tread the shadow-lands of eternity are returning good for evil by descending from their hunting-ground homes in the heavens, with balms of healing, and words of love and cheer. Hours, days, months, in the past, have we talked with Powhattan, through the organism of a medium friend, relative to the past, present, and future of the Indians upon this continent. 'Tis only justice to say, we have ever found this chief the very soul of simplicity, tenderness, truthfulness, and a genuine magnanimity. Blessings be upon Powhattan, Red Jacket, Tecumseh, Black Hawk, Thunder, Logan, Little Crow, Antelope, and all Indian spirits that are shedding their healing magnetisms and peace-influences upon the inhabitants of earth."

In April, he started with these commissioners for the Far West. This is an extract from an editorial reporting his experiences: —

"In Dakota Territory, near the confluence of the north and south forks of the Platte, we were privileged to sit with the Commission in an Indian Council. It was a novel scene, and every movement deeply interesting. The first glance at the Brulle Chief 'Spotted Tail,' the sub-chiefs and warriors present, inclined us to silently exclaim, 'What splendidly-molded forms! How dignified their bearing! *These* are truly men of health and of muscle; men of very large perceptive faculties, and magnificent noses,

— the Roman prevailing.' The tip-up and stub-noses that disfigure so many Hibernian faces characterize the features of none of the eighty thousand Sioux. The Cheyennes and Sioux are the enemies of the Pawnees. They fight very much like Christians.

"At the preliminary meeting the more prominent of the tribe, dressed in native costume (fancy colors as in our fashionable female society predominating), came in, decorated in beads, bones, buffalo-teeth, and glittering ornaments, — such as coils of brass wire, bands of silver upon their arms, and feathers in their hair, together with a long string of circular metallic pieces, graduated in size, and fastened to a leather strap attached and suspended from the back hair like a Chinese queue. The length of this is proportionate to an Indian's wealth and bravery, and, furthermore, indicates a sort of challenge. Thus adorned, they extended fraternal greetings, through the interpreter, to the Commissioners, Father De Smet, a Catholic priest, and others present. A general running talk then followed.

"At twelve o'clock, the Council met, the Commissioners fronting a rude table, interpreters and reporters at the sides, and the Indians in circular form. Spotted Tail, Little Thunder, and White Eyes, facing Gen. Harney, Gen. Sheridan, Col. Tappan, and the others, formed the inner circle. Back of the chiefs were the warriors; and behind these, in half-moon form, a large number of women and children. Having filled a huge pipe with yellow willow-bark and other ingredients, the Indians passed it from one to the other, each taking a whiff. It was the famous pipe of peace. All becoming quiet, Mr. Sanborn, acting chairman of the Commission, stated the purpose of the present mission from Washington, and the further peaceable aims of the Government toward the red men of the Western plains and mountains.

"Sanborn having closed his pleasant remarks, Spotted Tail, sitting a while in perfect stoic silence, at length replied, through Leon F. Pallarday, an interpreter twenty-two years in the Indian country. The speech, moderate, distinct in enunciation, and full of gestures, showed great practical common sense and sound thought mingled with much native shrewdness. He said in substance, —

"'We are glad to meet the representatives of the great father in Washington. I remember the talk we had together last year I have kept my word: neither my old warriors nor young braves have fought the white man since. I have tried to make the chiefs of the bands to the north understand that peace was better for all parties than war. I want peace; for all of us are brothers, and the Great Spirit smiles upon us all in the sun and stars alike. My daughter loved the whites, and is buried among them at Fort Laramie. I like peace. My old men and squaws like peace the best. I have unstrung my bow, broken my arrow, laid aside the war-paint, and felled trees across the war-trail.

"'Your great father must be rich, or he could not build the long, fiery trail, and send his braves so far to our council. We are poor; our pappooses' hearts cry with hunger. White men have killed some of our chiefs, destroyed our game, burned our timber, and dug our lands; and now you must give us a big heap of presents. We take the words you say to us in our hands; but some things you promise slip through. White men do not always keep their word. They cheat, and their presents are not *good.* Our fathers, many moons in the past, gave white men meat, buffalo-skins to keep them warm, and guided them through the mountain-passes toward the far-off sunset. Our hands to-day are warm, and our souls true to all true and peaceable pale-faced men; but we are *poor.* You must give us, blankets, arms to shoot the game, hatchets to hew poles for tents, and *many presents;* for our squaws and pappooses are hungry, and rain comes from their eyes.

"My braves are not children. They do not fear to die. They do not ask for pity or sympathy; only for *justice* and good feeling. Remove your soldiers from our hunting-grounds, and peace would come to us all. I will go with you to Laramie to induce Red Cloud, chief of all the war-parties, and Ogallala, to make peace, as Satanti, Black Kettle, and other chiefs have done. The old *chief*, Man-afraid-of-his-horses, is for peace; and he gave Red Cloud his daughter in marriage, early last fall, to keep the peace. I do not want to see the white man's blood flow, but want to live in peace with him, and in peace with all my brother tribes, and, dying, enter the peaceful hunting-grounds of my fathers. Tell your great father we were glad to see you. It made our hearts feel good. The Great Spirit looks down into our peace-council, and is pleased.' "

. . . .

"God has written upon every conscious heart the divine command, 'Thou shalt not kill.' The noble, eloquent words of the editor-in-chief of 'The Banner' should be republished in every paper of the Union, — in allusion to this great question, — namely, that, —

"'We (Americans) should have learned ere this that justice to all — red, white, and black — is the highest statesmanship, the greatest political economy, the safest foundation of a government, the surest guaranty of peace, liberty, progress, civilization, and order; the grandest conception, and most sublime action (as it should be the greatest pride) of a free people.'

. . . .

"Sitting by the side of a staff-officer who was fixing the strap to his pistol-casing, he inquired of us where we joined the Commission?

"'At Omaha, Nebraska.'

"'What for an outfit have you?'

"A little verdant in the army style of conversation, we replied, 'A shawl, and trunk, containing some clothing, books, papers, &c.'

"'Oh! I meant implements of defense, such as they use out here to pick off the red-skins.'

"'I never carry fire-arms, and could not be induced under any consideration to take the life of a human being.'

"'If those hostile Indians knew that, they'd have your scalp.'

"'Well, they could not take my *spiritual scalp*.'

"'What in the *devil* is that?'

"'Why, you know the apostle Paul speaks of there being a "natural body and a spiritual body," clearly implying a physical and spiritual organization throughout; and accordingly, though the earthly head were scalped, I should still live immortal, and could perhaps better serve the Indian and others of the down-trodden in spirit-life than this.'

"'Then you are really a non-resistant.'

"'In the sense of killing human beings, I certainly am, — believing that any true man *unarmed* is the most thoroughly armed; his motto being, it is better to endure wrong than to do wrong; better to be murdered than to murder; and better to suffer unhappiness than to make others unhappy.'"

Suffice it to say, that this expedition, though beneficent in design, accomplishing some good, was soon followed by renewals of war, being instigated by the whites' depredations. After Gen. Grant was installed President of the United States, Mr. Peebles wrote several articles indorsing his policy in sending to the Indians a band of peaceful Quakers, under Col. Parker's superintendence; and *there* is a lingering hope.

CHAPTER XX.

LOVE–LIFE.

"Sing to my soul the sweet song that thou livest!
Read me the poem that never was penned, —
The wonderful idyl of life that thou givest
Fresh from thy spirit, O beautiful friend!"

"Love was free,
Nobly unselfish, as an angel's pure." — BRISTOL.

THERE is a religion in which all agree, — the religion of the love of truth, beauty, music, goodness, purity. No theology can destroy or stain it. It belongs to all eras, all races, all worlds. It is the heart of heaven. It is as free as the sunlight; free as the fragrance of flowers, the bird's song, and the angel's dream. "Now, Jesus loved Mary and Martha." Was not that love free and holy?

"Whereso'er he met
The soul of a true woman, beautiful
In innocence, and heart devoted to
Humanity's high interests, — and, withal,
Upon her breast humility's pure pearl, —
He worshiped at that shrine, as true men must
Who meet with such a spirit."

In all his speeches and writings, Mr. Peebles is careful to draw the distinction between animal desire and spiritual love. His moral indignation is intense when he reads or hears an argument defensive of a loose and unrestrained socialism.

His idea is, that the functional uses of the passions are administrative subordination under the guidance of an enlightened morality, to develop and spiritualize the whole being, and the propagation of the race obedient to the dictates of the highest wisdom, that all children may be welcomed and cherished as earth's angels, born right, and therefore living right.

This extract from an article written for "The Progressive Age," 1863, is a true transcript of his opinion on this subject: —

"In cerebellum soil are the germinal types, buds even, of lilies and oceanic flowers, struggling to rise from their sedimental graves into the free, fresh sunlight of heaven; so are there mortals that live away down in the back-brain apartments of their soul-house. Let us aid such to ascend to the summits of the moral and spiritual faculties into which angels delight to gaze! . . .

"Physical gratifications can never supply heart-wants. Spiritual loves, pure and holy, can fully feed the strong soul. . . .

"If spirits teach 'promiscuity,' it speaks sadly for the medium, and a thousand times worse for the controlling influences. Such spirits must be recently from the central sinks of New York, or the 'Seven Dials' of London.

"All the brain organs and germinal forces of the soul are beautiful and divine. Even amativeness, disrobed of earthliness, resurrected and actualized in angelic life, is the synonym of love, — love pure and divine as God's; working with and inspiring the morality and spirituality of those higher faculties for all us mortals who can comprehend the purity and divinity of love. The fountain is infinite. It flows out spontaneous from regenerated souls towards all humanity, — man, woman, child; field, flower, mountain, and star; free, full, and unconfined."

His is the sentiment of "our brother" Geo. S. Burleigh: —

"By the loves which mark us human
We are verily divine.
True Messiah is every *true* man,
True Madonna each pure woman,
And their home the holiest shrine."

He is perfectly charmed with the child-like affection of the Shakers; maintaining that they live the nearest to an angelic life of any sect in the world, everywhere advocating their cardinal principles as respects the freedom and function of love. He has frequently visited them in their homes to sun his soul amid their spiritual purities, and returns to the 'outer court,' as he calls our social life, like Jesus from the sweet cottage of Mary and Martha at Bethany, invigorated in body and mind for a loftier work. At their great meeting in Boston, in 1869, when their doctrines and objects were defined before the thinkers of that city, Mr. Peebles, by their special invitation, and agreeable to his deepest convictions of privileged duty, was present on the stand to indicate his heart-interest. His speech on the occasion so defensive of their system was admirable.

We can almost feel his heart beat in ours as we read his words, first published in the "Religio-Philosophical Journal:" —

"The apostle John said he knew that he 'had passed from death into life, because he loved the brethren.' This love can never degenerate into license, nor such liberty into anarchy; for it is a principle disrobed of passion, — a resurrection even of the low brain organs, on to the plane of divine purity and use. All men are my brothers;

all women my sisters; all children my children; and I am every mortal's child. I have an interest in every child born into earth-life. Its destiny is linked with mine.

"'One family, we dwell in Him,
One church above, beneath;
Though now divided by the stream,—
The swelling stream of death.'

"My country is the universe; my home, the world; my religion, to do good; my rest, wherever a human heart beats in harmony with mine: and my desire is to extend a brother's helping hand to earth's millions, speaking in tones as sweet as angels use; thus kindling in their breasts the fires of inspiration, and aiding them up the steeps of Mount Discipline, whose summit is bathed in the mellowed light of heaven. All the love that can be attracted from my inmost being belongs to the poor and the crushed; to you, the world, the whole universe. Some may not specially call this love out; neither can lead call fire from flint. The fault, however, is in the lead. Transmute it to steel, and see the bright fiery effect! It takes some conservatives a lifetime to learn the folly of trying to twist ropes from sand, or of coaxing ice to kiss buds into May-blooms. Jesus said, 'All mine are thine, and thine are mine;' and during that precious Pentecostal hour, when the divine afflatus streamed from angelic abodes, not only 'many believed,' but they were so baptized into those unselfish influences that obtain in the spirit-world, that they resolved to have 'all things in common.' When these universal love-principles are outlived, the soil will be free to all to cultivate as is the air to breathe; gardens will bloom for the poor, highways be planted with fruit-trees and orphans find homes in all houses. Bigotry, too, will perish; superstition furl its crimson flag; prison-walls crumble to dust; tyranny die on the plains of freedom; and the cannon's mouth be wreathed with white roses, — symbols of perpetual peace.

An alleged weakness (?) in the character of Mr. Peebles is his "giving, for ever giving," as the worldly charge runs. Never a beggar called at his door in vain; never a poor soldier did he meet but he had something for him, if it took his last cent, and also a word or look of love; never a needy man, woman, or child asked of him a favor, but he granted it, if in his power. Hundreds of dollars has he loaned to his co-workers in the Spiritual cause; hundreds has he so lost, misfortune overtaking them; hundreds upon hundreds has he given away. When his sympathy is touched, tears flow, and the pocket laughs with a benevolent wink, if there is any thing in it. Thus, thousands are endeared to him, feel under obligation to him; and everywhere is he blessed with earnest greetings and gifts. His earnings therefore, in the main, are large these days: but he keeps nothing, above family expenses; all is expended upon the unfortunate, or the enterprises of public improvement. How many Spiritual speakers and mediums are indebted to him for favors! Attracted by his sphere, young speakers are known to follow him from place to place, like the steel chained to its magnet, developing them to be "chosen vessels" of truth to the famishing world.

From the many testimonials we quote from a private letter of Cephas B. Lynn's: —

"His kindness toward young media, more especially those struggling for usefulness on the rostrum, has been a marked feature in his career as a teacher of the Spiritual Philosophy. In fact, he is looked up to with the utmost reverence, and loved most tenderly, by scores of young lecturers in our ranks. I could name ten or twelve who acknowledge that Mr. Peebles has been the leading instrumentality in advancing them in Spiritual graces, and inducting them into active public labors. Blessings upon him for this! I gladly affirm my indebtedness to him in this respect; and my prayer is, that the Spiritualists of the country will see the wisdom of placing funds at his command; so that through him young media suited for the Spiritual ministry may receive that discipline and culture so essential to success."

Seemingly he sometimes errs on the side of charity. To encourage a beginner, or a luckless brother or sister, amid the poverties and perils of mediumship, — victors at last, — he has spoken words through the voice and pen higher sometimes than just merit would sanction, — merit as viewed from the world's angle of criticism. Like the Nazarene, he has so often taken others' sins upon his shoulders; and with his "stripes were we healed." He has always been sure to see the angel side of human nature, and clothed it with deserving garments, that the world might feel the heart of the crushed and fallen to be as pure and heavenly as his own. His errors are errors of charity; and are they not virtues? In the judgment every day acting, how large are the credits in the life-book of his soul! Listen to his testimony again: —

"Beautiful in effect is the medium of love to the morally diseased. It works by an infinitude of methods, but always to redemptive ends. When fires, fagots, clanking chains, and gloomy penitentiaries had all failed to reform, the 'still, small voice' of love and sympathy has touched the heart-strings, opened a new fountain, and redeemed the most obdurate. Says a European writer, 'Love is the instrument that the Almighty reserved to conquer rebellious man when all the rest had failed. Reason he parries; fear he answers blow for blow: but love is the sun against whose melting beams winter cannot stand. This soft, subduing influence wrestles down the giant: there is not one human being in a million, not a thousand in all earth's huge quintillion, whose stony heart can withstand the power of love.' This principle, wielded by William Penn, tamed the Indian's soul, and tuned his heart to throb alone in kindness; wielded by the benignant Howard, it made prisons in Europe schools of reform; by the great-hearted Oberlin, it transformed many by-corners of pollution in the old world into gardens of beauty; and, by and through Elizabeth Fry, it filled the inmates in houses of refuge and 'asylums of outcasts' with those higher thoughts and purer ideas, as sure to produce those elevating influences as are the lightnings to do their missioned work.

Physical *force* may override, and powerful *nations* may conquer weaker ones; but love as a motive power combined with wisdom can alone subdue, promoting that harmony so indispensable to spiritual growth. It is all the power ever employed by God, Christ, or angels in the divine order of subjugating; being the deepest, divinest, and mightiest principle in the universe."

Wherever he goes, he is in the habit of taking little children into his arms, laying his hands upon their heads in blessing, as did the Nazarene, conscious that "of such is the kingdom of heaven;" and long he holds them to his bosom to catch the glow of their innocent hearts, when he rises refreshed for work again, like a bird that has slept in a bower of sunlight to be inspired with the loves of a sweeter song. In Battle Creek, Detroit, New York, Philadelphia, and other cities, he has christened children in the name of the angels by the laying-on of hands, and sometimes by sprinkling pure water; and such occasions are most hallowed and melting, scorned, of course, by the croakers, but approved by all who love the envelopment of spiritual spheres.

Walking the streets of Boston with him, locked arm in arm, he humming a tune as we elbowed our way through the jostling crowd, we met a youth, just in his teens, pale, nervous, and emaciated. "Boy," he said, with a piercing look and a tender tone of voice, "eat coarse bread, drink pure water, bathe in it every night, sleep on a hard bed, rise early, and work temperately. Remember, boy! for I love you." Going a few steps farther, we met a humbly-dressed woman, with her basket of fruit in her hand, passing to her market-stand for sales. "Well, my sister," he exclaimed, patting her gently on the shoulder, "now for business." She turned and met his gaze; and the feeling of rebuke changed to a blushing courtesy, and, determined not to be outdone on short acquaintance, seized him by the arm, and laughingly said, "Yes: come on; I need your help, — come, my brother;" and he had to tear away with a kind shout back, "I will risk you alone in your honorable fruit business." Walking the streets of St. Louis, he met a bright-eyed little girl, tripping along at a dancing pace, humming a tune and swinging her arms. Though a stranger, he stopped her, spoke a tender word, lifted her to his lips, pressed a sweet kiss, and bid her "Be good; for you are an angel of love." The girl was so happy! and he moved thence with a free, buoyant step.

In a Portland audience, 1869, where Mr. Peebles was lecturing, sat a negro contraband, John N. Still, listening most earnestly. At evening, the sable brother timidly introduced himself, stating that he saw him in a vision three years ago as the "Horace Greeley of Spiritualism;" that he was a school-teacher of Virginia; was ordered by the Spirit to "Go North, go North!" His spiritual experiences were most remarkable. After hearing them, and delivering his lecture, Mr. Peebles brought the Southerner to the stand, briefly telling his story for him, saying, "The Indian is my brother, the white man is my brother, the Negro is my brother;" and then he appealed to his auditors with a pathos that probed the very fountains of their hearts, raising for him a generous contribution; when Mr. Peebles bade him go on his way again to the South, rejoicing to "sow the seed of this gospel among the freed blacks." The good brother wept with joy, made a happy speech, and, under that light, returned to his task.

Here are some of the word-seeds sown in the bosoms of true friends, which we have found in forgotten letters. The clergyman referred to below is Rev. ——: —

"PHILADELPHIA, Feb. 6, 1869.

"Bitter were the tears I saw him shed more than once. His education in the English Church, and then as a Baptist, made him what he is. Spirits are trying now to unmake him, for the purpose of making him over in part; but I believe him a truthful, honest, sincere man, having about him streaks of *vanity* and other follies. Who is perfect? If the laziest devil in hell should roll over in his brimstone bed, and ask for help, I should help him. The public might not approve; but I know of no 'dear public' not constituted of individuals.

"It may be a weakness in me, but everybody must be aided, saved, by somebody; and then I have a deep sympathy for clergymen leaving the old shells of theology."

Our Pilgrim has passed into that degree of love which Jesus actualized: "Whosoever shall do the will of my Father who is in heaven, the same is my brother and sister and mother." Beyond the family circle, beyond church, sect, party, nationality, he enspheres humanity in his spiritual fellowship; and yet the fountains of this oceanic love are to him more sacred than ever, and cherished with a deeper retrospective reverence. Visiting his native home in Vermont, — that old framed house, that running brook, that forest and rocky height, where the silver cord of life first pulsed the latent music of his soul, — he mused and dreamed awake, and penned the poesy of his thought thus: —

"To-day I sit 'neath the paternal roof, and, in shadowy memories and quickly-shifting kaleidoscopic presentations, re-live the past, all gemmed in those earlier years with the dewy freshness of childhood's sunny morning. How mystic life's web! How strange the voyage, freighted with flowers and thorns, smiles and tears, defeats and victories, making it rich in experiences! A divinity truly 'shapes our ends,' a certain destiny overshadows each of us, and fate proves to be a mighty wrestler. The pathway may be crimsoned with bleeding feet, or baptized in tides of tears: yet beyond this mortal realm the star of eve shines, and the 'Queen of Morn' pours forth celestial harmonies, making 'music over all the starry floor;' and there earth's divinest ideals become the soul's eternal realities. . . .

"Oh, how many pleasant associations cluster around that word *mother!* Some one has said that '*mother*, *home*, and *heaven*' are the most beautiful words in the English language. I almost venerate my parents."

CHAPTER XXI.

ASCENSION INTO THE CELESTIAL HEAVENS.

"I think of that city; for oh! how oft
My heart has been wrung at parting
With friends all pale, who with footfalls soft
To its airy heights were starting!
I see them again in their raiment white
In the blue, blue distance dwelling;
And I hear their praises in calm delight
Come down, on the breezes swelling,
As I dream of the city I have not seen,
Where the feet of mortals have never been."—EMMA TUTTLE.

IF a plant or dew-drop is dusted and quickened by a sunbeam, it has virtually been to the sun. What matters it whether we have spiritual experiences through our own organism, or that of another through whom we derive a greater fullness of angelic truth? Spherally the medium we love is ourself conjoined with spirits. Where every interest is mutual, and magnetic touch responsive, our medium is the telescope through which we look at heavenly worlds.

Dr. Dunn the medium, Mr. Peebles the spiritual astronomer: these brothers attended vast conventions of angels and archangels, heard discussions upon the best methods of mediumistic control, ate by imbibation of the fruit that grows in those upper paradises till nourished in the substantial vitalities of spirit-life. Always the pre-requisite for these interviews was temperance, fasting, purity of habit. At one time Aaron Nite informed them of his home, "Pear-Grove Cottage," in the spirit-world; and Mr. Peebles expressed an earnest wish for the medium to visit it.

"Comply, then, with conditions," replied Aaron: "temperance in all things, fasting, and purity; read inspired poetry; attune your affections to the music of angel spheres."

In due time, obeying the request, the medium visited that heavenly residence, whose first forms of beauty were budded in the scenes of

Yorkshire, Eng., and described it so accurately and charmingly, Mr. Peebles exclaimed, "Plant me a tree in Aaron's garden: let it grow large and broad; for I shall sit with him under its shadow some sweet noonday of that happy world!"

Not long after this visit, the medium was deeply entranced, the body seemingly dead, pulseless. A momentary blank, and he found himself standing beside his body, — a very spirit clothed in shining garments, — when his guide, appearing, said, "Now you will accompany us." They went south-east, toward the tropical lands of morning; spiritually, the love-life of truth: and at length reached a real world of busy populations, and, in their rapid journey, caught glimpses of lakes of the most enchanted beauty, forests teeming with fruits, gardens in bloom, mountains encircled with prismatic clouds, that dropped down fragrant showers upon the prolific valleys, and crystal rivers, roseate with flowers and redolent with the music of birds; the inhabitants industrious, beautiful, and happy; a conscious harmony of ambition actuating every one to make those homes most beautiful and sunny. Charmed and electrified with such atmospheres and scenes, he arrived safe and invigorated at the residence of Aaron Nite, where he was required to change his garments for something more ethereal. Properly vestured, they ascended, piercing those atmospheres and terraces of light, till in the distance they discerned a brilliantly white sphere, that opened at length, when there stood before them two men and two women, clothed in purple robes, their countenances radiant with serenity of soul, and bearing in their hands flower wreaths of varied form, hue, and fragance.

"I will go with these four spirits," said the guide, "while the rest of our circle will have to return."

Separating, the medium queried why that was necessary. The question in thought was immediately answered by the spirits in accord, the voice of one being the opinion of all: —

"Because their spiritual bodies are not sufficiently ethereal. The laws of instincts are moral gravitations here: we can go only where minds are one in affection. There is a truth in the parable with which our friend and fellow-pilgrim is familiar. The one who had not on the wedding-garment, being on a lower plane, could not remain. They must first evolve from holier affection this higher sphere, ere they can find this rest. You, dear brother, could not advance one step with us, did we not weave around you our aura, — the vestment of angel-love. Guard well thy mediumship, if thou wouldst behold the glories to come!"

Taking the medium's hand, they approached a forest of surpassing loveliness, bordering which was a fountain, its banks adorned with sensitive flowers; for they reverently bowed as the spirits passed. Reaching the fountain, they found it three-graded, dashing a rain-bowed spray, having colors no earthly art can picture, or sunbeams paint in the cloud. In this the medium was baptized; and a sister spirit gave him a nectar to drink. The spray of this "Fountain of Purity," as it was called, inspirited him with a hallowed feeling.

"Be calm now," said the guide, "for we are approaching the sphere celestial of that immortal teacher for whom we have the most profound reverence."

Journeying onward amid new scenes, philosophizing by the way, the band paused, saying, —

"We can go no farther: other guides must now take you in charge."

Six spirits appeared, led by "Queen of Morn," all clothed in white, having golden girdles clasping their robes, and enflowering wreaths on their foreheads, with beauty of form and expression known only in immortal lands. Throwing a soft electric light around the medium, and giving him a "white vesture" like their own, they passed to an imposing mansion, arch on arch, glowing with splendor aflash with living mottoes. Dome above dome, circle encircling circle, — east, west, north, south, — all lit up with glory. High above the rest was a tower, consecrated to the fine arts. A door opening, they entered, and were greeted by a teacher of music, who said she had sung often to her "Pilgrim Brother." Here were musical instruments of strange construction, giving melodies such as angels only can execute; and sculpture and painting by artists long since departed from our world. Ascending a spiral stairway, they entered a department consecrated to science, poetry, and wisdom, where venerable sages were conversing with their pupils in the most soul-fraught enthusiasm. After inspecting all these attractions, the guide beckoned him to follow, and led him up spirally to a lofty dome, adorned with paintings and statues of ancient seers and sages; among which were those of the Nazarene, with a burning star over his forehead, and of the apostles, occupying niches in fine view, each having a sentiment circling overhead significant of his mission. Translated, they read thus, —

SIMON PETER, — "*Wisdom to be sought of God.*"
ANDREW, — "*Christ the Corner-Stone.*"
JAMES, — "*Let thy Prayers be unto all Men.*"
JOHN, — "*Charity is the rule of God's Judgment.*"
PHILIP, — "*The Truth giveth Freedom to the Soul.*"
BARTHOLOMEW, — "*Righteousness is the Glory of All.*"
THOMAS, — "*Knowledge expels all Doubt.*"
JAMES, SON OF ALPHEUS, — "*The Truth that dwelleth in us shall be in us for ever.*"
MATTHEW, — "*God's Mercy is over All, and to All.*"
THADDEUS, — "*The good Shepherd is alike mindful of all his Flock.*"
SIMON, — "*The Tree that hath no Root shall wither away.*"
JUDAS, — "*Fulfillment of the Law.*"

Here also was a rich library of ancient dialects, religious and philosophic. Many of the books were set in circular, movable cases, easy of access, by simply whirling the library round in search of the books sought. Near one of these, at a table, sat the celestial guide, — the loving disciple who leaned on Jesus' bosom, clothed in a white robe, glittering like burnished silver. His look was grandeur itself; calm in gravity, the same love-nature, swayed more by wisdom, that seemed as a light and glow of a heavenly sun. Though easy in manner as a child, persuasive and musical in tone of voice, there was an apparent, graceful reserve, inspiring reverence, that prevented any hasty approach. He recognized the medium and his relation with our pilgrim, and held a most happy conversation with his guide, respecting the wisest methods of spirit-control. This mansion, or temple, seemed to be a great central battery for spirits and mortals. The medium's guide had served in the capacity of a spirit psychologist for many years; and to him the spirits there assembled appealed as to an oracle for conclusive measures. Their earnestness upon the subject of mediumship was most serious and fervent, knowing as they did that it is pregnant with the most sacred hopes of all worlds. "What can be done to avert so many abuses? what to institute better conditions? what to inaugurate more spiritual and fraternal governments on earth?" were among the practical questions for solution. During the conversation of John with this guide about this all-absorbing theme, allusion was made to our Pilgrim, as well as to others, stating that his organic sphere is receptive of influence from that temple; that "John and James blend in affection:" and he would impress his brother of earth not so direct, but mainly through the mediumship of associated spirits, projecting upon his brain a loving thought, whenever the social conditions demand, the better to reach souls that "hunger and thirst after righteousness." Then, as if his words were direct, this beloved spirit said in language so oft-repeated, so lute-like in sweetness, to our pilgrim, —

"*All these shall be thine, child, when thou art worthy. To him that overcometh is the promise of the blessed inheritance.*"

"O hearts of *love!* O souls that turn,
Like sun-flowers, to the pure and best!
To you the truth is manifest;
For they the mind of Christ discern
Who lean like John upon his breast!

"What doth that holy guide require?
No rite of pain, nor gift of blood,
But man a kindly brotherhood,
Looking where duty is desire, —
To Christ, the beautiful and good."

CHAPTER XXII.

"BLESSED ARE THE PURE IN HEART."

"The tears of the compassionate are sweeter than dewdrops falling from roses on the bosom of earth." — BRAHMINIE.

"God hath been gradually forming man
In his own image since the world began;
And is for ever working on the soul,
Like sculptor his statue, till the whole
Expression of the upward life be wrought
Into some semblance of the eternal thought." — GERALD MASSEY.

THE confidence of men and women in our brother is most beautiful. Never did a child come closer to a maternal bosom than a troubled brother or sister to his heart. Eternal secrets contain sometimes the holiest morals: they always indicate the under-currents of love. We do wrong to hide the rarest pearls. Let the world see how good is man's or woman's heart, when guided by an angel's wisdom. Oh, how divine it is to trust the divine of human nature!

The case is one of unhappy marriage in ———: the man warm-hearted, the woman antipodal; both in a domestic hell. He loved another, — loved a maiden who reciprocated the heart's call in sacred trust. Unschooled in the philosophy of magnetic spheres, confiding as a nestling-bird, whatever the spirits said was to her law and gospel. When alone by themselves, he was unconsciously entranced by a positive spirit, who, "for the sake of health," as runs the subtile plea, suggested an utter disregard of the legal tie that imprisoned the unhappy husband and wife. It was temptation. Rallying her moral courage, she waved the allurement as woman only can. The thought would have been as disdainful, it is said, to him in his normal state as to her; but the entrancement was repeated at other opportunities, and the tempter was there with persuasive voice.

Again and again she parried the dart, tipped with a grain of sorrow. Love holding her, she faltered, wept, prayed, but kept her virtue. Her secret love had been whispered to Mr. Peebles, whom she chose as her spiritual guardian. In her trouble, she wrote him; told him all; asked advice; declaring with tender words that she was sinking, — sinking in spirit, death seeming inevitable under such pressure, if she did not yield. This letter, shown us when fresh with the pulsing aura of the hand that wrote it, was touching, sweet, pleading, heroic as a halting child that loves the flowers where the stinging bees are culling honey. Mr. Peebles's reply was, "Resist; die first in the struggle rather than plunge into an entanglement of even the legal claim of an unloving wife." He portrayed the social perils, the need of reverence to self-denial, the glory of martyrdom, such as angels love to witness, the divinity of such a death rather than the ignominy of such a life. "Weave not," he said, "your chords of holy love into the meshes of a domestic quarrel; wait until God and man shall sunder the false, and your triumph of heroism will give you, oh, such a rest of soul, approved by high heaven!" This counsel was what she anticipated. She rose from negation, feeling new tides of life-force through her whole being; her gratitude was inexpressible; her spirit, now buoyant, infused health into the deadened channels; and angels wrought to consummate a legal union on a plane where they meet, — in the purity of spiritual affection.

Read this heart-pleading letter and its answer. We weep over them. How the human heart can bleed, and yet live! How woman can suffer, and yet hope and love! When will men be watchful, enzoned in moral integrity? When shall we learn the perils of obsessing spheres? Oh, the soul-accounts to balance by and by! The sister who writes this is a beautiful medium, faithful and true, who has treasures in the spirit-world. Let all such, — so *many* such! — wrestle with the weeping angels: —

"DEAR BROTHER PEEBLES, — I write to you for aid, sympathy, and influence. My husband has become so infatuated with a young lady, that he says he does not love me, and that he will never live with me again. This is a terrible blow. I love him as *dear* as I ever did, yet I can have no control over him. I think he is either *obsessed*, or *deranged*. He has left me perfectly destitute; no home. I am now a dependent upon my friends, which, you know, is very *humiliating* to me. And now, dear brother, I want you to help me establish my home again, happy as it has been. It *can*, I feel; it *must* be done. He must not bring this reproach on Spiritualism, and a curse like this on his family. See him, and turn him right. For God's sake, help me! As I look at our four helpless little ones, it almost crazes me to know that I am left alone to protect and care for them. Dear brother, let me hear from you soon. I feel you can and will help me, and save him. I feel that the good and true spirits will, and are trying to aid and help me. I will not despair, though all seems of inky darkness, and the gulf impassable; yet I hope. Please let me hear from you at once; for my heart is almost broken.

"Your sister in trouble,

"CLEVELAND, O., Jan. 6, 1871.

"MRS. ———. *Dear Friend,* — Your communication of —— lies before me, inciting sadness of spirit. It is only one among many of a similar character reaching me each year. This social problem is to me a continual puzzle; and, while I mean to be charitable, I must be just. How your husband, possessing the instinct common to humanity, could thus leave you destitute; how he could leave those four little children, whom he had been instrumental in bringing into the world, leave them to look up with tearful eyes and call in vain for a father, a father to love and counsel, savors of a reckless inhumanity, bordering upon mental insanity. It is not the work, my sister, of Spiritualism, but rather of demonism, — a psychological infatuation thrown around him by the serpentine charms of that 'young woman.' Is he dead to common justice, dead to duty, dead to those holy and paternal relations that should unite father and child? He will awake some day, in this moral maelstrom, to feel those bitter, biting, galling regrets, — to feel that anguish that no painter can put on canvas, so sure as God is, so sure as there is compensation. He would evidently say to me, in pursuing this course, 'I am seeking happiness.' So does the slimy serpent, when leaving his frosty den to catch the first sunbeams of spring. Happiness based in selfishness can not succeed; neither can the priceless boon be obtained at the expense of a wife's happiness, and injustice done to four little children. Every child born on this earth has the right to demand honorable recognition, care, and counsel from the father as well as the mother; has the right to be loved by both parents; and the right to a sound, practical education. . . . Gladly would I assist you, were it in my power; but I do not know where Mr. ——— is, nor have I the means of finding him. Could I lay my hand upon his shoulder, and plead for those children, — those olive-branches, that need to grow up under the sunshine of home and sweet home influences, — perhaps I might induce him to return, prodigal-like, to his family. Does he not know there is such a principle as self-sacrifice? that it is noble to forget self for others' good? Rest assured that you have my sympathy, and may command my services in any possible way that will bring about reconciliation, and help secure the good of all concerned. . . . Most truly thine,

"J. M. PEEBLES."

Is there not a homeopathy in the spiritual science? What but this shall cure our magnetic gluttonies with which we are surfeited? This getting drunk on the spheres of spirits! *Promiscuous* magnetism are the hells of mediumship, — inductive to sensual pollution! The sun is coldest when nearest in winter. The fleshly contact may be the farthest from heaven. The most potent healing is when the mediumized hand touches not the person. Physical nearness may be spiritual distance. Hand to hand may be earthly; soul to soul is heavenly. The sensuous will jeer at this: let them! The hand is magnetically charged with the voiceless language of the heart! By thy *hand* thou shalt be known; by its touch thy secret shall be revealed. The kiss of the sensuous lip gives coloring to character.

The sacramental wine of fashionable Christians, touched by their dainty fingers, effervesces with pride of caste, and every participant is tainted with vanity: it is indeed the blood of idols. Beware of a magnetic satiety: it is a spiritual fever!

In a valuable article published in "The American Spiritualist," making distinction between mere "*Spiritists* and *Spiritualists*," Mr. Peebles says, —

"If in any way given to constructive thought, they [Spiritists] place the base of the pyramid in the air, and then seek to adjust the physical forces and relational magnetisms to the neglect of those divine principles that take hold upon heaven and eternal life. They insist that their bodies are their own, and they have a right to use them as they will. Another way this of asserting the right of 'passional promiscuity.' The slavering, staggering drunkard admires the argument. 'Have I not a right,' he indignantly exclaims, 'a *right* to use my body as I choose? to put any thing into it I please?' and down goes the poisoned dram of liquor! To state is to refute such a monstrous position. . . . "Through suffering, discipline, and painful experiences, these social errorists will learn that liberty is not license; that love is not lust; that psychological influence is not spiritual attraction; and that gratification is not happiness, nor the right way to obtain it, in any realm of existence where intelligences exist as moral beings. To 'him that evercometh' is the paradise of purity promised. Our angels teach us that sensualists, stung with mental suffering, people lowest conditions in the tartarean spheres of the after life. It is not much — it is not *all* — to be a mere Spiritist. Multitudes of wild Indians are Spiritists; millions of Chinamen have been Spiritists from remotest antiquity; the polygamy-practicing dervishes in Mohammedan countries are Spiritists, and their tests are absolutely astounding. Some Mormons are excellent clairvoyants Spiritists. But clairvoyance, tests, facts, phenomena, all combined, have not made them philosophers, — have not saved them. Alone, they will never educate nor spiritually redeem humanity. . . .

"On the natural plane, considered from the Adamic side of life, it is well and wise to 'multiply and replenish the earth;' and every child thus born has the right to demand an honorable recognition from the father as well as the mother, — has the right to be loved and cared for by both parents, and the right to a sound, practical education. Finally, these selfish, credulous, pompous, exquisite, faint-hearted, shiftless, sensuous, flirting Spiritists, generally quite content with the alphabet of disorderly phenomena, need the quickening influences of the Divine Spirit, need religious conviction and moral culture, need conversion to, and baptism into, the heavenly principles of *Spiritualism*. . . .

"*Genuine Spiritualists*, — there are multitudes of these. They already constitute a vast army. Bearing upon their foreheads God's seal of manhood and womanhood, they daily walk the Mount of Beatitude, and commune with the transfigured who glide along the love-lands of heaven. Having trust in God, faith in the possibilities of humanity, and a blessed knowledge of immortality, through the present ministry of spirits, they are a moral power in the world. They live to-day as though conscious of being already in eternity. They are above the commission of unworthy acts. Seeking neither praise nor fulsome flattery, they are practical reformers, doing good for goodness' sake. Candid and sincere, they take no selfish advantage of others' weaknesses. Broad and catholic, they can work with Unitarians, Free Religionists, Liberalists, *all* true workers. In method they are more constructive than destructive. Relating to books, Bibles, and spiritual teachings, they exercise their own judgment. Administering reproof in gentleness, slow to believe ill of others, they forgive as they would be forgiven. Accepting Spiritualism as expressing the outflowing love of God, the brotherhood of man, the divine principle of holiness, the indwelling Christ of love and wisdom, the Comforter promised in the New Testament, the divine guest crowned with immortality, — genuine Spiritualists, in this and all lands, strive to live pure, practical lives, that others may see their good works, and thus be induced to accept the truth of heaven."

"Touch me not with profane fingers," says the delicate rose, fortified among thorns. "Touch me not; for I am not yet risen to my Father," said Jesus to Mary. Retard not the spiritualizing work. "Let thine eye be single" is Mr. Peebles's motto now. His prayer is, "Give me a sunny room, pure air, pure water, orderly associations, flowers, a clean forest or glen, a Gethsemane under the palms for meditation, a mountain for transfiguration, an angel's breath soothing my fevered brain to sleep, and my *loved* angel waiting there, silently distilling dewy dreams of an 'Eden Home.'"

We have a lady friend in Greenbush, Wis., whose mother, pure and tender as a seraph angel, made her house-plants her pets to love. Watering with care, touching them often, and speaking child-like names, they grew thrifty and beautiful. When she sickened, the plants, though cared for with equal attention by her daughter, also wilted; and when she physically died, they too died, — no art could save them. Did she not take their souls with her? So our brother would do: be so spiritual, so close now to the souls of flowers, birds, children, men, women, angels, that, when emancipation comes, he may still be wedded to their souls, to make his heaven.

In his earlier years of mediumistic growth, Mr. Peebles requested to be entranced, that he might see and hear for himself, and so be more efficient in the work of the spiritual ministry; but his guides have demonstrated, that, with his refined organism, it would unfit him, though it might not others, for earthly use, and that the highest spirituality is, when every faculty is celestially polarized, leaving the mind in *outward* consciousness, too, for the attainment of fullness, wholeness, perfectness. He has sometimes been oblivious to this wise injunction of his band, more particularly in the presence of clairvoyants.

At a meeting in Fond du Lac, Wis., immediately following the "Wilson and Haddock Discussion," when the former gave public tests of spirit-presence, Mr. Peebles was completely enveloped in the magnetism of the dominant sphere, neutralizing that of his attendant angel, when some other materialistic spirit partially psychologized his brain. On the way from the meeting, he demanded of his spirits to entrance him, that he might the better convince the doubting world, seeking the light of this gospel. We argued against him. Instantly a ray shot through the obsessing sphere, and scattered it as the outburst of a sun from the cloud; and he reeled under it, like Saul on his way to Damascus, when "there shined round about him a light from heaven." Powhattan then bathed him in the rosy influence of sympathy; when he drooped his head, and wept, holding us by the hand tremblingly, and praying under the silent stars to be forgiven his mistrust of divine wisdom. That night, in a company consisting, besides us two, of Raymond Tallmage and wife, Mrs. Julia T. Ruggles (daughter of Gov. Tallmage), and Mrs. Barrett, Mr. Peebles was strangely influenced by an Indian, then by "Queen of Morn;" when he laid hands of benediction upon all present, whispering a prayer, till hearts melted into tears, and tears were windows of soul to see the angels. Never was reward for faith in love so beautifully and divinely illustrated.

Mr. Peebles encourages spiritual circles for the "manifestations," as a basis of mediumistic development; inspires the mediums to perseverance, and the people to protect them in their beneficent ministry of love from the angels, but demands order, sincerity, charity. Truth is sacred; and credit is due to all its revealers, of every age and race and calling. This position of his is ennobling. Divine is character, when its soul gives justice where it is due, — to books, mediums, governments, and religions.

Lecturing in ———, he was importuned several times to sit in a promiscuous circle that was really repulsive to him. Knowing his own sensitiveness, he politely declined. "No," said his friends, "you help the circle so much: you are too particular, too proud." Yielding, just to accommodate them, he became entangled in a magnetic web. It was earthly, painful, darkening. Unable to resist it there, and realizing his moral peril, he seized his hat, rushed from the room, and ran at night two miles through the city; where, reaching a lonely spot by a great rock, he kneeled down and prayed and wept like a child, speaking the language of Jesus in his temptation, "Get thee hence, obsessing spirit!" Then fell that gentle wave of light from his band, breaking the spell; and with a whisper a voice said, "Brother, the lesson is well: be wiser; keep pure the white vesture with which thou art robed."

Natural to his refined ideal, Mr. Peebles recommends that a congregation assembled for spiritual communion be arranged in the order of a spiritual circle, alternately negative with positive, the more mediumistic in front, as on the armature. He wants the hall a sanctuary, *consecrated* as a "holy of holies," and used for no other purpose; for a variety of uses is incipient to obsession. Like the temple of the soul, it must be single to holiness, orderly, architecturally beautiful, airy; no somber shading, after the Episcopal style, but full of light and the fragrance of flowers. Boxes, pulpits, and desks intercept the magnetic circulation. "Away with them, and give me a broad, free platform." He earnestly advocates settling educated and trustworthy speakers in yearly engagements. He is in favor of alternate readings between speaker and people, with the interblendings of congregational singing, harmonizing into oneness of spirit. This method he has tried with brilliant success. Only one speaker on the platform at a time is his demand. Forehead to forehead is the line of inspiration. He would have the exercises simple and impressive, lifting the soul to diviner purposes. He cares nothing now about proselyting: is more constructive than destructive. How shall we convert the world? By *living* example! "We have enough believers," he says, "three millions genuine. Is the world the better for it? That's the question!" Risen above the chronic egotism and self-inflation of mere sensation, to attract idle curiosity, he calmly waits his hour of heavenly illumination, and does his duty, and enjoys his privilege, scattering truth-seed, criticising severely, and lovingly replenishing. Making an effort in —— to engage there a month's labor for one of our worthy young speakers, he was refused, on the ground that it would not command "big houses." This species of spiritual hydrophobia, poisoning so many city societies, every sensible Spiritualist deplores. Alluding to this matter in a private letter, he writes, —

"The saying, 'Draw,' provokes me. Dancing jacks and fighting dogs often *draw* crowds."

In moments of trial, when all seems to go wrong, our brother writes to a confiding brother, showing his child-like trust in the higher life: "I am sick in heart, sick in soul, sick of the world, sick of grasping Spiritualists, but not sick of God, heaven, angels, Spiritualism, or you." This said and felt, he rises as an oak that has taken deeper root, indorsing the poet: —

"In the tempest of life, when the wave and the gale
Are around and above, if thy footing should fail,
If thine eye should grow dim, and thy caution depart,
Look aloft, and be firm and be fearless of heart."

It injures a magnet to let it lie beside pieces of iron and steel. It should be suspended alone, with armature on. Understanding this law, Mr. Peebles, these days, guards against introductions, just before speaking, as far as it is possible with the rules of courtesy. From some ante-room, where he sits silent to catch the inspiring force, he prefers to pass direct to the rostrum, so that the angel-sphere, inflamed by the sympathy of the audience, may envelop him; for the touch of an angular hand may depolarize the influence. Owing largely to this habit, Emma Hardinge holds so perfect sway over her hearers, lifting them up by the power of heavenly truth. If a speaker is submerged in the combined spheres of a mixed audience, no higher thought is uttered than what floats through the general mind; therefore little or no good is done except to equipoise the magnetism. The speaker on the rostrum should be spiritually insulated, handing down the truth from the ministering angels. When such worship is closed, and the hearts of the people are warmed in love of a purer life, he greets them most cordially, adopting the Quaker style of shaking hands with everybody, imparting in that friendly grasp the virtue which the spirit imparted to him. Truthfully said the Nazarene, adverting to this law, "And the glory which Thou hast given me I have given them, that they may be one, even as Thou and I are one."

As an instance illustrative of his strict fidelity to order, may be mentioned his experience at Sturgis, when dedicating the "Spiritual Church," some of the brick of which he carried in his own arms. When the vast congregation was seated, he noticed just in front of him a woman of gross sphere, dark to him as a "case of obsession." The occasion demanded his best efforts. The woman was a sister, whom he would not offend for his right hand. What should he do? To rouse undue will-force might be combative; there was danger of a failure. Mustering moral courage, he sent a request for her to vacate the seat, to be supplied by another, better adapted to a spiritual circle. The woman, understanding the law, gave heed with a commendable grace, which touched his sympathy and brought her immediately into the sphere of inspiration, when the house became a Pentecost, the Spirit hovering on the people as with "tongues of fire."

CHAPTER XXIII.

"QUEEN OF MORN."—A VISION.

"Heaven rests on those two heaving hills of snow."

"And like a lily on the river floating,
She floats upon the river of his thoughts."

"By the night visions," "In a deep sleep," "I was in the Spirit on the Lord's Day," "And his face did shine as the sun, and his raiment was white as snow!" What meaneth all this? The angel knoweth, not philosophy; and the angel, without our volition, hath ushered us within the pavilion of the Spirit to see and hear. Have we not touched the spheres of heaven? By some prophet-guardian, we have seen "signs in the stars," writings upon scrolls, celestial scenery, and angel forms arrayed in the beauty-light of immortality; have heard the mystic voices, and the music of seraph choirs; have had the perception of principles, and felt the deep impression of soul in the silence of spirit-thought, too holy for utterance. With Paul, we sometimes think the words heard "are not lawful to utter." God help us if we sin the sin of presumption.

Under such guidance, we have seen that nuptials in heaven are keyed to qualification. "When thou art worthy," is the invariable rule of the "Beloved John;" "They that are accounted *worthy* to obtain that world" is the moral lesson of Jesus. In spirit-life hearts are to be *earned* at a great price. Some dear angel looks down into our soul, and loves there divinely, and then weighs our soul in the scale of justice, poised on the pivot of harmony. Is it faithful? is it pure? is it the echo-voice of sacrificing love? Ah! what a sin to weep over, if we are jealous because a sainted angel loves that soul more than we do! Who have the strongest claims? They who love us the most morally, the most wisely, the most tenderly, the most sacredly, the most spiritually. So the hearts we would hold in our bosoms must be preserved with eternal vigilance. To win victory is to love with an ever watchful self-denial. What a momentous truth! what a solemn warning in our reckless, guilt-impassioned world! What saith the angel by our side?—

"There are exiled hearts, disappointed hearts, bleeding hearts, bruised and riven hearts, forgiving hearts that have secrets,—hearts so mournful, so spiritual, that when we hither come to see their purity, behold, it is to witness a crucifixion more pitiful than that of Calvary,—hearts never mated in your world, but kept in reserve till the bride or bridegroom cometh from the house of many mansions to meet the emancipated prisoner of earth,—hearts that are doves going forth *from* the ark with olive-branches to humanity, whose very oil of love is pressed out by suffering for others' good, blessing everybody else, but ever pleading to see face to face, and hold hand within hand, whom Divine Wisdom has anointed for 'nuptials in heaven.' Under the dissolving crimson of life's setting sun, it is indeed a privilege to be friendly to such hearts, to touch them down to the springs, and be silent. Here is a "Paradise Lost," whose melancholy solitude is pleasure; for the tears that fall there are dews, and forth from their refreshing will unfold an Eden in which the betrothed Eve shall walk to greet her beloved 'neath the Tree of Life."

Whilst in Washington, Mr. Peebles one day called upon his esteemed friend, H. Clay Preuss, who, in spiritual entrancement, improvised a beautiful poem, entitled "Isle of the Blest," soon after published in "The Banner of Light," and set to music in "The Spiritual Harp." The psychometric *connoisseur* will recognize here the corroboration of our vision:—

"I see an isle, like woman's smile,
That blooms on a silver sea;
And from its groves of angel-loves
Swells music wild and free.

"Prefigured here, in marriage sphere,
We catch faint gleams of bliss,—
Of the sweet control of soul o'er soul,
When sealed by God's own kiss."

No one, not even Mr. Peebles himself, ever unveiled to us the secret hidden in his interesting editorial in "The Banner of Light," entitled, "The Two Star-Sisters of France." It is another witness of the truth of our vision. He outlines the life-history of Ernest

Renan and his sister Henriette, and Louis XVI. and his sister "*Madame Elizabeth.*" Henriette accompanied Ernest and his wife on his scientific mission into ancient Phœnicia, where brother and sister were both seized with a malignant fever.

"They were two souls warm with harmonious thought, and hearts beating as one. She went with him on to the loftiest pinnacles of Lebanon's mountains, and across the desert sands that line the Jordan, exchanging ideas with him, and living his very life.

"A French writer says, 'Notwithstanding her delicate health, she traveled to average eight leagues a day, being both a sort of private secretary who divined her brother's thoughts, and a sister of charity who watched with angelic tenderness over a precious existence, which she justly considered as the effulgent glory of her family and her name.' Though these long, tiresome journeys greatly fatigued her, she continued to assist her brother in writing 'The Life of Jesus,' till she felt the approaches of malignant fever. The symptoms grew worse; she was dangerous: yet her courage, for a brother's sake, seemed to defy the death-angel's touch. Ernest, hastening from 'Le Caton' with the surgeon, fell dangerously ill with the same fever. There they lay, brother and sister, sick and alone in a foreign land, the brother summoning all his energies to minister to his sister; the sister hiding her agony, concealing her sufferings, and struggling against the fever that was burning to her being's core, to watch by her brother's sick pillow. They fought death together, fought for each other, fought till they became unconscious. The sister awoke in heaven. Owing to Renan's robust constitution he survived; and, coming to consciousness, his first incoherent words were, 'Where's my sister?' The tearful eye of the surgeon told the story! Here my pen may drop. A recent writer of France says, 'Hunting in a friend's library, I came upon a pamphlet whose every line drew a tear. I know nothing more touching, sadder, or more beautiful, than the master-piece of a great thinker who bids a last farewell to a noble soul,' — that a *sister!*'"

In telling this touching story, Mr. Peebles evidently intends to compare himself in thought to Renan, traveling in quest of truth, — his sister, his angel-guide, who passed on before him, long before him, but, returning found his heart beating with her own the same musical concord; and "lo! she is by his side, traveling with him to the land of Adonis, near the holy Byblus and the sacred waters where the women of the ancient mysteries came to mingle their tears, to rest in the bosom of God."

The second star of France is Madame Elizabeth, "Queen of Morn," the harbinger of Mr. Peebles's pilgrimage over this strange world of ours.

"The Queen of Morn," and "The Spiritual Pilgrim!" this relation is the enchantment of the life he lives, this the soul of experiences, that threads life's silver chords round the world whither he goes, this the "Chain of Pearls" that blossoms ever upon his bosom to make his pilgrimage beautiful and fragrant with a love that descends dove-like from heaven. We must let him tell the story of Madame Elizabeth, as gleaned from the history he found in that antiquarian library in Boston: —

"Just prior to the stormy days of the Revolution, there arose in the French firmament another star, shedding a silvery radiance over the royal family and the entire kingdom of France. We refer to the *princess*, Madame Elizabeth Marie Hellene Capet, sister of Louis Capet, the noblest of the Bourbon line, and known in history as Louis the XVI., the martyr-king. Louis ascended the throne loving his people with a fatherly tenderness. His warm heart throbbing for the best welfare of France, he inaugurated a system of reforms that resulted in his dethronement and death. So popular was he with the poorer classes and the more benevolent of those in the higher walks of life, that a number of the most eminent jurists and advocates in France presented themselves, soliciting the glory of defending Louis XVI. Among them were Cazales, Necker, Nicolai, Lally-Tollendal, Malouet, Mounier, &c. *Thomas Paine* defended Louis in the Assembly. The illustrious Schiller sent to the Convention from Germany a memorial in favor of the king. Other petitions from scholars and counts reached the French capital, pleading for his life. But the decree of death had gone forth. Louis was aware of it by a presentiment. He had seen a female form, clothed in white, walking in the royal apartment, and then disappearing, — signal that a reigning Bourbon was to depart to the land of the just.

"During his imprisonment in that gloomy tower, the Princess Elizabeth left her brother's presence only to comfort Marie Antoinette and educate Louis's two children, — the Dauphin (Louis Charles), and Marie Therese. In one of the king's last conversations with his counsel, he spoke of the kind and tender consolations he had received, and especially of the happiness derived from the caresses of an affectionate sister. He said, 'I will not speak of my children now, nor further of my sister, whose life has been one unvaried course of devotion, courage, and affection. Her alliance was sought by Spain and Piedmont; and, at the death of Christina of Saxony, the canonesses of Piedmont wished to elect her their abbess; but nothing could separate her from me. She clung to me in my misfortunes as others attached themselves to my prosperity. But I wish to speak of what gives my heart keenest pain, — the unjust opinion entertained by my subjects of the queen.'

"Madame Elizabeth's devotion to her brother and family, while incarcerated in that dungeon prison, — mending their garments in midnight hours, administering medicines, speaking encouraging words, forgetting self, breathing prayers of trust and hope, and catching each stray moment to educate the children in music, drawing, and the fine arts, and conscious all this time that she was under the ban of The National Assembly, and almost certain of a death upon the scaffold, — challenges an equal in all the historic ages. And withal, how brave! When the mock-trial of the king was in process, the Princess Elizabeth was the only member of the royal family able to get near him. This, being inspired with a sister's love, she accomplished by rushing from window to window, with all the daring of an Indian maiden. The furious mob, in the name of liberty, seeing her near the king, mistook her for the object of their hate, Marie Antoinette, and shouted, 'There's the Austrian woman, the queen: slay her! slay her!' The soldiers of The National Guard who were surrounding the princess endeavored to undeceive them; but the noble-hearted heroine turned to the soldiers, face calm as an angel's, and exclaimed, 'No, no! Undeceive them not! Let them *slay* me! Let their bayonets drain and drink my heart's blood, if 'twill save the queen!'

"Deep trials refine the soul-forces; and human nature, thus refined, and outlived in its highest estate, brings heaven down to earth. This princess looked upon her poverty and sufferings, all for her brother's sake, as blessings in disguise. She felt that sorrow was but the prophecy of diviner joy; and, the nearer she approached the fatal close of life, the more radiant grew the brightness of her virtues and the glory of her martyrdom. Her prayers, beatific in angelic fervor, were full of forgiveness for her brother's murderous enemies; and such of her letters as were preserved reveal a soul all aglow with purity and affection.

" 'Every sentence, oh, how tender!
Every line is full of love.' "

"To a friend, she closes a letter thus:—

" 'I enjoy, by anticipation, the pleasure you will experience in receiving this pledge of friendship and of confidence. To be once more with you, and to see you happy, is all I desire. You know how deeply I love you. I embrace you with my whole heart.

" 'Elizabeth Marie.'

"This beautiful woman, so full of sisterly affection, persuasive tenderness, divine forgiveness, pious enthusiasm, and genuine heroism, was guillotined soon after her brother, upon the charge of corresponding with the king's brothers, and being an accomplice to the crimes of the Bourbon family, as 'heir apparent' to the throne of France. Twenty-four others shared a like fate at the same time. Her composure and touching resignation edified and astonished them all. It seemed her mission to minister unto others. She continued to encourage them to the last with words of cheer, and the exhibition of a noble moral heroism. Passing before her, they all bowed low as they ascended the scaffold. Madame Elizabeth's turn had come. Behold the scene!—tenderness in her eyes, love on her dewy lips, life in her warm veins, and purity on her white bosom, that so gently, tremulously heaved. The executioner tears aside the robes from her chaste form. Her dark hair hangs loose and wavy. She kneels. Her fair, beautiful neck lays upon the block. The axe glimmers, falls: the princess is in eternity!

"The last words of her counsel's defence were, 'She who at the court of France was deemed the most perfect model of every virtue can not be the enemy of Frenchmen.' The historian, De Beauchesne, says, 'She was the best and most holy of friends, who, wearing heaven in her heart, and love in her eyes, soothed the most cruel pangs with the balm of her words, and with her angelic gaze ever re-assured the soul. . . . Her whole being was too beautiful, too lofty, not to forget itself when any other interest presented. Hers was the purest expression of that single-hearted candor, of that *holy affection*, which Raphael has given to the mother of Jesus,—an angelic grace, a Christian serenity, that never occurred to the imagination of antiquity.'

"Now, encircled in light, she treads the fairest fields of heaven. Her robes, reflecting her soul's purity, are bright with glittering sprays from the 'River of Life,' that John saw proceeding from the throne of God. Her harp breathes only harmonial thoughts, and the sweet love-strains of undying melody. Her tears have been crystallized into pearls, to adorn the faithful. Her sorrows have ripened into holy and heavenly sympathies; and, through her poverty-experiences of earth, she is better enabled to now enrich millions with wisdom.

"Souls do not forget. All love is immortal. Doubtless she oft descends to earth with holy evangels, to cheer the sad as they journey o'er the sands of time, yet trustingly look upward to the evergreen mountains of promise, and to those ever-flowing fountains that dot the plaza-lands of paradise."

Closing the recital of this sad history, so feelingly told by Mr. Peebles, our best thought is found in silence, meditating upon what the angel said, "There are exiled hearts!" The elegiac words of Phebe Cary, let us quote them for our "Pilgrim:"—

"O my friend! O my dearly beloved!
Do you feel, do you know,
How the times and the seasons are going?
Are they weary and slow?
Does it seem to you long in the heavens,
My true, tender mate,
Since here we were living together,
Where, dying, I wait?
'Tis long years, as we count by the springtimes,
By the birth of the flowers:
What are years, ay, eternities even,
To love such as ours?"

In the "Isle of the Blest," the "Queen of Morn" is associated in Mr. Peebles's spirit-band with "Celestia" and "Morning Star,"—"Sisters of purity;" who play together upon "the harp, lute, and lyre;" whose music, though not often *heard* by our "Pilgrim," yet is it *felt*, soothing his spirit, and lifting his affections to the life they live with the child-angels of God.

At the gray of a summer's evening, this angel of all his years, whose hand had touched him, whose influence had so often enchanted his hopes, this "Queen of Morn," vestured in white, accompanied by her sisters, rapt in the poesy of song, whispered in the clairaudient ear of Mrs. Nellie Smith of Sturgis these precious words, addressed direct to our weeping pilgrim:—

"Come with me, O my beloved! come away for a season from thy cares and weary work! I will await thee on the green banks of the beautiful river, and give thee love's welcome.

"I'll tune my harp to its richest measures, and sing thee to sweet repose.

"Life of my life, for ever near, for ever dear, light is darkness without thee, and music is mourning. Knowest thou something of love? I will teach thee more; will perfume thy throbbing heart with ecstasies of which thou hast not known. Oh! what can I not promise thee? Rich gifts are in my keeping, but through love alone.

"My beautiful, I have watched o'er thy steps, and have exulted in thy soul's fair expansion; have seen the tides of feeling accumulate force, and noble aspirations take loftier flights: while love, the crowning palm of thy rich nature, has sent its roots deeper and deeper into the region of thy soul's mines of iron and gold and gems, exhaustless and indestructible. I know thee well, true love of mine; and all thy yearnings for the perfect life are clear to my spirit-gaze. Earth does not satisfy thee, nor should it. Will my love in measureless waves allay thy thirst? Ah! what can I give thee more? What askest thou? Speak!

"We have held nothing back when thou hast called: we have robed thee in angel royalty, have filled thy brain with poesy's true spirit, and touched thy lips with flame. We have set thy feet in high places, and have given souls into thy hands. What wilt thou still? Love, praise, and honor are at thy feet as myrrh and incense. Ask, if thy deep soul desires aught else, and I'll fly through Nature's vast domains to do thy bidding, — to bless *thee*, loved and treasured one. Perhaps the humblest instruments only may be at my command: do not disdain them. The Father's love overshadoweth all. In love alone can I approach thee, to touch the springs of thy own love-nature. Yet ever am I near: in thine orisons and meeting, I sing solemn symphonies, and chant the high Te Deum. Like the sparkling waters round a golden isle would I circle thee with sleepless vigils. Ever the burden of my song is love."

CHAPTER XXIV.

A NEW CYCLE.

"Life hath its harvest morns,
  Its tasseled corn and purple-weighted vine,
Its gathered sheaves of grain, the blessed sign
Of plenteous reaping, bread and pure rich wine,
  Full hearts for harvest times." — ISA GILBERT.

AFTER four years of faithful service in the Western department of "The Banner of Light," Mr. Peebles resigned his editorship, which the publishers of this stable journal reluctantly accepted. Yielding with a most friendly spirit, the editor-in-chief, Luther Colby, penned a very beautiful tribute, fraught with tender words, and with angels' blessings invoked upon his attached brother. In his valedictory, Mr. Peebles says, —

"Though life is fraught with varied changes, — meeting to-day, and parting to-morrow, — friendship, inhering as a principle in the human soul, never perishes. It is only a germinal bud on earth, blooming into a sweeter, fresher fragrance in heaven. Cordial in our nature, never can we forget the friends cherished, hands clasped, or acquaintances formed during the several years of our editorial connection with 'The Banner of Light.'

"If competent of self-judgment, it has been our aim, our soul-purpose each week, to be just and impartial, — to benefit humanity by elucidating the phenomena, the philosophy, and practical tendencies of Spiritualism. If, in so doing, a sarcastic word has carelessly slipped from our pen, or a severe thought taken form on the eighth page, wounding a sincere soul, we deeply regret it. 'To err is human; to forgive, divine.'

"Not a link in the chain of mutual sympathy and good feeling between us lies severed or rusted. In the business capacity and strict integrity of Wm. White & Co., we have the most perfect confidence; and only the hope of wider usefulness inclines us to enter a somewhat different and more diffusive field of action."

The "field" to which he refers was the general supervision of another weekly, "The Universe," published by H. N. F. Lewis, then in Chicago, subsequently in New York. In entering upon this task, to which he was so cordially invited, as editor-in-chief of this radical paper, he says, —

"Freedom is the watchword of the age, and as applicable to periodicals as to speech; still, this freedom must not be allowed to degenerate into anarchy, nor liberty into wanton license. A brotherly interchange of the most diverse sentiments, however, is educational, beneficial, and beautiful in practical results. Full of faith in the divine consciousness of the race, and trusting much to the noble instincts and innate worth of each and all individuals constituting our common humanity, we shall nevertheless bear the responsibility of only our *own* weekly productions. The thoughts that throb for birth into outer life shall flow from our pen in earnest words. If they warm the heart, gladden with sunshine the soul, and, removing the rubbish, plant roses along the rugged pathway of life, well; if not, they must move on, the guests of more receptive natures."

Some of Mr. Peebles's choicest gems of thought were published in "The Universe." We make a few extracts: —

"Senators, representatives, and other officials of high degree, rise to power through political corruption. Is the candidate available? — that's the question. Court decisions are carried by intrigue. Money, or a 'valuable consideration' as the equivalent, has become the underlying method of conducting public affairs. Will it pay? is the inquiry. Human integrity, justice, are among the 'lost graces' in political circles: the question is, 'What will it cost to get the office, and what can I make out of it?' The late war intensified this demoralization. The back-brain inspiration, so thoroughly aroused by it, still lingers. . . .

"Education, justice, equality, are the watchwords of all advanced thinkers. Education should be not merely the learning of words, but integral, — a cultivation of the intellect, of the affections, of the emotions, of the higher intuitive powers, — all those qualities that make the good man, the good woman. The sexes should be educated together, each assisting in the mental and moral development of the other. The education of the future, if in accordance with the genius of the age, will popularize hygiene, art, music, industry, integrity, peace, freedom, and sanitary reforms.

"Science is sifting theologies. Buried Asiatic cities are being exhumed; Central Africa is being explored; cables are girding the globe; and the Rocky Mountains have dwindled almost to sand-hills for the laying of the iron trail, along which schoolboys will soon fly their kites, and over which graceful summer swallows will sing their vesper praises. With steam for breath, and lightning for brain, the winds and seas conquered, the rock-ribbed mountains at our feet, now who will give us an air-ship, some *aerial velocipede*, that, swiftly cutting those clear atmospheric strata that look down upon northern ice-belts, shall land explorers upon the inner shores that fringe the polar seas? Is not the Columbus born, that, leading the way, will enable us to clasp the hands of those inhabitants who, in isolation, have so long summered and wintered in the frigid regions of the North Pole? Every acre explored, the whole earth is to become the servant of man, with palms and dates flourishing in deserts, flowers blooming along the highways, and fruit-trees bending with matured sustenance, wide and extended as the avenues of travel.

"There is a coming millennium for humanity. It will be a practical age. Men and women will be kings and queens, — exact equals, and laws unto themselves. The principle of love will link heart to heart, hearth to hearth, hamlet to hamlet, and nation to nation, — a banded brotherhood and sisterhood of interests, restoring the poet's Eden. . . .

"It is grand to contemplate optimism from the standpoint of the deep thinker; but any loose, illogical, illy-explained system of optimism — that lumps moral qualities and immoral tendencies into one conglomerated mass, that seeks the destruction of all distinctions between vice and virtue, and inferentially says, that pirates, murderers, thieves, sensualists, vampires, impostors, are 'doing their work,' thus implying that their work is legitimate, orderly, beautiful, and divine — is deserving of little consideration. The advocates and adherents of such a theory are entitled only to pity.

"That pirates, impostors, and all such characters, are doing a 'work' is very evident; and so is the inebriate doing a work, when he pours into his body poisoned liquors. This work fruits out in blotches, diseases, poverty, wretchedness, and a general dwarfing of the moral nature. Had not all such work better be left undone? Is there no way to the enjoyment of the heaven of temperance, purity, and harmony, save through the winding way of drunkenness and debauchery? Such a dogma is, —

'A monster of such frightful mien,
That to be hated needs but to be seen.'

It is quite time for Spiritualists to sift the chaff from the wheat, the sense from the nonsense, afloat in their name, and, gathering up their precious truths, now 'lying around loosely,' put them into shape and system, for acceptance and practice.

"The organizing of harmonial associations — banded brotherhoods and sisterhoods, based upon equality — would, while destroying all antagonisms between stolen capital and daily toil, make labor attractive. Furthermore, sinking selfishness into self-sacrifice, they would do away with isolation, and this crushing poverty that so fearfully obtains in the great cities. Those united societies termed 'Shakers' have no poor; and, on the day of Pentecost, those baptized from the heavens were inspired to hold 'all things in common.'

"Three important needs are constantly pressing themselves upon the masses. They are necessities, and may be denominated by the common terms, physical, social, spiritual. As legitimate, looking to the supply of these needs so universally felt, why not organize associations, thus reducing the better theories upon this subject to practical life? Of what avail the ideal, unless it fruits into the real?

"Under physical needs may be classed home, food, clothing, labor, amusements; under social necessities may be mentioned families, friendships, sympathies, music, art, literature.

"Under the head of spiritual needs may be designated moral culture, education, progress, spirit-communion, and such inspirations as shall help each and all to near the heavenly life on earth. How many sweet associations cluster around the endearing word 'home,' — a home possessing all the foregoing comforts and requirements, a home ever vernal with heart-flowers of beauty, a home with cordial hands to clasp our own, a home where wisdom guides, and love is law!

"These homes, with agricultural products for a physical basis, would afford the choicest opportunities for mental and moral culture. Manufactures would express the forms of use connected with such progressive movements. Commerce would be a means of supply, or, rather, a transfer of commodities, upon the basis of equivalents. Certain homes of the brotherhood would necessarily be mostly agricultural; others, manufacturing; and others still would combine the two in connection with the educational. A chain of sympathy and common interest, looking to the good of all, would thus grow up between these homes, whether located in this or foreign countries.

"A social order, possessing these and other beneficial tendencies relating to the equality of the sexes and the strict administration of justice, will ultimately prevail throughout the world. The angels so teach; and those who have tasted the first-fruits of the kingdom, or rather the republic, of heaven, actualized on earth, so believe. The *Shakers*, Essenians of the nineteenth century, are already in the vestibule of this temple.

"Such homes should have one common and elegant building in the centre, for lectures, music, educational pursuits, gymnasium-exercises, amusements, &c. Around, and branching outward from this, there might be a system of cottage-buildings, all in form and order. Purity the reigning principle, and culture the common aim, the interests of one should be felt to be the highest interests of all. Each should seek 'another's wealth,' — that is, another's good,— and find supreme delight in serving all; and those entering into such an enterprise should do it with a life consecrated to human good and happiness."

CHAPTER XXV.

APPOINTED CONSUL.

"Better be cheated to the last,
Than lose the blessed hope of truth."

"Let this suffice
To show why I my pilgrim patronize.
It came from my own heart; so to my head,
And then into my fingers trickled." — BUNYAN'S PILGRIM.

SINCE being associated with spirits of the Eastern world, Mr. Peebles felt an unquenchable longing to travel thither in quest of truth. The discipline, thus far morally enforced, taught him that the *spiritual* beauties of Oriental Spiritualism lay hidden under the *débris* of more modern literature. He dreamed awake; awake he acted: go he must. His whole soul burned with a flame of love for classic lands, for ancient ruins, for Asian mountains, for the poesy and song that throb the sunniest under the rising sun. Like the other major events of his life, this purpose, evoked by the spirits, cast its shadow into his horoscope, and there was seen by different clairvoyants long before his plans were matured. While lecturing in Detroit, Mich., he met Mrs. R. G. Murray, now in the Summer Isle, whose husband was formerly a Presbyterian clergyman, but an earnest and noble Spiritualist now, ripening for the great harvest. This lady, upon becoming entranced by an Indian spirit, calling himself "Big Thunder," said, "A bright, pale-faced spirit tells me to say to you, brother, that you are to go over the wide waters before the leaves become many times green and sere again. You are to go in a great ship-canoe, and in an official capacity." He inquired, "Why do you say that?" The spirit replied, "Because the pale-faced guardian so says, and because I see in your hand state-papers, sealed with red wax, and circled with red tape."

About four years prior to Mr. Peebles's travels to the East, the following vision was given to him by a clairvoyant medium in Philadelphia, Dr. H. T. Child, an experienced Spiritualist and writer, being present. The lady entranced, looking into a rock crystal of peculiar shape, said, —

"I see you in a foreign country. The people must be English; for their dress and language nearly correspond with the American. You are traversing the country on some interesting mission. Now you stand beside a singular vehicle: it resembles a wheelbarrow. A lady — it is Mrs. Hardinge — with yourself grasp the handles, and seem trundling it up the hillside. How faithfully, zealously, you toil! How strange! This vehicle seems loaded with books, pamphlets, and periodicals. A short, stirring, sincere, and enthusiastic individual seems to be loading the wheelbarrow. Mercy! how he works!' If it be true that the worker wins, a golden harvest must await such consecration to a holy purpose." It needs no supernatural gift to identify in this worker Mr. Burns, of the Progressive Library, London.

Seasons came and passed. Mrs. Murray spoke to him several times of her vision, expressing perfect faith in its fulfillment; but he then was doubtful, deep as was his desire to prove her a true prophetess. Our life-lines, do not angels hold them, and fasten them where they belong, from the past out into the future?

Some time in July, 1869, Harrison Barrett, Superintendent of the S. and F. R. R., invited Mr. Peebles to lecture in Sheboygan, Wis. Through the generous auspices of Rev. Mr. Howard, the Unitarian church was open to him. At the close of his lecture, he informed the people that he should start in a few days for Europe. That was his last lecture in America before leaving. There we parted with mutual blessings invoked. Soon his resolution was reported to the Spiritual papers. Col. D. M. Fox, editor of "The Present Age," then President of the National American Association of Spiritualists, thus spoke of his intended departure, —

"We are sorry to learn that Brother Peebles can not postpone his embarkation for Europe until our Annual National Convention, as we very much desired the calm counsel and genial influence of one who has been so long identified with the Spiritualistic movement. Our best wishes go with him; for we know how long and anxiously he has desired to visit the scenes of the Old World, and his intense desire to delve in its grand old libraries, containing their millions of volumes of ancient lore. With us, thousands of American Spiritualists will unite in saying, —

"'Where'er thou journeyest, or whate'er thy care,
My heart shall follow, and my spirit share.'"

Hearing of his design, friends in Washington and elsewhere procured for him a consulate to Trebisond, Asia. It was not expected. Mr. Lewis, of "The Universe," said, —

"We announced last week that Mr. Peebles was to set sail on Saturday, July 31, in the steamship 'City of Brooklyn,' for Liverpool, intending to visit the various countries of Europe, and, if possible, to continue his journeyings into the Orient. It has been Mr. Peebles's fervent desire, for years, to visit the Holy Land; but it has been uncertain whether he could accomplish this on the present trip. That doubt has now been removed.

"We have the pleasure of presenting our readers with the following note from Damon Y. Kilgore, Esq., of Philadelphia, received after the issue of our last number, which will convey gratifying intelligence to thousands: —

"PHILADELPHIA, July 30, 1869.

"H. N. F. LEWIS, ESQ. *Dear Sir,* — You will be pleased to learn that I have just received a telegram from Mr. Davis, Assistant Secretary of State, at Washington, stating that J. M. Peebles, editor-in-chief of 'The Universe,' has just been appointed Consul at Trebisond. . . . Our good brother left my office yesterday for New-York City, in the best of spirits. God bless him! DAMON Y. KILGORE.

"Trebisond is a leading commercial city of Turkey in Asia; and the personal advantage to Mr. Peebles of this appointment will be at once seen. It is needless to say that the official duties of the post will be conducted with scrupulous fidelity. This appointment affords an instance of proof, that the United States government does not bestow its favors entirely upon political aspirants."

"The Banner of Light" congratulated the appointment thus: —

"It is a wonder he was not rejected on account of his belief in Spiritualism. This appointment gratifies us exceedingly, as it is a proof that bigotry is lessening its hold on the minds of men in authority, and that justice is sure to achieve victory in the long run. How will our ecclesiastical friends like this appointment? Not remarkably well, we opine. Progress is ever onward, however; and those who attempt to retard it, through selfishness or bigotry, will surely be crushed by its ponderous wheels. May success attend Brother Peebles in his new mission is the sincere wish of his hosts of friends!"

E. S. Wheeler, of "The American Spiritualist," wrote, —

"We were made aware of the action in favor of the appointment of friend Peebles when in Washington this spring, and are not surprised at the result. We do not consider it 'a wonder he was not rejected on account of his belief in Spiritualism,' happening to know it was rather a strong recommendation in some official quarters. Among the most respected and trusted government officials are open and avowed Spiritualists. The administration persecutes no phase of religious sentiments; and, in our opinion, this ceaseless cry of the unpopularity of our philosophy, the poverty of ourselves, and the persecution we meet, is as much out of taste and time as foreign to the general truth."

It saddens our soul to say, that, after Mr. Peebles had left for Europe, studied efforts were made by two or three individuals to underrate the beneficence of his mission. His friends sent him letters of unfaltering friendship. He received scores of them, condemning the cowardly innuendoes. It was a trial moment, which centered his trust in heaven. "The American Spiritualist" justly said, —

> "The laurels he has won are well earned, at a great price of self-sacrifice, — laurels of fidelity, not of pride; and they who tear them would also rend the stars from heaven, if they shine not specially for them. . . .
>
> "He has gone there with the noble intention of gleaning historic truth, under the guidance of his ministering spirits, from ancient ruins of once flourishing cities that projected a world's civilization, from the hieroglyphics of buried tombs, from obelisks, and the rocks of consecrated mountains and shrines, of exhuming psychologically the hidden pearls of wisdom, embodied again in living form, to add a new luster of moral wealth to the spiritual temple we are all trying to construct for a shelterless and impoverished humanity."

Just before Mr. Peebles started, we received a letter, from which we clip this sparkling gem of faith, —

> "The time draws near for sailing, Hallelujah! Up or down among green seaweeds, all the same. The Lord reigns. In him and angels is my trust. Sail Saturday."

CHAPTER XXVI.

IN FOREIGN LANDS.

> "Horsed on the Proteus,
> Thou ridest to power
> And to endurance." — EMERSON.

IN steamer "City of Brooklyn," — swift plow of the main, propelling three hundred miles per day. "Adieu, sweet native land!" — "Adieu!" is the shout of parting friends, waving their handkerchiefs, the hearts' white flags of truce. On board this nautical commonwealth were Sir John Barrington, Ex-Lord Mayor of Dublin; Judge Field, brother of Cyrus W. Field, *alias* "Atlantic Cable;" artists and actresses, poets and philosophers, — a literary world in miniature. Our "pilgrim" caught the civilizing psychology of the ocean. The waves were mad, the winds frowned, the steamer staggered. "Heigho!" was his shout. The passengers slunk away into their berths. Jonah's fish was not half as vigorous; for he challenged the storms and waves, rushed on deck, gloried in the ocean's revelry, and escaped the sea-sick contagion. "Grace aside," he writes, "it is grit that leads to glory on the ocean." At midnight he was out watching the stars, sailing under sidereal bowers, the spirits leading. He stroked the beard of old Neptune, and mounted on his shoulders, thence up to that other realm, —

> "Out on the sea of eternity."

On the 18th of August, the "Brooklyn" touched at Queenstown, Ireland, and in a few hours more landed at Liverpool, — the solid city that defies all time.

Letters sent from the Old Country by our brother are so admirably descriptive of his experiences there, we publish them almost entire.

LIVERPOOL, Aug. 23, 1869.

DEAR BROTHER, — Am safely in the Old World, yet feel new and fresh. Every thing seems unique, substantial, and solid. Liverpool looks cold, stone buildings being large and dingy. Visited St. George's Hall, Birkenhead Park, planned by Sir Joseph Paxton. How magnificent! Mine host is James Wason, an eminent barrister; who has taken unwearied pains to show me Liverpool in its greatness and beauty, and Chester, an old walled city, abounding in ruins. The walls were laid in the time of Julius Cæsar. The Cathedral here interested me deeply. In it are the remains of distinguished personages, even the sarcophagus of Henry IV. of Germany. English friendship is peculiarly attractive to Americans, as I find it in Judge Wason. Through his kindness, I was invited into the criminal court, where I saw judges and barristers attired in robes, wigs, and bands. Ancient, grave, they appeared, when spiritually sensed, as heartless as dignified. . . .

Isn't it queer to be under the government of woman? Wonder if I shall see the queen, — an English sister of mine?" . . . .

MANCHESTER, ENGLAND, Aug. 27, 1869.

MY AMERICAN FELLOW-WORKER, — The railway journey to Manchester is through a garden of hedgerows and flowers. English cultivation is admirable. Saw women in the harvest-fields, — women's rights! Traveling here is un-American: the engines are smaller, but more fleet. The English tunnel their hills and mountains. . . . Manchester is the Lowell of England. It numbers four hundred thousand. Its manufactures are vast; and its black-throated chimneys breathe out volumes of smoke, which, descending, cast a gloom over the city and its suburbs.

A century gone, the religious authorities of this city persecuted Dr. John Dee, permitted the rabble to indecorously treat John Wesley, throwing mud in his face, and imprisoned mother Ann Lee, the patron saint of the Shakers. . . . Yesterday, in company with Mr. Bealey, a poet and scholar, visited the palatial mansion of John Bright of Rochdale, — name dear to every American. He is a rare man, perfectly easy, approachable, and agreeable; in fact, I find this is the case with all English gentlemen. Our conversation was mostly upon peace, — the peace-movements of England and America. He intimated that the surest way to maintain peace, under the present status of civilization, is to maintain large standing armies. In this we differed. Standing armies imply readiness for war; and this incites the spirit of bloodshed. He spoke of American institutions in the highest terms. . . . I have lectured in Manchester several times on Spiritualism: but the mental soil seems hard and unimpressible. But few attended. Oh, how unlike those inspired meetings in America, where hundreds and thousands gather under the green forests and hills, to hear the angels' gospel! . . .

I find in Rev. John Hodgson a good, Methodist minister, who preaches Spiritualism: when attacked by secularists, he manfully defended my positions. . . . My mind to-day turns continually upon Aaron Nite and Dr. E. C. Dunn. Wonder if I can certainly identify Aaron at Yorkshire? Knowing as I do that there are obsessing spirits who assume false names for selfish ends, if I fail in this attempt, it will be the first time that I have doubted his individuality for many years. I shall go there, and thoroughly test the matter. . . .

YORK CITY, ENGLAND, Aug. 30, 1869.

MY TRANSATLANTIC BROTHER, — As I wrote you the other day, one all-absorbing thought has been on my mind. "To Yorkshire" has haunted me. "I *must*," I said, "see the ancient home of my spirit-brother, Aaron Nite." And here I am. It seems to me a sacred city. Am I a spirit-worshiper? — not worshiper, but lover. Eleven years since, Aaron told me about these very scenes which are now before my eyes. How wonder ful! Here are the River Ouse; St. Mary's Abbey, in ruins; the Minster; the beautiful window-designs; the location of the Virgin Mary, with the serpent under her feet; the rocks and lawns where he played when a mere boy, — all exactly as he many times pictured them.

Accompanied by Robert Green, Esq., of Brotherton, I hunted to-day in the "Annals of York," but failed to get any clue of identity, until a venerable antiquarian directed us to the "Will Office;" where, securing the services of the clerk in overhauling the records, I asked him to go back two hundred years, and search for the Knights, — a family famous for its clerical distinctions. He did so; and, to my joy and delight, he found the name of Rev. James Knight, the identical brother of Aaron. The test was perfect. Let me never doubt. He insists upon spelling his name in Anglo-Saxon style, — *Nite*. The *original* name was McKnight; and the family was connected with the McKnights who commented on the Gospels. I procured a full copy of the original record, with this translation from the Latin, —

"Twenty-fourth of October, 1714. James Knight, A.M., was ordained deacon in the Savoy Chapel, London, and priest in the same chapel on the following Sunday." — *From the Institution Book in the Archi-episcopal Registry, York, England.*

Oh, I rejoice in the fact that I have tasted of the ministry of angels! . . .

GLASGOW, SCOTLAND, Sept. 1, 1869.

BROTHER OF THE WEST, — . . . . Am in Scotland, — dear old land of my ancestors. It thrills my soul with joy to tread these hills, pluck the heather, ramble these woods, reminding me of Burns' "Cotter's Saturday Night," — of the homeward cotter from his rustic toil. Reflecting upon the configurations of this country, I can well understand what made a Burns, a Wallace, a Bruce, a Marvelle, and a Hugh Miller, who, in a vain attempt to reconcile the Book of Genesis with geology, became mentally unbalanced, and passed by his own hand to the better land. . . . My meeting on Sunday at Glasgow was a success: hall packed, Prof. J. W. Jackson in the chair. Stopping now with friend Nisbet. The Clarks, Browns, and Duguid, the spirit-artist, have called upon me: they are all good, genial Scotch. I already love them. Wonder if I shall think as much of the Londoners. . . . Should like to describe to you the scenes and my emotions whilst passing up the Tweed to Berwick Castle, and by the old town of Peebles, mentioned in Burns's poems, and rendered famous in Sir Walter Scott's novels. . . . Of Edinburgh, — what a beautiful city! — it is truly entitled to the appellation of "Modern Athens." After repairing to the publishing-house of William and Robert Chambers, I visited John Knox's house, one of the oldest buildings in the city. . . . Did I tell you that I was in Farnley Hall, seeing the paintings of Vandyke, Rubens, Turner, and other masters? They are superb. I saw Cromwell's broad-brimmed hat; the table at which he dined the day before the battle of the Moor, in 1644; the swords of that hero, and of Lambert and Fairfax. . . . Our "Day Out" down the Clyde, among the lakes, nestling among the mountains, how beautiful, sunny, sweet! The scenery equals any thing I have seen, though not on so magnificent scale. Queen Victoria was on the lake the same day; had a fine view of her majesty's highness. She is a good sister, a true mother, and, as ruler, exerts a good moral influence, and is dearly beloved by her subjects. . . . I have written Mrs. Peebles all about this, descriptive of the heather hills that bore on their ragged bosoms the hearts of our progenitors, and particularly of the good queen. Ever thine, J. M. PEEBLES.

London! — the great world of brain, the heart of commerce.

> **"These high things are lost and drowned and dimmed,**
> **Like a blue eye in tears."**

"So thou art, old city, for me, too, a wandering minstrel; who shall delight thee with a song, O Mother of nations?" Our "Pilgrim's" reception surprised him, — unlike American style. Less notoriety would have suited his taste; but he was taken by storm, and had to surrender to British tact. We clip the following from "The London Human Nature:" —

"The readers of that veteran and stanch exponent of Spiritualism, 'The Banner of Light,' have long been agreeably attracted towards the last page of that journal; on which was, till lately, printed the 'Western Department, — J. M. Peebles, editor,' — in which capacity this gentleman has been chiefly known to British readers. As a lecturer, 'The Banner' has also introduced him to this country by the copious reports of his orations on the Spiritual Philosophy which it has given from time to time. . . .

"Mr. Peebles reached the metropolis on the morning of Sept. 6; and, after an interview with Mrs. Hardinge, previous to her departure for Liverpool *en route* for America, he took up his abode at the Progressive Library and Spiritual Institution, desiring quiet and retirement, that he might prosecute his literary labors. A committee of leading London Spiritualists quickly resolved on giving their distinguished guest a public reception; and, accordingly, a circular signed by J. Burns was issued to the prominent Spiritualists of London and the provinces, stating that 'the arrival of Mr. J. M. Peebles, of America, in this country, has suggested the desirability of entertaining him at a meeting of welcome, on the occasion of his visit amongst us, and give a representative gathering of London Spiritualists the opportunity of exchanging fraternal greetings with an American medium and leading Spiritualist of culture and experience.' The meeting took place at the Spiritual Institution, 15 Southampton Row, W.C., on the evening of Wednesday, Sept. 15; when a most influential and harmonious gathering met to do honor to Mr. Peebles, and the movement and nation he represents. Amongst those present were Mrs. Macdougall Gregory, widow of the late Prof. Gregory of Edinburgh; the Countess Paulett; Mrs. George Thompson, whose husband is so well known in England and America for his active sympathies with the cause of human freedom; Mr. and Miss Cooper; Mrs. Tebb; Miss Santi; Miss Houghton; Mr., Mrs., and Miss Dornbusch; Prof. Palmer of St. John's College, Cambridge; Mr. Russell of the University, Cambridge; Rev. M. D. Conway; Rev. S. E. Bengough, M.A.; B. Coleman, Esq.; A. B. Tietkens, Esq.; Dr. R. Colquhoun; Dr. Wilmshurst; Mr. Hannah; Mr. Mawson, Mr. Armfield, &c.

"Letters from eminent Spiritualists were read, — from William Howitt, D. D. Home, J. W. Jackson, Dr. Nichols, Rev. F. R. Young, S. C. Hall (editor of 'The Art Journal'), and others.

"Mr. Coleman, in opening the proceedings, said, —

"'LADIES AND GENTLEMEN, — I have just been requested to take the chair on this occasion. We are met here, as you are aware, to give a welcome and greeting to our friend Mr. Peebles; and, to those who are acquainted with American literature, his name will be familiar. I have known him by reputation for many years; and I am free to say, I know no man more unselfish or more earnest than our friend Mr. Peebles. I may also say, that though I cordially respect my friend, and highly appreciate his earnest working in the cause, yet I might not be able to agree with him in all the views he might take of our movement; but as we can all agree to differ, and respect the differences of opinion which exist amongst us, that does not prevent us from thanking him for his presence amongst us this evening in the cause of Spiritualism.'

"Mr. Tietkins was then called upon to read the following

"'ADDRESS TO MR. J. M. PEEBLES, OF AMERICA, BY THE SPIRITUALISTS OF LONDON.

"'DEAR SIR AND BROTHER, — We have the greatest pleasure, on the present occasion, in welcoming you amongst us, and in extending the warm hand of brotherhood to you, as an eminent representative of the millions on the Western hemisphere who share with us the beautiful teachings derived from spirit-communion.

"'Peace, wisdom, and inspiration be with you, and the highly-enlightened nation of which you are a distinguished citizen! We perceive in your life-work, as inspirational medium, teacher, author, and editor, an apt illustration of the genius of modern Spiritualism. In your learned researches, you have shown that the stream of human progress has been fed ever, in all ages, from spiritual sources; that this divine influx is inexhaustible, and ever present; that it is confined to no age, race, sect, or form of belief; and that its redemptive work will yet extend to the complete development of man from all angularities and imperfections.

"'We welcome you also as an authorized delegate from the friends of peace in America, and as an active promoter of individual and social reform and human welfare in every sense.

"'We shall be glad to hear from your lips some account of the present position of Spiritualism in America, its upward struggles, its achievements, and its future tendencies; also, the status of mediumship most prevalent and useful, and any other information which the impressions of the moment may furnish.

"'We shall be glad if you can extend your sojourn amongst us, and help us in the great work which we have scarcely yet begun. We cordially invite you to our platforms in the metropolis and chief cities of this country. The people require much teaching concerning our principles and motives; and the leaders of our movement would be benefited by your guidance in the matter of organization, and the best means of promoting the popular diffusion of Spiritualism.'

"'Wishing you a prosperous and safe journey to the consular appointment in Asia which your government has been pleased to confide to you, and praying that you may be the recipient of those blessings (in this and other worlds) which flow from the soul's most cherished treasure, — the possession of truth, — we are sincerely yours.'

"Mr. Tietkins concluded by moving a resolution that the address be adopted by the meeting, and presented to Mr. Peebles.

"The Rev. S. E. Bengough, M.A., of Christ's College, Cambridge, seconded the resolution, and at the same time desired to say a word with regard to his own feelings in welcoming a gentleman from the Far West. He owed a great debt of gratitude to the mind of America; because much that had led to his improvement, and added to his manhood in the truest sense, had been derived from those writings which had emanated from the other side of the Atlantic. He thought no Englishman could become conversant with such writers as Emerson, without being the better for it. He was very anxious indeed to become acquainted with the book on the table, entitled, 'The Seers of the Ages.' In looking over its pages, it promised a rich feast. From it he observed that Spiritualism has been known in all ages, and to all nations, — in Persia, Greece, Rome, and Palestine; and this led him to notice one fact with regard to Spiritualism: It seemed that we could not possibly separate opinions from national character, and that our national character influenced our conception of every thing, and Spiritualism among the number. 'How very different, for instance,' said Mr. Bengough, 'is the tone of French writers on Spiritualism to those born in England, and partaking thoroughly of the English spirit. This holds true of every nation. Then in what respect are we to derive especial advantages from American Spiritualism? They speak our language, while at the same time their thoughts are not confined within the barriers which of necessity confine, in a certain measure, our own, and prevent the true development of the spiritualistic idea; and I think, therefore, when we have brought prominently before us by the first minds of America these great truths, we are likely to have many of our narrow opinions broken down, and new life imparted to us. Therefore, for my part, I shall listen with great interest to Mr. Peebles.'

"Miss Houghton said, 'We are most happy to see Mr. Peebles, and to welcome him to this country.'

"Rev. M. D. Conway being called upon, said, '*Mr. Chairman, Ladies, and Gentlemen,* — I have great sympathy with you in giving welcome to a genuine American thinker and laborer in good works. Not being a Spiritualist, I have no claim upon the generosity which has invited me here except the great respect I have for truth. I am more friendly with Spiritualists than with spirits; and I acknowledge a large number of very dear friends in that body. There has not yet been a complete and thorough attempt to bring the scientific men of London to the point of testing the great and important claims of this movement. No one can travel through America or Russia, and mix in any company, but he will find a Spiritualist present, — persons perhaps of great intelligence and refinement, — barons and princes, and persons who have studied in all languages; and no individual can for a moment doubt their integrity. The subject has not been sufficiently decided by men of science and culture, except such as were Spiritualists; and few are capable of strict scientific investigation. The most of people can only believe what they can *bite:* more, they can not understand. Of course I know what the Dialectical Society has been doing; but the public will have no more faith in them than they have in any of you, gentlemen: and, when they come out with their report, no one will respect it. The only thing in the world for the skeptic mind of this age will be when two or three well-known scientific men can report that they have seen the manifestations. As for Mr. Peebles, I have long known him as a liberal American and an earnest man; and I am obliged to those gentlemen who have so kindly enabled me to meet him.'"

Mr. Burns also addressed the meeting in a most felicitous manner, also C. W. Pearce, both alluding to the progressive library for the diffusion of Spiritual literature.

"Mr. Coleman then put the address to the meeting, which was carried with unanimity.

"Mr. Peebles then rose, and in an off-hand manner said, —

"'MR. PRESIDENT, LADIES, AND GENTLEMEN, — The privilege of meeting you upon the present occasion affords me intense pleasure. Personally strangers; yet for years I have known some of you, — at least through your public lectures, authorship, and contributions to the English and American press: and I am exceedingly happy this evening in the privilege of clasping your warm hands, looking into your earnest faces, and coming into closer relationships with you socially and spiritually. Delegated by the "Universal Peace Society of America," planting my feet upon your soil, I held in my earnest right hand the olive-branch of peace; and the other day, numbering one of that thirty or forty thousand assembled in the Crystal Palace, and seeing suspended over those eight thousand choralists the national flags of England, Ireland, Scotland, and America, responding seemingly in holy quietness to the melody of Oliver Wendell Holmes's peace-hymn, so touchingly rendered at the Peace Jubilee in Boston, and immortalized melodies from Handel, Mozart, Beethoven, Mendelssohn, Rossini, and other masters, my soul throbbed in gladness: and for the moment I fancied myself in Syrian lands, listening to the echoing refrain, "Peace on earth, and good-will toward men." Your own Lord Brougham said, "I abominate war, as unchristian. I hold it the greatest of human crimes." England and America, as elder and younger brother, united by the common sympathy of race, speaking one language, and connected by thousands of commercial interests, should never breathe the word war. All nations should settle their civil and international differences by arbitration and congresses of nations. The genius of the age calls for the practice of these divine peace-principles."

. . . "'I am very happy this evening in seeing before me Mrs. George Thompson. I speak of George Thompson as an old friend, never forgetting the pleasant conversation we held together at the residence of J. C. Woodman, Esq., Portland, Me.: in fact, there is a common sympathy, which tends to make our philosophy, our science, our spiritual gospel of reform, in this age a practical one; and we should bring it down to every-day life, and live it, that others may see "our good works, and be led to glorify God." The principles of Spiritualism are marching on rapidly in America, and gaining attention in every circle of society. It has been estimated that there are eleven millions of Spiritualists in America: this, probably, includes those still in the churches, and whose religion simply recognizes the fact, that spirits *can* communicate. The lowest estimate, however, is four millions. We have a National Association, several State conventions, hundreds of organized societies and progressive lyceums, which that highly-illumined seer, Andrew Jackson Davis, first saw in the spirit-land. In these progressive lyceums, to the importance of which many of our American Spiritualists are not yet educated, our children are taught to develop their whole being, mentally, morally, physically, and spiritually. The great power of the sectarian churches consists in warping and training the young in their superstitions and dogmas; and the Roman Catholics know, that, if they can get the charge of the children for the first few years, they need have no fear of their becoming Protestants, — a hint which Spiritualists should turn to good account. If we would liberalize the race, we must educate the young; and this Spiritualists should accomplish through children's progressive lyceums, progressive libraries, new educational institutions, the support of our periodical literature, and the encouragement of mediums and speakers: and thus the work of progress would go forward on a broad liberal basis of sympathy and harmony, laboring to educate and spiritualize ourselves and our race.

"'The Rev. Mr. Bengough, M.A., of Christ's College, Cambridge, who has just taken his seat, deeply interested me, as did the subsequent stirring words of Rev. M. D. Conway, so well known in the Unitarian circles of America. His well-timed sentences reminded me of a half-day spent in the library of Emerson. . . .

"'Whittier says, "The destroyer should be the builder too;" and Carlyle insists, that he who "goes forth with a torch for burning," should also carry a "hammer for building." Many have yet to learn the full import of the term *toleration*, the meaning of the word *charity*. Intellectually we may, we necessarily *must*, differ; but our hearts, all touched and tuned to the Christ principle of love, may beat as one. The angels do not ask, What do you believe? but, What do you do? what are you life-aims? what practical work have you wrought for humanity?'"

Mr. Peebles published editorially in "The Universe" lively descriptions of English scenes, entertainments, institutions, and civilizations, continuing them throughout all his Eastern travels, — enough to make a large volume, unlike any thing ever before written. Because of their historic researches and psychological conclusions, they are invaluable. At our suggestion, he contemplates writing a series of works, dating from his past and future travels, entitled, "The Spiritual Philosophy of History."

Learning that there are a hundred and sixty-five thousand paupers in the city of London, with their concomitant degradations glaring out on every side, — observing the rule, where royalty is, is poverty, the two extremes of society, — and painting an editorial picture of the cost of monarchical crowns, that of Queen Victoria being worth a hundred and twenty-one thousand pounds, he exclaims, "O Christian England! feed your hungry, educate your ignorant. . . . Queen Victoria, sell your crown, and give the proceeds to the honest, struggling poor! "

At the house of Mrs. Gregory, a literary Spiritualist, Mr. Peebles saw the photograph of the Catholic sister who was the instigator of the "Immaculate Conception." Her name is Bernadette, of Lourdes, among the Pyrenees, in the South of France. Mediumistically she saw the Virgin Mary seventeen times in a vision, who told her she was "immaculate." Priests hearing her confession, and perceiving the idea could be made a dogma profitable to the Church, declared her a saint. In grave council, the Catholic dignities pronounced it a dogma; and quite sensible it is, provided it applies to *all* children conceived in spiritual love.

In London, Mr. Peebles had an opportunity to corroborate the affirmations of his ancient spirits respecting civilizations, recalling his conversation with "Aphelion," who "lived 16,000 years ago." Calling on Dr. Birch, the Egyptologist of the British Museum, then reading hieroglyphs relating to the "Books of the Dead," he was informed, that, "the farther we go back in Egyptian history, the higher is the culture and civilization."

CHAPTER XXVII.

"LA BELLE FRANCE."

> "Star of the brave! thy ray is pale;
> And darkness must again prevail!
> But, oh, thou rainbow of the free!" — BYRON.

LEAVING London about the 1st of October, Mr. Peebles crossed the English Channel, from Dover to Calais, in a steamer good as the best, which he styles "filthy, and positively detestable." The project of tunneling the channel he made a matter of scientific prayer. The French soldiery, the peasants in their harvests, the luxurious gardens, the entrance into Paris, — "Queen of the Beautiful," — assured him he was surely in a foreign land. "How unlike England!" he exclaimed. "There all is solid: here all is gay and volatile." During four weeks' residence in Paris, delighting his senses with the purity of its air and the floral exuberance of its fashionable streets, walking the Boulevards in meditation, he thus summed up the warning lesson of his prophecy in a letter to "The Universe," dated Oct. 6, 1869, —

> "Paris is France. Sundays are its gala-days. The citizens are proud of their fountains, gardens, beautiful Boulevards, and massive libraries, — all open to the public. Under this display and grandeur, however, lies a maddened volcano. Its fire and flame already cause a half-subdued rumble. Gog and Magog are sharpening their weapons. That Napoleon's health is frail, none dispute. The sins of his youth are fruiting out into fearful pains and penalties. The grave invites his body to hasten: a rich worm-feast is promised. Then comes another revolution: mark the prophecy!"

Ere a year rolled by, what he prophetically foresaw is *now* fulfilling in the unparalleled war between France and Prussia, — Napoleon a prisoner, the empire broken, Paris in a siege, a republic organized; and struggling for life, and all Europe in a political ferment. What the augury? Ask the spirit oracles. "Poor France! weep for Paris! weep for the slain of thy sons and daughters! She will rise again rejuvenated!"

Whilst in Paris, Mr. Peebles was the guest of Mr. Gledstanes, an English gentleman of position, engaged in Spiritual literature. Having traveled extensively in India and China, he gave him many valuable items of Oriental politics and religion, for future discourse. He says, "I am ever at school, — a pupil."

Leon Favre, then Consul-General of France, brother of the distinguished Jules Favre, both Spiritualists, became his fast friend. They locked arm in arm, embosomed in deep friendship, his French brother descanting so fervently upon the "new religion." — "Fifty thousand, Monsieur Peebles, — fifty thousand Spiritualists in Paris alone!" exclaimed he, with a rapture of light in his countenance; and then, in graver aspect, he informed him of "a reign of blood close to the doors," — scenes which the spirits had sketched in prophecy, exactly as impressed Mr. Peebles whilst before walking the Boulevards. America had to emancipate her slaves on a crimson sea, ere the Spiritual religion could be planted: so France, with the guilt of fashion staining her moral character, enervated by luxury, can rise only by the force of arms, breaking her monarchy, and marching to education and liberty.

In company with Mr. Gledstanes, he strolled into *Petite Pères*, Church of "Little Fathers;" where M. Jean Baptiste Vianney, Curé D' Ars, exercised his wonderful gifts of healing by the laying on of hands in the name of the Virgin Mary. The names of thousands he healed are there inscribed on elegant tablets: so the place was holy to him, not because of the temple, but because there holy deeds were done by spirit-power.

But these deeds of the Catholic healer he found equaled, if not excelled, by those of Henri Auguste Jacob, of our Spiritualistic times.

"Jacob was a Zouave and musician, playing upon the trombone while in the army. Having avoided intoxicating drinks, soldiers' slang, and other vices common to military life, and, withal, being very kind-hearted, he was exceedingly popular in the ranks of his fellow-soldiers. He is nearly six feet high, has black hair, dark hazel eyes, regular features, and a head rounding up in the coronal region, something like that of A. J. Davis. He is about forty years of age, and in religion nominally a Catholic. He sees spirits, feels their presence, and, guided by their inspiration, prays to them and God. Some twelve years since, while marching through the streets of Paris with his regiment, he saw a poor crippled child being drawn in a carriage by its parents. The child had not put its feet to the ground since it was two years of age. An irresistible influence seizing Jacob, he went to the child, and, placing his hands on it, said firmly, '*Get up and walk;*' which, to the joy and astonishment of the parents, it did. Hundreds who were standing near witnessed this. The next day a score came to him, all of whom were healed or improved.

"The French are an excitable people. Soon hundreds flocked to him daily from all ranks of society, troubled with 'all manner of diseases,' as in Christ's time. It is calculated that he cured fifteen out of every twenty who came to him. Impossible to receive the crowds in the barracks, a friend, M. Dufuget, a prominent citizen and merchant in Rue de La Roquese, opened his house, business-place, and workshop for the reception of sufferers. A thoroughly good man, M. Dufuget himself became developed as a healer The throngs eventually increased to 2,000 a day. This blocking the streets, he was warned to desist. Not heeding the policemen's warning, he was arrested, and thrust into prison, — all of which might have been expected in Imperial France. How it reminds one of those old apostolic times, when Peter, James, and John, and others, exercising spiritual gifts of healing, were 'cast into prison!' Through the influence of friends, he was after a time released, remaining *incog.* If using his gifts, it was in private. Prejudice gradually gave way. . . .

"Five minutes before the hour for healing, he steps into the room, takes a peculiar attitude, clasps his hands, requests perfect silence, and, asking them *all* to engage in silent prayer, he departs. He is naturally a reticent man. Coming into the presence of his patients the second time, he looks at each intently (not allowing them to speak or point out their ailments), and then touching each, tells what he *can* and can not do for them. His powers are much greater when there is a throng present. He does not insist that people are healed when they are not. His remarkable powers, he continually affirms, come from God, through good spirits and angels. The masses that come to him are of the common people. It was the 'common people' in Bible times that 'heard Jesus gladly,' — fishermen and herdsmen. This is the 'second,' the *continuous* coming of Christ. . . .

"None accuse him of being mercenary. His mission is an important one; and he is working it out beautifully, for the good of humanity. Blessings upon the French Zouave!"

Knowing that the enlightened *governments* are Spiritualistic, in America the *people* accepting the new religion, and in Europe the kings and queens, he writes, "Alexander II., of Russia, is worthy of his title, — 'liberating father.' The emancipation of millions of serfs was concordant with the genius of Spiritualism. The angels ordered it: they are our saviors!"

Departing from England was leaving *brain;* coming to France was finding *heart.* With M. Pierart, the scholarly editor of the "Revue Spiritualiste," and author of the popular "Drama of Waterloo," he enjoyed a feast of soul, — everybody was so polite, so obliging! Anna Blackwell, a lady of high social position as a literary writer, introduced him to Madame Kardec, the "beloved" of Allan Kardec, whose works are so valuable for reference on the question of re-incarnation; and there he procured, and subsequently published, the remarkable career of this medium, known for his virtues.

Introduced to M. Pierart, a scholarly Frenchman, he was again reminded of the truthful words of "Aphelion," inspiring deeper confidence at every step in life in the wisdom and fidelity of his spirit-band, encircling him so lovingly during those foreign experiences. This savan said, —

"Egyptian civilization was in a hight of glory 15,000 B.C. There was no *adultery.* Marriage was probationary seven years: if then agreeable, to continue fourteen years; and then, if desirable, through life. After fourteen years, no separation. Children of divorced parents took the mother's name, and were the intellectual and moral property of the government, educated at the public expense. 'Plato,' he added, 'drew his best conceptions from those ancient Egyptians.'"

On hearing these statements, Mr. Peebles exclaimed to himself, — "O Egyptian hierophants! lead me to your sunny clime, and teach me the wisdom of modesty!"

Under the courteous escort of Baron de La Taille des Essarts, celebrated for mediumship, Mr. Peebles rode through the panoramic scenes of the country, passing the Park St. Cloud, the River Seine, Montmartre, Arc de Triomphe, Place de La Concorde, Notre Dame, Hotel des Invalides, the Pantheon, flower-gardens, and fountains. He said of this journey to Versailles, "In fulfillment of a spirit-prophecy, this is one of the happiest days with which the Infinite Father has ever blest me." A *prophecy?* Yes: long years ago, in his early Spiritual experience with Dr. Dunn, Madame Elizabeth promised him the privilege of visiting the scenes of her earthly home in the palaces of the kings in Versailles. Thither now! "Is not destiny a reality?" he asks. "Are we not the subjects of higher powers? Do not angels shape our lives as do geographers meridian lines?"

He walked in those "six miles of picture-galleries in these old Bourbon palaces, — finest in the world!" Here he found a picture of the angel as she was in her girlhood, copies of which he procured for such a worship as a loving heart only knows how to offer in acceptable service. Mr. Peebles argues the claims of the Bourbons! Why? Ask "Queen of Morn" — why.

"There is a grandeur in the soul that dares
To live out all the life God lit within."

Weeks rolled by with the swiftness of days amid the gayeties of Paris; but "Stay no longer" came the spirit-order: "hurry to Asia." On the way, *viâ* Lyons, he entered the valley of the Rhone, charmed with its beauty, ruined walls, and castles of feudal times, querying as to the cause of such blight; when, tracing it to the Church, he exclaimed, "God save America from Roman Catholicism, or any other priestly power!" In that manufacturing city, after visiting the museum, botanical gardens, halls of sculpture, and St. Pierre University, — the "redemptive agencies of Lyons," — he paused before the *Place de Serreaux*, where in 1794 so many were sacrificed to the so-called Goddess of Liberty by the guillotine; when the shout of "Down with the Bourbons!" was followed by a dynasty more fearful and bloody. He seemed to hear the cry of martyrs from the ground, pleading "for free education to all the masses as the only safe guarantee of equal rights. Change the shout to 'Down with Popes!' and burn all guillotines!"

Stopping a few hours at Marseilles, he improved them by a survey of its spacious harbor, its vineyards, and olive orchards, the crowds of idle men and women, the Catholic priests parading the streets in gorgeous gowns and robes, himself the gazed of all the gazers; for his disgust of such lassitude made him taller in dignity than ever.

His steamer, classically named "Ilissus," was to him the world in miniature; for among the passengers were Sicilians, Frenchmen, Greeks, Nubians, Syrians, Arabs, Armenians, himself a long-bearded "Spiritual Pilgrim," of America, — all attired in their several national costumes. That suited him exactly, — "unity in diversity: there I studied God!"

Selecting from the many idioms, he there most heartily indorsed the opinion of Madame de Staël; who said, —

"If I were mistress of fifty languages, I would think in the deep German, converse in the gay French, write in the copious English, sing in the majestic Spanish, deliver in the noble Greek, and make love in the soft Italian."

Entering the straits of Bonifaccio, they sailed by the shore of Corsica; when the very air seemed to report the destiny of bloody heroes, of which the fated Napoleon the First is an example. Remembering he was commissioned to the Old World as a peace representative, he wrote, —

"My mind reverted to that 'man of destiny, born and nurtured on this rugged shore, whose star, after culminating to the zenith, sank extinguished in blood at Waterloo, to rise no more. Was war well for him? was it well for English Roundheads to behead Charles I.? was it good in the excitable French to murder Louis XVI., Maria Antoinette, and the sainted Madame Elizabeth? . . . . Kindly-tempered justice, goodness, and love are the only redemptive powers in the universe. 'Love your enemies: bless, and curse not!' said the sweet-souled Nazarene."

Seeing Caprari on the north and east, where Garibaldi retired to the quiet of a farmer's life, after gaining a crown for Victor Emanuel, he said in one of his letters, "Italians will never rest in spirit till Pius IX. is dethroned, and Italia's sun shines upon a united Italy, with Rome for its capital." Little did he then think, whilst sailing the Mediterranean, that within a year nearly all these prophetic words would be literally fulfilled. Let us keep records of prophecies: they are banners of liberty to the revolutionists.

What a history soon rolled wave-like over the memory! Piræus, the port of Greece, beckoned him: there was Salamis just past it; and off that coast the valiant Greeks defeated the Persian fleet of Xerxes, 480 B.C. In imagination he saw the battle, and saddened at the thought, that two thousand years of Christianity have not since obliterated the curse of war. Has not the force that built up Greece blasted its prowess? So he reasoned. Landing and sensing the decay around him, he exclaimed, "The Greeks of to-day are ancient Greeks no more! What wrought the change?" — "Ask dead priests!" solemnly whispered a spirit by his side. He stood before the Acropolis at Athens, passed up the propillion, or grand entrance, and surveyed Mars Hill, where Paul preached the "Unknown God" to the Athenians; touched the massive pillars of Bacchus, spiring above the ruins; gazed down into the subterranean passage leading from this temple of spirit-rites into the vast amphitheater. What a hollow sound! Do not the dead voice their sorrow here?

"Let there be light! said Liberty;
And, like sunrise from the sea,
Athens arose! — Around her born,
Shone like mountains in the morn,
Glorious States; and are they now
Ashes, wrecks, oblivion?"

He found the ruins of the temple of Minerva, the temple of the Winds, the temple of the Muses, and the temple of Jupiter Olympus, "many of whose proud columns," he writes, "having defied the storms and devastating forces of time, remain as standing signals of architectural splendor and perfection." There, too, were the remains of Hadrian's Arch, the bed of the Ilissus, the monument of Lysicrates, the theater of Bacchus, the temple of Theseus, the magnificent Parthenon, and the shattered arts of Pericles and Phidias, "stripped by Venetian, by Turk, by earthquake, by time, by Lord Elgin for the British Museum, still serene in their indestructible beauty."

"Fair Greece! sad relic of departed worth!
Immortal, though no more; though fallen, great!
. . . Oh! who that gallant spirit shall resume,
Leap from Eurostas' banks, and call thee from the tomb?"

Studying the causes of such magnificence, even in ruins, tracing the life-links of civilizations to configurations and climatic magnetisms of country, shaped and toned into practical order by civil and religious institutions, he credited the master spirits that anciently inspired scientific Spiritualists to think, to construct, to dare. He writes, —

"Under the shadow of an unspiritual church, science was neglected, the oracles abandoned, and Grecian civilization recoiled into brooding silence among these ruins! What is required, then? Philosophy with phenomena, science with marvel, and *reason* crowning all. I stood over the prison-cave where the Greeks confined the Spiritualistic Socrates, the iron gate still there, — a gloomy den, to converse with a Crito and an Alcibiades. Judea and Greece awarded to their inspired teachers crosses and hemlock draughts. Such was gratitude! Have the times only in methods greatly changed?

. . . . "It seemed strange to walk the streets of Athens, and compare its sparse and degenerate five thousand inhabitants with its enlightened and cultured populace of long ago. There stands the Parthenon, unrivaled still. There are to be found the relics of architecture, poetry, and sculpture, that tell of the transcendent genius of those departed masters. To-day our scholars and our devotees of the fine arts flock to that ancient seat of genius and learning, to borrow the inspiration that seems even yet to sanctify the place. From these testimonies to intellects whose incarnate forms have long since vanished off the earth, we turn and look upon the present living people, and ask ourselves, Is this progress? — these degenerate descendants of illustrious ancestors? Progress, triumphant elsewhere, stands aloof from Greece; only retrogression there. From Athens I desired to go back to Marathon and Corinth, but was told that it would be unsafe; for brigandage is rife in that region, and is secretly countenanced by the officials of the country."

Boarding the steamer again, he entered the Dardanelles, the ancient Hellespont, and glided close to the crumbled ruins of historic Troy, where blind Homer begged his bread, — a beggar once, now what? Oh, why must all great geniuses be crucified, ere they can be justly esteemed? Up the Hellespont. "There, right there, is the locality," said the captain, "where Byron swam across these waters, May 3, 1810, from Sestos to Abydos; where the young Venetian, Leander, years before him, performed the feat, to secure the hand of his lady-love." Byron records it, —

"He swam for love, and I for glory."

CHAPTER XXVIII.

PILGRIMAGE IN THE ORIENT.

> "'Tis the clime of the East, 'tis the land of the sun!
> Can he smile on such deeds as his children have done?"

> "Government, like dress, is the badge of lost innocence: the palaces of kings are built on the ruins of the bowers of paradise." — THOMAS PAINE.

ONE October morning, at its first gray, our "Pilgrim" sailed around the Golden Horn, and lo, Constantinople! Describing the scene in an editorial, he says, —

> "The sun now colors the eastern sky with gold. Rising, it tips and turns the minarets to fire. The buildings, the vessels, the mosques, are all illuminated.
>
> "If Geneva has been called the proud, and Naples the beautiful, Constantinople may rightly claim for herself the title of magnificent. Seated in gardens, it is not strange Constantine should have desired to have removed the capital of the Roman Empire to the site occupied by this imperial city. No soul alive to the beautiful in nature, or the exquisite in art, could fail of admiring its lofty and imposing position, its domes, its minarets, its sheltering groves of cypress, its hills in the distance, now crimsoning into the sear of autumn, and the blue waters that lie at the feet of those Moslem splendors. . . . The Sea of Marmora is deep and beautiful. . . . What a magnificent harbor it would make, with Constantinople for the central capital of Europe, Asia, and Africa!"

The conception of such a capital is grand: the future will tell whether it is prophetic. Surveying the tower at Pera, the flotilla upon the Golden Horn, the Bosphorus with its suburban villages, the palaces of the Sultan, the peopled hillsides upon the Asian coast, the hospital scene of Florence Nightingale's womanly work during the Crimean war, he shouted aloud on the deck of the steamer, "What a great, cosmopolitan city! my soul thrills with intense delight!" But

> "Distance lends enchantment to the view."

Landing, the spell vanished.

"No omnibuses," he says, "no conveyances of any sort, offered us their accommodations; only sedan-chairs were on hand for the ladies, and hammals for the carrying of trunks. The most obvious feature of this city is its dogs. Constantinople is the dog's paradise. There are two ways in which you can insult a Turk, viz., spit on his beard, or kick a dog; for that animal is sacred: the bark of a dog once saved the city, by betraying the enemy."

Of his observations and experiences in Constantinople, this is his statement, reported in "The Universe," —

"The religion of these Moslem millions, little understood and frequently misrepresented, is in one of its theoretical aspects, at least, eminently Unitarian. Their first article of belief declares, that 'God is great: there is but *one* God, Allah!' Mohammedanism is *not* a comparatively new religion. M. de Percival, speaking of its antiquity, says, 'This was not a new religion which Mohammed announced, but the ancient religion of Abraham restored to its primitive purity.' The prejudices of Christians are heartless and soulless. That the followers of Mohammed 'do not believe women have souls' is an imported missionary falsehood, black as night; that they do not permit their women to go into their mosques for prayers and worship is another pious falsehood equally malicious. With a good pair of eyes, we saw them bowing, kneeling, worshiping in the Mosque of St. Sophia, and also in that magnificent one erected by Sultan Ahmed. That they practise polygamy is true, though in a moderate degree compared with the 'wisest man' of the Bible, — Solomon. They profess to get their authority for having a plurality of wives from the Old Testament. Christian writers have approved of it. St. Augustine observes, that 'there was a *blameless custom* of one man having many wives; which at that early time might be done in a way of duty.' Pope Gregory, in the year 726, justified polygamy in some cases. Bernardo Ochinus, a Christian writer of the sixteenth century, published dialogues in favor of the practice. The celebrated Christian poet, John Milton, defended polygamy in his 'Treatise on Christian Doctrine' (p. 237, *et seq.*). After quoting several passages from the Bible in favor of the practice, he says, 'Moreover, God (Ezek. xxiii.) represents himself as having *two wives*, Aholah and Aholiah, — a mode of speaking which Jehovah would by no means have employed, if the practice which it implied had been intrinsically dishonorable or shameful.' Spiritualists do not advocate the right, nor believe in the practice, of such sensualism.

"The Mohammedans recognize both dispensations, — the Jewish and the Christian. The more intelligent followers of Mohammed always speak reverently of Jesus of Nazareth, regarding him as an inspired prophet, sent to teach. Mohammed, they assure us, was the promised 'comforter' that 'should come.' They insist that our Christian Scriptures have been thoroughly corrupted in the original text. This few scholars doubt. The Moslems further say, that in the palace, the old Seraglio, there were, among others, a hundred and twenty large Greek manuscripts and important commentaries upon the New Testament by the early church fathers. The Roman Catholics believe this, and have offered large rewards to obtain them. The Koran is made up largely from the Old and New Testaments, united with the doctrines of the Magi and Soofees, of Persia and Arabia, and the teachings of the angel Gabriel, who frequently visited the prophet Mohammed.

"Literally speaking, the Sultan is the head of the Mohammedan religion. He never fails of repairing to the mosque on Friday. Next to him come the moolahs and muftis, corresponding to churchal bishops, and then the ulemas, who are their priests. They have no fixed ritual. In all countries worshiping the Crescent, they bow towards Mecca, the Holy City, and put their faces to the ground when pronouncing the word *Allah*. Friday is their holy day. With the face toward Mecca, the worshipers bow forward, placing their hands at the sides of the head, covering the ears, signifying, 'May no depraved word reach my ears!' then bow forward again, covering the eyes, meaning, 'May no sight of evil reach my eyes!' then the hands are laid upon the breast, the body bent reverently forward as before, in token of acknowledgment, that 'Mohammed is the prophet of God;' last, the hands are extended toward the ground, the body lower bent than in the previous positions, indicating adoration of Allah, 'There is no God but God; and Mohammed is his prophet.'"

So beautiful and significant is this prayer, our "Pilgrim" delights to repeat it in deep sincerity, and to adopt the Moslem form of social greeting, placing the hand quickly upon the forehead, recognizing God as witness; then upon the heart, recognizing Mohammed as an inspired prophet of God; then grasping a neighbor's hand so cordially, as if to say, "I greet thee in peace."

One day, near the hour of twelve, M., he ascended a minaret, surveying the city below; when the muzzein came out from near the summit, summoning the people to prayer, intoning the words in a plaintive cadence, "*Allah Akbar, Allah Akbar, La illa il Allah, Mohammed resoul, Allah, Allah, Akbar!*" He knew not the meaning; and yet standing in silence, he caught the spirit of devotion from the high minaret, and repeated in English, "*God is great. There is no God but God, and Mohammed is the prophet of God. Come to prayer: come to security and peace. God is great. There is no God but God.*" Mornings he heard the muzzein's cry, "*Awake, awake, and pray! It is better to pray than to sleep. There is no God but Allah.*" And the spirit of the summons he invariably obeyed, feeling the need of a similar custom in Christian lands, — a call upon the people to prayer with the angels; and he would have this trinity evoked, — *God, angels, humanity:* "God is love, angels are his messengers, and humanity is his prophet." Speaking of the character of the Mohammedans, he writes, —

"All good and true Mussulmans go to some mosque; where there is something corresponding to a discourse, although the most of the service consists in repeating and chanting portions of the Koran. The Turks are perfectly Catholic in feeling, freely tolerating all religions in their country. It is universally conceded here in the East, that the old Mohammedans, in no way tinctured with the Christian civilization of Europe, are the most honorable people in the world. The present Sultan neither smokes, nor tastes of liquors nor wines. I should feel infinitely safer in a dark midnight hour, wandering among straggling Turks, than in the drunken 'Five Points' of New York, the 'Haymarket' of London, or anywhere in Christian Spain. . . . Among the natives here, I met many who are Spiritualists, and was the recipient of their hospitality. The Turks are a wondrously hospitable people. When you enter the house of a Turk, he provides you with a mat, urges you to partake of his coffee and fruits, saying, 'My wives are your servants. I am your slave. My house is your house. All I have is thine. I greet thee in peace.' Such is the hospitable nature of these people, that to-day I could travel all over Turkey at little or no cost beyond the pay of an interpreter. The better classes, however, live back in the country."

Having received his *Exequatur* from the Turkish government, in recognition of his consulship, he was now able to find access to political and religious authorities, moving in their ranks, the better to glean the information for which he came to Oriental lands. The Suez Canal was about to be opened. The occasion brought to Constantinople several imperial dignitaries from Europe; and among them was Francis Joseph, Emperor of Austria; also Prince Amadeus, son of the king, known as Duke of Aosta, since elected king of revolutionized Spain, and the Crown Prince of Prussia, *alias* Frederic William, with all of whom he had the pleasure of forming acquaintance. Prince Amadeus wished information concerning the different phases spiritism had assumed in America.

With the Crown Prince, standing unshod, he witnessed the worship of the dancing and howling Dervishes, cutting themselves with knives in monstrous gashes, but the next moment healed by the magnetic touch of the sheik. They walked upon the sick, pathetized them, made them put their hands within "Mohammed's brass hand," and, wonderful to know, were instantly restored! On talking with this and other venerable sheiks, on other occasions, he was surprised to learn, that these wild worshipers fasted before coming into these sacred circles; that the origin of their worship was spiritual, in obedience to the same laws practised in America and Europe, under the enlightenments of science. Taking notes of these and other facts, he there resolved to write the "Spiritual History of the Mohammedan Religions," that the Christian world may no longer falsify with impunity the Spiritualism of Mohammed.

The Crown Prince stood by Mr. Peebles in the Mosque of St. Sophia: they conversed freely and responsively of the "new religion." The Prince invited his friend to Prussia. Mr. Peebles looked deep into his soul, as if there to read the future destiny of his gallant country. They parted in the Crescent City, — the "Pilgrim" to go on his errand of peace, the Prince to prepare for war against France!

The French Empress having arrived in Constantinople *en route* for the Suez Canal, Her Imperial Majesty, the Emperor of Austria, and other official personages, were specially invited to attend worship with the Sultan on Friday, the Mussulman's Sunday. Just before twelve, from the minaret of the palace, the muzzein called the faithful to prayer at Dolma-Baktche; then moved the grand procession, according to rank, — Empress and Emperor, Dukes, Princes, Ambassadors, Ministers, Consuls, Pashas, on Arab steeds, the Sultan with body-guards from all races in the Empire. How strange a sight!— Mr. Peebles among these officials, attired in courtly Turkish costume, going to the worship of Allah! Writing of this pageant, Mr. Peebles says, —

"The shipping was gay with colors, flags, and banners. Everybody seemed to be in the narrow, dirty streets, — cripples and beggars pleading for piasters, flaunting their rags in the presence of lace, red tape, and royalty: it roused my American blood to a high pitch of excitement. How long, oh! how long, is pampered royalty, kingcraft, and priestcraft to crush the lowly, continue caste, and curse the earth? . . . Remember that Christian nations uphold this Sultan's throne as the French bayonets do the pope's! . . . Can there be a more hateful theological mongrel, a more horrid moral spectacle, than effete Mohammedanism veneered and polished with French Catholicism? . . . .

"It was little pleasure to see, and less to be officially 'toted round,' mingling in that gay throng of rulers and diplomats. The forms of reception, the display, the pageantry, were so anti-American; the salutes from the land-batteries, the thundering of cannon, the flag-dressed men-of-war, were so repulsive to my *peace principles*, — saying nothing of the military bands, and the review of thirty thousand Turkish troops, — that I longed to get away from plumes, feathers, and epaulettes, away from gilded buttons, dangling swords, red ribbons, and the glittering trappings of royalty, away into my library, or on some mountain, with God, angels, and birds. Is the story, — the Christian world's prophet-songs of the 'Prince of Peace,' and a millennium of love and harmony, — all a dream? What hinders the consummation? Kingcraft, priestcraft, *ignorance*. Down on them! Too long have they cursed this world, made so beautiful by the Father of all. Put down kings, and put up the people! People implies men and women. I repeat, Put down all princes, potentates, and powers that subsist upon the sweat of honest industry! put them down, not by revolutions, not by frantic mobs, not by sword and blood, but by educating the people, *all* the people — to govern themselves, self-government lying at the foundation of all government.

"Though forced by circumstances, now and then, into the midst of consulate officials and princely rulers, my heart is with the poor, with the suffering, with God's dear humanity. If this is not good consul talk, it is certainly practical, and comes from a soul that throbs in deepest sympathy with every conscious intelligence of earth and heaven.

'Wandering by the classic river
In its soft mysterious flow;
Murmuring, as it rolls for ever,
Of the myths of long ago.

. . . . .

'From many a proud cathedral,
Turkish mosque and minaret,
Turn mine eyes with fond devotion
To the brow of Olivet.'

"They turn thither, because from under those olive-trees speaks a brother; whose voice, echoing along the uneven spaces of nearly two thousand years, says, 'My kingdom is not of this world.' 'I testify of myself.' 'My peace I leave with you.'"

Among other happy acquaintances formed in Constantinople, he mentions M. Repos, a French attorney, a zealous Spiritist; and M. Sillerman, a Spiritualist, in a German mercantile establishment, and from them learned how rapidly Spiritualism is diffusing itself in Asia Minor and Syria. He found excellent media in Constantinople, and, invited, addressed the Spiritualists in the hall of the *Chambre de Commerce;* and their interest was truly inspiring.

In Stamboul, the Turkish portion of Constantinople, Mr. Peebles noticed an Egyptian obelisk, having inscriptions engraved five hundred years before Christ, freshly representing the Delphian Tripod. There, too, was a spring once flowing, over which the Tripod was placed; on which sat a mediumistic priestess, invoking some god or goddess of Delphi, uttering oracular words of inspiration. Everywhere he found the relics of ancient Spiritualism, reviving now in more practical form.

It is Mr. Peebles's custom in visiting cities, especially in foreign lands, to inspect their cemeteries; where the traveler accurately can decipher in the inscriptions upon tombs and graves the plane of religion, and the hope of the bereft. He thus poetically relates an incident coming under his eye whilst in the cemetery of Scutari, near Constantinople, —

"It was a calm October day, afar up the Levant. For several hours I had been wandering in that famous Mohammedan burying-ground, Scutari, Asia. This cemetery, three miles in length, and somewhat irregular in shape, is tastefully surrounded and beautifully shaded with tall cypresses. The scenery was so strange, so half-entrancing, that time passed unheeded. The sun now low in the West, I left the speaking monuments of mortality around me, and hastening to the shores of the Bosphorus, to take the steamer for Constantinople, saw a venerable appearing Turk, tall and turbaned, distributing coins and fruits to a group of ragged children standing by the wayside begging. The beneficence was as suggestive as patriarchal. When through with the deed of mercy, several of the children, stepping forward, bowed, and kissed the giver's withered hand. Smiling, he asked Allah to bless them, and then passed quietly on his way. The scene, purely Oriental, so touched my heart that my eyes were immediately suffused with tears. It was a moment of transfiguration. Under the inspiration, my soul so warmed into love and sympathy for humanity, that I, too, in spirit, kissed the old man's hand, — *kissed*, knowing it to be the hand of Ishmael, wrongfully said to be 'against every man.' Ay, God, whether known as Brahm, Allah, or Father, is good. Human nature is good: *all* is good; and love is omnipotent. Seldom offending the critics with attempts at rhyme, because believing most efforts to voice sentiments in poetry could be better expressed by the use of plain, substantial prose, I trust to the kindly nature of the reader this once for the following: —

"The Orient sheds its shimmering haze
O'er field and garden, sea and isle;
And Asia's arch is red with rays
That turn to gold each Islam pile.
My heart is filled with warmth again:
I feel for Moslems in their thrall;
I only hate the hate of men;
I love the heart that loveth all.

Each soul hath stemmed some fearful storm;
Each heart is chafed with wasting scar:
My life-boat wrecked in manhood's morn
Now drifteth like a shooting star.
But oh! I have not lost the power
Of sympathy at sorrow's call;
For love inspires each fading hour, —
That love which feels, then gives to all.

Oh! think it not a vain conceit,
That angel-echoes linger still
In hearts whose chords of music sweet
The pangs of earth can never chill.
Ay, there are souls with holy love,
Who like the circling stars may fall;
But, falling, rise to heaven above:
I kiss the hand that helpeth all."

About the 1st of November, 1869, Mr. Peebles expected to arrive at Trebisond, Asia, to enter upon his official duties. He soon grew restless, in these Turkish cities, of so much filth. He reports himself to American readers, through "The Universe," after this style: —

"Are not Americans naturally nomadic? A year ago last March, I sat in an Indian peace council, with the Congressional Committee and several army generals, at the confluence of the North and South Platte Rivers, in those Colorado regions. The week following I was on the summit of the Rocky Mountains, standing on the highest railroad eminence between the two oceans. To-day I am near the eastern extremity of the Black Sea in Asia; and what of it? Where next? Why live in the world and never see it?

'Behold, we live through all things, — famine, thirst,
Bereavement, pain, all grief and misery,
All woe and sorrow: life inflicts its worst
On soul and body; but we cannot die,
Though we be sick and tired and faint and worn.
Lo! all things can be borne.'

"Trebisond is an important fortified seaport town of some fifty thousand inhabitants, over thirty thousand of whom are Mohammedans. The old city was built upon a sloping hill, facing the east. The lower portion is horribly shabby and filthy. The Turks have been on the descending portion of the cycle of progress for centuries. Within the walls are old ruins and mossed monasteries, — remnants of Grecian and Mohammedan wars. The nationality of the city is Turkish. The intermingling medley is composed of Persians, Arabians, Georgians, Armenians, and some Mesopotamian wanderers. It is a choice place to study the Shemitic world in its decline. The English shipping is comparatively small, the American virtually nothing. The houses are of stone, and in style Asiatic, with roofs nearly flat, covered with tiles. They are generally surrounded by small gardens, some of which are very neat, and tastefully arranged. The business streets are narrow, crooked, and disgustingly filthy. Packs of dogs — sacred animals with the more ignorant Turks — are the scavengers. The city contains twenty mosques, and nearly as many Greek churches, the worship in which corresponds with the Roman Catholic. The Greek Christians, however, deny the authority of the Pope and the papal power of the West. From the year 1203 till the subversion of the Eastern Empire, Trebisond was the capital of an extensive dominion, reaching from the Phasis to Halys.

"Mr. Palgraves, the gentlemanly English consul in Trebisond, and a ripe Oriental scholar, has been to Mecca, explored Central Arabia, and made himself thoroughly acquainted with Persia, together with the nations lying east of it. He speaks thirty languages. No one would do well to talk of Greek originality in his presence. Have the so-called enlightened ages given the world any thing new in the line of morals or metaphysics for the past two thousand five hundred years? *That's* the question. Russia, France, Prussia, and other European nations, have consuls located in Trebisond.

"The American consulate was created with the design of opening an extensive trade with Persia and contiguous nations. Treaties and methods to this effect were discussed under Buchanan's administration, but never adopted. The position is of little importance compared to that of Constantinople. A railroad is now in process of construction from the eastern borders of the Black Sea to the Caspian. One hundred miles are already completed. Russians own the stock. Besides vast quantities of *bitumen* and kindred substances south-east of the Black Sea and along the borders of the Caspian, there are petroleum oil-springs bubbling up in various localities, thus prophesying of inexhaustible stores. They are worked, so we are informed, in a most clumsy manner. The Turks are very jealous of the 'Franks,' and fearful of English and American enterprise. American ingenuity and energy may yet develop these treasures, and others, under Asiatic skies. Asia Minor is exceedingly rich in minerals of various kinds. The coal-mines are immeasurable. Lead ore yields seventy-five per cent. There are silver and copper mines. Wild fruits, figs, pomegranates, olives, grapes, &c., abound in great luxuriance. There is perhaps no country upon the globe, if we except Africa, so little understood or appreciated as this portion of the Asiatic world...

"Decline and decay characterize the present Turkish nation. A deathly torpor has seized its vitals. It is truly the 'sick man' of the Orient. Russia wants the vast domain. England and France say, 'Hands off!' Prussia and the central nations of Europe think it well to maintain the balance of power as it is. May not the more modernized phase of Turkish theology have something to do with this stupor? The Moslems are *fatalists*. One article of their faith reads thus (see J. P. Brown's Derv., p. 11., pars. 5–6): —

"'It is God who fixes the will of man; and he is therefore not free in his actions. There does not really exist any difference between good and evil; for all is reduced to unity: and God is the real author of the acts of mankind.'

"These are square statements. We relish them, because entirely free from those bungling twistings and turnings that distinguish Calvinists and certain Spiritualists, who hold and advocate the same doctrine. Fatalism in this bald form is considered by a large class of progressive Moslems as an innovation, however, and other than an original dogma. The only hope for Turkey is, to inaugurate a vigorous system of education. The Sultan, when visiting France, doubtless became aware of this; accordingly, within a few weeks, a new educational code has leapt, like Minerva, fully armed, from Sultan Abdul Aziz-Khan's brain. The course of public instruction marked out by the Porte is exceedingly elaborate, including primary and preparatory departments, normal schools, and universities."

Noting the hospitality of the Turks, their earnest devotions, their fidelity to nationality, their natural vivacity and honesty, their abstinence from "swine's flesh and wines," their religious toleration, their mediumistic qualifications, their revered relics of an original, pure spirituality, and contrasting these with governmental corruption and bribery, with enormous taxation upon the people to build and support palaces and harems, with the insipid condition of the women, — the future mothers, enslaved to men's pleasures and passions, — surveying all this, and considering a remedy, he prints these telling words, —

"The complete overthrow of all authoritative polygamy-sanctioning Bibles — such as the Old Testament of Jews and Christians, and the polygamy of the Koran — is the first step towards inaugurating reform movements in these Eastern countries. Then, instead of sending whining, lazy, money-making missionaries from America, to convert Mussulmans to sectarian Christianity, send the American plow and the American schoolhouse, American enterprise and American Elizabeth Stantons, to advocate woman's rights, woman's suffrage, woman's equality with man."

Smyrna, where was located one of the seven churches of Asia, to which the apocalyptic angel promised "a crown of life" if she continued "faithful," contains 150.000 souls; and among them walked one day our lonely "Pilgrim," in quest of Polycarp's tomb,— Polycarp, the martyr and bishop, and "friend of John the Beloved." Mr. Peebles stood over it in deep reverie. What emotions thrilled him! He seemed to hear the voice of the burning bush at Mount Horeb, "Take off thy sandals; for the place whereon thou standest is holy ground!" These were some of his inspirations: —

"At my feet have lain matchless ruins, and rolled tideless rivers; around me have stood monuments of valor and patriotism, and the scattered remnants of Hellenic grandeur; such was Greece to me: but here, under Asian skies, on this November day, mountains bear winter upon their heads, spring upon their shoulders, autumn upon their bosoms; while summer, with bud and blossom, is ever resting at their feet. How naturally adapted all these regions to poesy and prophecy! Such lands ever produce seers, seeresses, and sibylline oracles. How sacred is this place!"

At Smyrna he found several Spiritualists, — M. C. Constant and M. E. H. Rossi, the more prominent, — who hold spiritual *séances* during the winter months, the angels organizing their forces at the seat of one of the "seven churches"!

> "God sends his teachers unto every age,
> To every clime and every race of men."

Dining at the home of Mr. Smither's, the American consul, so hospitable, he reclined upon the Turkish divan, and relished the rich soup, the seedless raisins, nuts, grapes, pomegranates, figs, apricots, and oranges, — all native to that sunny clime. "Asia Minor," he said, "is the paradise of fruits." Turks, Albanians, Persians, Englishmen, Frenchmen, Americans, were represented in this city, all much inclined to Turkish habits. With the rest, he wore the fez, and occasionally the Turkish costume, — which he brought home, — and talked with the Persians, through an interpreter, about the land of the "fire-worshipers," — the most stately and graceful people he ever met, so tall and dignified, attired in their pyramidal-shaped turbans, and long dresses girdled with gaudy sashes. All his boyish school-ideas about a caravan were realized here; for one came into the city, hundreds of camels in a train, — patient creatures, led by a lazy Turk, — heavily burdened with cloths, madder-root, olive-oil in goat-skins, opium, figs, &c. These products opened to his vision the vast resources of wealth in that country, waiting for American emigration and industry to develop.

Riding donkeys is in fashion there: so he mounted one when going to see some ruins. "My 'cavasse,' — Turkish guide, — insisted," he says, "upon my riding his animal, as my lean, half-fed horse had several times stumbled. Ay, Americans, you ought to have seen me upon that long-eared fellow! Carefully surveying my long legs and general build, I came to the sage conclusion, that I never could look graceful upon the back of a little donkey!" We wonder those Smyrnians did not shout, as the miners did in California, "There goes old Pilgrim's Progress!"

Conversing with Mr. Macropodari, a native of Boston, a wealthy resident of Smyrna, as they rode together through the gorgeous scenery of the city suburbs, he learned that "less crimes are committed by the Turks than any people in the world: their word is *good*. A shake of the hand closes a contract, to be *kept* strictly as any written document." All American and English consuls with whom he talked say the same. But the Turks, like our poor Indians mingling with the whites, are being vitiated by Greek and Roman Christians, — by "shrewd, cunning, money-getting Christians!"

Ephesus, the old Ionian city, famous for its stadium, theaters, and temple of Diana, recipient of a Pauline epistle and the personal ministry of the apostle John, — that he must visit. The journey lay sixty miles into the country. Hiring a "cavasse," armed like a brigand, he started, and soon stumbled upon a party of Americans, bound for the same place, all from Chicago, — Dr. J. S. Jewett, Lecturer in the Medical University; Charles G. Haskins and Wells C. Lake, — traveling thither in quest of information, gathering cabinet specimens, exploring ruins, and taking a general topographical survey of the country. Our "Pilgrim" was overjoyed. Americans are closer brothers in a strange land.

The following beautiful letter, bubbling over with soul, addressed from that Asian city, must ever blossom in the memory of the reader: —

"EPHESUS, ASIA MINOR, Oct. 25, 1869.

"*Brother* ——, . . . The sun of the New-Testament epistles is John, — the sainted John, that lovingly leaned upon Jesus' bosom. In youth, he was my ideal man. To-day, he is that angel in heaven whom I most love. Not Arabia, then, nor Palestine, but classic Ephesus, is my Mecca.

"'Unto the angel of the church of Ephesus write, These things saith he that holdeth the seven stars in his right hand, who walketh in the midst of the seven golden candlesticks.'

"A pilgrim under a scorching Asian sky, I rested this afternoon, leaning upon one of the pillars that Christian and Moslem tradition unite in declaring marks the apostle's tomb. It was a consecrated hour! Its full history will in the future be written. While standing by this tomb, on the verge of Mount Prion, looking down upon the marbled seats of the Ephesian theater, — relic of Hellenic glory, — with my feet pressing the soil that pillowed the mortal remains of the 'disciple that Jesus loved,' ere their removal to Rome, no painter could transfix to canvas, no poet conceive suitable words to express, my soul's deep emotions. The inspiration was from the upper kingdoms of holiness; the baptism was from heaven; the robe was woven by the white fingers of immortals: while on the golden scroll was inscribed, '*The first cycle is ending: the winnowing angels are already in the heavens. Earth has no secrets. What of thy stewardship? Who is ready to be revealed? Who, who shall abide this second coming? Who has overcome? Who is entitled to the mystical name and the white stone? Gird on thine armor anew, and teach in trumpet tones, that the pure in heart, the pure in spirit only, can feast upon the saving fruitage that burdens the tree of paradise.*'

. . . "From the summit of Mount Prion, the Isle of Samos may be distinctly seen. Gazing at this in the distance, and nearer to the winding course of the little Cayster towards the sea, at the scattered remnants of temples, marble fragments, broken friezes, and relics of every description, I could not help recalling the prophetic warning of John, in the Book of Revelation, 'I will come unto thee quickly, and will remove thy candlestick out of its place, except thou repent!' —(Rev. ii. 5.)

"It is generally admitted that the apostle John lived to be one hundred and four years of age; and all we know of his later days is linked with Ephesus, — accurately described by Herodotus, Pausanius, Pliny, and others, — outside the records of the church Fathers. It is not known how long St. John resided in this portion of Asia: suffice it, that his memory still lingers here, enshrined even in the Turkish name of the squalid village about two miles from the ruins of the old Ephesian city, — '*Ayasolouke*,' which is a corruption of the Greek '*Agios Theologos*,' the holy theologian, the name universally given to this apostle in the Oriental Church.

"The mosque here, which is magnificent, even though in partial ruin, was undoubtedly an ancient Christian church, probably the identical one which the Emperor Justinian built on the site of an older and smaller one, dedicated in honor of St. John; who at Ephesus trained the disciples Polycarp, Ignatius, and Papius to preserve and disseminate apostolic doctrines in Smyrna and other cities of Asia. In the erection of this church edifice by Justinian, upon the spot where the venerable apostle preached in his declining years, were employed the marbles of Diana's temple. Visiting these scenes — Asian cities and churchal ruins — strengthens my belief in the existence of Jesus, the general authenticity of the Gospels, and the profound love-riches of John's epistles. It is the land of inspiration, of prophecy, and of spiritual gifts. Even the skeptical Gibbon, writing of the 'seven churches in Asia,' virtually admits the fulfillment of the apocalyptic visions. After recounting the final subjugation of the provinces of Bithynia by Orchan (A.D. 1312, &c.), he proceeds: 'The captivity or ruin of the seven churches of Asia was consummated; and the barbarous lords of Ionia and Lydia still trample on the monuments of classic and Christian antiquity. In the loss of Ephesus, the Christians deplored the fall of the first angel, — the extinction of the first candlestick of the Revelation. The desolation is complete; and the temple of Diana, or the church of Mary, will equally elude the search of the curious traveler. The circus and three stately theaters of Laodicea are now peopled with wolves and foxes. Sardis is reduced to a miserable village. The god of Mohammed, without a rival or a son, is invoked in the mosques of Thyatira and Pergamus; and the populousness of Smyrna is supported by the foreign trade of the Franks and Armenians. Philadelphia alone has been saved by prophecy or courage. At a distance from the sea, forgotten by the emperors, encompassed on all sides by the Turks, her valiant citizens defended their religion and freedom above fourscore years, and at length capitulated with the proudest of the Ottomans. Among the Greek colonies and churches of Asia, Philadelphia is still erect, — a column in a scene of ruins, — a pleasing example that the paths of honor and safety may sometimes be the same.' —(Gibbon's 'Decline and Fall,' chap. lxiv.)

. . . "Eusebius and others tell us of the profound reverence that all the early believers in the doctrines of Jesus had for this aged and loving saint; who sorrowed with Christ in the garden, stood by him at the cross, received in charge Mary the mother of Jesus, and clairvoyantly beheld him ascend to the homes of the angels. This sentence from his pen will live for ever, 'God is love.' When he had become too weak and infirm to walk to the old primitive church edifice in Ephesus, his admirers, taking him in their arms, would bear him thither; and then, with trembling voice, he could only say, 'Little children, love ye one another.' These and other well-attested historic recollections, rushing upon my mind, lift me on to the mount of transfiguration. I am happy. Could I have my library and a few congenial souls present, should be resigned to live under these soft, clear skies of Asia, till, putting off my pilgrim's sandals, I hear the voice, 'Thou hast finished thy course: *come up higher!*'"

CHAPTER XXIX.

NAPLES AND ROME.

"Oh, for a touch of the Olympic games!"

FINDING Turkish countries socially uncongenial, the autumn and wintry winds from the Black Sea injurious to his lungs, his spiritual nature unsatisfied, he obeyed the inspirational promptings of his spirit-guides by resigning his consulship. Through our consul-general at Constantinople, Mr. Goodnowe, of Portland, Me., the resignation was accepted, but not until after his commission had received confirmation in the Senate. Leaving Turkey, he took an extensive tour through Asia Minor. . . . "'Mid evergreen isles waves a sapphire sea. I am entranced in meditative delight," he said, as his steamer circled westward, bound through the Archipelago, — "classic sea of antiquity." Sailing out of the Dardanelles, there was Clazomenæ, once a famous center for commercial cities; then Scio, Byron's "rocky isle," where the Christian crusaders massacred the Turks in the name of the "Prince of Peace;" then Samos, home of Pythagoras; then Cos, of mountain-peaks; then sainted Patmos, where John was banished, but was "in the spirit on the Lord's Day;" and Rhodes, too, with its ruined Colossus; then classic Syracuse, which Strabo said was once "twenty-one miles in circumference," sacred to the memory of Æschylus, Demosthenes, and Archimedes; then Mt. Ætna, Sicily, belted below the equator with snow, towering up eleven thousand feet, with three distinctive zones of vegetation. Full of enthusiasm, he started with his guide to ascend; but the weather, changing, imperiled life: so he retraced his steps, pondering whether the New Atlantis, sunk nine thousand years before Plato's time, was not located in that volcanic section of the Mediterranean. Other islands are gradually sharing a similar fate. Santarena has nearly disappeared. Dating these facts, he called to mind the promise of that ancient spirit, "Aphelion," that media would yet clairvoyantly disclose a submerged continent, the relics of its civilizations still preserved in its swashing brine.

He was now on Italian soil, in the city of Messina, Sicily, the guest of Mr. Behn, the American consul, — land of Tasso, Columbus, Galvani, Perasee, and other geniuses ascended! were they not his companions? The very thought of it hallowed every instinct to grateful meditation. Noticing the papal monasteries and churches, the superstition of the lower classes, removing their hats before the priests, the devoutness of the wild brigands, "equal to American Christians at eight-o'clock prayer-meetings," and invoicing the French bayonets that guard the papal throne and the Romish machinations of Empress Eugenie, "the Pope's Imperial Nuncio," he concludes his lesson in these memorable words, —

"Educate the people, permit women to vote, and republics like Edens will cover all isles and continents."

This feeling was evoked mainly by the following experience in Messina, an episode which he afterwards related in one of his American lectures upon his "Oriental Travels:" —

"The sound of a band of music attracted me to the street, where I saw a small procession carrying sacred images, and surrounded by a crowd, which idleness, curiosity, or religious enthusiasm had induced to swell their ranks. It was St. Agatha's Day; and being a stranger, and curious to know what was going forward, I joined the procession as it entered the Plaza, and there witnessed the performance of a variety of ceremonies. Not seeing as distinctly as I wished, I mounted a block, steadied myself in my place by a branch of a tree, and, to use an American phrase, was 'enjoying it hugely,' when all at once I became conscious that the attention of the crowd was diverted to and concentrated upon me. They began to talk to me: I couldn't understand them. They gesticulated fiercely, — for the Italians, like the French, talk as much with their hands as their tongues, — still I did not know what they meant, nor what to make of it, and made up my mind that I had better retire from the scene. With this intention, I stepped down from the block; but the throng pressed round me with louder words and wilder gestures, as if to frustrate such an attempt. Then I thought of calling the police to my aid. I had learned Italian enough for that: it was an essential that I took care to acquire the first thing after my arrival. I shouted till I brought one to the ground, and he, too, began to talk to me with an astonishing severity; which, incomprehensible as it was, warned me that I must look further for safety. In this strait, a lucky expedient suggested itself. I threw open my coat, displayed the badge of the Progressive Lyceum that I fortunately wore, struck it with the air of a man who proclaims himself to be somebody, and signed the policeman to follow me to the 'Hotel de Victoria.' The effect was magical. Impressed with a sense of my importance, and a conviction that there was a mistake somewhere, the throng fell back, the policeman at my urgency accompanied me to the proprietor of my hotel, by whose aid I succeeded in making him understand that I was an American consul. The explanation of this popular demonstration against me was, that they had mistaken me for Father Gavazzi, who was reported to have recently landed on the island, intending to harangue the people against the pope's infallibility. Gavazzi, you may recollect, was at one time a priest; but, latterly apostatizing from the church, he drew upon himself the righteous fury of all its devoted followers. For some unaccountable reason, I was regarded as in league with Garibaldi, — the very unruly anti-churchman; and so I was! and the excited mobs were shouting, '*Down with the agitator! Away with Padre Gavazzi!*' The moral to be derived from the adventure is this: If you would insure your safety in a foreign country, keep out of crowds."

Voyez Naples et mourez. "I change the traveler's motto," said Mr. Peebles, "See Naples, but *never* die!" Boarding a neat Italian steamer, he was among the monks; — cowled, crossed, cloaked *beggars!* "They not only looked fat and sleek, but drank wine and smoked cigars very much like sinners in gin palaces, dirty and lazy too!" Passed close to volcanic Stromboli, the ancient Æolus, revered by Pliny, the exiled home of Charles Martel, famous with the Crusades; and, landing, he found rooms in the Vico Carminillo, — former residence of Robert Dale Owen while American minister there. The odor of his good name still lingers in that city. At rapid glances, he analyzed the kaleidoscopic scenery; and his soul enlarged in reverence for the beautiful of other days, still blooming amid ruins. We catch some of his sunbeams of thought, —

"The waters of the Bay of Naples have a cerulean tint, crescent-shaped, backed by an amphitheater of hills and mountains, with rocky slopes covered with sunny villas, sprinkled with orange and lemon, fig and oleander; Capri, loveliest of isles, in front, — a silver slipper; caves and grottoes in it; Sorrento, gleaming through the waves, — home of Torquato Tasso; the streets narrow and dingy, paved with lava; badly constructed dwelling-houses, iron gates, flat-roofed; insolent carriage-drivers, — villainous misrule of Catholics!

"O Pius IX! you so rich from hoarded taxes, — Peter's pence and foreign purses laid at your feet, — feed the people! . . . Get your sleek bishops and priests to plowing, sowing, and cultivating the fields for your beggars' sake, instead of mumbling prayers for 'Christ's sake.' Who with brains cares a fig for the decisions of your Ecumenical Councils? The people are above all councils. Who cares whether there be one, three, or thirty thousand gods, provided they are all good ones? Who cares whether Jesus was begotten by a holy or unholy Ghost, allowing he was well-begotten, and lived (as I believe he did) a beautiful and divine life? Who cares whether Jonah, of Nineveh memory, swallowed, or was swallowed by, a whale, providing the bones of neither obstruct the navigation of the Suez Canal? Pope Pius, no more of your dictatorial bulls, nor muttering of formal prayers in Latin! FEED THE BEGGARS! EDUCATE THE PEOPLE! No more pretensions to infallibility, or wasting of kisses upon that brazen toe in St. Peter's. FEED THE BEGGARS! EDUCATE THE PEOPLE! No more bowings, twistings, crossings, before a speechless image or golden cross. FEED THE BEGGARS! EDUCATE THE PEOPLE! No more confessions from sinning Catholics to equally sinning priests and popes. FEED THE BEGGARS! EDUCATE THE PEOPLE!"

With Samuel Guppy and lady and others, — all intelligent, hospitable Spiritualists, of high-toned character, — Mr. Peebles improved this Neapolitan visit in inspecting the historic places and ruins in and about Naples. Starting on a warm December day, they soon reached *Virgil's tomb.* Over it he stood and mused, reading the inscription to his memory, best engraved upon the hearts of all scholars. Reaching a mountain, they rode through the *Grotto di Posilipo*, cut by the ancients, — magnificent, arching eighty to ninety feet, and two thousand three hundred and sixteen feet long, and twenty-two feet wide, — tunnel for a railroad; drove to Pozzuoli, — Cicero's "Rome the lesser," founded 558 B.C., now dim in its ancient splendor; stood on the jutted mole whereon rested the famous bridge of Caligula; saw the remains of the temple of Augustus, with its fragments of Corinthian columns; studied the figures *in basso relievo* upon the white marble monument in the square of Pozzuoli, personifying the fourteen cities of Asia destroyed by an earthquake. As these were executed two or three thousand years ago, he inquired naturally, "How and in what direction have men progressed? Has this century produced any thing original in art or metaphysics?" Pozzuoli was the ancient *Puteoli* of Paul (see Acts xxviii. 13), who here walked; and here he may have preached the re-appeared Christ. "Brother Paul fell into a trance; was a missionary in Ephesus, Rome, and the Isles of the Mediterranean; had visions; was a healing medium."

The amphitheater, there it was, amid the mold of Pozzuoli! — the place of Nero's gladiatorial sports, himself in the arena when Tiridates, king of Amedia, was his royal guest. Five hundred feet in length, one hundred and forty in breadth, in form of an ellipse inclosed in a circle, it could seat fifty thousand spectators! Our "Pilgrim" walked over it, — a *silent* spectator now, — the very stones voicing his thoughts of this strange world of ours, — life budding on the stalk of death! He ascended its marble steps and over its four tiers of seats. Far below, under the marble flooring, were the stalls for the bears, lions, and tigers; the deep wells; and on the sides were the visible entrances for the gladiators and animals. There, too, was the imperial seat, distinguished by Corinthian columns of black marble. What brooding meditations were his! —

——"Where dead men
Hang their mute thoughts on the mute walls around,
He lingered, poring on memorials
Of the world's youth."

Sibyl's cave, beyond the ruins of Baiæ! how weird to our "Pilgrim!" Over the earthquaked soil, — over Lake Avernus in the socket of an extinct volcano's eye, — hot water boiling up from its center; on its verge the cave, eight feet wide, and six feet arch; "it was a deathly-silent retreat." He describes it, —

"The mosaics, the old Roman fresco inscriptions on the stone stairway, the rock-hewn path, the weird throne on which the sibyl sat while giving the oracles in a trance ecstasy, together with the niche and aperture for the use of the individual receiving the oracular responses, were to us deeply interesting. Many of those sibylline oracles — ancient Spiritualism — are still extant, and have often been referred to in settling church controversies."

Nero's baths! He penetrated thither, several hundred feet into the winding passage of a mountain, narrow and black. "The stream is hot; boils eggs in three minutes. The descent is certainly fearful: few go down to the edge. Bathing my forehead in the boiling water, and examining the rocky bed on which gouty, rheumatic old Nero used to rest after his bath, I came out quite exhausted." Mr. Peebles plunged into Nero's dungeons, cut in the tuffa-stone mountain, "where this cruel emperor used to imprison rebels and captives." What a somber spell came over him as he inspected them! How they psychologically voiced the long ago! "How," he thought, "does rock and stream record the deeds of men, never to be effaced!" "History is a grand lie!" said Voltaire. A truer statement was never made. Only the Spiritual psychometrist can correctly write it. He alone can unriddle its fables and its churchal hypocrisies, written on so-called "sacred books." "Who is able to loose the seals?" The psychometrist! Said M. Dupotet, "Whatsoever thou shalt have thought shall be known to all who wish to know of it." Said Prof. Babbage, "The air is one vast library, on whose pages are for ever written all that man has ever said or woman whispered." Said Wm. Denton, the Spiritual scientist, "The very rocks drink in the character of the people of the country in which they exist," — startling truths, which the Spiritual Philosophy reveals! Most wonderful will be its developments, when wisely-disciplined media, standing on the places memorable in history, inspired by the acting spirit risen to heights of perspective, shall read the "soul of things" and the soul of events, magnetically engraved on ruins, rocks, and dust.

The Catacombs, — subterranean burial-places, those of Naples anciently extending nine miles in one direction and thirteen in another, entered now by the church of *Gennero dei Poveri:* down, *down*, he and his friend D. descended to this "nether world," led by two solemn-visaged guides, — "the living city over our head, a dead city of bones under our feet." There they were, "coffins, sarcophagi, tiers of tombs, rotten boards, rusty nails, nameless heaps of skulls, spines, arms, ribs, — a frightful aspect! There, too, were urns, vases, crosses, and the remains of the altar and church of St. Januarius, of the third century. This saint and his believing companions, being Christians, were thrown into the arena of the wild beasts, by order of Emperor Diocletian, but were not harmed. "Some psychological or spiritual influence may have saved them, as in the case of the prophet Daniel." In the year 305, he was beheaded on an eminence between Pozzuoli and Solfatara. He is the patron saint of Naples. "During the festival days that commemorate him, — the 3d of May and 19th of September, — his preserved blood is said to liquefy in the presence of the people. That the liquefaction takes place, Protestants admit; but is it blood, the genuine blood of the martyr, or a chemical preparation? That's the question. The purported miracle is performed in the cathedral." Mr. Peebles wanted to take away a skull as a relic, but was refused. "They are the skulls of *Christians*," said the monkish guide: "it would be sacrilege!" Afterwards finding a nice skull down several hundred feet, having a large frontal development, he convinced the guide, "it is *Pagan*, because of large reasoning faculties and full benevolence and conscientiousness:" so he was permitted to take it. Whose the skull, he has hope of yet tracing mediumistically, with a history therewith connected.

Solfatara, — the *Forum Vulcani* of Strabo; what a sight to our "Pilgrim!" It is nearly extinct; but, near the edge of the crater, he noticed "a fearful, fiery orifice, belching out steam, gas, and sulphur-impregnated smoke, half strangling us." He cast down a stone upon the crater-flooring: hearing its deep echo, and looking over, he called it the "mouth of hell." He thus suggests a Yankee enterprise, — "Let Elder Knapp and other revivalists ship this fire-mountain to America, and exhibit it as a foretaste or practical illustration of the *bottomless pit.* The Church could make money out of it."

Vesuvius, — volcano of the centuries! Mr. Peebles stood upon its summit, and gazed down into its awful vortex. There rolled before him visions of the past, time's tides, life's beats, civilization's cycles, religion's decay and resurrection; "and I, — am I a fated child too?" he asked. He walked the streets of exhumed Pompeii, and, with torch in hand, descended into buried Herculaneum, wondering at the grandeur of the amphitheater whose columns have braved the decay of two thousand years. In Pompeii, every thing seemed fresh, of yesterday.

"I am brought," he writes, "into actual relations with the temples, altars, paintings, mosaics, pavements, houses, and social life of men and women that thronged these chariot-groved streets two thousand years ago." In the wonderful museum in Naples, he found "Papyri, Etruscan vases, surgical instruments, agricultural implements, necklaces, ear-rings, brooches, chains, combs, gold lace, and ornaments of every kind; loaves of baker's bread, with name of the manufacturer thereon stamped; honey-comb, grains, fruits, eggs, bottles of wine and oil, hermetically sealed, — all these preserved since the eruption of 79, showing the high state of civilization the Pompeians had attained before the Christian era." Well does he exclaim, "Life is everywhere! Living men are constantly touching responsive chords that will vibrate for ever! The kingdoms, cities — ruins of the agone ages — are many-tongued and voiceful. The present is the hyphen that connects the past and future."

"Yet this is Rome,
That sate on her seven hills, and from her throne
Of beauty ruled the world! . . . .
Hear me, ye walls, that echoed to the tread
Of either Brutus! — once again I swear
The eternal city shall be free!"

"Is this Rome the seven-hilled, the mosaic of St. Peter's, the eternal city?" was our "Pilgrim's" thought, on his first waking in the morning after his arrival, — "Rome! still proud and imperial, the moss-fringed panorama of prostrate columns, tumbling arches, splendid palaces, ivy-encircled towers, — Rome! relic of nearly three thousand years of the world's history?"

Here meeting Prince George de Solms and Dr. F. H. L. Willis, "the true-souled brothers," the latter traveling in Europe in quest of health, he felt at home. Together roamed they the city: stood on Palatine Hill; talked in spirit with Romulus, — who marked the boundaries of the city with a plow, — with Cicero, Numa, and Tarquin, with Brutus and Cassius, with Cæsar and Mark Antony; ascended to the roof of the Capitol, and surveyed the square city, — "the ruined Forum, the Temple of Jupiter, the Temple of Concord, the Arch of Septimus Severus, the Temple of Antoninus, the Arch of Titus, the mighty Colosseum, the Appian Way, fringed for miles with the tombs of the citizens of old Rome, and the Seven Hills on which the city is built, dotted with churches, convents, palaces, gardens, fountains and tropical plants." They saw the "Tiber rolling along its muddy tide, as in old historic periods;" on its banks, the columns of Trajan and Antoninus, crowned with the statue of St. Paul, the dome of the Pantheon; over the bridge, Hadrian's Mausoleum, and the old palace of the Vatican, "whence have gone edicts shaking kingdoms, and making crowned heads tremble. Thank God and the good angels, popish bulls are quite harmless now." . . . "Oh, the towering dome of St. Peter's, mightiest of earth's temples, reaching toward the sky!" Within the walls they noticed the old aqueducts and baths, each more than a mile in circuit. Away stretched the eye over the Campagna, — "the gently-sloping Alban Hills, the Apennines with crests piercing the blue sky, the Sabine Hills suffused with dark purple, and the Etrurian plains extending far beyond the vision's reach."

The next day they visited these noted places for minute inspection, and found a world of art, ruins, beauty, filth, beggary, and everywhere the tracery of ancient glory and renown. They crossed the bridge of St. Angelo; paced the Borgo Nuovo; stood under the Piazza; and there was the gorgeous St. Peter's! covering eight acres, on the spot where Nero had his Circus, just where the apostle Peter was martyred. "See the unspeakable grandeur!" writes Mr. Peebles. "Stand under the firmament of marble, and cast your eye along the richly-ornamented nave, along the statue-lined transepts, and up into that circling vault, that wondrous dome, supported by four piers each two hundred and eighty-four feet in periphery, and then you feast upon the fullness of its magnificence. . . . It occupied a period of one hundred and seventy-six years in building, and three hundred and sixty years to perfect it!" They saw the papal throne, the master paintings of the renowned artists, — Raphael's and Angelo's, — the "Gift of Tongues," the "Feast of Pentecost," and the "Transfiguration," —the last great work of Raphael; "who seems to have been conscious then of standing upon the very verge of the summer-land."

Walking out to the Protestant burial-ground, beset by Catholic beggars as usual, as if there they might breathe a freer air, they found the tomb of the poet Shelley, having the simple inscription, "*Concordium;*" and beyond it that of the poet Keats, bearing this inscription, —

"*This grave contains all that was mortal of a young English poet; who, on his death-bed, in the bitterness of his heart at the malicious power of his enemies, desired these words to be engraven on his tombstone, 'Here lies one whose name is writ in water.'* Feb. 14, 1821."

Commenting upon this, — for the record touched his heart, — Mr. Peebles writes home, —

"A pack of prowling, cowardly critics, incompetent of writing poems themselves, and actuated by a low ambition, — a sort of mental dropsy, — pounced upon the sensitive young Keats, and hunted him into his grave. He lives: they are forgotten."

The Ecumenical Council, the twenty-first of the Latin Church, that pronounced the Pope "*infallible*," was holding its sessions during Mr. Peebles' visit to Rome; consisting then of fifty-five cardinals, eleven patriarchs, six hundred and forty-seven primates, archbishops, and bishops, six abbots, twenty-one mitered abbots, and twenty-eight generals of monastic orders. These fathers he saw in St. Peter's on Christmas Day. Speaking of the august ceremony there performed, and of friends, he writes in a private letter to us, dated Rome, Dec. 26, 1869, —

.... "Two of these days in Rome I have spent mostly with Prince George, — a magnificent man, every inch a prince. He accompanied me to the Vatican, St. Peter's, ruins of Cæsar's palaces, the Pantheon, Pincian Hill, and several of the most distinguished churches. On Christmas Day, saw the Pope borne through the broad aisle of St. Peter's upon eight men's shoulders, the Catholics dropping suddenly upon their knees as if he were the Almighty himself. Saw the seven hundred bishops kiss the brazen toe. Beholding the miters, crosses, imperial robes, and heartless ceremonies, I said, 'Is this the religion of Jesus, *the meek and lowly?*'...

"My dear brother, Dr. Willis, is with me. How happy our acquaintance in years past, when we were laboring together, he in Cold Water, and I in Battle Creek, Mich.

"Kindred natures indulge in few formalities. Especially is this true when meeting in foreign lands. Our evenings in the city are generally spent together in fraternal fellowship. Unseen visitors — unseen to self, at least — are often in attendance, with heavenly words of truth and love. The panoramic vision of the spiritual temple, with the mediumistic workers engaged thereon, given to the doctor upon one of these occasions, is literally ablaze with all the characteristics of a revelation. Heaven grant his speedy restoration to health!"

CHAPTER XXX.

FLORENCE.

> "All houses wherein men have lived and died
> Are haunted houses. Through the open doors
> The harmless phantoms on their errands glide,
> With feet that make no sound upon the floors." —
> HENRY W. LONGFELLOW.

GLORY of the middle ages! Florence! beautiful, freshened by the Arno, whose banks Milton trod; the spiritual battery once of the fiery Savonarola, hurling thunderbolts at the Pope; famous for sculpture, painting, and poesy, — how charming to the "Pilgrim"! He hastened to the Franciscan convent, and then to the Old Bastion, and gazed and gazed enraptured. He visited the pride of the Florentines, — the Santa Maria del Flore, of which Michael Angelo said, "I may equal, but I can not surpass thee." He walked its solemn aisles, "haunted with pious, speechless ghosts," the gloom like its theology. The old masters have paintings here: one is "Paradise;" opposite "Hell," black and fiery; and "Purgatory" is quite "respectable, showing genuine benevolence in the artist." What is the attractive power of the Catholic Church? Delaage, a zealous Catholic, answers, "The sublime and ravishing harmony of her chants, the bluish wreaths of her ascending incense, the pictures and statues with which she adorns her cathedrals and churches, and the magnificent and impressive ceremonies of her worship!" Is there not a lesson for Spiritualists to learn here? Goethe says, "The beautiful is higher than the good; for the beautiful includes the good within it, as a part." In the Church of Santa Croce he walked amid tombs, and "conversed with souls that yet speak through the sister arts, — painting, sculpture, architecture." He read on some of the monuments the names of Galileo (over whom the church begins to repent), Boccaccio, Marsuppini, and Michiavelli.

What memories thrilled him as he read the registry of their virtues, and caught the baptismal light of their spirit-presence! And did he not there sense the soul of Dante, once frantic under the abuses of enemies, now dusting his brow with poetic glory? Here was that Spiritualist's favorite retreat, near this church. Our "Pilgrim" visited the spot, and felt what kindred souls only feel, and recalled Rogers's words, —

—— "On that ancient seat,—
The seat of stone that runs along the wall,
South of the church, east of the belfry-tower,
(Thou canst not miss it) in the sultry time
Would Dante sit conversing, and with those
Who little thought that in his hand he held
The balance, and assigned at his good pleasure
To each his place in the invisible world;
To some an upper region, some a lower:
Many a transgressor sent to his account
Long ere in Florence numbered with the dead."

He entered the galleries of painters' portraits. Here were Titian's face of "deep expression;" Leonardo Vinci's, "full of beauty, grandeur, and majesty;" Michael Angelo's, "sour, harsh, and gloomy;" Raphael's, "easy and graceful;" Angelica Hauffman's, "young, dreamy, and winning;" Joshua Reynolds's, "hard and stern."

"A writer in 'Household Words' says, 'The face being the outward index of the passions and sentiments within, the immortal dweller fashions and molds the plastic substance of his home, and helps form and alter the architecture of its house, like the bees and birds.... The spiritual principle writes its own character on its exterior walls, and chronicles from time to time its upward aspirations, or its more complete abasement.'"

Understanding this *spiritual* art, another thought suggested itself to the mind of our brother, whilst philosophizing upon these symbols of soul, whether the molding influence of the love of the beautiful is not often measurably neutralized by the adversities of life? True, no doubt! The touch of early frost destroys the violet's beauty and sweetness. Artistic geniuses, soaring above the sensuous of earth, "dreamy and impractical," as they are called, sensitive to every touch of mind, persecuted for their innovations, inevitably clash with popular opinions and consequent misfortunes, that render passion a battle, and love a storm: so that a sweet spirit, limning itself in physical form, may appear as Angelo's, "sour, harsh, and gloomy;" but, in the freer world of angels, be as the Nazarene's, — "shining as the sun.' Let Spiritualists, then, institute their educations and their social relations in such a manner as shall foster, reward, and protect true genius; then shall we see the robe of divinity and the privilege of angels in our redemptive world.

The leaning tower of Pisa, of boyhood's wonder! he sat under its shadow; "take care, surely it must fall!" He mounted the spiral staircase, one hundred and eighty-seven feet, and looked off upon the city of fifty thousand, once double that, once the rival of Genoa, and the competitor of Venice for the sovereignty of the sea. But the tower! "While on this elevation, your thoughts naturally revert to Galileo, who used the inclination of the tower to find the measure of time, and develop his theory of the fall of heavy bodies. Here, too, he demonstrated that the earth sails round the sun. Daring man, — a heretic! The Church has ever persecuted the scientists."

In *Cimiterio Inglese* he found the grave of Theodore Parker. On the way, he passed the monument erected to the memory of Mrs. Browning, the poetess and Spiritualist. All that is on it is, "E. B. B." So the sculptor *nearly* remembered her own wish, so sensible, —

"A stone above my heart and head,
But no name written on the stone."

"Under the cypress-trees, and having a plain brown marble monument, repose in this cemetery all that is mortal of one, who, not only in America, but in all enlightened lands, lives on earth immortal. The slab has this inscription, —

"'*Theodore Parker, born at Lexington, Mass., U.S.A., Aug.* 24, 1810; *died at Florence, May* 10, 1860.'"

What emotions thrilled his heart! He recalled the Church's persecution against him, and the Church's repentance, now that his truth and justice prevail. "I am proud," he says, "that I had known him in life, — proud that he was an *American*. . . . The true worker continues his work in the land of souls."

Wherever Mr. Peebles goes, he is sure to find the principal literary characters, and sound the depth of their minds, to learn their worth in the world. Such acquaintances are so many steps to the paradise of universal truth. At Florence, he was introduced to T. Adolphus Trollope, son of the celebrated Mrs. Trollope, who years ago traveled in the United States, on a tour of observation, writing a book of us and our institutions. He is an author of literary fame. Mr.

Peebles visited his elegant mansion, gardens, and massive library; which, he says, "bound my soul as with a magic spell. Books, *books!* Bury this frail body under a pyramid of books!" He found this gentleman an earnest investigator of Spiritualism, having witnessed remarkable tests of spirit-presence through Dr. Willis, at Villa Trollope, Ricorboli.

Stepping into the studio of Hiram Powers, the world-renowned American sculptor, he studied the gospel of the fine arts, — their influence upon national character. With Mr. Marsh, our United-States minister, he listened in rapt delight to Mr. Powers's practical good sense upon the necessity of developing in young minds a loving ambition for sculpture and painting, as a most powerful instrumentality of national progress. Our carving of the beautiful carves the soul in its divine image. The busts of "Eve," the very perfection of art, and "Our Saviour," so exquisitely finished, were only companions of Longfellow, Everett, Webster, Franklin, and Jefferson. This is right, —

"No high, no low, no rich, no poor,"

in the kingdom of the good and true. Mr. Powers, a firm Spiritualist, "would see our spiritual literature of the highest order."

Baron de Guldenstubbe, "is the unassuming and thoroughly individualized." Through this gentleman's mediumship, Mr. Peebles obtained new phases of spirit-writing most wonderful. "Placing writing materials upon monuments, sarcophagi, in the Louvre, and places consecrated to certain saints, he obtained proofs of spirit identity. He published sixty-seven fac-similes. The handwriting of Marie Antoinette and others was immediately recognized." The baron published these writings in "Thoughts from beyond the Tomb," and the "Reality of Spirits."

Salvadore Brunetti, formerly a professor in a Syracusean College in Sicily, is a brother in whom he found a friend of liberty; imprisoned by Francis II., emancipated by Garibaldi, and now a wandering *improvisatore*, — a poor and homeless medium, blessing the world by his spirit songs and poems.

Baron Vincenzo Caprara is a great scholar, imprisoned for republican sentiments, persecuted by the Catholic priesthood, succored by the angels, disinherited by mortals, enriched by the gods. "Pleasant are our memories," says Mr. Peebles, "from writing and mingling with him in the social circle. If Italians do not, future history will do him justice."

Girolamo Parisi is editor of "The Aurora," in Florence, a periodical devoted to the spirit sciences. A "truly generous man," writes Mr. Peebles, remembering his many kindnesses.

Signor G. Damiani, of ducal family, a political agitator like the rest; once a Catholic, now a radical Spiritualist; "a daily missionary of uncommon scholarship, preaching the ministry of spirits in the best social circles of Italian, English, French, and German society," inviting and challenging the greatest scientists of the world, such as Profs. Lewes and Tyndal, to a trial of Spiritualism, — how highly does our Pilgrim prize him!

Baron Kirkup, venerable and noble, a painter, friend of the beautiful William Blake, his daughter a brilliant medium, his library priceless, his genius most golden, his attendant angel *Dante*, crowned by the king of Italy as a "knight" [*La Corona d'Italia*], for his restoration of the painting of Dante, under the inspiration of the poet himself, is soon to be crowned by the angels in the gallery of paintings in the spirit-world. "How I love this generous brother of large soul!" exclaims our "Pilgrim" again.

"He who would be the tongue of this wide land
Must strike his harp with chord of sturdy iron,
And strike it with a toil-embrownèd hand.
Such, such, is he for whom the world is waiting,
To sing the beatings of its mighty heart:
Too long hath it been patient with the grating
Of scandal-pipes, and heard it misnamed art."

"The Anti-Ecumenical!" As this council runs parallel with that of the Roman, that pronounced the Pope "*infallible*," — a council that was the outburst of free thought, prophetic of papal decline from that very hour, — we publish its entire proceedings as reported. The following note was tendered Mr. Peebles whilst in Florence: —

"ASSEMBLEE DES LIBRES PENSEURS
DEVANT SE REUNIR A NAPLES
LE 8 DÉCEMBRE 1869.

BILLET D'ADMISSION.

ORDRE DU JOUR DE LA SÉANCE D'OUVERTURE.

"1. Discours d'inauguration;
'2. Compte-rendu du Comité provisoire, et lecture des principales lettres d'adhésion;

"3. Appel nominal, et enregistrement des membres présents;
"4. Election du Comité central défininitif.

"Mr. James M. Peebles, à qui le présent billet d'admission a été délivré, pourra se faire représenter par un délégué, dont il écrira le nom au dos de cette feuille, en le faisant suivre de sa signature. Il est prié, en outre, d'accuser réception de ce billet dans le plus bref délai, en écrivant à Naples à M. J. Ricciardi, Député au parlement d'Italie, *Riviera di Chiaja*, No. 57.

"*Pour subvenir aux frais considérables de l'œuvre, un droit d'entrée de* 50c. *sera payé par le porteur du présent billet.*
"*Le lieu et l'heure de la réunion seront indiqués par les journaux.*"

Previous to this meeting, Mr. Peebles was introduced to Count Riccardo, through Signor Damiani, and spent several evenings with him and other distinguished cosmopolitan gentlemen; during one of which the Count, turning to him, and speaking in plain English, said, —

"America and American institutions are not convulsed with the intrigues of Church and State. No, sir! liberty is the American watchword. Freedom, political, social, and religious, constitutes our 'Trinity.' We have letters of sympathy from distinguished men and women in all parts of Europe, from St. Louis, Chicago, Cincinnati, Milwaukie, and other portions of the United States; but as you are the only personal representative, so far as I am aware, we should be happy to have you sit and deliberate with us in our public council."

We clip the following from the Naples and Florence "Observer:" —

"SATURDAY, Dec. 14, 1869.

'MEETING OF THE ANTI-CONCILIO, OR CONGRESS OF FREE-THINKERS, IN NAPLES.

"The first meeting of the 'Anti-concilio,' organized by Count Ricciardi as an opposition and demonstration to the Ecumenical Council now being held in Rome, took place on Thursday in the theater *San Ferdinando*. The stage was occupied by the foreign delegates, the president, his secretaries and supporters, and the representatives of the press; amongst whom we noticed Mr. Daniel, the special reporter of 'The New-York Herald,' U.S.A.; Mr. Peebles, United-States Consul to Trebisond, Asia, and editor of 'The Universe;' M. Carl Ludeking, correspondent of two German-American papers, and other foreign correspondents. . . .

"Then followed reading of telegrams from several cities in Italy, from Vienna, from France, from Trieste, Temesvar in Hungary, from Spain, and from other European cities. That which came from Trieste was received with great warmth, as also were the Hungarian and the Spanish, some passages which censured in bitter terms the French occupation of Rome, producing the most unbounded applause.

"A very spirited speech was then made in Italian by M. Ovary, a Hungarian delegate, in which he alluded to the stupidity of propounding the syllabus in the nineteenth century. He said, 'The papacy is the principal obstacle to liberty, and the scourge of society.'

"Personally he was there intrusted to represent the opinions of twenty-five thousand of his fellow-countrymen; and a friend, also present, was delegate for an equal number. He protested against the iniquities of the papacy, and ended by reading a short address in Hungarian and Italian; which stated that the Magyar race were heart and hand with Count Ricciardi in the work he had undertaken.

"A letter from Gen. Garibaldi was then read. It was written in the usual pungent style of the general, alluding to the priesthood, commencing with '*Rovesciare il mostro papale.*' He said, moreover, that he belonged to the religion of truth, and the true religion of God; expressed his concurrence in the object of the meeting, and regretted his inability to attend. Letters were then read from Henri Martin, Victor Hugo, Edgar Quinet, Michelet, the German professor Moleschott, and other *savans* of Europe.

"Gen. Mata read an address in Spanish, and was saluted at the close by cries of '*Viva il Messico!*' . . .

"The roll-call was preceded by some few speeches, one of which was by Mr. Peebles, editor of "The Universe," Chicago, U.S.A.; another by Mr. Carl Ludeking, of St. Louis; another by an aged German professor; a fourth by a young republican from Belgium; and a fifth by Garibaldi's old chaplain."

In his admirable report of the council, Mr. Peebles writes to "The Universe," —

"At the general opening of the anti-council, the president delivered the address, which was pronounced learned and logical. His gestures were graceful and easy. The Italian language is music itself. Closing, he submitted the following questions to the Congress assembled, as suggestive of discussion: —

"I. Of religious liberty, and the best means for rendering it full and permanent.

"II. Of the complete separation of Church and State.

"III. Of the necessity of a code of morals, independent of religious belief.

"IV. Of the establishment of an international association to promote the principles of freedom, and the general *good*, intellectual and moral.

"The officers chosen and committees appointed, the secretaries read letters of adhesion and approval from Garibaldi, Victor Hugo, and many other distinguished patriots, authors, thinkers, in Europe, Mexico, United States, Brazil, Chili, West Indies, the Grecian Isles, and important cities in Asia and Africa. Between two and three thousand individuals' names were enrolled, a majority of whom, being in attendance, answered for themselves when called by the secretaries. Occasionally, when some celebrated lady arose, and responded 'present,' or offered a few encouraging remarks, the cheering of the multitude would be deafening.

"The vast audience, so orderly, yet so enthusiastic, presented a magnificent spectacle. It has never been our privilege to behold a nobler class of youth than those Italian students in attendance, representing universities and other institutions of education in the kingdom of Italy. The women that so bravely answered to their names were *mothers*, *wives*, *sisters*, that do not fancy the manipulations and liberties that Romish priests often take with their daughters at private confessions. In the United States, Roman Catholicism, gentle, cooing, and cunning, presents upon the surface a very amiable and dove-like appearance; but, under that silken plumage, there skulks the demon of despotism, superstition, and a bloody inquisition, waiting a hoped-for ascendency in America.

"A Polish patriot, who fought with the Italians against the Austrians, was greeted upon taking his seat with prolonged applause. His burning eloquence thrilled every heart present.

"A soldier, whose body bore the scars of many battle-fields, spoke against kings, popes, and priests with the same earnestness that he fought for a united Italy.

"When Garibaldi's old chaplain arose to speak, the clapping of hands and enthusiastic shoutings seemed like the 'voice of many thunders.' He declaimed against Church and State, Popish infallibility, the baseness of a French soldiery in Rome, the advantages taken by priests in 'confessions,' and the despotism of the Catholic Church.

"Mr. Peebles called, he addressed the meeting, the president translating a portion of his remarks, —

"ITALIANS, BROTHERS, — Made, by virtue of an invitation extended by your distinguished president, a member of this Congress of free-thinkers, and requested to participate in your deliberations, I most deeply regret my inability to address you in your native language, — a language so naturally adapted to music, to the sentiments of poetry, and the principles of philosophy. Freedom of conscience underlies the very foundation of the American declaration of independence. Our Constitution, giving the preference to no religious creed, does not even mention the word *God*. Rightly interpreted, it considers man above *all* institutions, — man and his innate rights above cardinals and popes, churches and kingdoms. With the exception of a few clergymen and their willing dupes, the united voice of America is eloquent in behalf of the inalienable rights of man, — the right of each to think, to hear, to believe, and to judge for himself upon all questions, civil, political, and religious; and no priest has any business to say, 'Why believe ye?' or, 'Why do ye thus and so?'

"History warrants the declaration, that, wherever papal influences and Bibles have gone, there have followed in the wake war, persecution, bigotry, and oppression. Sectarian Christianity has deluged the earth in crimson streams for opinion's sake. It kindled the fires of Smithfield. It bolted the dungeon doors of the inquisition upon Savonarola. It rung bells of rejoicing on St. Bartholomew's Eve. It persecuted Tasso, Copernicus, Galileo, and stabbed to the heart other apostles of science and men of letters. It sacrificed two millions of men during the Crusades. Christian steel has drunk Christian blood in all lands. The sword of Pope Pius IX., upheld by the bayonets of a Christian nation, is already edged for further rapine and death. Only two years since, he decapitated young Tognetti for alleged political conspiracy. This youth, fired with the inspiration of freedom, loved Italy, loved *human rights*, more than the temporal power; and, by the Pope's order, he was executed: and his two brothers are in this assembly as mourners to-day. Down on such Christianity as this! Down with your red-handed popes, and up with science! Down with priests, and up with the people! Down with bigotry, and up with toleration! Down with churchal authority everywhere, and up with individual freedom! Italians, send American, *all* missionaries, back to their native lands with their *Bibles* and rot-eaten *tracts*, and invite them to return with patent washing-machines, school-houses, and libraries, with the ax, the spade, and the plow, and, when returning, use them with ungloved hands. Practical industry cools missionary zeal. Shame on these American bishops who go from a country of freemen to papal Rome, to vote the Pope infallible. Such assumption is the quintessence of impudence on their part, weakness and dotage on his.

"The central idea, the prime thought, of cultured Americans, is free speech, free press, and free religion. The generous hearts of at least twenty million trans-Atlantic citizens beat in full sympathy with yours to-day. As an individual, I tender you the affections of a warm heart, the clasp of an open hand, and the fellowship of a soul that has sworn eternal hate to priestcraft and oppression.

"President, I am a mystery to myself. When I 'would do good,' like an apostle, 'evil is present with me.' When I would subdue by love, then, looking down upon an assemblage like this, and listening to the recital of wrongs, of chains, of prisons, and of papal murders, my tongue, my lips, break out, *On with the battle! On* with *fire* and *sword* and the black-throated *artillery* of death! The *people* are the Christ of this century; Rome is the cross; popes, cardinals, and priests are the crucifiers. Down, then, peacefully if possible, but down, with *despots* and *tyrants!* Then the cordial brain-region — the divine nature gaining the ascendency, my soul speaks — speaks in tones equally firm, but more humane and angelic, *On* as the highest wisdom may dictate! *On* with the artillery of tongue and pen! on! remembering that love — the divine principle of love — alone subdues!

"Reason is God's seal of true manhood. Though there are socialists and secularists, rationalists and materialists, the Spiritualists, numbering several millions, form the central column in the progressive religious movement of America. Scientists and radical Unitarians constitute the right and left wings of this army.

"Not empowered to speak authoritatively, I feel that I do the free-thinkers of my native country no injustice in the declaration, that negatively they deny the fall of man,' 'the trinity,' 'total depravity,' 'vicarious atonement,' 'endless punishment,' 'a general judgment;' 'the plenary inspiration of the Bible,' and the personality of either a human-shaped God or devil.

"Affirmatively, this aggressive body believes in the divine existence, the intelligent life-principle of the universe; in the innate moral worth and progressive tendency of humanity; in the certainty of a compensation, ever acting in consonance with the fixed laws of nature; in political, social, mental, and religious freedom; in a true life, founded upon the highest intuitions of the soul and the moral consciousness of the race. Because more intimately connected with it, I feel a more perfect freedom in speaking of Spiritualism as a great motive power in America.

"Under some name, and in some form, Spiritualism, as demonstrated through phenomena, and substantiated by unimpeachable testimony, has constituted the basic foundation and been the motive force of all religions in their incipient stages. The Spiritualism of to-day, in America, England, and all enlightened countries, differs from that of eighteen hundred years since, in Judea, only in the better understanding of its philosophy, the general conception of its naturalness, and its wider dissemination through the different grades of society. It has been and is God's visible seal of love to all climes and ages.

"As a general definition of Spiritualism, the following is submitted: —

"Its fundamental idea is God, the infinite spirit-presence, imminent in all things.

"Its fundamental thought is joyous communion with spirits and angels, and the practical demonstrations of the same through the instrumentality of media.

"Its fundamental purpose is to rightly generate, educate, and spiritualize all the races and nations of the earth.

"Spiritualism, considered from its philosophical side, is rationalism; from its scientific side, naturalism; and, from its religious side, the embodiment of love to God and man, — a present inspiration and a heavenly ministry. In the year 1900, it will be the religion of the enlightened world.

"It underlies all genuine reform movements, physiological, educational, social, philanthropic, and religious; and, spanning all human interests with holy aim, it seeks to reconstruct society upon the principles of a universal brotherhood and the strict equality of the sexes.

"Desirous of greater knowledge touching the relations of spirit with matter, and of men with God, and the intelligences of the surrounding world of spirits, Spiritualists study and reverently interrogate the laws and principles that govern the phenomena and occult forces of the universe, the histories of the past, and the experiences of the present, anxious to solve those psychologic and spiritual problems of the ages, — man's origin, capacity, duty, and final destiny.

"Interrelated with spirit and matter in their varied evolutions, and with the highest interests connecting all worlds, Spiritualism is neither supernatural in philosophy nor sectarian in tendency; but broad, catholic, and progressive, — the voiced truth of God through nature to the rational soul, — a science, a philosophy, and a religion.

"Contemplated from the mount of vision, it may be compared to a temple whose outer foundations are upon earth and whose golden dome is in heaven. Its facts, its workmanship, are embellished by the fingers of angels; and its principles are upheld by the hand of God.

"Thanking you for your patience in listening to a stranger in a language that few of you understand, I close with this sentiment: —

"May Italians speedily possess all Italian territory! May proud, historic Rome be its capital! May capital and country constitute one united republic! and may that republic be sustained by the enlightened influences of education, justice, universal suffrage, the equality of the sexes, and the beautiful peace-principles of love and wisdom."

On a rich silken banner or standard, behind the platform, were inscribed the names of the countries represented by delegates, or letters of approval. The motto upon the banner was decidedly significant: —

"THE NATIONS OF THE CIVILIZED WORLD MADE BROTHERS BY FREE THOUGHT."

The word *Rome*, though in gilded letters, was veiled in black crape.

"Near the close of the second evening's session," writes Mr. Peebles, "while a talented French delegate was speaking eloquently of Republican institutions and *free religion*, declaring that Rome was kept from the Italians against the will of Frenchmen, hundreds of voices joined in the cry, '*Long live Republics, liberty of conscience, free religion!*'

"When up rose an officer, scarfed and ribboned, and said, '*In the name of the laws I pronounce this meeting dissolved!*'

"Murmurs half-suppressed, agitations, intense feeling of indignation, as though a fearful mental storm was ready to burst, and President Ricciardo rising said, 'I beg of you to disperse quietly, — quietly, and in good order.'

"It seemed like a dream. An immense assembly in attendance, — a French orator in the midst of a thrilling speech, an enthusiastic people cheering and rejoicing, the meeting dissolved, the lights extinguished, a horde of policemen prowling about, the people crowding into the streets.

"Shame on such despotism! My whole being was on fire. O beautiful, sun-kissed Italy! O wretched, bleeding, pope-cursed Italy! I mingle my tears with yours, with Perasees and the angels, asking how long, oh! how long, before your day of deliverance?"

At this council, Mr. Peebles was awarded with a significant and splendid medal for his speech, and the interest he manifested in its grand objects, and was afterwards elected an honorary member of the *Societa Florantina de Spiritismo*, presenting him a diploma written in Italian, and dated Feb. 28, 1870.

CHAPTER XXXI.

WORK IN THE BRITISH ISLES.

> "'Tis the voice
> Of infant Freedom! and her stirring call
> Is heard and answered in a thousand tones
> From every hill-top of her Western home!" — GEO. D. PRENTICE.

> "Character is what God and angels know of us." — THOMAS PAINE.

LEAVING the Neapolitan cities of Italy, Mr. Peebles returned to London in January, 1870; and, obeying the promptings of his spirit-friends and the invitations of English Spiritualists, with J. Burns proceeded immediately to the organization of Sunday meetings at the Cavendish Rooms, Mortimer Street, Regent Street. His first lecture was delivered on the third Sunday in January, to a comparatively small audience. He continued his Sunday labors four months in London, and week evenings in the provincial cities, the interest constantly augmenting into fine assemblies, composed of the best English minds. He instituted order by religious services interspersed with music, allowing inquirers at first to question him at the close of his speaking. The evening meetings were the more inspirational; and frequently plenty of rappings were heard near seats occupied by media, but not loud enough to interfere with the proceedings.

Occasionally absent in other cities, his desk was supplied by J. Burns, E. D. Rogers, F. R. Young, H. D. Jencken, A. C. Swinton, T. Shorter, and others, with excellent success. The general drift of his thought, and the good accomplished in that brief time, will be found in these summary extracts from the British Spiritual press. The following are from that able journal, "The Spiritualist," edited by W. H. Harrison: —

"Mr. Peebles, according to a system he has long carried out in the United States, preceded his lecture with a short religious service; and he began by giving out a hymn, which was sung by the large number of Spiritualists and others present. He then offered up a short prayer to the Almighty, giving thanks to him for the blessing of direct communication with departed friends, and for having planted within every human being the seeds of endless growth and eternal progression.

"Mr. Peebles then said, that, in one of the epistles of Paul, there is language something like this, 'Be ready to give to every man a reason for the hope that lieth in thee.' Reason, he said, is a divine gift, — one of the greatest characteristics of true manhood; and, as God has been pleased to make us reasonable beings, we ought to exercise these reasoning powers to the best advantage. We should sanction no theology, no moral teaching, and no deduction of science, till we have brought the subject to the test of reason. Wherever there is an effect, there must have been a cause; wherever there is motion, there must have been something to produce it; and, wherever there is a house, there must have been a builder: so, where we see millions upon millions of bright and glorious worlds circling in their orbits, there must be some intelligence guiding them by immutable laws. . . .

"Mr. J. M. Peebles, American Consul at Trebisond, lectured at the Cavendish rooms on Sunday evening, Feb. 27. He commenced, The inspired Psalmist once said, 'Oh, worship the Lord in the beauty of holiness!' It is not more in harmony with nature for water to seek its level, or the mystic needle to point to the North Pole, than for man to worship. Wherever man has been, he has left marks of his worship of God. The power to ask the question, 'What is God?' implies to some extent the power to answer it; and God is infinite life and truth and gladness and intelligence and love. God has implanted in man a belief in a superintending existence, guiding all worlds. We do not comprehend him: we can not even fathom ourselves. We can only grasp and digest what is inferior to ourselves. He supposed that God is not a personal being with a definite shape, but that God is in the universe, and just as much present to-day as in the days of the patriarchs. Directly you personalize God, you localize him: whatever you localize you limitize; and whatever you limitize is imperfect, and may be destroyed. He could only say with Jesus, 'God is a spirit.' He thought that man physical is the ultimate of the rest of the earthly creation, and that all the lower forms of life and matter are focalized in him, from the oyster to the monkey upwards. He did not mean that man is made of the primates, but of the spiritual ultimates of the primates. There is reason to suppose that there is a portion of the Spirit of God in every human being, and that this divine portion never becomes impure: it is only when this innermost purity tries to externalize itself through the spirit body and the material body, both of them containing and being surrounded with inharmonious conditions, that troubles and sorrow and suffering afflict the progressing mortal.

"The lecturer next stated, that the condition of man is one of endless progression. If they asked, 'Is God a progressive being?' he would answer at once in the negative. But if God does not progress, and man does, will not man in the end reach him, and be lost in him? No; for the progression of man is finite, and no number of finite movements will reach the infinite. It is a fact capable of mathematical demonstration, that two lines may continually approach, yet never meet; also in the attempt to divide the number ten by three, on the decimal principle, one may keep on carrying figures until the whole universe is filled with them, yet never get to the end. No aggregation of finites can make up infinity. A man should never bow down in sackcloth and ashes before his Creator, but stand up in the glory of his manhood, as a being destined for eternal progression in the spheres. Spiritualism does not teach that God is a tyrant and angry with man. . . .

"Spiritualism does not say, 'Believe my creed,' but 'Feed my sheep;' does not say,

'Worship in my church,' but, 'Worship as your own conscience dictates;' does not insist so much upon the saying, as the doing of prayers, that the heart's best affections may be baptized into a love holy and heavenly: in fine, Spiritualism is that 'other angel,' that the revelator John saw 'flying in the midst of heaven,' and preaching the everlasting gospel of immortality, — the gospel of 'peace and good-will to men.'

"He loved the living gospel of Spiritualism, because it shows so much of the kindness and love of God. Pain is only an angel, leading us back to nature and truth: sickness purifies the physical organization; and disappointments strengthen individuality of character. Even Jesus, it is said, was purified by suffering; and there is no eternal endless evil in the universe. He was so organized that he could not love a hateful object. Human love is a thing which comes out like the flowers, to drink in the dew-drops, and to rejoice in the sunlight of heaven. Human love is a great reforming power; and its binding influence was never more plainly shown than when William Penn made his treaty with the Indians, by the rolling river, under the old elm-tree's shade."

"The Medium," a chaste, pungent sheet, edited by J. Burns, reports the evening service, —

"Mr. Peebles's discourse at the Sunday-evening services in the Cavendish rooms, on the 27th ult., was one of the most powerful, in some respects, that we have ever listened to. The subject was 'Heaven and hell: what are they? where are they?' which was characterized by cogent reasoning and great moral power. A curious fact should not be overlooked in estimating the cause of the singular influence which this address had on the hearers. Several seeing mediums who were in the meeting gave corroborative descriptions of spirit-forms which were seen behind the speaker. A venerable-looking sage, with very long hair and beard, stood on a mound apart from the speaker, the space between whom and this spirit was filled with a white ethereal substance. A female spirit stood to the right, and a male spirit to the left of Mr. Peebles, while an Indian stood right behind him. Streams of light proceeded from the grave-visaged sage to the attendant spirits; and, when the ideas were bright and forcible, the color of these streams was golden; but when of an ordinary kind, they were silvery in appearance. The attendant spirits took hold of the streams of light proceeding from the sage, and placed them on the head of the speaker, sometimes in the region of ideality, and sometimes that of veneration and benevolence. The Indian spirit made very long passes with his hands all over Mr. Peebles's body, from the head downwards, as if to give him force. These are very interesting facts, and require no comment."

At this meeting he electrified his audience by relating some of his experiences with the Indians during his tour with the "Peace Commission," —

"Some one thousand Indians met in council, drawn up in half-moons, near the confluence of the Rivers North and South Platte: the discussion then began; and old grievances were brought up. Gen. Sherman, a kind-hearted man, but shrewd withal, put some questions about one point, in which the Indians had broken a former treaty; and these questions rather puzzled the chief speaker on the other side, who was known to the whites as 'Old Spotted-tail.' Being puzzled, he refused to give an immediate answer, and summoned to his side a young Indian, who directly afterwards ran away; and, for nearly one hour and a half from that time, not a single word would the old Indian chief, or any subordinate chief, lisp: but, when the young man came back,

Spotted-tail made a most eloquent speech. He (Mr. Peebles) afterwards ascertained, that, nine days before the council met, a celebrated medicine-man among the Indians had begun to prepare himself to hold converse with the Great Spirit, and to give advice to the tribes. By being calm, meditative, and taking little food, he became passive and negative enough to enter the clairvoyant state; and thus the advice was given. There was not a single Indian youth to be seen in all that council; and, on inquiry, he was told, that, three days before it began, orders had been issued that all young Indians should absent themselves from the camp, because the chiefs did not wish them to become contaminated by the vices of the Christian whites."

Finding Spiritualism in the British Isles nearly as rudimental as in America a number of years ago, Mr. Peebles was thrown back to first principles, and, being well versed in them from large experience, was able to cope with any difficulties. As a general rule, the spiritual manifestations excelled those he had formerly witnessed in his disciplinary years. Among others he mentions those of "seeing spirits in crystals;" upon which Prof. Kenneth R. H. Mackenzie, discoursed, at the rooms of J. Burns. Mr. Peebles wrote home, —

"Magic rock-crystals are exceedingly expensive. The late Earl of Stanhope, who nearly completed the great reflecting telescope, six feet in diameter, and longer in focus than Lord John Rosse's giant instrument, gave much time to crystal seeing. A crystal mirror, or crystal spheroid, is placed before the eyes of the sensitive or medium, who first sees a dense cloud form in the mirror, followed by total blackness: afterwards come flashes of electric fire or light; and then come psychologic visions of distant places, persons, and spirits. The crystal, giving the condition of passivity, affords at times wonderful tests. It is a species of clairvoyance."

On the evening of April 11, a *séance* was held at the house of Mr. Everitt, 26 Penton Street, London, attended by Mr. Peebles, Mr. Maurice, Mr. and Mrs. Taylor, Mr. Mylne (from India), Mr. Scott, &c., and mediums, Mrs. Everitt, Mrs. Burns, and Mr. Shepard, when the spirit "John Watt" spoke in audible voice. The spirits scattered perfumes through the room. The seers saw a female spirit standing by Mr. Peebles; and he himself heard her gentle voice. She was recognized as the spirit "Josephine." The spirits wrote on paper and walls without human hands; and, in several instances, they carefully lithographed messages. They shook the house, partially shattering it, till it required repairing.

On other occasions the spirits spoke through tubes, played on instruments, and scattered again the delicious odor of spirit-flowers. "Mr. Peebles was suffering from pain in one of the lungs; and three Indian spirits were seen to approach him. Mrs. Burns and Mr. Shepard distinctly saw a spirit drawing out a dark, diseased substance from

Mr. Peebles's breast; after which, another spirit flooded him with a white substance, which soothed the pain, and re-invigorated him."

At a meeting of Mrs. C. Berry's circle, on Wednesday evening, Jan. 19, Mrs. Perrin and Mr. Child, media, together with other ladies and gentlemen, including Dr. Ashburner and N. F. Daw, Mr. Peebles had an interview with John King, by audible conversation. This spirit identified himself as the King who struck him those heavy blows at the *séance*, in Cleveland, Ohio, of the Davenport boys, in 1856. The spirit also re-called the interesting incidents of that occasion; when Mr. Peebles remarked to the astonished circle, "To John King I owe my final conversion to Spiritualism."

Thomas Reeves, reporting Mr. Peebles's and Dr. Newton's successes, in "The American Spiritualist," — flowers from the seeds these gentlemen sowed, — among others mentions the names of John Blackburn and J. Morse, as mediums, and the spiritual demonstrations following the agitation of Mr. Peebles's lectures: —

. . . "It is certain that the impetus given by this gentleman's visit has imparted an activity to Spiritualism that was not previously possible.

. . . "The spirit-voice is heard at quite a number of circles; and, at Mrs. Everitt's, the curious manifestation of lights has been seen by all sitters, including those who are in no degree clairvoyant. A few evenings since, balls of fire were observed much larger than heretofore; and those in whom the spirit-sight was somewhat developed were able to see the spirit form emerge from the lights, and enlarge itself to the size of a human being. Mrs. Berry's circle is also sitting weekly; and Mr. Robson, at Mr. Weeks's, has obtained some very curious communications from spirits of olden times, including poets, writers, politicians, artists, musicians, and the whole array of developed intellect, as well as from soldiers from the battle-fields of the Continent.

"But Spiritualism is rapidly going beyond the mere phenomenal or matter-of-fact phase. The Children's Lyceum is budding, and bearing fruit. A lyceum instituted during the past summer in the new lyceum building at Keighley, Yorkshire, is being pushed on with great vigor; and the leaders and children are anxiously awaiting the arrival of the new 'Lyceum Guide,' which is being imported from Boston. This movement is being imitated in other places; and, indeed, before the season is over, these schools will be materially increased.

"The labors of the Hon. J. M. Peebles have borne fruit; which will show itself more and more as time goes on."

At Bradford, after an electric lecture, a lawyer popped up, and said, "The able gentleman has told us about spiritual things: now we would like a test. Show us the *ghost*, and we will believe;" and sat down, amid a sensation. Mr. Peebles, seldom at a loss for a reply, rose and replied, "The gentleman believes in God: will he show us God? He believes in Jesus Christ: will he show us Jesus

Christ?" The audience was in a perfect foam of enthusiasm at this happy hit. "I am a lecturer on Spiritual Philosophy," he added: "my mission is to instruct by the gift of knowledge, not to show a *ghost*."

Walking the street the next morning, his ears were greeted with jeers and taunts; one man vociferating, "There goes the long-haired devil-rapper!"

An English clergyman, special reporter for "The London Daily Telegraph," a paper in the interests of the crown, gives quite an elaborate review of Spiritualism, represented by "three remarkable spiritual mediums, — Dr. Newton, Jesse B. H. Shepard, and Rev. J. M. Peebles." After summing up the doctor's beneficent mission, and Mr. Shepard's musical *séances*, all in a most sarcastic style, he dispatches our "Pilgrim" thus: —

"The Rev. Jabez Burns, D.D., a Baptist minister of Paddington, considerably surprised us all by mounting the platform, and indorsing the claims of Dr. Newton and the teaching of Mr. Peebles. So very complimentary was he to Dr. Newton, that the doctor could not bottle up his beneficence, but begged pardon for interrupting the speaker, and greeting him with a brotherly kiss! Mr. Peebles spoke little; but what he said was a *multum in parvo*. As the mission of Dr. Newton is fatal to pharmacopœias, so is Mr. Peebles destined to demolish doctrines, creeds, and churches, at one fell swoop.

. . . "Mr. Peebles, at the Cavendish Rooms, succeeding to the mantle of Mrs. Emma Hardinge, discourses of Spiritualism to the accompaniment of approving raps, presumably from Hades."

"Human Nature," a scholarly monthly journal, edited and published by J. Burns, says, among other important reports of spiritual movements, —

"The work is extending itself into the provinces. Mr. Peebles has visited Norwich, and addressed earnest, intelligent, and influential meetings. He is invited to Halifax; and other places are making arrangements. Where there are two or three Spiritualists in a place, they need be under no misapprehensions in making arrangements for Mr. Peebles. The first two meetings should be called by special invitation, and be held in some gentleman's drawing-room or parlor. Another Spiritualist might invite his circle of friends to his house on the following evening; after which, a modest public meeting might be ventured on, to be followed by a second, which might be considered enough for a beginning. From such safe and agreeable proceedings, useful organizations would certainly spring up, and great good be effected. Mr. Peebles is just the man for this important work, — a work which is sternly demanded in England, and which every earnest reformer sighs for."

"The Norfolk News" reports his lecture in St. Andrews Hall, Norwich, on Thursday evening, Feb. 15, as a news-item. At the close, some one rose and asked, "What is the use of Spiritualism?" Mr. Peebles replied, —

"That is a Yankee question. [Laughter.] We should not say, 'What is the use of it?' but, 'Is it true?' The use of it is to show that there is a future life, and to corroborate the Bible histories. The use of it is to roll up the curtain, and show to us those we love. It teaches us that there is no death. The lecturer, in conclusion, made some telling observations in relation to the restraining influence that would be exercised over the viciously inclined by the thought that there are present with them, watching them in all their doings, the pure spirits of those who love them."

Noticing some portly gentlemen, who, it might be inferred, were accustomed to wine, evidently desirous of having the spiritual gifts, he related an incident of California experience; when a person of animal habits interrogated him,—

"'Can I become a medium?' I replied that it was needful, in the first place, that he should cleanse his body; secondly, avoid liquors; thirdly, take no tobacco into his mouth; next, avoid swine's flesh, and all coarse and gross language; and then three evenings a week go into his closet, and sit down in prayer, passive and calm, for one hour: and, before six months had rolled away, he would see the loved ones, or hear their voices, or have some other demonstration of their presence. The man went away sorrowful; for he could not endure to do all these things."

Reporting the efforts at Halifax, Yorkshire, the editor of "Human Nature" says, —

"On Monday morning, March 14, we left Mr. Peebles at the Great Northern Railway, *en route* for Halifax, where he has had a most successful course of lectures. The friends of Spiritualism in that town are thoroughly active and in earnest, as all Yorkshire men are when they take up a good thing. They accordingly hired the finest public hall in the town — the Mechanics' Hall — for Mr. Peebles's lectures, charged 1s., 6d., and 3d. for admission, Sunday, 2d. The meetings were small to begin with, and it is an immensely large hall; but the interest increased: and much excitement was created by the free discussion and questions answered by the lecturer each night. It is reported that five clergymen were present on one evening, and three on another, one of whom had the good breeding and 'Christian' charity to call the lecturer an 'infidel' to his face. The consequence of all this is, that the committee have cleared their expenses with something over; and everybody is extremely pleased except the 'devil and the Orthodox.'

"Spiritualism has attained a position in Yorkshire which is not dreamed of by the people of the South. The Sunday meetings at Halifax are held in a nice snug hall, capable of seating three hundred, has a fine organ, and some one that can play on it. Similar good news hail from Keighley. Mr. Weatherhead is building a handsome hall at his own expense; and this ancient headquarters of progress seems determined to maintain its supremacy.

"We rejoice in the success that attends the labors of our friend Mr. Peebles: no man can more fully deserve it. We require such a speaker and mediator between truth and the people amongst us at all times. Those who desire a visit from him should make arrangements without delay."

When that minister at Halifax called Mr. Peebles an "infidel," he rose calmly and said, —

"You call me an 'infidel.' Sir, do *you* believe in Jesus Christ?"

"Yes," answered most emphatically.

"Do you believe in the gifts of the Holy Spirit, promised to believers?"

"I do most assuredly," replied the minister very coolly.

"Very well: I test you by Christ's own words, 'These signs shall follow them that believe, They shall cast out devils; lay hands on the sick, and they shall recover; make the blind see, the deaf hear, the lame walk,' &c. Do these signs follow *you*, sir?"

"*Ahem*, — well, — no!"

"Very well; then you are not a believer: you are an *infidel!*"

At this crisis, another clergyman, seeing the predicament of his brother, volunteered his services, saying, "I wish to ask the speaker one question. You took your text from the New Testament. Are *you* a believer in Jesus Christ?"

"Most assuredly, my brother," replied Mr. Peebles.

"Do any of these spiritual gifts follow you, Mr. Speaker?"

"Certainly: and, among others, I have 'the gift of knowledge,' and have come to teach *you*," answered Mr. Peebles, as the audience surged in laughter, and cheer on cheer echoed through the extensive hall.

A writer in the "Unitarian Herald," London, thus speaks of Mr. Peebles and his Halifax lecture: —

"Mr. Peebles is a tall man, with a high forehead, large features, and a long grayish beard; which, joined to his strange dress, give him a look that is not of this world. The shape of his head and face reminded me much of Mr. Baxter Langley, in spite of the difference of manner and complexion.

. . . .

"I heard Mr. Peebles's lecture at Halifax during one of his provincial sojourns; and he left on my mind a strong conviction of his sincerity and originality. I believe that I saw before me a man who had studied human life and religious ideas in strange and unwonted aspects; had dared to read God and nature with his own eyes, and to tell the world what he had seen there. I had met men before who had the courage to think the truth, and one or two (possessed of large private fortunes and very submissive wives) who even dared to speak it; but I have never seen a man who would give up his life to the work of spreading an unpopular religion over two continents. I listen respectfully when Strauss, Renan, Hase, Neander, Prof. Seeley and Mr. Liddon tell me all that they have found out of manuscripts and lexicons as to what the life of Christ *must have been;* but I shall drink in every word that Mr. Peebles, resting from his apostolate, will tell me as to what the life of Christ *is*, and perchance find in 'Jesus, Myth, Man, or God,' a living solution of the greatest of life-problems.

. . . .

"He expatiated on the diversity of religions that he had seen in his Eastern wanderings, and the multiplicity of sects amongst Christians. He sketched several of the sects sarcastically, not sparing even the poor Unitarians; and finally, 'There is the English bishop, a nice man, with very white hands, and a very fine house, and a fine park, and a very fine fortune. He drives every Sunday in a very fine carriage to the church, where he will ascend a very fine pulpit, and preach with eloquence and vigor from the text, "It is easier for a camel to go through the eye of a needle than for a rich man to enter into the kingdom of God.'"

"He said to us, 'You call yourselves Christians, and profess to believe in Christ and the literal truth of all his sayings. If there is a Christian within the sound of my voice who has sold all that he had, and given it to the poor, let him get up and shake hands with me. He paused; but all was quiet. He added, shaking his head, 'I am sorry to find that you are all unbelievers.'

"He read several curious passages from old sermons, to illustrate the belief in eternal punishment. One described the satisfaction of the saints at the sight of the tortures of the damned in hell, and said somewhat as follows, 'The redeemed husband shall see the damnation of the wife that lay in his bosom, and shall shout *Hallelujah!* and the child shall cry *Amen* to the tortures of the mother who bore it!' And he read the once popular American hymn, concluding, —

'And hell is crammed
With infants damned
Without a day of grace.'

"The most interesting part of the evening was the discussion which followed the lecture. Several warm opponents attacked Mr. Peebles; and the dexterity with which he answered, or at times evaded, their arguments, was a curious contrast to the earnestness of his earlier manner. The vociferous enthusiasm with which several female auditors received all his sayings, even the most destructive, was highly amusing, and somewhat significant.

"One man got up and said, 'How can you say that Christ never taught the doctrine of an eternal hell, when you know the text, "Where their worm dieth not, and their fire is not quenched"?' At this the gallery — the gallery was acidly Orthodox — felt that a poser had been launched, and applauded vigorously. Mr. Peebles looked up at them and said, 'The gentleman has quoted a text which he thinks, and you think, says that most men will suffer horribly to all eternity; and, as soon as you hear it, you applaud with great joy. *I am sorry you find any cause for delight in such a prospect.*'

"One opponent demanded if Mr. Peebles believed in the Bible, and expressed great horror when the latter answered, that he believed such parts of it as his reason and conscience approved. Peebles then said, 'Does my questioner himself believe in any more? I will ask him if he believes the passage I am going to read.' He then turned to the chapter in Numbers, and read the precept, to slay the Midianites with their wives and children, and to reserve the young women for the benefit of the Israelites. The passage took us all by surprise; and there was an audible and very general cry of horror from the audience as he read it. 'Does my questioner really believe that God ever ordered such a thing as that?' The man got up very much puzzled, and very cross at the turn things had taken! 'It is disgraceful to quote such a passage as that. No infidel could use a baser quotation.' Here a woman's voice, audible throughout the room, softly said, 'But *isn't* it the Bible?' and a universal laugh followed. However, the Orthodox champion went on: 'I do believe that passage; I do believe that God gave that order. And I believe that the Judge of all the earth must do right, although Mr. Peebles may not understand the manner of his working. This is just the sort of text that infidels quote; and Mr. Peebles is simply an infidel in disguise.' When all was quiet, the lecturer said, 'The gentleman has just called me an infidel. I fancy the children of Israel said that Moses was an infidel, when he suggested that they should leave Egypt. Certainly the good, temple-loving, synagogue-going, hypocritical old Pharisees said Jesus was an infidel. And so the priests and monks said about Martin Luther; and so the Church said about John Wesley: they were all infidels. I am much obliged to my friend *for putting me into such good company.*'"

On Monday, March 21, James Lingford and others invited Mr. Peebles to lecture in Leeds, a city of about two hundred and twenty thousand inhabitants, out of which about a dozen only could be gleaned willing to hear the truth. But the good seed was sown in some honest hearts, to be gathered when we are old. He also lectured in Corporation Row, Clerkenwell, with great power of conviction. R. Pearce, Secretary of the Association, sent him a handsome letter of thanks for his "able services."

Continually questioned about the "indignity of the manifestations," Mr. Peebles furnished his enemies with the following "biblical pill" in "The Medium:"—

"It is often said by the opponents of Spiritualism, that the moving of furniture, the producing of rappings, and all physical manifestations, are utterly unworthy work for immortal intelligences. Will such consult the following passages of 'Sacred Scripture?'

'At the same time spake the Lord by Isaiah, saying, Go and loose the sackcloth from off thy loins, and put off thy shoe from thy foot; and he did so, walking naked and barefoot.'—*Isa.* xx. 2.

'And the Lord came down to see the city and the tower, which the children of men builded.'—*Gen.* xi. 5.

'And it came to pass that in the morning-watch, the Lord. . . . took off their (the Egyptians), chariot-wheels that they drave them heavily.' . . .—*Exod.* xiv. 24, 25.

'And Gideon said unto God, If thou wilt save Israel by mine hand, behold, I will put a fleece of wool in the floor; and if the dew be on the fleece only, and it be dry upon all the earth besides, then shall I know that thou wilt save Israel by mine hand.

'And it was so; for he rose up early on the morrow, and thrust the fleece together, and wringed the dew out of the fleece, a bowlful of water.'—*Judges* vi. 31, 37, 38.

"Now, then, if the Lord, according to the Scriptures, commanded Isaiah to go barefoot and 'naked,' came down to examine a 'tower' that men had built, took off the Egyptians' 'chariot-wheels,' and wet Gideon's 'sheep-fleece,' it certainly should not be considered either undignified or unworthy of exalted spirits—our immortal brothers—to lift furniture, and 'rap out' communications in demonstration of immortality. Any thing that can subserve divine use, or tend to the amelioration and spiritual enlightenment of humanity, is by no means unworthy of an angel from heaven."

At London, Mr. Peebles received a lengthy and terse criticism on his "Seers of the Ages," by E. S. Wheeler, of "The American Spiritualist," who claimed that Jesus is nothing but a made-up character; also a criticism, equally pointed, by William Howitt, who, admiring the work, regarded one feature of it as Christianly unsound, in that it teaches the Unitarian doctrine of the *humanity* of Jesus. Christian Spiritualists in and about London also criticised him severely, because of his "anti-Christian teachings." Some one sent him the following letter: —

"BISHOPSGATE STREET, March 15, 1870.

"MY DEAR SIR, — It is not from a desire to wound your feelings, but to serve the truth, that I write to you upon this occasion.

"Spiritualism, to become successful in the kingdom, must be managed by men of cultured minds, and with a becoming Christian prudence. We neither want the re-incarnation theory of French Spiritualism nor the infidel Spiritualism of America preached in our midst.

"I have heard five lectures from you during the past few months; and in not one of them did you mention Christ, — Christ as the only name given under heaven whereby we must be saved.

"Any teachings of Spiritualism not in strict harmony with Christian doctrines and influences, though taught in fluent American style, and by a United-States consul, will not be received by our English people. This was Mrs. Hardinge's fatal mistake: with her lecture against the Trinity, comparing the Triune Godhead to the Rule of Three, and her remarks upon Christ's sacrifice for sin, went her influence for good. Also there are very serious objections to reserving seats, giving shilling *séances*, and paying salaried speakers, even though imported from America, which erroneously claims to have originated Spiritualism! Paying mediums leans to deception, and the practice of trickery for gain.

"I can not give my adhesion to the most pretending of the spiritual arrangements, as they are now being manipulated in London. I do not question your sincerity nor ability to teach; but your doctrines are not acceptable to the Christian portion of true believers.

Respectfully yours,

"AN ENGLISH SPIRITUALIST."

Under these criticisms, Mr. Peebles proceeded immediately to write a book, entitled "Jesus, Myth, Man, or God," published by J. Burns. He gave it his best thought; enriched it with historic research, furnishing proof of the personal existence of the man Jesus outside of the Christian Fathers or the Gospels; reviewed Trinitarianism without quarter, and exposed the corruptions of the Christian Church, from the time of Constantine to the present. He subpœnaed the priesthood, and charged them with atrocities and vices from which there is no escape. The book is interspersed with sharp hits like this: —

"Warned, therefore, by the blood-crimsoned banners that have floated and still float over Christian lands, in the name of the imprisoned and beggared, the burned and persecuted for Christ's sake, in the name of the skinless skeletons of fifty millions of slaughtered victims, slaughtered and piled on the bony back of *churchal Christianity*, I protest, as one among sympathizing millions, against having '*Christian*' dragged in and imposed upon Spiritualism!

"Sectarian Christianity is becoming more and more a moral stench in the nostrils of all great and noble souls. Scientists in every enlightened country spit upon its creed-stuffed and priest-patched carcass. Profound thinkers make merry over its shattered, withered, and *soul-less* body!

Thus using the two-edged sword against anointed falsehood and evil, the author, defensive for purity, crediting a man for what he is morally worth, says, "Jesus' sympathetic character was certainly sweeter than that of the masses of men. His aspirations were exalted: angels breathed directly upon him. No continued moral perversions impaired the delicate perceptions of his nature, chilled the fountain of his feelings, nor the currental flow of his soul's affections. Married by the inexorable law of affinity to humanity, he could not be chained while on his missioned work to another individuality. Quick to feel the sorrows of others, the sensitive tendrils of his loving heart, constantly attuned and tremulously responsive, vibrated to every child of human suffering. He identified himself with sorrow and disgrace, with humanity in its lowest estate, that he might the more successfully exert the healing, saving love-power of his soul in the redemption of the erring."

Being evidently somewhat disturbed at the wrangling over the term *Christian*, as a proper prefix to Spiritualism, and wishing to strip the word from all unnecessary adjectives, he said in one of his London lectures, in words that seemed to pulse in the hearts of his hearers, —

"But differ as we may in our theories, when pushed into the mythic realm of speculative theology, our facts are one. On this common ground, then, this broad platform of tolerance and good-will, let us stand a banded brotherhood of true souls, — stand like polished shafts of light and truth in the temple of the eternal.

"As a Spiritualist, striving to conserve the good found in all religions, past and present, seeking constantly to lead a holier life, looking trustingly for higher unfoldings of truth and fresher developments in the fields of science, I extend the fraternal hand of fellowship to each and all; and in this hand buds and blossoms the olive-branch of peace. 'By this,' said Jesus, 'shall all men know that ye are my disciples, if ye have love one for another.' What matters nationality, clime, or dogma to God, who beneficently 'sendeth rain upon the just and the unjust?' What cared the Good Shepherd of Judea about the color or names of the sheep constituting the flock? 'Other sheep I have,' said he, 'which are *not* of this fold: them also I must bring; and there shall be one fold and one Shepherd.' What will it be to angels when the curtain of immortality is uplifted, and you stand in the presence of those glorified hosts? The question will not be asked, Were you a Christian Spiritualist, a radical Spiritualist, or a re-incarnation Spiritualist; but did you live up to the light you had received as soul-convictions? Were the heart's affections right, and the life-purposes pure? Did you feed the hungry, clothe the naked, provide for the orphan, sympathize with the sorrowing; or, scripturally expressed, did you 'go about doing good'?"

During his stay in London, Mr. Peebles received the following note from Mr. Sen, the distinguished Hindoo temperance advocate, scholar and divine: —

"4 WOBURN SQUARE, W.C., 20th April, 1870.

"MY DEAR SIR,—I shall be happy to see you here on Tuesday next, at any time between two and five, P.M. I remain, my dear sir, yours truly,

"KESHUB CHUNDER SEN.

"J. M. PEEBLES, Esq."

"The Medium" reports the interview that succeeded this cordial invitation:—

"Our readers will have heard of the arrival and cordial reception in London of this gentleman, who is a native of the East Indies, and an enthusiastic religious reformer. His object is to establish the primitive religion of a belief in the one spiritual God, and a practical duty of education, and works of progress and philanthropy. Already a number of churches are in existence in Hindostan; and the movement is being carried on with great enthusiasm, renouncing idolatry in every form, breaking down caste, and promoting knowledge and mental freedom. On Tuesday afternoon, Mr. Peebles and Mr. Burns had an interview with this distinguished visitor, and gave him to understand, in the name of the Spiritualists of Britain and America, that they deeply sympathized with his mission; which was in most points identical with the objects sought by Spiritualists. They informed Mr. Sen that Spiritualism had the same monotheistic basis as the 'Brahmo Somaj,' of which he is the distinguished leader, and that Spiritualists labored to disinthrall mankind from sectarian caste, social caste, property caste, and from the galling bonds of ignorance and superstition, forged for society for many ages by an ignorant, bigoted, and self-interested priesthood, and the slough of misery and vice entailed on the people by the unwarrantable dominance of rulers and aristocrats over property and personal liberty. Our friends found in Mr. Sen an intelligent man, and a brother, whose social and theological views are far in advance of the popular theology of this country. Mr. Sen gave some information respecting the supernatural beliefs of his countrymen; who are superstitious, and require to be educated and directed. He is well acquainted with Spiritualism, knew our departed friend, the late Mr. Nelson of Calcutta, also Peary Chand Mittra of Calcutta, the leading Spiritualist of India. We wish India could afford to send over a good supply of such missionaries, to teach the true religion which thousands of years ago originated on the banks of the Ganges, but which Pagan emperors, licentious kings, popes, bishops, priests, and parsons have degraded into a mercenary trade, to suit their selfish interests."

An aristocratic wedding: of course he would attend. This note was cordial:—

"Lord and Lady Otho Fitz-Gerald request the pleasure of the Rev. J. M. Peebles's (United-States consul) company at St. Martin's Church, on Thursday, 12th of May, at eleven o'clock, and to the wedding-breakfast afterwards at one o'clock, at No. 8 Carlton-House Terrace."

About two hundred distinguished guests assembled,—lords, dukes, reverends, honorables, marquises, marchionesses, &c.; who lavished choice presents upon the bride, step-daughter of Lord Otho Fitz-Gerald, comptroller of her Majesty's household, and also upon the bridegroom, "The Rev. George Cockburn Dickinson, married to the Hon. Ursula Elizabeth Denison." Their bridal tour was to the Holy Land. The "consul" enjoyed it vastly, thinking all the while that hearts are all royal where true love is.

The merits of our brother's work were recognized in Paris, by making him an honorary fellow of the "Société Parisienne des Études Spirites," as will be seen by the following letter: —

"*The Paris Société for Spiritual Studies. Founded at Paris on the* 1*st of April,* 1858, *by Allan Kardec,* 27 *Rue Molière.*

"PARIS, May 28, 1870.

"SIR AND DEAR BROTHER, — The Paris Society for Spiritual Studies desires me to thank you for the present which you have made thém of one of your excellent works, 'The Seers of the Ages.' One of their members will report on it at a forthcoming *séance* of the society.

"They, moreover, are grateful to you for the intention which you appear to have of making the books of Allan Kardec known in America. You are thus working towards a unity of belief which can only be accomplished to the extent that the lofty doctrine of re-incarnation is made clear, on the basis of a rational theory concerning life and progress.

"It seems to us a matter of great importance, that, without regard to differences of nationality, all those who share in a common belief should be in constant communion of heart and intellect, and that Spiritualism should take an international character.

"Our society would be proud to count you among those belonging to them. They beg you to accept the title of honorary and corresponding member, which they are pleased to offer you. Accept our, &c.

"E. BONNEMERE,

"*President of the Paris Society for Spiritual Studies, Member of the Literary Society, and of the Society of Dramatic Authors.* 31 *Rue de Boulogne, Paris.*

"MR. PEEBLES."

Mr. Peebles was invited into literary circles represented by the Brights, Masseys, Howitts, Tennysons, Ashburtons, Jacksons, Burnses, Tyndalls, Lockyers, Varleys, Crookes, Wilkinsons, Cooks, Wallaces, &c., and was unexpectedly elected a member of a scientific society of distinguished influence. "The Medium and Daybreak" says, —

"When our friend Mr. Peebles went to the East last autumn, he had instructions from the Anthropological Society of London to gather whatever facts came under his notice relative to the science of man. To this end he was appointed a local secretary for the East. His speedy return to Britain prevented his credentials reaching him in Asia; but, since he arrived in London, he has attended some of the meetings of the society, and has been presented with a diploma of honorary fellowship and of local secretary for Trebizond or elsewhere. Mr. Peebles has ample scope for making anthropological observations in America, where he has come much in contact with the Aborigines."

The following is a copy of his diploma: —

"ANTHROPOLOGICAL SOCIETY OF LONDON.

FOUNDED IN 1863.

"The Anthropological Society of London, at a meeting held this day, elected J. M. Peebles, Esq., United-States consul, a Local Secretary for Trebizond, Asia; in virtue of which the present diploma is delivered.

"J. M. PEEBLES, F.A.S.L., *Honorary Fellow.*

"JOHN BEDDOE, *President.* J. BARNARD DAVIS, *Vice-President.*
DUNBAR ISADORE HEATH, *Treasurer.* C. STANISLAND WAKE, *Dep. Director.*

"LONDON, Nov. 30, 1869."

Availing himself of the courtesies of the *Royal Institution*, Mr. Peebles attended the meetings of this scientific body. The London "Pall-Mall Gazette" reports one of the lectures upon "The Solar Spectrum;" which to our Pilgrim was of great utility, illustrative of the effect of spirit-spheres upon mortals, —

"Last Saturday afternoon, Mr. J. Norman Lockyer, F.R.S., delivered his third lecture, at the Royal Institution, upon 'The Sun.' Prince Christian presided; and among the listeners were her Royal Highness the Princess Louise, Lady A. Stanley, Prof. Tyndall, Lady Ashburton, Dr. J. H. Gladstone, F.R.S., Mr. J. M. Peebles, American Consul at Trebizond, and Sir Henry Holland, Bart., M.D., F.R.S., President of the Royal Institution.

"A parallel beam of light from the electric lamp was passed through a vertical slit, from which it emerged into the dark theater. A glass double-convex lens was then placed in the path of the light; and, after passing through the lens, the rays were sent through two hollow glass prisms, filled with bisulphide of carbon. By this arrangement, the different colors in white light were disentangled from each other, and spread out upon a screen; where they appeared like a slice cut out of a rainbow, with the red color at one end, gradually melting in succession into yellow, green, and blue, till the violet of the other end of the spectrum was reached. He then told how the white light of the sun, when similarly treated, does not give quite a similar spectrum ; for, instead of the colors being continuous, they are cut here and there by vertical dark lines, of which two in the yellow part of the spectrum are very prominent. Incandescent gases do not give a continuous spectrum under ordinary conditions; and ignited sodium vapor gives a spectrum consisting of two bright yellow lines only and no other color. The two bright lines of sodium fall upon exactly the same part of the spectrum as the two dark lines in the spectrum of solar light; and it has been discovered, that the two dark lines just mentioned are produced by sodium vapor between the eye of the observer and the sources of the light of the sun. In proof of this, Mr. Lockyer threw a continuous spectrum upon the screen, the carbon points inside the lamp being well impregnated with sodium, to intensify the yellow rays. Then outside the slit, and in the path of the rays, he burnt some metallic sodium; so that the light from the lamp had to pass through the ignited sodium vapor before reaching the screen. It was then seen that the vapor absorbed some of the yellow rays, so as to produce a dark band upon the screen; but it

18

did not intercept rays of any other color. Incandescent vapors, therefore, have a tendency to absorb the rays which they themselves emit; wherefore the two dark bands in the yellow of the solar spectrum are believed to be caused by an atmosphere of sodium vapor between the eye of the spectator and the source of a portion of the yellow light of the sun. On the same principle, the presence of other substances in the sun has been proved."

These private letters to us from Mr. Peebles are so descriptive and fraternal, we deem them worthy of a place, —

"London, Feb. 24, 1870.

"Dear Friend and Brother, — . . . Am now speaking every Sunday in London, attempting to build up a society. It is the first continuous effort to establish spiritual meetings upon a religious basis. All previous took the form of lectures.

. . . "Next week I purpose visiting Victor Hugo, the French exile. He is a reputed Spiritualist: certainly his words are all aglow with soul. In funeral orations, I think he excels all other men.

. . . "Soon as possible I desire to write a book on "Mohammedanism and Spiritualism of the Orient." It would delight my soul to live in some Oriental country. There could I find the promised rest to the weary.

"Love to Olive, Henry, Hattie, Freddie, Willie, — buds on the life-tree.

"I received letters from my dear Dunn, my bosom boy and brother; and how do I delight to hear about his excellent wife and two intelligent, sunny children! Our world is so full of loves, it ought to be beautiful and good." * * *

"London, April 3, 1870.

"Friend Joseph, — . . . One sentence in yours pains me. You ask, 'Have you forgotten the obscure brother, living away here among these snowy hills of Wisconsin?' Forgotten! do you not yet fully know me? I have never yet forgotten a friend. Would sacrifice any thing for you, for your family, for all friends. . . . I am tired, weary. It is exhaustive, this speaking in London Sundays, and week-day evenings in the provinces. I admire these Englishmen. All my prejudices have faded away like the morning mists. There is a solidarity in the English character. Slow, but sure, their friendship is permanent. Next week I purpose to visit the Isle of Wight, seeing the poet Tennyson, and speaking perhaps one evening. It is rumored there are several Spiritualists upon the Isle. Last week, visiting, I tarried a day and night with William Howitt and family. Mary, his wife, is an angel. His library is very extensive. His lawn and garden abound in beautiful walks. His head is a living cyclopædia, filled with the wise sayings of thinkers in all ages. Next autumn they celebrate their golden wedding. Their home seemed to me an earthly paradise." . . .

* * *

"London, April 17, 1870.

"Brother, — . . . The wise man and just considereth all circumstances and contingencies before he scoldeth (Gospel according to James, chap. i. verse thousand.)

"Your favor of March 30 *unbottled* its vitriol upon me; the 17th, I was glad to get bottle, vitriol, and all. The effect was as delightful as storms and whirlwinds. The sky evidently feels better after spilling out hurricanes. Doubtless you are in good health now. You tried to complain in your last, but did not succeed. The Christ in your composition is continually gaining victories over Adam. Surely, when you would do evil, *good* is present with you.

. . . "Dr. Willis left us yesterday for America. He took a good portion of my heart with him." . . .

* * *

"LONDON, April 18, 1870.

"DEAR BROTHER, — . . . Spiritualism has performed its first cycle. Curiosity for the phenomenal is subsiding. Another angel will soon sound an alarm in the heavens. This will awake us to the moral necessity of embodying the practical with the fundamental principles. Thinkers and scientists are searching for the harvests of these twenty years' sowing. . . . 'Watchman! what of the night?' I am recruiting a week in Hammersmith at the home of Mrs. Morris, a cousin of Robert Dale Owen. She has a private library of four thousand volumes. What a feast!"

* * *

"LONDON, 15 SOUTHHAMPTON ROW, W.C., May 13, 1870.

"DEAR BROTHER,— A veil, a deep veil, has hung like a pall over me for several days. Causes, great mental labor and earnest opposition to my efforts from secularists and a few Christian Spiritualists. When shall we all learn to practice toleration? Some Spiritualists here believe in the vicarious atonement and other churchal dogmas! How long must I, a peace-man, be forced to fight with tongue and pen? I confess I weary of life's battles, and sigh for a hermit home with only books, paintings, flowers, and my sweet angels. . . . My inspiration leads me to ignore all prices for speaking; to go into the by-ways and lanes and the very church-doors, crying aloud, and sparing not. My heart is with the people. I take no pleasure in preaching to saints. Are there any? Did not Jesus come to 'save sinners, of whom I am chief?' . . . To-morrow I return to the residence of J. Burns and family, — good, faithful workers. Never can I forget their kindnesses. Note the beautiful penmanship of my amanuensis, Thos Reeves. He is the soul of integrity."

* * *

CHAPTER XXXII.

EUROPEAN CORRESPONDENCE.

"Life can be as lovely as its best moods. . . .
In the wine of love is the truth of life." — GAIL HAMILTON.

EARLY in 1870, Hudson Tuttle proposed to Mr. Peebles that they publish "A Year-Book of Spiritualism;" the former editing the American department, and the latter the European and Asiatic. Appreciating its need, these gentlemen corresponded with the leading Spiritualists throughout the world, and ushered in 1871 with a beautiful eclectic work, published by "The Banner of Light" Company, statistical, representing Spiritualism in all its phases by its scholars Each year they will issue a new volume, marking the progress oi the angels' gospels.

Mental impressibility, conversation, and public speech, epistolary correspondences, and the press, are the methods of Spiritual commerce. Mr. Peebles employs them all. Whilst in Europe, his correspondence was immense, as in America. At times he was obliged to engage an amanuensis. Aside from the personages herein noticed, he received valued letters from Mrs. DeMorgan, author of "From Matter to Spirit;" M. Martin Tupper, author of "Proverbial Philosophy;" Mrs. McDougold Gregory, wife of a distinguished professor of Edinburgh College, who, in the spirit-land, sends to her the angels' wisdom; Mrs. Max Müller, wife of the great Sanscrit linguist; Gerald Massey, the Spiritual poet; Tennyson; Baron von Schickh, the Austrian Spiritualist; Baron Guldenstubbe; Rev. John Page Hopps; Robert Chambers; Prince George de Solms, introducing him to his grace, Bishop Bugnion, who is one of the greatest scholars in the world. These mementos of love, flowering with Spiritual thought, and so beautifully haloed in friendship, we have no right to publish.

"FLORENCE, Dec. 13, 1869.

"MY DEAR PEEBLES, — . . . I am very impatient to meet you. I have told you before how my soul has been drawn towards yours. But do try and stay weeks in Rome: in two or three days you can see literally nothing of its many wonders. I shall want to be with you nights while you are there, and share the same apartment with you: for there will be so much sight-seeing days that we shall have no time to give to the discussion of the many matters I wish to talk with you about; and I love dearly to talk a while after retiring. I hope you will not deem this a very strange request. The Guppys are very kind-hearted and generous.

"I was persuaded into giving a *séance* the other night at the villa of a beautiful countess here, — one of the loveliest women I ever saw. The manifestations were most marvelous. . . . I shall want you to see Prince George de Solms while you are in Rome. He is genial. Our acquaintance has ripened into a sincere friendship. I have a letter from him every week. He bears his princeship in a sensible way. Give my love to Damiani. . . . God bless you, my dear brother! Fraternally thine,

"FRED. L. H. WILLIS."

"FLORENCE, Jan. 1, 1870.

"MR. J. M. PEEBLES: *Dear Sir*, — Under the guidance of the spirits, charged by Providence to direct the movement that will conduct humanity to regeneration, you are perhaps the chosen instrument in America. Could I, in my naughtiness, trust to the many assurances of my Spiritual guardians, I might believe myself to be a chosen one for this side of the Atlantic. Vanity, self-love, pride, have nothing to do with the thought: the belief to be such an instrument may be cherished without any sentiment of worldly purpose; and what if erroneous, if it gives a holy strength to perform what tends to explore and work out always for the diffusion of truth, if it induces even to the sacrifice of one's self to attain the glorious aim?

"Well, dear Mr. Peebles, if you have for the arduous work the confidence in my aid that I feel entirely in yours, let us work together, you from the West shore, I from this side of the ocean; and we shall in spirit stretch our arms, and meet to grasp strictly our hands, and form the bridge upon which, according to the ardent wish expressed by the spirit of Allan Kardec, may be laid the chain of union between the American and the European continent-schools of Spiritism.

"'The Aurora' ('Daybreak') will be ready about the 15th or 20th of this month. I will direct some numbers by post to Mr. Burns; and a parcel of fifty I may send from Leghorn to New York, directed, if you will let me know. In America are many Italians, through whom much good may be done in the way of spreading our dear doctrine. An opportune distribution *gratis* will be the best means.

"Believe me, dear sir, yours very sincerely,

"GIROLAMO PARISI."

"16 RUE DE LA BIENFAISANCE, PARIS, Thursday.

"MY DEAR FRIEND, — I envy you; wish I could be as useful in this great Spiritual movement as yourself. It is a glorious thing to be doing God's work, and help extricate humanity out of its benighted darkness. You can have the five works of Allan Kardec for ten shillings.

. . . "I will try and get you a photograph of Favre. The young Baron did not send you the one he promised, because he could not procure it as expected.

"I shall be glad to be kept posted as to your movements in the East. I have not relinquished the idea of visiting America, and should like nothing better than to accompany you to that land of promise.

"I would like exceedingly to hear your lectures in London. Remember me to the worthy Burns and family. I am, my ever dear brother, yours very sincerely,

"GLADSTANES."

"Our Sargent," of Boston, traveling then in Europe to recuperate his health, is a full-orbed Spiritualist of literary rank, being author of "Peculiar," "Planchette," "The Woman who Dared," and other popular works. His letter is sunny with good sense and energy: —

"CANNES, A.M. (FRANCE), March 21, 1870.

"MY DEAR MR. PEEBLES, — . . . I see that the Spiritualists of England have given you a most affectionate welcome; and I cordially wish you prosperity in your gallant efforts to spread the truth as you see and understand it. If more men and women had but courage to speak their convictions, how many social and dogmatic shams would have their day of death accelerated! But there is so much fear of treading on the toes of conventionalism! The great work of Spiritualism will be, to emancipate thought, to take us out of time-worn ruts, and make us breathe the exhilarant, divine air of liberty, calling no man master, and swayed neither by spirits in the flesh nor out of the flesh (though their name be Legion) to accept what violates our reason and our sense of right.

"But the wide, the unbounded prospect spreads before me. I must close.

"Affectionately and sincerely,

"EPES SARGENT."

Countess Mde. Medina Pomar, a devoted Spanish Spiritualist, in a friendly note of encomiums upon Mr. Peebles's labors in London, adverts thus to the doctrine of re-incarnation, —

"We were much disappointed not to have the pleasure of your company last Sunday, whom we waited for so long in vain. Can you not come next Sunday evening? I am anxious to meet you, and have a long conversation with you upon that branch of Spiritualism entitled re-incarnation."

"STRADA FIORENTINE, No. 9. NAPLES, April 12, 1870.

"MY VERY DEAR BROTHER, — . . . 'The Year-book' you intend publishing appears to me to be a great boon to Spiritualists. . . .

"You ask a paragraph from me on the state of Spiritualism in Italy. I will write as you wish, at the first opportunity, if it be only half a page. I shall also do all in my power to contribute to the financial success of your 'Annual.'

"I have read with intense interest the accounts of your Sunday-evening discourses in the metropolis of England. Oh, how I regret not being present at those rich feasts of mind! Go on, dear brother, with the grand work of re-generation; and may the dear spirits strengthen your body, thus rendering your task easy!

"You have no doubt by this time seen the good queen of England; whom, I am sure, you must have admired for her great affability: but, if she had none of those graces which distinguish her, the fact of her being a Spiritualist forms her greatest claim to our love and admiration.

"Pray, take care of your precious health, and believe me to be your true friend and brother,

G. DAMIANI."

Elder Frederick W. Evans, English by birth, through the church into materialism, and this into Spiritualism, and thence by his own mediumship into the "resurrection state of true believers," termed Shakers, — the Essenes of this century, — addressed Mr. Peebles a lengthy communication whilst in England. We extract from its sweetness, —

"MT. LEBANON, April 29, 1870.

"J. M. PEEBLES: *My much esteemed Friend,* — I often think of you since you began your Old-World ramblings; am glad to learn that the 'Auto' reached you safely. I know of no one whom I should prefer to have it. You are one of a class of souls who are inspired from the seventh heaven! Spirits from thence follow you continually; and once in a while, in the stillness of your soul, they minister the elements of the '*Harvest Home,*' — a joyful sound in the rural districts of Old England. Grand idea, beautiful type is *that,* when the last load of wheat from the harvest-field is coming in with the laborers, on the top of the golden mountain, as it moves along towards the garners of the husbandman, joyfully shouting at the top of their voices, 'Home, home, harvest home!'

"But what language of mortals shall describe the unutterable joy and glory of the final *harvest home* of earth's inhabitants, when the last sheaf, a human soul, shall be brought into the resurrection state, and 'the *end,*' the *end,* has come?' 'The harvest is ended, and all are saved! shall be shouted from one heaven to another.' Home, home, at last! The harvest of earth is gathered; and we shall all together raise the shout of 'Harvest home!' . . .

"Accept of the love of our order, and of your friend the writer in particular. Good angels have you in their keeping, and will guide your feet aright towards the Zion of God as your final home; and in due time after *you* will come the souls whom you have quickened in their spiritual germs to seek a new life.

"Farewell. From your brother laborer in the Lord's vineyard,

"F. W. EVANS."

This German correspondent is a scholarly Spiritualist; and "Luos" referred to is a most powerful spirit of rare intelligence and acuteness, —

"BADEN, GERMANY, May 13, 1870.

"FRIEND PEEBLES, — . . . It is a great blessing to be in communion with such an elevated spirit as 'Luos,' who has now been in communication with us for about fifteen years, and who formerly enabled my wife to perform wonderful cures by the laying-on of hands. Spiritualism has only a beginning here, through our initiatory means; but at Leipsic it is all rife through the energy of Count Poninski, who has been lecturing there. I am told a circle has been formed at Dresden, and a Spiritual journal published in Saxony by Dr. Berthelen. At Vienna a Spiritual circle exists; but progress is exceedingly slow at present in materialistic and priest-ridden Germany. *You* have done great things in England; and it is therefore a misfortune you are obliged so soon to return to the United States. Clerical, sectarian orthodoxy is a sad dead-stop to progress; but it will have to give place eventually to the divine revelations of Nature, and the teachings of the 'angels of the Lord who encamp round about them that *love* him.'

"My wife unites with me in expressing to you that loving attachment which only real Spiritualists can be truly sensible of.

Ever yours,
"A. KYD."

Invited by influential citizens, Mr. Peebles intends at some future day to visit Australia, "The Continental Isle," and sow the Spiritual seed. Messrs. Naylor and Terry speak of many efficient media there. Mr. Naylor is editor of the new Spiritual journal, "The Harbinger of Light," —

"MELBOURNE, AUSTRALIA, May 15, 1870.

"J. M. PEEBLES: *My dear Sir*, — . . . I read your 'Seers of the Ages' with avidity, and made use of your valuable information in several lectures; which I delivered last year, copies of which, together with 'Glow-worm,' shall shortly be forwarded to you.

"I am, my dear sir, yours fraternally,
"B. S. NAYLOR."

"MELBOURNE, VICTORIA, AUSTRALIA, May, 1870.

"J. M. PEEBLES, Esq.: *My dear Sir*, — Spiritualists here are not very demonstrative: but we have many earnest workers, preparing the ground, and sowing the seed; which is already springing up in many unlooked-for places. We wait our time to organize, and expect, when we do so, to have the requisite material to secure strength and cohesion.

"Yours fraternally, W. H. TERRY."

Making inquiry of Anna Blackwell about the Kardec books, Mr. Peebles received a beautiful letter, from which we extract a few thoughts. Her writings grace the pages of English magazines.

"PARIS, Wednesday, 1870.

"DEAR MR. PEEBLES, — . . . These views of re-incarnation purport to be given by the spirits of the Evangelists, sent by Christ (our planet's presiding sidereal spirit), to explain what the ignorance of the time compelled him to leave under a veil. . . . Christ lived right from the beginning, which we have not done; he reached the sidereal degree eternities before us; he is divine only in the figurative sense in which we all shall be when we reach that degree, thus giving its final death-blow to the polytheism of which the first Christian form of belief is the last example. For, when once the world comes to see that *that* most glorious and beautiful spirit is no more "God" than we are; that he was made, tempted, educated, just as we are, though "without sin," — there will be no danger of any other polytheistic notion obtaining credence!

. . . Yours very truly,
"ANNA BLACKWELL."

Inquiring of Mr. Sammons about Spiritualism in South Africa, Mr. Peebles was informed there had been a little agitation in that isolated spot. We extract a paragraph: —

"CAPE OF GOOD HOPE, SOUTH AFRICA,
CAPE TOWN, May 20, 1870.

"J. M. PEEBLES: *Dear Sir*, — . . . I have followed you in many of your sayings and doings, since you have been in England, and read with great pleasure the object and first attraction that drew you there, — which was a singular proof of faith and confidence. . . . Believe me, dear sir, your obedient servant,

"W. L. SAMMONS."

"SAGNA LA GRAND, ISLE OF CUBA, Feb. 14, 1870.

"MY DEAR FRIEND, — . . . Spiritualism is not widely known here, though many are inquiring. I have long known you through 'The Banner' and your published works. While wandering, why not come to us, bringing with you a good test-medium? thus giving us both phenomena and philosophy. You would meet with a cordial reception in this country. . . . I am a Spaniard, coming to this country fourteen years ago. I have been in your country twice. I am anxious to become developed as a medium; then I should have the knowledge within myself. I am very anxious to form your personal acquaintance. . . . Most sincerely thine,

"EULOGIO PRICTO."

The following, addressed to Mr. Peebles in deep mourning, indicates the appreciation in which he was held in London by those especially most in need of the heavenly light. Mrs. Morris is an esteemed cousin of Hon. Robert Dale Owen.

"8 THERESA TERRACE, HAMMERSMITH, W. LONDON.

"MY DEAR FRIEND, — I am honored and delighted to find that you will come and visit a poor widow, who will give you a hearty welcome to her *humble*, *quiet* home. . . . How I prize your glorious work 'The Seers, &c.'! Your Spiritualism is exactly, I think, like mine. What glorious thinkers and writers you have in America! . . . There is so much *Orthodox Church cant* and all kinds of uncharitableness against those who do not swallow, or rather pretend to do so, all the absurdities of Trinitarian doctrines, that the Spiritualists form here two antagonistic branches.

"How beautiful was your discourse last Sunday! It ought to have been preached in some of our grand *empty* city churches. With God's blessing, may you soon recover is the prayer of your friend! CAROLINA H. MORRIS."

As we read the following, the soul is stirred, for we think of the ancient brother-seers who made "Vishnoo" a study. India is a soul-mother of religion. May the morning-sun of the Spiritual Gospel rise again upon her sacred lands! —

"CALCUTTA, 11th June, 1870.

"J. M. PEEBLES, Esq., Southampton Row, London.

"*My dear Sir*, — I must ask you to pardon me for the delay I have made in replying to your favor of the 4th April last. Though I have been a Spiritualist for many years my knowledge of the Spiritual circles existing in the different parts of the country is very limited, and I fear I can not be of much use to you. I have never taken any interest in external manifestations, and have devoted my entire attention to the study of my soul and its varied phenomena in connection with the external world, and the nervous system, and its subjectivity by itself, or by freedom from phenomenal states. This study is ennobling inasmuch as it raises us above all creeds and sects, and brings us into intimate communion with God, his will and providence. I have got to say a great deal on the subject of Spiritualism from my own experience; which with me is an accomplished fact. Though I have read a large number of books on Spiritualism, I confess I have found in most of them a great deal of error, or, in other words, what I have known otherwise from my own experience. I shall be delighted to see you here.

"Yours fraternally,
"PEAR CHAND MITTRA."

"Sept. 25, 1869.

"MY DEAR SIR, — . . . Thank you for your very splendid lecture on Spiritualistic belief. Of course, we do not agree in *all* points; but we do in the grand principles of a spirit intercourse, and that will progressively open up to us all the rest.

"Wishing you a prosperous journey, I remain, my dear sir, yours faithfully,

"WILLIAM HOWITT.

"J. M. PEEBLES, Esq.

"P.S. We had a most interesting *séance* at the Everitts'. 'John Watt' talked like a philosopher, and, what was better, like a Christian philosopher. The Everitt mediumship is eminently satisfactory. "W. H."

The following is an extract from a note sent Mr. Peebles by a distinguished professor of Oriental languages in one of the English Universities: —

"SEPT. 25, 1869.

"MY DEAR MR. PEEBLES, — I have been for the last few days so much engaged with the Nawâb of Bengal, that I have been unable to write to you before. . . . Should you come here, which I hope you will soon, I shall be happy to show you all the attention and hospitality in my power. I will keep a look-out for any traces of Spiritualism in my Oriental reading, and send you them from time to time. For the present I send you two instances, which I think will interest you.

"Mr. Pearce tells me you have been good enough to give him a copy of your 'Seers of the Ages' for me. I am extremely obliged to you, and shall read it, I am sure, with much pleasure, and because it is memorial of a very pleasant acquaintance which I hope will continue." * * *

Having visited Scotland and Wales, Mr. Peebles resolved to know something from personal observation of "The Emerald Isle." Writing, he received the following from two distinguished gentlemen of Dublin, both patriots and liberalists, the one ex-lord-mayor, Sir John Barrington: —

"GENERAL PRINTING-OFFICE, DUBLIN, IRELAND, April 30, 1870.

"JAMES M. PEEBLES, Esq.: *Dear sir*, — . . . So you have a touch of the 'Round-tower-*aphobia!*' I had a slight attack once myself, but a dose of sound practical sense recovered me. I am a disciple of O'Neill, who says, 'They were evidently built by the ancients to puzzle the moderns.' There was never a greater success. In the libraries of the British Museum is his great work on the 'Ancient Crosses and Round Towers of Ireland.' Command my services at any time. . . . Truly yours,

"IVER MCDONNELL."

"DUBLIN, May, 1870.

"J. M. PEEBLES, UNITED-STATES CONSUL, IN LONDON: *Dear sir*, — I was glad when I read your note this morning, and to find that you had not forgotten your promise to visit Ireland. I shall be happy to see you, and do what I can toward showing you any thing of interest in Dublin and its neighborhood.

"Believe me, yours faithfully,

"JOHN BARRINGTON."

Through the mediumship of Dr. Dunn, the spirits affirm that these "Round Towers" were erected by the ancient Medes, though built about the time of the origin of Christianity. The crosses sometimes found near or in connection with them refer to the cross-bows used in the warfares of the Medes and Persians. The openings at various distances were simply lookouts, and apertures for arrow-shooting upon the approaching enemy.

After a close scanning of the conditions of the Irish, during his rustications in their beloved country, Mr. Peebles indites the following, —

"DUBLIN, IRELAND, May, 1870.

"MY DEAR FRIEND, — . . . Though my rambles over this city and into the country, and my observations in other localities, are quite limited, yet at a glance can I discern the general grade of the English government here, and of the Irish character. O my soul! come into judgment. How I pain over misrule! The eagle becomes filthy when caged: give him liberty, and how grand on the wing! The history of Ireland is the index of her capacity. Such poets as Thomas Moore, such patriots as Robert Emmet, O'Connell, O'Brien, and the like, are the magic of her redemption yet. But look at her degradation now; at the ignorance and superstition of her toiling millions; at the grinding, debasing effects of Papacy upon her devotees! My God! is there no spot on our green earth where the oppressor's foot has never trod? . . . When will legislators learn that governments are for the people, not people for governments? and that no government on earth is worth a single human life? Come, angels, and help us reverse the rule; making man, as Henry C. Wright says, 'superior to his incidents.' It is so strange to me that kings, queens, and presidents do not see this simple law, — that fealty is best secured where the people's rights are best secured. Guaranty by law, executed in fidelity, the God-endowed right to 'life, liberty, and the pursuit of happiness,' to all the people, and educate them up to a just appreciation of these principles, and behold the grandeur of patriotism and the peace and prosperity of the nations! . . .

"Whilst walking these streets, I seemed to be touched with the fire of the immortal Emmet, who, when condemned to the gallows by grave judges because he struck for Irish independence, asked for no epitaph over his grave, but 'the charity of its silence.' What burning words in his last plea before Lord Norbury, ringing still in every Irish heart that loves Erin's isle! — 'When my country takes her place among the nations of the earth, then, and not till then, let my epitaph be written.' The execution of that orator smothers my soul: but it finds vent in tears when I remember his love for the daughter of Curran, the great Irish barrister, — how he imperiled his life to breathe one word of affection into her soul; how she wilted and died in far-off Sicily when her hand was given to another; for she loved only as woman can love the patriot Robert Emmet. I recall the mournful melody of Erin's poet, Thomas Moore: —

'She is far from the land where her young hero sleeps.'

"Pardon me my deep feelings, brother; for I am hopeful as I weep over martyr-dust. Defeats will yet prove successes. Our William Lloyd Garrison, America's friend and patriot, suffered a thousand deaths whilst fighting for Afric's sons and daughters; but he triumphed at last; our nation rose to glory, and his name is now sacred. Our tears — oh, may they spread a rainbow over this isle of the British sea!

'O Erin, my country! thy glory's departed;
For tyrants and traitors have stabbed thy heart's core.
Thy daughters have laved in the streams of affliction;
Thy patriots have fled, or are stretched in their gore;
Ruthless ruffians now prowl through thy hamlets forsaken;
From pale, hungry orphans their last morsel have taken;
The screams of thy daughters no pity awaken.
Alas! my poor country, thy Emmet's no more!'

"Thy brother, J. M. PEEBLES."

CHAPTER XXXIII.

THE FAREWELL IN LONDON.

"Gather up the fragments, that nothing be lost." — JESUS.

"Storms purify the air we breathe. Rains that rust the corn revive the grass. The refuse of the yard makes the peach and pear grow more luxuriantly. Stars that fade from our skies only pass to illume other portions of the sidereal heavens. The dewdrops that glisten in morning-time from million plants are only exhaled by sun-kisses, to form clouds in aerial regions, to fall in copious showers gladdening the earth, while moving on in rills and rivers to the ocean again. Nothing is lost. Our loved ones, whom the world calls dead, have only passed to the Summer-Land before us, to return again as ministering spirits."

How applicable these words of our Pilgrim to himself! Hardships in Asia, fogs and damps in London, together with severe mental labor, had bleached his locks to a venerable gray, — a change in which he takes a strange pride; longing for the day, close at hand, when they will be white as snow. Friends in America entreated his return home. Friends in England with equal assiduity plead for him to remain, if consistent, thinking the summer-flowering might recuperate his wasted energies. He carried the question up to the oracles; listened to the still voices of his ever-faithful guardians; and concluded to return, for there were pressing duties in the Spiritual work claiming service in his own America. Learning his purpose, the Spiritualists of London resolved upon some token of their gratitude, and appreciation of his labors in the Queen's realm. His farewell address, delivered on Sunday the 29th of May, was replete with his most inspired thought. We select an extract to indicate its drifting wave: —

"The philosopher sees in the falling and decaying of a leaf, even, the action of life-forces, which speak eloquently of resurrections and reconstructions upon the higher planes of vegetable existence. Newton, in an autumn day, lying beneath a tree laden with golden fruit, saw an apple fall to the earth; and the law of gravitation flashed across his mind. Franklin, with kite and string, called the electric fluids from heaven, and threw an eternal fact into the face of all past ages.

"Now cables stretch across oceans, and magnetic wires girdle the globe. A psychologic star appearing in the Syrian skies of the East directed the clairvoyant eyes of wise men — magi, or seers — to a lowly manger, within which lay concealed causes that should ultimately usher in a better and more harmonial era.

"A tiny rap was heard in the Fox family, near Rochester, N.Y., — in and of itself, a minute event; and yet behind those mystic sounds were hidden living, tangible demonstrations of a future existence through the present ministry of spirits. The rapidity with which this truth has diffused itself into poetry, history, philosophy, and the theologies of the different denominations, astonishes even its most enthusiastic advocates. Its banner floats to-day beneath all skies. It is kindling a new light in Asia, shining in beauty upon the hills of Hindostan, sparkling over the plains of Farther India, beaming in splendor throughout the courts of Europe, sounding an alarm from the distant isles of the ocean; and each tone is musical with the living fact of immortality,— immortality for all the races of men. The army of Spiritualists is constituted of millions of devoted followers. It is throwing from the press, constantly, books, pamphlets, monthlies, and weeklies. It has in America six weekly organs, and others which devote some space to the subject; between one and two hundred organizations, denominated Children's Progressive Lyceums; besides a National Association, several State Conventions, and thousands of societies supporting regular Sunday-services. The soundest jurists, the most logical thinkers, some of the most distinguished Congressmen, and certainly the most eminent of American poets, are Spiritualists.

"In England you publish 'Human Nature,' 'The Spiritual Magazine,' 'The Spiritualist,' and last, but not least, the stirring weekly, 'The Medium and Daybreak.' Each admirably fills its own legitimate position; and in the kingdom of Great Britain, the realm of thought, there is room for them all. The Macedonian cry comes from all quarters, 'Come over and help us!' Send us mediums; forward us periodicals; furnish us lectures; give us food, — even that bread of God that cometh down from heaven, and giveth life to the world. Our friend Burns is sending books, not only to the Continent, not only to Australia and New Zealand, but to the farthest isle of the ocean. Surely the heavens are opened, the angels are in the clouds of heaven, and ministering spirits are working with us for the world's redemption. Lift up your heads, O faithful souls! for your redemption draweth nigh.

. . . .

"The apostle Paul, when about to leave an Asian church for Rome, wrote thus: 'Only let your conversation be as becometh the gospel of Christ; that whether I come and see you, or else be absent, I may hear of your affairs, that you stand fast in one mind, with one spirit, striving together for the faith.' And, as I am about to leave you for my native land, I feel, while appreciating your many kindnesses, to beg of you to let your conversation — that is, your daily moral deportment — be such as to honor the divine principles you profess; so that whether I come and see you, or be absent, I shall hear of your affairs, that you stand fast in one spirit, and that the spirit of harmony and charity, with a mutual co-operation for the upbuilding of Spiritualism. It seems not only opportune, but providential, that Dr. Newton, at this particular hour, with his wonderful healing powers, and yet abounding with the love of the angels, the gifts of the spirit, should appear in your midst. But gifted and consecrated as he is to the apostolic work of causing the lame to walk, the blind to see, the deaf to hear, he (like the gentle Nazarene) has not where to lay his head. O London, London, busy, bustling, selfish, sordid city of millions, how little you appreciate the brother whose hands are as palms of healing for the nations of the earth! It matters not what the people, nor what a catering public press, may say: God and God's angels are with him, and that to bless humanity.

"I see before me Mr. Shepard, who, aided and instructed by immortals, has himself become the very soul of music: I further see Mr. Morse, ever controlled to breathe trance-utterances, rich in philosophy and wisdom; Mrs. Everitt, whose mediumship has convinced thousands of immortality; and other mediums who are also present, and are sowing the seeds of heavenly harvests. And, further, I can not let the moment pass without speaking of the Progressive Library, under the supervision of our friend James Burns. This is 'The Banner-of-Light' institution of Great Britain. It is a center, a grand rallying-place, for Spiritualists from every point of the compass; and as you love Spiritualism, as you love the promulgation of truth, and as you appreciate my feeble labors during the past four or five months, I beg, I entreat of you, to sustain and encourage Mr. Burns in his noble work. Few know his labor, his self-sacrifice, and devotion to the principles of our philosophy. In early morning he is at his post of duty; and often the midnight hour and the small hours of morning find him inditing articles, furnishing editorials, planning *séances*, and devising other means for the propagation of a broad, free, unsectarian Spiritualism.

"But now comes to me the saddest hour of the past several months. It is to thank you for individual and social kindnesses, and confess to you a deeper appreciation of Englishmen and English character the more thoroughly I have been brought into social relations with you for the advancement of a common cause. Not a jar has marred our general harmony. Those who were faint-hearted when these religious meetings commenced are now strong and united, awaiting the return of the distinguished worker, Mrs. Hardinge, to carry them on to still greater victories. Though far across the blue waters, I shall delight to hear of your affairs, — to learn of your temporal and spiritual prosperity, and know that Spiritualism has become an acknowledged power in this great world's metropolis. With me, friendship is no idle word: I do not like, but I love my friends with a true soul-affection. Such friendship buds upon earth only to bloom in heaven. I shall never, never forget you, good friends, nor the many happy hours that I have whiled away in your society as a fellow-worker; and from my heart of hearts I can only exclaim, 'God and his good angels keep and bless you!' If in the enthusiasm of my nature I have said one harsh word, or breathed one unkind thought, forget and forgive. 'To err is human; to forgive, divine.'"

"The Medium and Daybreak" thus reports one of Mr. Peebles's Sunday meetings in London: —

"It would be difficult to imagine a place more completely packed with human beings than the Cavendish Rooms were on Sunday evening. Dr. Newton was expected, and the Spiritualists and sympathizers turned out in a body to meet him. The usual attenders dropped in early; and the arrangements were so admirable, and the friends so helpful, that no discomfort or disappointment was experienced. Thanks are due to Mr. Humphrey for his efforts to seat the hall as thoroughly as possible. Mr. Peebles delivered an admirable sermon, exactly suited for the occasion, of which we can give only a few extracts. He said that in the Gospel as recorded by John, we find this language: 'You shall know the truth, and the truth shall make you free.' 'As I lift my eyes as far as I can, and take a moral survey of the universe, I see, or seem to see, men thrusting out their soul-feelers, and asking anxiously for the highest and best form of truth. It is no more natural for water to find a level, it is no more natural for the magnetic needle to turn to the north pole, than it is for the human soul to search for truth; and it is a fact, that truths must not only be born in mangers, but they must be crucified, and that, too, frequently between thieves. They must be baptized in tears before they can become mighty forces, swaying the masses, and leading them on step by step to higher and more divine planes of mental and spiritual life. We are created in God's own image; and it thus becomes us to use those reasoning faculties that we thereby inherit. Hence we should sanction nothing fresh in science, no dogma of the past or present, until the same has been carefully investigated and candidly weighed in the balance of reason; and thus we shall be ready at all times to give to every man a reason for the hope that is within us.' Mr. Peebles said that the natural man is composed of two elements, — the physical and the spiritual. The physical body is merely an echo of the more real one it represents. The flesh, blood, bones, and hair are merely the outward signs of an inward and spiritual man. When Crito came crying and weeping to Socrates, just after he had drained the hemlock cup, and asked where they might bury him, Socrates, though in the agony of death, smiled, and said, 'Verily, just where you please, if you can catch me.' Socrates knew they could not bury him; only his shell. Spiritualists sometimes speak of burying a person: but this they should not do; they should speak out and live out their philosophy, that others may hear and see it. Spiritualism gives us a correct idea of a spiritual man and the spiritual life. In stating that there is no such thing as death, Mr. Peebles said he had lately been shown a letter from Mrs. Hardinge, in which that lady said she had recently been speaking in Bridgewater, United States, where lived a Mr. Kingman, a venerable old man, who was an ardent admirer of Mrs. Hardinge, and who had expressed a wish, that, whenever he passed away, Mrs. Hardinge might attend his funeral. On the evening of her address, the old man went to the hall before it was open; and with much enthusiasm he took his seat with his family; and, just as Mrs. Hardinge entered, he fainted. Some one told her that Mr. Kingman had fainted: but she said, 'No: he is dead.' They replied, it was not possible; but neither water nor fanning nor magnetism could bring him back to physical life. He was in the spirit-world; and yet he spoke to Mrs. Hardinge within five minutes of his departure, saying, 'I shall hear your lecture now;' and, during the lecture, there came two tremendous sounds upon the desk, that startled the whole audience. Mr. Kingman had been an excellent man, and much respected, and his friends wished that Mrs. Hardinge should speak a few words to the mourners; but the churches were refused for that purpose. At length one was procured, but on the condition that only ladies should have admission. The address was announced; and a great number of persons came to hear, the road being literally filled with carriages: and in that church Mrs. Hardinge delivered a grand and eloquent discourse, and withal so simple and touching, that nearly every eye was bathed in tears; and, when she arrived home, she heard the voice of Mr. Kingman say, 'I have heard every word of your lecture.' 'Thus,' said Mr. Peebles, 'there is no death. The immortal loved ones live, and walk in white; and, if we would live more spiritual lives, we should be able to walk and talk with them more readily than we do now, and thus be able to prepare ourselves for the future life.'"

One Thursday evening, June 20, a meeting, convened to bid farewell to Mr. Peebles before his departure, was held in the Cavendish Rooms;, H. D. Jencken, barrister-at-law, presiding.

The ladies had arranged all in exquisite order for song and recitation between the intervals of the speeches. Mrs. Varley, Miss Keene, Mr. Shepard, Mr. Peele (reciting a poem of Mrs. Mary Howitt),

Mrs. James Hicks, Mrs. Morris, and others, constituted a musical and recitative orchestra of a most enlivening inspiration. The room was beautifully decorated under the artistic management of Mr. Lander, Mr. Taylor, Mr. Slous, Mr. Hockley, Mrs. Berry, Mr. Henderson, Mr. Dixon, Mr. Duguid, Mr. Everitt, Mrs. Varley, Mr. Rippon, Miss Hay, Mr. Childs, and Mr. E. T. Bennett, who contributed objects of interest.

The report of this ever-memorable meeting is from "The London Spiritualist:"—

"The president, in his opening remarks, stated the purpose for which the meeting had been called, and spoke highly of the capacity for work and the disinterestedness of Mr. Peebles. He told how Mr. Peebles had organized the Sunday-evening meetings in the Cavendish Rooms, and that not upon a sectarian, narrow type, but upon principles which would admit all kinds of Spiritualists. He had also aided similar institutions in other towns, and had been endeavoring to found Children's Lyceums for the education of children. . . .

"Of late years, Spiritualism has been spreading very rapidly in England; and he was indebted to Mr. Harrison, who sat by his side, for the idea that at first Spiritualism, like a stone thrown into the water, made only a small ring, but gradually threw out larger and larger circles, till at the present time it covers a very extensive area, and before long it will begin to clash with vested interests. When that is the case, there will be considerable agitation and disturbance."

The president read the following resolution:—

"That this meeting heartily expresses its warm appreciation of the distinguished services of Mr. J. M. Peebles as a lecturer, author, and eloquent expounder of the important truths and high moral teachings of Spiritualism."

In his commendatory remarks, Mr. Thomas Shorter said,—

. . . "He (Mr. Peebles) has presented truth in the spirit of truth, which is the spirit of charity. He has given us an example of absolute mental independence,—the utmost freedom of thought and expression, combined with the most reverential feeling, and with all respect for those whose theological opinions may, in some important respects, differ from his own. He has shown not only that these qualities are compatible, but that they blend in perfect harmony; that the one is the natural product of the other: for an enlightened reverence, that highest reverence we owe to God, naturally leads us to respect all whom he has formed in the image of his own divine nature, and who, therefore, are measurably partakers of his Spirit. This union of knowledge and reverence, this blended action of free intellect and religious feeling, seems to me preeminently the great need of our present age. We have many men who know much of many things; who can count the stars of heaven, and classify the products and inhabitants of the earth and of the sea; who can tell you why the grass is green, and why the sky is blue; and talk learnedly of the genesis of life and its developments; but who seem touched with no sense of awe and unutterable wonder at the mystery which life presents, no feeling of reverence as before an Infinite Presence, a Holy and Eternal Love, which, like the blue sky, bends over all: One in whom we live and move, and have our being; One with whom we can hold communion, and in whose faithfulness we can trust, —a consciousness which, when deeply felt, thrills the heart, causing it to raise the grateful prayer, or hymn of praise, or to muse in silent worship. On the other hand, how many persons there are of sincere and fervent but narrow piety, with no ample stores of varied knowledge, no large and liberal culture, no intellectual expanse, with horizon stretching out toward the infinite, but who sluggishly move through life, pacing round and round, and never passing out of or beyond the old narrow tracks of custom and tradition! We want neither an undevout science nor an ignorant devotion. It is not good, but most harmful to the individual and to society, for either the spiritual offertories or the intellectual faculties to remain thus torpid. Let us not pamper any one portion of our nature, and allow another to go lean and starved. We want both mind-culture and soul-culture.

"'Let knowledge grow from more to more,
But more of reverence in us dwell,
That mind and soul, according well,
May make one music.'

"He has sought to allay irritation of feeling, to soften the asperities of controversy, to exorcise the evil demons of anger and resentment, to do the blessed work of the peace-maker, and to enforce the importance and urgent need of working out those essential truths in which we agree, instead of wrangling over those things concerning which we differ. There is one consideration which qualifies the pleasure of our present meeting. This is a *farewell soirée*. There is always a tone of sadness in that word *farewell*. And yet it has another side. It is a word very beautiful, and full of meaning: with us, at least, I am sure it is most appropriate and expressive; for wherever our friend may be, whether personally present with us or absent from us, our hearts' sincere wish toward him is, and ever will be, fare you well! It is true, we anticipate with lively satisfaction that our friend will ere long return, we hope with renovated health, to carry on the good work he has so well begun, not only here in London, but in the provinces. It is, however, barely possible that all within the sound of my voice will ever on earth meet again; but it is one of the consolations of our philosophy and our faith, that no bodily absence, no mountain-barrier or interposing ocean, or even change of worlds, can effectually separate those who are one in sympathy and in soul. The 'communion of saints,' affirmed by the Church, is but the theological form of expression of a universal truth. It is to me one of the most beautiful and beneficent dispensations of Providence, that gradually, as we advance in life, the balance of attraction changes, drawing us, with steadily-increasing force, rom the natural to the spiritual world. In the early hours of our brief day of mortal life, we are surrounded by kindred and playmates, and friends and lovers. All is hope and promise. Flowers spring up in our path; the lark carols joyfully his matin-song; and no cloud dims our bright, blue sky. But as the sun passes its meridian, and the shadows lengthen before us, and the cool hours of eventide draw on, friend after friend departs; the father's protecting arm is no longer around us; we feel not the mother's nightly kiss upon our cheek, nor hear the ringing laughter and the merry voices of our early home: the balance has turned, and now dips ever more heavily to the other side. As this world recedes from us, the other looms larger, and draws nearer: and, as our pilgrim-feet near the broad and shining river that rolls between, loved voices call to us, and the angel-forms of the departed stretch forth eager arms to welcome us; and we are ready to exclaim with Simeon of old, 'Lord, now lettest thou thy servant depart in peace.' We need not, however, wait for the death-angel to usher us into the heavenly kingdom: we may, if we will, enter into heaven here and now; or, rather, we may let it enter into us; for, as a great philosopher has said, 'Certainly it is heaven upon earth for a man's mind to move in charity, trust in Providence, and rest upon the poles of truth.'

"Mr. W. Tebb then seconded the resolution, and reviewed the work performed by Mr. Peebles during his stay in London. He said that Mr. Peebles had given his hearers most hopeful views about the other life, although he had said little about such dogmas of worship as total depravity, original sin, and endless misery, and, instead of such subjects, had said a great deal about those divine enunciations contained in the 'Sermon on the Mount.' Mr. Peebles also had said very little about the sins of the Jews, and a great deal about the short-comings of Spiritualists; which plan he thought quite as calculated to do good as those teachings which the English public are accustomed to hear. (Hear, hear.) At the present time, there are certain political difficulties between this country and America; and if there is one nation to which we are bound by closer ties than to another, it is America. He, however, had no doubt that the differences would be amicably settled.

"The chairman then put the resolution to the meeting; and it was carried amid loud applause. He afterwards read the second resolution, placed in his hands by the Rev. Jabez Burns, D.D., of Paddington:—

"'That Mr. Peebles be cordially invited to return to this country again as soon as convenient to him, to further the good work of Spiritual enlightenment and organization in London and the provinces which he has so devotedly and successfully inaugurated during the last four and a half months.'

"Dr. Burns said that he was exceedingly pleased with both the resolutions which had been read by the chairman; and that he had listened with very much pleasure to the address which had been delivered by Mr. Shorter, for it met his own views as to the right method of promulgating truth of any and every kind. He had not heard much that Mr. Peebles had said; but with such of his teachings as he had read he was delighted. Whatever was true in Spiritualism would abide; and whatever was not true in the movement, those who were listening to him did not wish to abide (hear, hear, and overwhelming applause): therefore he (Dr. Burns) was of the same opinion as themselves. All being thus desirous to gain truth, it must be remembered that truth is never gained except at a sacrifice; and, in buying the knowledge of truth, many cherished and preconceived views must be surrendered. As for the theologies of the day, he wished that every form of theology might perish that had not truth in it. Just in proportion to the amount of truth which they contain should those theologies live: when they are not true, let them die; and the sooner they die, the better. (Applause.) Those who have truth should be manly enough to profess what they believe, and not be ashamed of it; though this course of action sometimes requires great courage to follow. He was very much pleased with what had been said in Mr. Shorter's address about charity and love; for these virtues should be used even in the promulgation of truth. Mr. Peebles had once done him the honor to come to a meeting over which he (Dr. Burns) presided; and, directly he saw Mr. Peebles, he fell in love with him at first sight: for many years ago he had learned some phrenological truth; so that, when he looked at Mr. Peebles, he could not help admiring his noble head, with so much benevolence and affection written thereon. At the present meeting, he had marked with delight the gentleness of countenance which Mr. Peebles displayed to everybody. He loved him because of his lovable spirit. He felt that there was communion of mind between them; and should, for one, be rejoiced to hear when Mr. Peebles came back from America. . . . He prayed for uninterrupted peace between America and Great Britain. He would rather have the healing power to remove sadness and sorrow from human beings than be the monarch of the universe.

"Mr. J. Burns seconded the resolution, and spoke of the devotion and labor of the ladies in getting up the meeting, which was entirely their work. He did not repine at Mr. Peebles's leaving them, but was rather thankful that he ever came: to grieve would be selfishness, ingratitude. His heart was full of joy and gladness at the wealth of affection which he felt for the guest of the evening. Mr. Peebles had done a great work, not only in England, in London, but throughout Europe and the East. He was a living embodiment of the cosmopolitan genius of Spiritualism, which owned all men as brothers, and the wide universe of God as the home of the human soul. Every man gave off an influence as he moved about in the world; and, if it were one of love and goodness, then to travel amongst various nations would unite them all in one bond or net of sympathy. He hoped to see Mr. Peebles in London again soon. His return had been predicted by spirit-agency. Mr. Peebles was in every respect a Spiritualist: he called his teaching by no other names, and kept it pure from all creeds. He was almost constantly under spirit influence and direction as regards his writings and speaking on this subject. Even in matters of health and daily life, he was the special care of dear friends in the spirit-world, who, through him, had a work to do for humanity. He felt, therefore, that it would be well with their friend wherever he was. God and good angels were with him.

"Dr. Newton said that in Mr. Peebles his hearers had received not only a righteous man, but a prophet who had given them evidence that the same power exists now which existed years ago. Among the spirits aiding him in his (Dr. Newton's) work of healing the sick was Jesus himself. 'These signs shall follow them that believe, — they shall lay their hands upon the sick, and they shall recover.' Are these signs in the churches? Do they follow the churches? He (Dr. Newton) had been sent to this country more for spiritual healing than for healing the pains of the body; and this power of healing would do a great work in England. The dough has already been raised: soon the bread will be put into the oven, and be brought forth for the benefit of those hungry souls who have been fed on husks, and who dread an angry God and a burning hell. It is a happy knowledge that the brightest spirits that ever walked the earth are with us by day and by night, and that their love becomes more intensified because they are in spirit-life.

"Mrs. C. F. Varley then stepped upon the platform, and presented Mr. Peebles with a handsome purse upon a crimson cushion, saying, 'I am desired by the ladies of the committee to present you with this purse as a mark of gratitude.' The purse contained rather more than twenty-five pounds, the proceeds derived from the sale of tickets of admission to the meeting. The chairman repeated Mrs. Varley's words to the audience. As this was totally unexpected by Mr. Peebles, he was for the moment evidently overcome, and unable to collect his thoughts. Some friends present also presented him with an album containing good portraits of many of the chief celebrities in Europe.

"Mr. J. M. Peebles then said, 'Mr. President, ladies, and gentlemen, it seldom falls to the lot of a mortal to experience a moment so full of real enjoyment as this, when rising to return thanks for the honor you have done me upon this occasion, — an occasion to me of both joy and sadness. It is not so much myself you intend to honor as the heavenly principles of the Spiritual philosophy of which I am but a humble advocate. Your terms of commendation, I fear, are above my deserts, however sincerely and conscientiously I may have advocated the truth, and discharged my duty as a public teacher. Still, fully appreciating them, I shall most gratefully treasure your kind works and expressions of good will in the silent memory-chambers of my soul's sanctuary, — treasure them as the generous overflow of hearts that beat in unison with mine, and whose aspirations are to promote the best mental and spiritual interests of a common humanity. It is not my purpose to make a speech: infinitely do I prefer listening to others. Looking around, it quite overjoys me to see so many familiar faces, so many noble-minded Englishmen, some of whom have already made their mark upon this illustrious age in science and literature; so many kind-hearted and earnest believers in the ministry of angels, — those angels of God who delight in returning to earth to demonstrate immortality, and to aid their mortal brothers and sisters in their weary journeyings toward the shores of the better land. The sympathy and friendship of such a congregation as I see before me this evening constitute the proudest laurels a man can win. Be assured I shall wear them in my heart of hearts till I meet you in the upper kingdoms of eternity, where affection is power, where love is life, and life a perpetual growth in the good, the beautiful, and the true. The address of the chairman, so clear and cogent; of Mr. Shorter, sound and well-timed; of Mr. Tebb, breathing the spirit of sincerity and good-will; of the Rev. Dr. Burns, rich, racy, eloquent, and full of charity; of Mr. James Burns, earnest and truly heartfelt, — these, coupled with the excellent remarks of others, bountiful in expressions of a general soul-sympathy, all tend to bind your better natures to mine with that threefold strand not easily broken. The presentations are most acceptable. I shall endeavor to prove myself worthy, not only of your friendship, but of the valuable gifts which you have been so kind as to tender me. The address of the Rev. Dr. Burns, when speaking of Whitefield, reminds me of this anecdote. Whitefield, when speaking once in one of the States of America, suddenly stopped, and, turning his eyes heavenward, exclaimed, 'Father Abram, are there any Baptists in heaven?' — 'No,' was the response. 'Are any Methodists in heaven?' — 'No.' — 'Any Presbyterians?' — 'No.' — 'Any Churchmen?' — 'No.' — 'Any Unitarians?' — 'No.' — 'Who are in heaven, then?' — Father Abram replied, 'They are all Christians; that is, good men. They have left their sectarian names and dogmatic theologies all behind them.' It is not faith, not metaphysical belief, but works and good deeds, that entitle to happiness. Beautiful is this spirit of charity which crops out from progressive souls in all lands and climes. I can not let this occasion pass without thanking the ladies for their efficiency in conceiving and executing the arrangements upon this occasion. It has been truthfully said that woman is first in every good word and work: it is certain that she was last at the cross, and first at the grave of the risen Savior. Woman's influence has swayed scepters, dethroned rulers, and ever exercises an uplifting, a healing, and holy influence. Though oceans roll between us, though mountains lift their hoary heads to separate us, I shall never forget the warmth of English hearts, nor the social enjoyments of English homes; and, though I should never meet you again face to face upon the shores of mortality, it is to me a beautiful thought, that I shall meet you, know you, and love you, in that world of immortality where farewells are never heard, and where friendships and soul-unions are eternal.' "

CHAPTER XXXIV.

WATCHMAN, HO!

"Watchman, what of the night? . . .
Lo! the morning cometh!"

"There is a tide in the affairs of men."

"Awake, thou that sleepest! — arise from the dead!"

ALL souls we touch into quickened life are ours to love. Improve the opportune moment; ride in upon the rising wave; let the pulse of inspiration rebound in thy soul. Shall thy enemy occupy thy sacred rights? Beware of procrastination: it steals from reform. Behold, another angel is flying in the midst of heaven; and her voice is as the voice of a trumpet on the Mountains of Transfiguration, — "Come hither and build!"

After a rough and stormy voyage in the steamer "City of London," from Liverpool, Mr. Peebles arrived in New York on the evening of the 21st of June, 1870. The Spiritual press of America welcomed his return. "The Banner of Light," his old tried friend, said, —

. . . "Mr. Peebles remained in London four and a half months, where he lectured on Spiritualism with marked effect; and much good will be the result. He will be warmly welcomed by his many friends on this side of the water. He left New York immediately for his home in Hammonton, N.J.; where he will remain a week or two, and then proceed to Washington on business connected with the Government. It is Mr. Peebles's intention, we believe, to return to Europe at no distant day, there to continue the good work he has begun."

Emma Hardinge immediately sent him the following kind greeting. She has since, with her husband, gone to London, further to perfect the work inaugurated there by Mr. Peebles, and with vast success.

"CHICAGO, June 24, 1870.

"MY DEAR FRIEND, — . . . Accept my most hearty congratulations on your trip, its results, your safe return, and mental satisfaction with all that has passed. You have surely done a most noble work in my native country, for which God and angels will bless you."

Saddened over the suspended life of "The Universe," but "patient in tribulation," ever preserving the equanimity of charitable fortitude, he went right to work again, after a few days' rest in his own home, with renewed energy and resolution. Westward, lecturing by the way in Milan, Ohio, in Battle Creek, he arrived in our "beautiful retreat," in Glen Beulah, the last of July, for quiet and literary labors. "Rest?" — as well ask the ocean to rest under the Euroclydon of America's free air. Under the auspices of the Missionary Movement in Wisconsin, he was with us at great mass-meetings of Spiritualists held in Manchester, Ill., — "The feast of continual baptism," — and in the Wisconsin towns of Fond du Lac, Glen Beulah, Omro, Neenah, Fox Lake; and, week-evenings, lecturing in other towns on "Social Life in Turkey;" everywhere commanding popular patronage, and enforcing the truths of political and domestic liberty.

On the evening of Aug. 14, during the mass-meeting in Omro, being then at the residence of E. Thompson, a circle was held, consisting of Mr. Peebles, Dr. Dunn, and our self; when the Indian Powhatan appeared with Dr. Schwailbach, Dr. Willis, and Michael O'Brien, each of whom entranced the medium, and spoke in his characteristic dialect. Powhatan demagnetized the room, and introduced a spiritual atmosphere, hanging up magnetic curtains in the corners to protect "distinguished visitors" from mundane influences, and with great reverence ushered in "John," "Queen of Morn," and "Morning Star," whom he seated in magnetized chairs behind these invisible curtains. As usual, Aaron Nite was the speaker. That hour was hallowed: a holy awe pervaded our souls. Life was reviewed; its pilgrimage made golden in reminiscence. Their address exceeded even our thought to grasp its deep spirit-eloquence. A lever of light lifted us higher. We were in heaven! They said a council of many spirits had recently been held in their world to devise ways and means for the inauguration of a more "efficient system of culture" among Spiritualists. In the summary, they suggested two principles in the "social structure:" —

1. That the basis be *moral spirituality*, as the *fundamental* force of education; to which Spiritual phenomena shall be simply *incidental*, as streams from its fountain.

2. That the outward sign and seal of such society, or system of union, be a declared disposition to attain such spirituality.

On the occasion of his last lecture in Omro, portraying the hidden beauties of angel ministry, and the imperative duty of cultivating them, ennobling life with its divine virtues, he seemed, as Sister Brown of Ripon said, "the apostle John, acquainting us with God and heaven." But an hour before, we had retired like a turtle within its shell, self-condemning, weeping, in fact, over our mistrust, for the moment, of higher inspirations, yet yearning to be freer in expression of soul to help bless the starving millions with this manna falling from the angel-skies. For this we received a deserved rebuke, and encouragement to overcome a "sinful modesty," as he called it. When rapt in the pathos of his theme, the vast congregation eager and grateful as flowers in the baptismal sunlight, and his mind rose higher on wing of ecstasy, just as he was using a beautiful figure to illustrate the burning thought, he was suddenly wheeled round ere the sentence was finished, and rushed to us upon the stand, and spreading his hands in benediction upon our head, unconscious of his act or words, saying aloud in the hearing of the people, "Brother, *brother!* never, *never*, NEVER again mistrust thyself! Let thy light shine! Give to mortals thy inspired truths! for God hath chosen thee. Bless the needy, relieve the distressed, heal the sick and wounded hearts, console the sad, forgive the unfortunate, and show forth the record of a faithful ministry in the gospel of the angels." Then he passed to Dr. Dunn, and invoked a blessing upon him, charging him with counsel exactly adapted to his spiritual needs; praying that we might both bear the mantle of peace together, after he, "the Pilgrim, has passed higher." That melting scene will never be forgotten, nor its wise lessons imparted by the inspiring spirit. "Never mistrust thyself" is a text that will ring in our ears, even when we cross over to the reward of duty done.

Following his successful labors in Wisconsin, Mr. Peebles went to Chicago, filling a monthly engagement, enforcing the ardent object of his heart, — the construction of Spiritualistic society upon a basis of moral and devotional culture; from Chicago to Battle Creek and Sturgis; and thence to Cleveland, and there, too, pursuing the same policy, that the gazing world may soon be gladdened with the better fruits of Spiritualism. Cleveland was his radiative point in all directions; lecturing nearly every week-evening, during the fall and winter months, in Norfolk, Ohio, Clyde, Kelley's Island, &c.

In January, 1871, by the urgent request of the parties concerned,

Mr. Peebles entered into the editorial copartnership of "The American Spiritualist" with Hudson Tuttle, A. A. Wheelock Managing Editor; hoping, as he says, "to aid that faithful organ in its great struggle for the position it deserves." It bears the imprint of his great love-nature, taking broad and fraternal ground with "The Liberal Christian," "The Index," "The Radical," and public organs and speakers and mediums that have hearts as offerings for humanity.

The following incident, appearing in his editorial column, contains so fine a moral recommendatory to fidelity with all reformers, we extract its general wave-thought: —

"An amusing scene occurred the other Sunday evening at our Spiritualist meeting in Cleveland. Reaching Lyceum Hall, a gentleman said to us, 'A lady has gone into the hall after you in great haste.' — 'Ah! any one sick or dead?' — 'No; but Mrs. —— wants you and your audience to adjourn, and go over in a body to the Universalist meeting in Garrett's Hall.' Entering Lyceum Hall, we saw our excellent sister — a firm Spiritualist — zealously engaged in persuading Spiritualists to leave their meeting, and attend that of the Universalists. Some had left. At length, approaching, she pleasantly urged us to dismiss our meeting, hinting that it would necessarily be 'very slim,' and all go over and hear Mrs. M. A. Livermore preach a Universalist sermon. Our comic side was touched. The missionary-business is ever in order; but for a Spiritualist to serve as a missionary for recruiting a sectarian church finds its parallel in the man who 'put a penny into the urn of charity, and took a shilling out.'

"Taking our seat upon the rostrum, wet and drizzling as was the weather, we found there were a hundred and seventy present. When rising to speak, the number had increased to over two hundred. Voting is testing. We asked all who favored adjourning to Garrett's Hall to rise: *not one arose!* When ready to commence speaking, there were full three hundred present. The lecture finished, Mr. Lawrence, a firm and consistent Spiritualist, rising, and making some very happy remarks, complimenting the assembly for their adhesion to principle, and the speaker's good sense of propriety, asked such as approved of the lecturer's course to rise; and, with the exception of something like half a dozen, the entire audience rose to their feet, and rose, too, with a right good will. It was a complete triumph for consistency, decision of character, and fixedness of principle."

After canvassing the treatment which several Universalists received from their sect, and the creedal basis of their belief, mentioning among other practical things the folly of an unstable policy, he quotes from "The Cleveland Leader" a paragraph of Mrs. Livermore's discourse, with a review: —

"The good man and the bad each have their punishment here. For the future of the former nothing need be feared; no more for the latter: their eternity is alike. When the bad man enters the other world, he leaves his body, his sins and mortal part, behind, and goes a new soul, and commences under the tutelage of God to live a new life."

"Every Spiritualist (says Mr. P.) who believes or realizes any thing of spirit-communion knows that these creedal positions are false; and yet they are invited to listen to and sustain them by their influence and money. Many Spiritualists are doing this silly thing to-day all through the country. . . .

"Spiritualism is progressive and catholic, embracing the good and the true of all creeds, climes, and worlds."

Burns's "Holy Fair" seems appropriate here. The Peebles of his time has evidently lost no virtue in his representative brother of to-day: —

"In good time comes an antidote
Against sic poisoned nostrum;
For Peebles, frae the water fit,
Ascends the holy rostrum:
See! up he's got the word o' God,
And meek and mine has viewed it."

Mrs. Livermore, a patriotic and vigorous agitator of Woman's Franchise, and elevation to the highest trusts in the gift of the people, is a consistent example of the very wisdom Mr. Peebles recommends, — concentrative, constructive, defensive of her own "household of faith;" and therefore succeeds, honoring, no doubt, the man who thus contends for the triumph of what he believes is truth and right: —

. . . "Things should be called by their right names. This worldly policy is contemptible. The clown that made the attempt to ride two horses at once fell into the mud.

"Sects we repudiate. Paper creeds are hardly fit for spittoons. Whenever Spiritualists fix upon a form of belief, and pronounce it a finality, they may count us out. 'Good for this day only' should be the first article of every confession of faith. For radical Unitarians, Free Religionists, Shakers, and Liberalists, in all lands, we extend the warm fraternal hand of fellowship, and ask to be considered their co-worker.

"Had every mortal left the hall, Sunday evening, we should have remained at our post. With God and angels present, none are alone. When Spiritualists support genuine mediums; when they will cease chasing up every passing novelty, and stand by their convictions of truth; when they will cease supporting sectarian churches, and sustain regular meetings of their own; when they will encourage lyceums, good music, order, liberal giving, religious culture, acknowledging and working with God's ministering spirits for redemptive purposes, — then will Spiritualism become a mighty moral power in the world."

During his successful labors in Cleveland, a mass convention of Spiritualists and Shakers was held, about the beginning of the year 1871, in the Lyceum Hall of that metropolis. Mr. Peebles was elected president. Among the very interesting incidents connected with this meeting, "The Cleveland Herald" reports: —

"Rev. J. N. Still (the same brother who met Mr. Peebles about two years before in Portland), a colored itinerant Spiritualist, arose in the audience. He was invited to the stage, and made a few remarks. He told of what he had seen through visions, saying among other things that he saw 'that brother' (the chairman) in the spirit three years before he saw his face; and he was led from the wilds of Virginia to Portland to meet him. He also had a clear view of all the events in the history of Spiritualism that are now taking place; and he wrote a book about it. Ever since he saw that new light, he had been traveling every day upon his great mission, begging his bread wherever he went. He believed Spiritualism to be the great system that is to enlighten and purify the world. He felt a burden of spirit upon him for his own race; that he was the apostle commissioned to tell them the glad tidings.

"As he closed he was loudly applauded. The chairman said he met him (Mr. S.) some years ago, and believed him to be a true and faithful advocate of Spiritualism, acting under the control and direction of the spirits. As he descended the stage, an elderly Shaker gave him his seat, the man sobbing at the general expression of sympathy."

Here were gathered representatives of a class of Spiritualists under the once-ignominious name of Shakers, that hold property in common, having "no saloons, no brothels, no swearing, no manifestations of ill temper, no rant, cant, nor hypocrisy, — a people living quiet, simple, spiritual lives, always devout, happy, and serene." Upon the stand were Elders William Reynolds and Oliver C. Hampton, of Union Village, Warren County, O.; Elder Frederick W. Evans, Mt. Lebanon, N.Y.; Elder George Albert Lomas, Watervliet, Albany, Elder James S. Prescott, North Union, O.; Elder Ephraim Frost, Lebanon, near Dayton, O.; and several elderesses; besides a fine band of singers, and thirty or more Shaker laymen from North Union; also W. W. Bloom, Carrie Lewis, Mr. Peebles, and other Spiritualists.

This conventional action of the Shakers indicates the moral heroism of their inspiration. Coming from their recluse to win some to their simple-minded purities is the experiment which an angel may try at his peril. If their virtues corrode not with this magnetic touch, it will prove that here is power of redemption against which "the gates of hell shall not prevail." But it is the divine way: good shall not be hidden. The sweet bud must blossom, though it die in the expending of its fragrance.

The sentiments of these speakers are so lofty in spirit, under the hearty indorsement of Mr. Peebles in the chair, we deem a few extracts a beautiful adornment here: —

"Love is of God, — pure, holy, free. Lust, apostolically speaking, is 'earthly, sensual, and devilish;' and those who could not and did not distinguish between love, *free love*, and *lust*, only reveal the degrading depravity of their natures. Love, under the guidance of wisdom, is the great redemptive power of the universe. 'If ye love me,' said Jesus, 'ye will keep my commandments.' Freedom and love walk hand in hand in the resurrection-state, — a state attainable in this present life through self-abnegation, and holy consecration to the good and the true.

"Shakers and Spiritualists are one in their knowledge of immortality and the primal objects of existence. Through the influence of Spiritualism, sectarianism, with its bigotry, intolerance, and tyranny, will be swept away. Neither Spiritualists nor Shakers should be afraid of abuse, slander, and ridicule; for, if their doctrines were correct, they could only be strengthened by opposition. Believers — meaning the Shakers — have come into order. Their baptism is from the heavens. The disorderly, disintegrating fanaticisms prevailing to some extent among Spiritualists bring dishonor upon the truth. There is no point upon which the Shakers are so misunderstood as marriage. This is the lion in the way. But believers are not opposed to those on the Adamic plane in the world 'marrying and being given in marriage.' This is well. But there is a Christ plane of purity above it. Their warfare is against the abuses of marriage, the expenditure of the seminal forces, the social evil, and the monopoly of private property.

"The Children's Progressive Lyceum is a live institution, bound to progress as one of the reforms of the nineteenth century. It doth not yet appear what it will be. God bless the effort!

"The Bible is a compendium of the history and literature of the Jewish people, and is no more the word of God than is the bible of any other nation. Let us accord the same respect to the Koran of the Mohammedans, the bible of the Chinese, or that of any other people.

"When woman shall have attained her full social and political rights, she will be the balance-wheel of government: wars will cease, and the political arena will be purged of its uncleanness. Shakers do not fight: they are an example of what would be the result if women were put on an equality with men. The 'social evil' is everywhere perplexing the legislatures and municipal authorities. We declare against war, — the killing of hundreds of thousands of men, and entailing untold suffering upon widows and orphans, to gratify the whims of politicians. There is in every human soul the germ of a spiritual life, that, when quickened into activity, will lift persons up into the Christ sphere, where the animal natures and propensities are entirely subdued.

"It is perfectly right and proper, that, on the earthly plane, people should have husbands and wives, as much so as that they should have wealth; and they only sacrifice that for something better in the higher sphere. There is wealth enough in the world to give every human being enough to place him above want. The Shakers have proved that, under the community system, all have enough and to spare. We yearly feed thousands of poor who never do a stroke of work for us.

"When these principles, of fraternity become practicalized, the long-promised age of peace and plenty, of love and good will to men, will have dawned; yea, it will have been fully inaugurated upon earth, angels walking hand in hand with a regenerated humanity. Spiritualism is a call for higher religious observance in life: hence we find the highest class of Spiritualists organized in the heavens and on the earth, with self-denial as their savior, a divine life their basis, and the practical operation of the Sermon on the Mount their religion. True Spiritualists do not under-estimate self-denial: they see the elements of eternal life in a celibate life, and freedom from war, slavery, sickness, and destitution, by living a life above the plane of mere earthly loves and sensual excitements. Let Spiritualists organize on the principles of eternal, never-changing life, and they will see the shackles of marriage, war, private property, and disease, — all the relations and conditions of temporary corruption, — fleeing as does the dew before the rising sun, - the sun of the millennial day. The great lights of Spiritualism admit two distinct orders of life, — the natural and the spiritual: the one belonging to the earth, earthy; the other to the heavens, heavenly. And, as heaven is a condition of purity and holiness, it should be inaugurated on earth. This was the prayer of Jesus, — 'Thy kingdom come.' This divine kingdom, or high spiritual condition, had come to Jesus. It will come to all, when, like the believers called 'Shakers,' they appreciate and enter into the resurrection-state. 'I am the resurrection and the life,' said Jesus."

Working faithfully in Troy, N.Y., then in Boston, lecturing before the popular audiences of Music Hall, Mr. Peebles, by urgent request, went to New Orleans, La., sowing there and in other Southern localities "the precious seed." The interest was electric. The Southern heart is exceedingly genial. Freed now from the incubus of oppression, the Caucasian and sable races, under the domain of the same "stars and stripes," are greeting this morning of a new day with hallelujahs that find tongues in the very waves of the great Gulf. East, west, north, south!—so rolls on the tide of inspiration; and the lilies of our truth are blossoming in every isle, continent, and sea.

The city papers favorably noticed his successes there. The friends were encouraged. In "Editorial Etchings," published in "The American Spiritualist," he writes, —

... "Our rooms are in the St. Charles Hotel. Have already met several of the friends. The Southern heart is warm and generous. How easy to find the good, the beautiful, and the true, when we search for them! ... There are many Spiritualists in New Orleans. ... They need, as everywhere, system, method, and unitive work. ... We have met noble, ay, royal souls in this city. The South abounds in them. It has gladdened our heart to clasp their hands, receiving favors and personal kindnesses. Acquaintances of this character ripen into enduring friendships. All the memories of the month, connected with our lectures upon Spiritualism, are pleasant. Long will they remain in the treasure-chambers of the soul's sanctuary. Dr. J. W. Allen, a most excellent man, is the president of the Spiritualist society. ... A confession. — At two o'clock, accompanied by a friend, long known to us in Michigan, started for a Spanish cock-pit, to witness some gaff and spur gymnastics. It was daylight: why not see all sides of the world? The building, at the corner of Roman and Dumaine Streets, bears some resemblance within to a theater. The patrons were mostly Spanish and French, with a fair sprinkling of city officials, and three members of the legislature. Though the fowls fought well, the sight was disgusting and hateful beyond description. The young lads smoked; the men betted, cheered, and shouted. A strange world, — cocks fight in New Orleans, bulls fight in Spain, and men fight in France; the motive force and purpose of the combatants being victory. Those French and German Christians did bloodier fighting, however, than do trained birds in the South, or bulls in Spain. Civil and national wars will prevail just as long as the animal predominates over the moral nature. War for any cause is utterly opposed to the whole genius and tenor of Spiritualism. No practical Spiritualist can buckle on the martial armor, and go out to murder his fellow-beings."

We quote again, from a private letter to us, dated Goldsborough, N.C., May 4, 1871.

. . . "So, brother, I have visited every State in the Union, except Arkansas, Texas, and Florida. Spoke in Mobile on Monday evening. Had a pleasant time in Maysville, S.C. Here is a *military school.* Had a pleasant argumentative interview with some of the military students. The contest was on peace and war. They thought if all Northern men had cherished and practiced 'peace principles,' there would have been no war, North and South.

"Last evening I spoke in Goldsborough, — expect a crowd to-night. Bros. N. F. White and E. V. Wilson have spoken here to large congregations.

. . . "I ought to have said, that in Mobile, Ala., a gentleman, John Bowen, threw open his parlor-doors, and we had a large and enthusiastic meeting. On the whole, I am delighted with the South. The people are cordial, warm-hearted, and noble, and very *liberal* in theologies.

. . . "I have just dined with Rev. H. Bain, Universalist minister here in Goldsborough. He is a firm and out-spoken Spiritualist, and his daughter is a medium. Love to Olive, 'Uncle Harry,' and children."

Lecturing a month in Baltimore, his old battle-ground, now enflowering from the spiritual seed of his sowing, Mr. Peebles returned to Cleveland, from which city he writes in private : —

"Brother, I am going to Europe again; sail 1st of July. The London people insist upon my speaking while I am there. Oh, my dear English friends, how I love them! They beg of me to come and spend the winter, as Emma Hardinge returns to America. This I can not do, as I am engaged for October in Louisville; then for four or five months in Memphis, New Orleans, Mobile, and Washington. Bro. A. J. Davis has just written me a long and beautiful letter, full of good words to bear to the English Spiritualists, &c. It was dated, Orange, June 11, 1871. In it he says, —

"'Mary and I always read your articles in the different journals and books you publish, and find you surely on the right side of *truth, justice,* and *love.* I was particularly interested in your late article in "The Present Age," on "Pymander," showing how exactly the human mind makes a circle every three or four thousand years in the perception and declaration of ideas.'

"This letter reminds me of William and Mary Howitt of England, whose hearts are in their hands. When shall I see them again? There is not a wrinkle on their souls; and, owing to a pure life, their foreheads are so spiritually beautiful, we forget, and scarcely see any wrinkles there."

Sunday evening, June 25, "The Children's Progressive Lyceum," of Cleveland, with other generous friends, accompanied Mr. Peebles to the cars, where with "Angels bless you" he started for Europe. He is now in England, making arrangements for the publication of "Higgin's Anacalpysis," gathering facts for the "Year-Book of Spiritualism for 1872," consulting English and French Spiritualists relative to a future world's convention of Spiritualists, and lecturing there occasionally. Elder F. W. Evans, editor of "The Shaker," published under the auspices of the Mt. Lebanon Association of Shakers, is with him in England, — two brothers in the spirit.

As Mr. Peebles physically wears away, and approaches the spirit-world, he is more sensitive and sympathetic, distressed at times over the raging waves of human passions. This life looks to him more and more an exile from his native land. In a private note to us is this ebullition of soul, —

. . . "Earth is hell, rimmed now and then with a scattering rose-bush: a valley of dust and dry bones, touched now and then by a breath from the summer-lands of heaven. Marching through this valley, I often weary and faint. O my brother! when will our labors end?

. . . "In one of your letters you ask, 'When are you coming home?'

"How much meaning in that question!

"Home! strange word, inciting in my bosom queer and quivering emotions! My earthly home is in Hammonton, N.J.; my spiritual home is in Rockford, Ill., under the white wing of Dr. E. C. Dunn's spirit-circle; my celestial home is in the Shaker fraternities, where reigns the Christ-spirit of purity and peace; and my general home is the universe. To-day I am at home in New Orleans, this Crescent City of summer flowers and sunny skies; but I sigh. Oh! how my soul sighs for that home above, eternal in the heavens!"

"Thy earthly work," say the angels to the "Spiritual Pilgrim" "has not yet reached its zenith; thy cup is not full; more trials await thee; thou art not spiritually ripe. Be patient for the harvest, when we shall call for thee."

Wherefore are the rocks clad in blossoming vines? wherefore is the trodden dust so fragrant? A spirit has walked there; immortal pilgrims have carried there the virtue of their light. "How beautiful are the feet of him that bringeth good tidings of good!" An exiled John has been in every clime, "in the spirit on the Lord's Day." He bears the burden of duty as a joyous privilege. Grayed by the storms of adversity, with staff in hand, his eye scanning the terraces of progress, his head dusted with the evening sunlight, he is rapidly nearing the spirit-world; he is climbing the mountain of life, on whose crest is his "Angel of Love," beckoning, "Come up hither!"

O ye faithful! take courage in the battle. Our bloody sweat enriches the Gethsemanes of human sorrow; our tears are mirrors to see the glory to come. Plant love-seeds where our dear brother has wrought in the hours of spring. Lo, the birds of paradise are in grand oratorio! The celestials say of us, —

"BEHOLD THE CHAIN OF PEARLS!"

www.ingramcontent.com/pod-product-compliance
Lightning Source LLC
LaVergne TN
LVHW020245110826
845151LV00003B/1025

9781425529208